Contemporary Politics in the Middle East

Fourth Edition

BEVERLEY MILTON-EDWARDS

polity

First edition published in 1999 by Polity Press
This fourth edition published in 2018 by Polity Press

Polity Press
65 Bridge Street
Cambridge CB2 1UR, UK

Polity Press
101 Station Landing
Suite 300
Medford, MA 02155, USA

ISBN-13: 978-1-5095-2082-4
ISBN-13: 978-1-5095-2083-1 (paperback)

A catalogue record for this book is available from the British Library.

Names: Milton-Edwards, Beverley, author.
Title: Contemporary politics in the Middle East / Beverley Milton-Edwards.
Description: Fourth edition. | Cambridge ; Malden, MA : Polity Press, 2018. |
    Includes bibliographical references and index.
Identifiers: LCCN 2017023463 (print) | LCCN 2017025588 (ebook) | ISBN
    9781509520855 (Mobi) | ISBN 9781509520862 (Epub) | ISBN 9781509520824 |
    ISBN 9781509520824q(hardback) | ISBN 9781509520831q(pbk.)
Subjects: LCSH: Middle East–Politics and government–20th century. | Middle East–
    Politics and government–21st century.
Classification: LCC DS62.8 (ebook) | LCC DS62.8 .M55 2018 (print) | DDC 956.05–dc23
LC record available at https://lccn.loc.gov/2017023463

Typeset in 9.5 on 13 pt Swift Light
by Toppan Best-set Premedia Limited
Printed and bound in Great Britain by CPI Group (UK) Ltd, Croydon

For further information on Polity, visit our website: politybooks.com

Contents

Tables and Figures

Tables

Figures

Preface to the Fourth Edition

The first edition of *Contemporary Politics in the Middle East* was published in 1999 at a time when the region – like the rest of the world – was on the cusp of a new century and great change and development seemed increasingly likely. The second edition came in 2006 at a time when the region was in fact gripped by great uncertainty, conflict and turmoil. In addition, in 2011, as the third edition was just being published, the Middle East and North Africa were convulsed in a popular people's uprising against autocratic and corrupt rule, which became known as the Arab Spring. I remain deeply appreciative of the positive response that the publication of the previous editions of this book elicited from readers. This fourth revised, updated and expanded edition of the book is a response to such readers and a reflection of their appetite for the study of the politics of the Middle East.

This book aims at providing a general introduction to the contemporary politics of the Middle East and in the following chapters a number of major issues or themes are identified that have shaped and characterized the variety of political systems and social relations which exist across the region. For the purposes of this book, 'the Middle East' refers to nineteen states, from Morocco on the Atlantic seaboard to Iran on the Asian continent. This book is written explicitly with the non-specialist reader in mind. The themes that are examined, therefore, are broad, linked to particular cases or events and interwoven with the other topics under discussion to provide a comprehensive account of the factors which influence and shape the development of politics in the region.

The first and chronologically significant theme is the impact of colonialism on the region, particularly during the latter half of the nineteenth and first half of the twentieth centuries. Chapter 1 outlines the relationship of domination and subordination established by the West (Britain and France in particular) over the Middle East. It looks at the nature of political rule and government and the prevailing economic motive behind this imperial and colonial relationship. It has been argued that the colonial experience has had a lasting impact on the region, and the role that the West played, as part of its colonial ambitions, in carving out the state system of the present-day Middle East has seriously disrupted political life in the region since this time. The colonial experience in the Middle East also raised a number of significant debates about the economic and social impact of such strategies, and the extent to which the experience has altered or disrupted pre-existing socio-economic relations and patterns. These debates have, in turn, informed academic analyses of modernization and associated theories of development. These theories and concepts have also led to a growing interest in the processes of state formation initiated by the West and the legacy for Arab attempts at state-building in the twentieth and twenty-first centuries.

One of the first indications of this impact is discussed in chapter 2, which charts the rise and development of Arab nationalist ideologies, such as Ba'thism and Nasserism, that characterized many populist regimes in the region in the 1950s and 1960s. The historical overview of this theme is put in context in relation to current theories of nationalism. The growth and popularization of nationalist ideologies in the Middle East are important in understanding the concomitant secularization of politics in the region and the impact of western-style political ideas such as nationalism and socialism on patterns of politics. In addition, recent debates about the historiography of Arab nationalism, particularly during the so-called era of independence and personified by figures like the Egyptian leader Gamal Abdel Nasser, will be addressed.

Ideologies aside, the importance of oil and associated issues of political economy, including the political and strategic competition for other scarce and valuable natural resources such as water, are addressed in chapter 3. The focus on political economy, and more specifically the politics of oil and the wealth this has generated in the area, resonates in relation to the nature of political systems within the region. As I shall argue, it is no coincidence that political life in wealthy Gulf States is governed by the same elites who own the wealth derived from the oil fields of Arabia. This chapter will also examine other issues of political economy vital to any understanding of the region, including the debate about rentier economies, policies of economic liberalization – or *infitah* (opening), as they are referred to locally – and the poor economic performance of the region as a whole in the global market. The immense wealth and patterns of distribution have altered relations within as well as outside the region and, as I explain in chapter 4, go some way to explain the nature of conflict that has characterized the Middle East in the contemporary era. While the Arab–Israeli conflict has dominated the region, other conflicts have played their part in undermining the stability of the area as a whole. Thus, sectarian, economic and territorial disputes, as well as the Israeli–Palestinian conflict, are examined along with specific case studies that also invoke the increasing threat of terrorism that has marked the region in the past decade. The perspectives of conflict outlined in the chapter are by no means conclusive but they do highlight associated issues such as the role of international actors, the role of the military in politics and issues of internal legitimacy, and traditional state-to-state rivalries such as those between Iran and its Arab neighbours.

In many respects, the themes addressed in the next three chapters of the book – political Islam, women, and ethnicity and minorities – reflect the concerns of non-state actors and say more about the politics of 'below', or the politics of protest and discontent, than about the ruling regimes of the region. In chapter 5, the impact of political Islam is discussed at length. I argue that the manifestation of political Islam encompasses a far broader political spectrum than we are encouraged to believe in the West – indeed, that one is talking about many political Islams and dimensions of Muslim politics that incorporate debates about women, human rights, democracy, state and politics, liberalism and fundamentalism, and violence. Linked with the apparent resurgence of Islam as a political force, the debate addressed in chapter 6, on democratization, first outlines the initial emergence, fall and partial rebirth of democratic politics in the region. The chapter then focuses on recent debates about democratization that have been promoted from outside the Middle East as a means of combating tyranny within the region, particularly the perceived anti-democratic nature of political Islam. This section includes a review of current analyses of democratization and the argument forwarded by some theorists relating to the culture of receptivity to ideas about democracy which are largely western in inspiration and practice. The next two chapters of the book address issues which hitherto have remained on the margins of formal politics in the region – women, and ethnicity and minorities. For a number of decades, however, the role of these groups in the political life of the region has been an increasing focus of attention and debate. Largely, systems of governance have ignored, suppressed and even attempted to eliminate the politics raised by women or by ethnic groups such as the Kurds. I will, therefore, examine some of the recent literature that addresses the interpretation of the role of women and ethnicities and minorities in the Middle East. Such studies have paid more attention to the private than the public political arena: the politics of the family, issues of leadership in households, and debates about women's status and reproduction. They reflect studies in general, recognizing new methodologies that place greater emphasis on gender politics, and ethnic or ethno-nationalist ideologies. This in turn links back to the debate which currently rages in the Middle East: to what extent can primordial definitions of ethnicity, religion and tribe explain the relative resistance of Middle Eastern societies to the institutions and ideologies of the West?

The next chapter, on international – but primarily American – foreign policy in the Middle East, explores the deep and intimate relationship between the United States of America and the various states of the region in terms of American national interest and the wider ideological debates of the twentieth and twenty-first centuries. The chapter also examines the role of Europe, and more specifically the EU, in the Middle East, highlighting the important part this plays in the politics of the region. The re-ascendant role of Russia, particularly in Syria, is examined in this chapter. This highlights how global power balances impact the region. The final chapter is about the Arab Spring and the events which have unfolded from it since the first outbreak of protest in Tunisia in December 2010. It examines and provides analysis of the factors which drove protest, the nature of protest, and regime responses to a form of crisis which has afflicted large parts of the region. Since 2010, the region has been shaped by the politics of transition, authoritarian resilience, new conflicts and an era of uncertainty.

This book, then, paints a broad picture, not of a monolithic Middle East populated by the caricature figures of Arabs, Israelis, Turks and Iranians that we are familiar with through our own media in the West, but a richer vista which includes significant groups of political actors which, in the past, have either been ignored or severely misunderstood in an attempt at reductive accounts of this fascinating region of the contemporary world.

I hope that readers of this book remain as stimulated by this newest edition as I have been in terms of revisiting the topics and themes of this book and looking at them afresh. I would like to offer my thanks to all those cited in the earlier editions of this book, plus Charles E. Kiamie III at George Washington University for a timely prompting, and Heather Wilson, a former student of Middle East politics, who worked to provide research. I am also very grateful to all my colleagues at the Brookings Doha Center and in particular the Director of the Center Tarek Yousef, as well as Nadine al-Masry, Sumaya Attia, Fatema al-Hashemi, Noha Abdoueldahab, Françoise Freifer, Baha Omran, Ranj Alaldin, Firas al-Masri, Bill Hess, Kais Sherif, Luiz Pinto, Kadira Pethiyagoda, Abdel Abdel Ghafar, Sana, Thana, Hamad and Walid from Georgetown University and the Qatar Foundation, who not only fully supported me but gave me an opportunity to be located in a place where I could learn and benefit from world-class expertise on the Middle East and North Africa. I want to express my appreciation to H. E. Cristian Tudor, Romania's Ambassador to Qatar, a student of the first edition of this book who has also fortified me with his interest in the topic. I want to extend my thanks to all my students at Queen's University Belfast, whose enthusiastic interest in this topic constantly encourages me. Many of these students today are in professions and careers where not only their knowledge of, but their ability to analyse, the Middle East region contribute to better forms of understanding. I am deeply appreciative of the assistance offered to me by Fahad al-Dahami. Fahad's sojourn into the world of the contemporary politics of the Middle East allowed me to look anew at the topics and debates in this book.

To Johnny, I offer my thanks for his support. His loyalty has made a world of difference to me. My wonderful children Cara and Joshua have always encouraged me in my scholarship – their thoughts and wisdom are a true inspiration. My particular thanks are extended to Louise Knight at Polity for her unstinting support and encouragement, and to Leigh Mueller for her conscientious attention to copy-editing.

Beverley Milton-Edwards
Queen's University Belfast, Northern Ireland, and Brookings Center Doha, Qatar

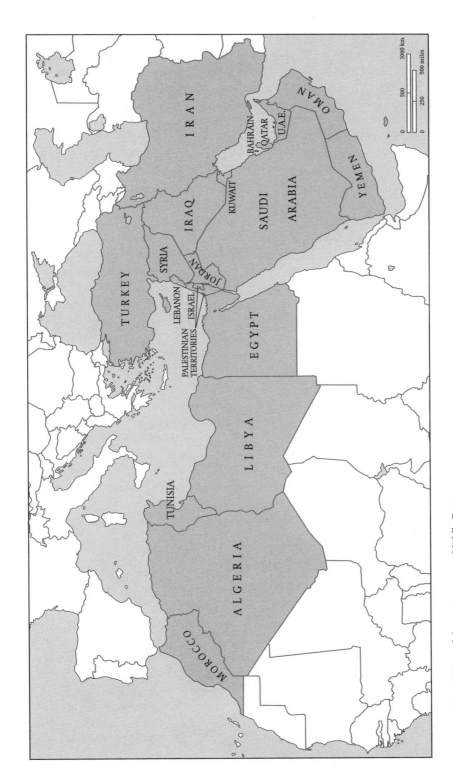

Map 1 *Map of the contemporary Middle East*

Introduction

This book is designed to act as a useful introduction to contemporary politics in the Middle East from the end of the Ottoman Empire at the start of the twentieth century to the present day. The definition of the Middle East that I adopt in this book refers to the following nineteen countries: Algeria, Bahrain, Egypt, Iran, Iraq, Israel, Jordan, Kuwait, Lebanon, Libya, Morocco, Oman, Qatar, Saudi Arabia, Syria, Tunisia, Turkey, United Arab Emirates and Yemen. We can also include Palestine, recognized by the UN as a 'non-member observer state' in 2012, as a twentieth state. Politics here is not just about the state, the politics of government and institutions, or party systems – the obvious point here being that this doesn't inform us well enough about the nature of politics within and across state boundaries in the region or take into account the political impacts of non-state actors.

My approach is to look at the region through a number of important themes, without which any understanding of politics would be meaningless. Thus, as well as charting a chronological path, the book will address such themes as political Islam, democratization, gender, ethnicity and political economy. The connection between these themes is apparent because they are all interrelated in a series of dynamic and intricate layers. Thus, in order to understand the politics of a state and its people, such as Lebanon, one can examine specific themes such as ethnicity, minorities, colonialism, nationalism and Islam, as well as conflict. The justification for the themes that I have chosen for analysis is that simply to study the state in isolation from such dynamics or to look at one perspective rather than a series of other viewpoints misleads the reader.

By 'politics', I mean something broader than the mechanisms of power that relate to and revolve around the modern nation-state and its institutions. This permits us to look at the politics of other non-state actors and elements such as Islamists, women or ethnic groups like the Kurds. How, for example, could one truly understand the politics of Iraq after the fall of Saddam Hussein without understanding the impact of ethnic issues, the sectarian dimension, democracy promotion, conflict and political Islam, in the forms of al-Qaeda and ISIS, on this fragile state? The connections that emerge from the study of such themes will become increasingly apparent to the reader and allow them to determine independently which factors or theoretical frameworks are most effective in terms of wider regional comparisons. In other words, I am offering an emancipation mechanism to the reader so they can determine their own perspectives and analysis.

Traditional studies of the politics of the Middle East have tended to focus overly on the state and its associated actors. This approach has its value but it limits the scope for the study of the political dynamic in a wide geographic region such as the Middle East, and ignores key factors as outlined above. Other approaches have centred on a country-by-country study and this too has its value in terms of looking at power distribution and analysis, but is restricted in terms of a comparative overview of the region. With the themes that I have selected, the reader can take a comparative overview or look more specifically at a country through the tool of the case studies and recommended reading sections. Indeed, I hope to avoid overgeneralization by presenting case studies in each chapter to illustrate the issue at hand. Each chapter will also contain questions for discussion and highlight useful sources of recommended reading, so that students of the subject will be able to grasp quickly the important conceptual frameworks constructed around the region which help support patterns of scholarship and research. In this way, we will avoid falling into the trap of assuming that all politics in the Middle East is alike, and give ourselves an opportunity to see the various forms of politics that operate.

The contemporary Middle East is still portrayed by the western media as mysterious, a region of intrigue and war, the cradle of terrorism, religious extremism and barbaric rule. Journalists and news reporters regularly appear on the airwaves to relate stories of unending conflict and dispute, the abuse of privilege and power, and the desperation behind popular calls for reform and political change. A sample of news stories from March 2017 highlights the almost perpetual framing of the Middle East in stereotypes by the western media. In the UK, for example, the *Daily Mail* tabloid newspaper carried news stories of a visit by King Salman of Saudi Arabia to Indonesia. In the reporting, the King arrived in a 'gold-clad plane', travelled down a 'golden escalator', was flanked by 'flunkies' who were 'armed' with 'umbrellas' (Davies, 2017). From Mosul in Iraq, western war reporters wearing body armour were covering the rout of ISIS. Syria's war was 'recognized' at the Oscars with an award for the makers of the film *White Helmets*, followed by an HBO screening to American TV audiences. And though it is true that not all media portrayals point to such stereotypes, the media do still continue to frame the Middle East as being unique or part of a package of exceptionalism. However, it is not.

The Middle East, like many other regions of the globe, suffers in part from the effects of persistent authoritarianism, lack of political participation, poor economic growth, foreign indebtedness to the West, competition for resources and increasing urbanization. As authors such as Berger and Weber (2014) and Svolik (2012) highlight, there are no myths to explode: in many respects, the Middle East is like other developing regions and characterized by similar forms of politics. In sum, it is not as unique as many authors would have us believe. Some generalizations, however, cannot be avoided, and are particularly necessary and useful in helping students new to the subject understand the Middle East and make sense of cultures, histories and politics so very different from their own. Most people new to the subject already carry with them a generalized – and often stereotyped – view that has played a part in their decision to find out more.

The students I have taught in the last two decades often come up with the buzzwords presented in figure I.1 below when we first talk about the politics of the Middle East.

There is nothing wrong with this as long as biases are acknowledged and the further acquisition of knowledge is based on sound academic reading. Newcomers to the subject tend to see the region and its politics in the following way: as hot, bearded camel riders; desert-like; poor, undeveloped, backward; governed by Muslim fanatics and tyrants; characterized by rich Arabs in London and Arab terrorists blowing up planes. In some respects, this is a frozen image – as demonstrated by the image in figure I.2 – which was formed hundreds of years ago and often remains unchanged.

In the age of the millennials, the perception of the Middle East being a region characterized by war, violence, conflict and terrorism has grown as western powers have become increasingly militarily, diplomatically, and in terms of humanitarian intervention, embroiled in the region. It is important to recognize that we in the West do bring preconceptions and biases with us when we start to study the Middle East. It is no use pretending that we have no knowledge; our opinions, information and views will have come from sources as diverse as Sunday-school Bible stories, our Judaeo-Christian cultural context, presidential calls for a ban on Muslims, news of ISIS-perpetrated massacres, our own citizens becoming jihadis fighting in Syria or Iraq, social media, YouTube, films, books and television programmes. So we should, at the outset, stop for a moment and think about our own image of the region and the representations we have received. The objective of this

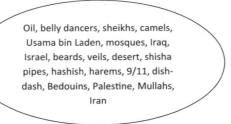

Oil, belly dancers, sheikhs, camels, Usama bin Laden, mosques, Iraq, Israel, beards, veils, desert, shisha pipes, hashish, harems, 9/11, dish-dash, Bedouins, Palestine, Mullahs, Iran

Figure I.1 *Middle East buzzwords*

Figure I.2 *Frozen in time: the Middle East*

book is to re-examine these images, see how they differ from reality and build a new store of knowledge that is more balanced and informed around the prejudices that we already hold.

In recent decades, the growing interest in the region has been accompanied by an increasing number of academic journals, texts and books devoted to the study of the area. Students of politics in the twenty-first century are able to access material through well-stocked libraries, journal collections and the World Wide Web. It is questionable, however, to what extent the proliferation of materials on or from the Middle East has encouraged an expansion of prejudices or new perspectives on the region. Views on the Middle East have hardened and narrowed.

The Muddle East?

It's a play on words of course – the Muddle East. Yet often, for the first-time student of the politics of the region, this is what their introduction to the topic can feel like. Students are asked to engage with a vast region characterized by forms of politics which they may not have encountered before. What we mean by the Middle East and where it starts and other regions end may initially seem a rather inane question. Nevertheless, these very basic terms of reference need to be discussed and examined from a number of perspectives. The political events taking place in the Middle East today are the subject of considerable attention and interest from across the globe. The region is fascinating, providing rich contrasts in political, cultural, social and economic spheres. The contribution of the peoples of this region to history, civilization, art, culture, science, religion, music and politics can no longer be neglected or ignored.

Ancient civilizations also have their roots in the Middle East. In addition, the three great monotheistic religions, Judaism, Christianity and Islam, were established in these lands. Throughout history, great empire-builders, political rulers, religious leaders, poets and scientists have emerged from the area to influence and inform European cultures. The golden age of Islam witnessed the spread of the religion to Europe in the West and Asia in the East. The rich heritage of literature, through poetry and story-telling, informs us of immense empires under the Muslim Umayyad, Abbasids and Ottomans, of just rulers, corrupt tyrants, dynastic power struggles, feats of military daring and scientific endeavour. In the nineteenth and early twentieth centuries, the Middle East was subject to external colonial competition resulting in widespread processes of modernization and development. But the colonizers did not always find what they imagined of the Middle East. Commenting on the British occupation of Baghdad during the First World War, Iraqi novelist Khalid Khistainy mused:

Box I.1 Baghdad messpot!

Well, Baghdad was a terrible disappointment to them because they came with the story of Baghdad of the Arabian Nights and all the glory of the Arab states. And when they entered the city they really found only a big village. No more. There was no ... not one single public road, no schools, no services, no hospital and one secondary school in the whole of the city. There was really very little in Baghdad to be proud of. And there were no paved roads at all, just little medieval lanes and when it was raining it was a terrible mess there in the city. I must say the English soldiers when they came to Baghdad they were told of course that the name Iraq did not exist at the time. They were told they were going to Mesopotamia. And they had one look at the city, the city of Baghdad and they said 'Oh, this is Mesopotamia ... This is a messpot!'

(Khistainy, 2002)

The impact of this foreign intervention was apparent in the emerging map and attendant state structures of the region in the wake of the First World War. Straight lines appeared on the maps of the region and government systems dreamt up in Paris and London were imposed as new states (see map 1). 'Iraqis at the time', remarks Khishtainy, 'they regarded themselves as Muslim subjects of the Sultan in Istanbul and the country itself was divided into three provinces and they were not linked to each other, so there was no sense of nationhood in Iraq' (Khistainy, 2002).

Varieties of modernization have occurred within the region, many externally influenced and driven, some internally propelled as part of idiosyncratic visions of social, political and economic engineering involving whole societies. An example of this is best illustrated in the case of Libya's development, under the rule of Muammar Gaddafi (1969–2011), which involved the whole of Libyan society in a grandiose modernization project which was ultimately doomed to fail.

The Middle East is also a source of some of the world's most valuable energy sources: oil and gas. For high-energy consumer states like the USA, for example, access to oil reserves in the Middle East has been a national security concern vital to the nation's economy and survival. The discovery and subsequent export of oil and gas in the region have led to unimaginable wealth for some Arab states, the impoverishment of others, problems of import–export substitution, and the rise of rentier economies that have impacted on political rule. In addition, the production of so much oil and gas has shaped the relations the region enjoys with other parts of the world and its role in the international community, and impacted on capital markets.

Geographically speaking, the region is vast and its borders and boundaries are still open to debate – meaning different things to different people. The geography of the region reflects territorial and spatial dimensions which are being challenged, and re-shaped. National boundaries have proved impermanent and are being re-territorialized by new political challengers such as ISIS. Depending on which definition of the Middle East is used, the area stretches from Morocco in the west to Iran in the east, and can include sub-Saharan Africa, Turkey, Afghanistan and the Arabian/Persian Gulf. Colonial and neo-imperial cartographers display a penchant for redrawing the boundaries of the region in debates about solutions to problems posed by past enthusiasts. Within this region, territory has always been given meaning politically. The physical geography of the Middle East includes vast deserts, modern cities, snow-capped mountain ranges and important natural resources. Many states in the contemporary Middle East are relatively recent creations, their boundaries and borders being the product, one way or another, of the era of colonial interference in the region. Iraq, for example, is a twentieth-century invention of British officials who 'united' three provinces of ancient Mesopotamia and imported a new Arab monarch from the Hejaz of Arabia to sit on a British-inspired throne. The British then proceeded to squabble among themselves with respect to the cheapest and best way to manage the 'native' Arab population. We get such insights from the private letters of significant colonial figures such as Gertrude Bell (who herself invented Iraq and prevailed upon British officials to bring her dream to fruition). The following is an extract from Bell. The letter, in addition to discussions of the weather and who she has taken tea and dined with, also addresses the politics of the day and her frustration at the policy-makers back home – including a decision from London to cut and run from Iraq:

Box I.2 Extract from a letter home: Gertrude Bell in Iraq

... If we retain the mandate we must spend the money on it which it demands. There's no 9d for 4d – or 9d for nothing at all ... but will rogues like Winston [Churchill] and Lloyd George use that honesty to the public? I'm afraid there can be no doubt of the answer. They will go on with their hanky panky until it leads to terrible disaster to this country ... and possibly to very great inconvenience, if not worse, to ourselves – for I doubt our capacity to withdraw scatheless through anarchy. I shall not, however, mind what happens to us. We shall have deserved everything we get.

Father, think – if we had begun establishing native institutions two years ago! By now we should have got Arab government and an Arab army going; we should have had no tribal revolt; all the money and lives wasted this year would have been saved.

(www.gerty.ncl.ac.uk/letter_details.php?letter_id=4490)

As Bell highlights, political space was fluid and subject to competing interests. Furthermore, the independence of the majority of these states (such as Gertrude Bell's beloved Iraq) is a phenomenon located in the middle to latter part of the twentieth century and linked to the independence movement throughout the Third World and patterns of international politics and relations which subsequently resulted from these global changes. But by and large the independence movements were about breaking the power of foreign rulers, foreign influence and interference in domestic politics of the region.

The region is also the home of many religious groups. Among Muslims, there are Sunni, Shi'a, Sufi, Alawite and Druze. In the Christian community, there are Catholics, Greek Orthodox, Mandean, Sabaean, Maronites, Armenians, Coptics, Assyrians, Protestants, Anglicans and Melkites, to name but a few. In addition, Jews have populated the region, not just in the Holy Land but in countries like Egypt, Syria, Morocco and Yemen (Shabi, 2009). There are also small religious minority groups such as Yazidis and Samaritans. The religious importance of the region cannot be underestimated, as billions across the globe turn to it for prayer, pilgrimage and worship. They also venerate religious sites that are thousands of years old. Located in Mecca in Saudi Arabia is the Kaaba – the most revered spot in Islam. In Jerusalem, Jews pray at their most holy site, the Wailing Wall or Kotel; Christians worship at the Church of the Holy Sepulchre where they believe Jesus Christ was crucified and buried; and Muslims at al-Aqsa mosque, the third holiest site in Islam. In Bethlehem, Palestine, the birthplace of Jesus Christ is marked by the pilgrims at the Church of the Nativity in Manger Square.

Religious diversity, therefore, actually characterizes the region, though the Muslim faith enjoys primary status in many countries. Within the region, the religious tag is still used as a means of identifying and setting boundaries between people (Barth, 1969). Diversity has often led to difference within a particular faith, leading to breakaway sects or schisms, as well as between faiths, witnessed more recently, for example, by an upsurge in Muslim – Coptic Christian tensions in Egypt, or the state of near civil war in Iraq.

Ethnic and minority identity is an important and increasingly pertinent issue affecting the politics of the Middle East. Until the end of the Cold War, the Gulf crisis and the disintegration of the former Soviet Union, the ethnic dimension in politics was relatively neglected, largely suppressed and ignored. The emergence of ethno-national conflicts throughout the globe, and the subsequent resolution of some of them, have impacted on the Middle East in a variety of ways. Ethnic and minority diversity is a feature in the majority of its states and characterizes modern nation-states such as Israel (Jew – Ashkenazi or Mizrahi – and Arab), Syria (Arab, Kurd, Christian, Alawi and Druze), Iraq (Arab, Kurd, Christian, Yazidi, Turkman and Marsh Arab), Iran (Persian, Arab, Kurd, Azeri, Baluchi and Circassian) and Algeria (Arab and Amazigh). Thus, Arabs, Amazigh, Kurds, Marsh Arabs, Jews, Persians and Circassian all come from distinct backgrounds, embracing unique characteristics deemed fundamental to identity. In addition, some forms of ethno-national identity are relatively recent constructs created in response to the threat of annihilation or assimilation. Such ethnic differences have played a large part in shaping the identity of the inhabitants of the region, many of whom find themselves residing in a modern nation-state to which they feel little loyalty, remaining as marginal forces on the fringes of society. They oppose rule from an alien centre and agitate for a range of changes, from more ethnically sensitive policies on education, or the preservation of certain linguistic traditions, to outright secession and self-determination.

No discussion of the contemporary Middle East should ignore the enduring power of tribal, clan and family ties in explaining politics in the region. Despite modernization and globalization with their attendant homogenizing features, tribe – as a foundation of political, social and economic power – endures in many countries of the region. Colonial powers frequently perceived the tribe as an impediment to state-creation. Clan and family ties are mobilized in weak states and become the refuge for citizens who feel as if they have no stake in the state. Tribe, clan and family ties also maintain 'insider'–'outsider' distinctions in the manifestation of power among ruling families, state systems and presidential dynasties across the region. Tribe, clan and family account for the legitimacy claims of the Hashemites in Jordan, the al-Saud in Saudi Arabia, the al-Assads in Syria, the Hariri in Lebanon, the al-Sabah in Kuwait, al-Qasimi in Sharjah, al-Maktoum in Dubai, al-Nuaimi in Ajman, al-Nahyan in Abu Dhabi, al-Thani in Qatar, the al-Khalifah in Bahrain and the tribal confederation of the Hashid in Yemen.

The Middle East, as described above, is different from the Arab world, which is composed of all of the aforementioned countries except Turkey, Iran and Israel. The Arab world is something different again from the Muslim world, which includes all of the aforementioned except Israel, but also encompasses countries such as Turkey, Pakistan, Afghanistan, etc. Other terms applied to the region include the Near East, and the Fertile Crescent, which refers to the area from Lebanon in the north, to Syria in the east and Israel/Palestine to the south. The Levant or Mashreq is also commonly used to describe Lebanon and Syria. Labels such as the Gulf states, the Arab-Afro states, the Islamic states and the Maghreb – which refers to the North African states of Morocco, Algeria, Tunisia and sometimes Libya – are also frequently applied both within and from outside the region. Also within the region we can talk about the existence of other worlds, such as Jewish, Islamic, Christian, Arab, Afro-Arab and southern Mediterranean. The use of these labels has more to do with the diffuse notion of identity that often pervades the region than anything else. They also highlight the way in which the region interacts politically as well as in other spheres with these 'other worlds'.

At the heart of this debate about the labelling of the region is a subjective/ objective setting of boundaries, and the social and political space between the peoples of the region and the rest of the world (Barth, 1969). Borders have been artificially set but boundaries in the region remain contested and challenged in terms of tribal, class, gender and religious differences. Here, 'the Middle East' as a label becomes an exclusive term identifying a particular set of states distinct from others. Within the region, the issue of labelling also becomes one of identities, where the nation-state seeks to create and establish identities which compete with other group identities focused on tribe, family, gender, ethnicity or religion.

Who invented the Middle East?

The term 'the Middle East' is a relatively recent one, a product of contemporary rather than historical interest in the region. Previously, those from outside the region who had an interest in it referred to it, or parts of it, as the Near East, Persia, Mesopotamia, the Orient, the Levant, the Maghreb, Zion or the Holy Land. These terms have encouraged a particular association of ideas or a view of the region which is often simplistic and the product of crude reductionism and stereotyping. The Orient, for example, was a term that grew out of European fascination with the Middle East, particularly in the eighteenth and nineteenth centuries. Oriental society, however, was portrayed in a negative manner and seen as symbolizing everything the West was not. As Turner (1994) argued, 'Oriental society can be defined as a system of absences – absent cities, the missing middle classes, missing autonomous urban institutions and missing property' (p. 40). Other terms and labels, such as Zion and the Holy Land, were used to convey a romanticized and reductive vision of certain parts of the region that had much to do with a utopian vision of redemption for Jew and Christian alike and resonated with Islamophobic constructed 'memories' of the Crusades.

The 'Middle East' label, then, was invented by individuals from outside the region who sought to make sense of or understand orders of political, economic, social and cultural relations in a geographic region stretching from Morocco to Iran. The cartographers of the Occident then set about – and continue to this day – re-drawing and re-fashioning the borders of the region to incorporate their own ideas of statehood, belonging and nation (Neep, 2015). It was not a term that those indigenous to the region used, though today it is self-referred to as *al-sharq al-awsat* (Middle East). Common usage of the label can be located in the Second World War when the British military established a 'Middle East Command' in the area under the authority of the War Office. It was an invention of the war, a military necessity, but it remained long after British – and, for that matter, French – influence in the region declined and was replaced by the superpower competition between the USA and the former USSR. The term also entered the lexicon of diplomats, academics and the media and increasingly replaced the usage, in Europe, of the 'Near East' that in the USA is still used to describe what I refer to as the Middle East. Turkey is sometimes included in this construction of the Middle East and for the purposes of this book is considered part of the region. Use of this label by those who study the region from outside its geographic boundaries has led to debate about the assumptions and prejudices they bring with them from their Eurocentric perspective and biases. By applying this label, the diversity of the region is reduced. Its cosmopolitan status and rich cultures are overlooked. This debate was largely initiated following the publication of a text that challenged prevailing western scholarship and perspectives on the region.

Orientalism – the enduring debate

In 1978, a Palestinian Arab academic living in the USA published a book entitled *Orientalism*. The author, Edward Said, aimed to challenge, criticize and shake the foundations and assumptions at the heart of western-based academic study of the Middle East. He set out to describe the symbiotic relationship which scholars had ascribed to the Orient and Occident, in which the Orient symbolized the negative, the backward and the barbaric, and the Occident the positive, the enlightened and the progressive. Said argued that westerners had long depicted the Orient as societies with uncivilized values, repositories of supine rulers, and an area of sexual exoticism. In turn, as Said argued, this allowed for the West and the westerner to remain signified by superiority. He contended that this construction of the Orient masked European ambition for power over the Middle East. As Said stated,

Box I.3 Orientalism

Orientalism [is] a Western style for dominating, restructuring, and having authority over the Orient ... Orientalism, therefore, is not an airy European fantasy about the Orient, but a created body of theory and practice in which, for many generations, there has been considerable material investment.

(1978, pp. 3 and 6)

Any student with a serious interest in the study of the Middle East should read Said's exposition in *Orientalism*, and his later work entitled *Culture and Imperialism* (1993a). While Said may not have been the first scholar to highlight orientalist scholarship (Turner, 1994), in essence he develops a three-pronged line of attack on western scholarship of the Orient. This Orient is geographically located in the Middle East and is primarily Muslim in religious character. First, Said criticizes western scholarship for its essentialist perspective on the region, and the way in which it both treats and presents Muslim society as one homogeneous and monolithic mass. Second, he argues that western scholarship on the region is politically motivated, and in particular was and remains associated with the political and economic ambitions of colonialism and imperialism. As such, western domination of the Orient is the political motive, according to Said, behind most scholarship on the region. Finally, Said presents an argument that academic tradition on the subject in the West has resulted in and created a body of 'authoritarian truths' which must, he argues, be challenged by new scholarship and new thinking. Ultimately, Said is asking the West to rethink its relationship with the 'Other'. He constructs a critique of western assumptions about every aspect of the Middle East, whether cultural, political, religious, social or in the sphere of economic relations.

Does Orientalism persist in the present? Does domination persist in the cultural, political and economic relationship between the Middle East and the West? Cultural and media representations, it can be argued, still throw up such negative stereotypes. Popular TV and film franchises continue to depict unreconstructed and patronizing prejudices of the Middle East, its cultural mores, specific countries and its citizens. A new generation which is now aware of these factors continues with this rigidity within the realms of conventional scholarship and persists in characterizing the Middle East in ways basically unchanged since European domination was first established over the region. In a 'critique of academic scholarship', Hisham Sharabi (1990) identifies three fields of scholarship on the Middle East: Orientalism, area studies and liberal humanism.

As Sharabi declares, the point of his argument is not to undermine conventional discourse on the region but to present a meaningful critique of the way in which it is conducted, the hitherto unquestioned assumptions held by western scholars even in the present day. Thus, two principal assumptions are questioned: the first, 'the specifically western experience of transformation and change understood as progress ... The second ... from the view that non-western cultures somehow belong to a different order of existence and develop according to a different impulse' (Sharabi, 1990, p. 4).

Orientalism persists, but has been challenged by successive generations of young scholars and students of the region. For liberals and post-orientalists, the term (rather than the associated attitudes) is a thing of the past; they are conscious of their 'westernness' and struggle to dissociate themselves from the old lackeys of Orientalism. The debate persists. In 1993, Edward Said and Ernest Gellner engaged in a very public row about the persistence of Orientalism and Eurocentric bias in the study of the Middle East. In a review of *Culture and Imperialism*, Gellner accused Said of 'inventing a bogy called Orientalism' through which rigid lines of good and bad in the study and characterization of the region could be drawn. Gellner questioned this methodology, pointing out that some figures castigated by Said as orientalists had brought positive benefits to the region through the accompanying forces of industry and technology (Gellner, 1993, p. 4). Said's rebuke was vociferous. By this point, he had himself become a poster-boy for this movement of study, and a progressive voice for post-colonial analysis. At one point he remarks: 'Let him [Gellner] delight in his sophomoric patter by all means, but let him not at the same time fool himself that what he says about Islam, or the formerly colonized world or imperialism or postmodernism, has anything to do with what any of them are really about' (1993b, p. 17). Said's arguments, Said's work and Said himself drew many contesting critics and the helpfulness of *Orientalism* continues to be questioned to the present day (Varisco, 2017).

In the wake of 9/11, the rise of al-Qaeda threats across the globe and new military interventions in the Middle East by the West, attitudes did harden again. Political leaders employed the vocabulary of a war on terror as a war of values, pitting the apparently superior values of the West against the Middle East epitomized by the hate values of jihadi terrorists and leaders like Usama bin Laden and Omar al-Baghdadi. Today the same processes are evident in how Arabs and their politics are viewed by and in the West (Hom, 2016). The process of 'othering' has been mutual – many extreme religious fundamentalists now stereotype the West in a negative fashion and argue that the chasm between them is too wide to repair (Hegghammer and Nesser, 2015).

The academic row, symbolized by Said and Gellner, over the way in which the Middle East should be studied, is as important today as it ever was – if not more so. It is important because the primary lenses through which the Middle East is still represented in the West are filtered through a variety of online activities including gaming, the media and social media, which is highly reductive (Höglund, 2008). Other leading academic figures have come into conflict with Said's approach, among whom Bernard Lewis stands out. In his own work, including *Islam and the West* (1993b) and 'The question of Orientalism' (1982), Lewis argues that Said's success in writing *Orientalism* lay in its anti-western, pro-Third World perspective that served a purpose for those leftists and others intent on undermining American foreign policy. In addition, he criticized Said's work for simplifying and reducing complex problems affecting the Middle East and the Muslim world. Fred Halliday defined himself as falling into neither one camp nor the other, and instead criticized both for failing to recognize 'what actually happens in these societies' as opposed to their approach of writing about 'what people say' (1996, p. 201). The debate continues with academic and ideological foes on either side of a divide about the way in which the Middle East should be studied, its influence and its relation to power (Adib-Moghaddam, 2010).

Studying the Middle East, then, leads one into a world of often opposing and critical scholarship where the student of the subject must always be aware of the agencies that motivate its scholars. The Middle East, incorporating as it does the Muslim world, Arab and Turkish people, the rich and the poor, ethnic groups – such as Kurds, Amazighs and Marsh Arabs – women, religious minorities including the Jews, the developed and undeveloped, citizen and refugee, urban and rural, religious and secular, powerful and weak, remains essential to any future configuration of the global system. Indeed, global politics, the fate of world economic markets and trade balances are all significantly affected by the Middle East and its varying political strata. The very future and security of the globe are believed to be threatened by Arab and Muslim terrorists from the region. As I have shown in the debate above, how we choose to study the region matters very much to our understanding of it.

State types: making sense of multiplicity

Once the difficulty of defining a few basic terms of reference has been overcome, it is also useful to present a classification of the state system in our study of politics in the contemporary Middle East. The establishment of nation- or sovereign states in the region is a contemporary phenomenon associated with the defeat of the Ottoman Empire in the First World War and the rising power of Europe over the region in the post-war period. As Roger Owen (2004) remarks, 'As far as the Middle East was concerned, it was generally the dominant colonial power that first created the essential features of a state, by giving it a capital, a legal system, a flag and internationally recognized boundaries' (p. 13). The model of the state that the European powers sought to export to the region descended from the state types evolved in their own societies, reflecting a separation between temporal and spiritual powers. The models of statehood applied in the region also reflected the prevailing philosophical saliency in post-Enlightenment Europe of concepts of sovereignty, democracy, liberalism and secularism, as well as the change in economic modes of production from agrarian to industrialized societies. These factors all played a part in shaping the particular types of statehood which were exported to the Middle East and used in the construction of new states, nations and capital-driven economies. As Hobsbawm (1997) points out, state-creation in the Middle East has been about processes of 'decolonization, revolution and, of course, the intervention of outside powers' (p. 178).

The subsequent political independence of such states is also a relatively recent event, mostly achieved following the decline of European influence in the region after the Second World War and before the increasingly powerful ascendancy of the competition between the USA and the former USSR for influence in the region. Yemen was the first state to achieve independence in 1918, and the United Arab Emirates (UAE), Bahrain and Qatar the last in 1971. Most of the territory of the region has known foreign rule in one form or another under the authority of outside European or western powers. Therefore, independence and the further development of the nation-state and nation-building are relatively dynamic manifestations (Lustick, 1993). In some countries, the state- and nation-building experiment is still under way, often underpinned by the military or occupation by foreign forces, and by limited opportunities for mass-based politics. In Iraq, since the fall of Saddam Hussein in 2003, the Ba'thist state has been entirely dismantled and the Allied-led experiment in new nation-building has been deemed highly problematic. By 2017, as Iraqi forces prepared to capture Mosul from ISIS, political debate was also animated by the prospects of even holding the state together. Momentum for Kurdish independence has grown.

The states and state system of the region are diverse and subject to competing typologies drawn and established by academics on the subject. These are useful in that they help us ascertain political patterns of governance and the state, and the increasing sense of the artificiality of many state systems in the area. The nation-state in the Middle East has manifested itself in a number of ways and its elite has gone a long way to promote characteristics of national – whether Syrian, Iraqi, Kuwaiti or Egyptian – identity within a distinct territorial entity. On the other hand, the nation-state – or rather nation-building – has also been increasingly recognized as failing many so-called citizens, ignoring other stronger identities as the homogenizing of the state is brutally imposed from above. Such was the case in Iraq, where ethnic and other identities were suppressed, first under the banner of Ba'thist ideology and then under Saddam Hussein's myopic vision of 'nation without difference'.

Before we examine these typologies of the state, it is worth remembering some of the more universal features identified as creating a sense of cohesion in the Middle East before the advent of the European colonial powers and their accompanying political models of development for the nation-state. Under the Ottoman Empire, ruled from Constantinople (modern-day Istanbul), which preceded the era of 'grand interference', loyalty and identity in the region were bound together through a variety of factors including a unified code of law, political system and taxation, as well as by religion, clan, tribe, family, class, language and ethnic group. Common languages, including Turkish and Arabic, and common religion – Islam, Christianity and Judaism – played an important part in forging a sense of identity, even if it did not always result in unity at a political level (Hourani, 1991).

In the present day, however, it has been argued that some features of the modern nation-states of the region work against these unifying factors, often fracturing homogeneous groups with shared ethnic, religious or linguistic traditions. It is argued that the state system has created fissures and artificial systems of governance based on political traditions and thought that are not indigenous to the region, but instead are the legacy of the period of foreign domination. This is a region where the state is less rooted than in others, and is therefore weak in terms of its moral weight and legitimacy (Hudson, 2015). As a result, the inhabitants of the region have encountered many problems with their state systems. For the most part, the problems are attributed to the synthetic nature of the state and its western-influenced roots. As Saouli reminds us, 'In the Arab world, the state seems to be an ephemeral condition awaiting modification, either by the proponents of sub- or supra-state ideologies or through external design' (2012, p. 5). Scholars working on the subject of the state and establishing typologies of the state system in the region are aware of these difficulties, and have incorporated them into their models – conscious that they can never be fixed, only dynamic.

Typologies have been devised by a number of scholars, including Giacomo Luciani and Ilia Harik in Luciani (1990), Roger Owen (2004) and Simon Bromley (1994). Other authors on the subject include Nazih Ayubi, Fateh Azzam, Michaelle Browers, Ahmad Dallal, Steven Heydemman, Michael Hudson, Philip Khoury and Joseph Kostiner, Ian Lustick, Adham Saouli and Sami Zubaida. While all of these writers may differ in the perspective from which they work, or in certain methodological techniques that they engage in, or in the arguments they construct on this subject, they all recognize the state, Arab or otherwise, in the region. Before proceeding further, however, a working definition of what is meant by the state is worth elaborating here. The modern nation-state is usually construed as a territorial political unit. It is not a virtual invention, rather it consists of a claim to authority, sovereignty, institutions of rule and government, means of raising state revenue through taxes or other sources, international recognition, a flag and a capital. As Owen (2004) points out, while there can never be one precise definition of the state, and nor is the nation-state in the Middle East a purely western product, the general features outlined above can be recognized as common to the typologies outlined below.

It is worth looking in some detail at the useful debates outlined by Luciani and Harik in Luciani (1990), Owen (2004), Bromley (1994) and Ayubi (1995). Although such studies may appear to be quite dated in terms of when they were published, they remain relevant to the large majority of states that presently exist within the region.

Owen takes a structuralist approach, focusing on class and economic relations, both internally and externally generated. Through this particular lens he identifies three state types that are common in the region:

Box I.4 Owen's typology of the Middle East state

1 The colonial state, which existed in the post-First World War period in countries such as Egypt, Syria, Lebanon and Iraq. The colonial state, according to Owen (2004), was distinguished by the following three features: 'central administration; the policies of the colonial power; and colonialism as a conduit for external influences' (p. 13).

2 The immediate post-independent state, where national liberation movements struggled to consolidate a state system based on western forms of government through supporting socialist or other ideologies.

3 The authoritarian state, where participatory democracy is absent, and one-party rule supported by a strong military and internal security structure dominates.

Under this typology, Owen addressed one-party states (e.g. Syria and Iraq), family rule (e.g. the Gulf states) and even the examples of Libya under Jamahiriyyah rule. Owen's approach is concise in execution and allows a variety of political circumstances to be incorporated into the three broad headings that he outlines. Absent from his approach is the accommodation of states such as Israel in the region.

Luciani (1990) also identifies important features of the Arab state (rather than the Israeli, Iranian or Turkish state) which echo Owen's typology. Luciani believes the first distinguishing feature of the stable state is 'the position of the central strongman, leader or orchestrator, the Great Patron or Manipulator'. Second, he introduces the idea of 'periodicity', where leaders 'sweep clean the government'. Third is the 'politics of limited association', where political activity exists but is ultimately limited by the ruling elite. Fourth, a broad middle class rules the state. Fifth, Arab states are weighed down by large bureaucracies; and, sixth, the state acts as 'an organization of control or regulation'. Finally, Luciani remarks that the 'orientalist tradition' would identify the influence of Islam on the Arab state system (pp. xxvii–xxx).

Harik (1990) establishes a useful typology, which differs from Owen's by arguing that many contemporary Arab states (Harik cites fifteen) are indigenous products of the region rather than colonial creations. Here Harik acknowledges the more informal patterns of politics that have remained in the region, evolving and currently resisting the homogenizing ideologies of socialism and capitalism that have been utilized to serve the nation-state and its elites as it attempts to create new identities and loyalties. Harik (1990, pp. 5–6) identifies five traditional Arab state types:

Box I.5 Harik's typology of the Arab state

1 The imam-chief system – 'authority in a sanctified leader' (Yemen, Oman, Hijaz).

2 Alliance system of chief and imams – 'authority is invested in a tribal chief supported and awarded legitimate authority beyond the confines of his tribe by virtue of his identification and/or alliance to prominent religious leaders' (Saudi Arabia).

3 Traditional secular system with 'authority invested in a dynasty free from religious attributes' (Qatar, Bahrain, Kuwait, Lebanon).

4 Bureaucratic-military oligarchy type. Authority originates in urban-based garrison commanders, who in time develop an extensive bureaucratic apparatus. Monopoly of the means of coercion in the hands of an administrative caste is the major feature of this state type (Algeria, Egypt, Tunisia).

5 Colonial-created system. States carved out of the now-defunct Ottoman Empire on the basis of foreign imperial interest in the absence of a credible local base of authority to erect new structures (Iraq, Syria, Jordan, Palestine, Israel).

Harik's typology is useful for the alternative perspective it encourages us to take and the less formal patterns of politics – such as the political power of the tribe, ethnic group or religious leader – that it highlights, alongside more formal power bases such as the military.

Ayubi (1995) works from both a political economy and comparative approach, seeking to explain why Arab states are 'fierce and hard' in one respect but ultimately feeble in normal state activities such as tax collection and welfare provision. Using the political economy perspective, Ayubi brings the work of authors like Antonio Gramsci and Guillermo O'Donnell into his analysis of the Arab state in the Middle East. He argues that all Arab states are, to one degree or another, authoritarian, engaging in coercive measures against citizens, while also remaining distant from them. In addition, he identifies two state types: the revolutionary *thawra* (revolution) state, based on populist, radical, socialist and nationalist rhetoric, and the *tharwa* (wealth) state type, 'relying for survival on kin-based relations, but above all else on financial capital, or wealth' (1995, p. 447).

More recently, scholars like Saouli have also attempted to reformulate the study of state-formation and endurance in the Middle East. Basing his approach on definitions of the state, he addresses their creation and destruction in terms of Weberian ideals. He acknowledges that the evolution of the state system in the region is not linear and that the state is derived just as much from social realms as from economic and other factors. He also notes the need to reflect on ethno-national, geopolitical, economic and cultural dynamics in the categorization and re-categorization of states in the region. In the wake of the Arab Spring, Saouli also offers a timely reminder that 'the process can reverse ... when we talk about a state we are in essence referring to a regime ... that dominates other forces within a social field; not a public organization' (2012, p. 20)

In the chapters that follow, the three basic themes outlined above (what is the Middle East?; the debate on Orientalism; and the concept of the state in the Middle East) will resonate in the thematic discussions of colonialism, Arab nationalism, political economy, conflict and lack of peace, the impact of political Islam, the debate about political participation and democratization, women, and ethnicity. The themes and issues affecting the contemporary politics of the Middle East are inextricably interwoven in a fascinating and rich tapestry in which individual threads may be unravelled only in the context of associated themes. The issue of gender in the Middle East, for example, cannot be fully understood without grasping the nature of the state – state type, the make-up of the elite and other power-holders in society, the pros and cons of the debate about Orientalism in representing the 'other': all apply equally to the gender theme and highlight the inextricable links between the essential issues discussed in this book.

Questions for discussion

- Is the Middle East an artificial construct of the West?
- In what ways does Said's description of Orientalism as an exercise of cultural power align to political power in the Middle East?
- Is the nation-state doomed to failure in the Middle East?

Recommended reading

- Albert Hourani (1991) offers the most comprehensive introduction to the history of the Arab people, which reflects many of the issues raised here. Cleveland and Bunton (2009) also offer a good basic introductory text on the history of the region, with a useful focus on the Ottoman period and twentieth-century political history.
- Choueiri's (2005) edited companion history of the Middle East is very valuable in terms of its breadth and depth – the individual chapters address such themes as formative Islam, cultural traditions and social structure, dynastic rule, independence and nation-building. Gelvin (2007) provides a very strong 500-year history of the region and addresses formative eras and periods such as the 'Great Transformation' through an engaging narrative which is helpful for first-time students of the area.

- Ilan Pappe (2005), while still chronologically surveying the contemporary history of the region (from the end of the Ottoman Empire), provides his reader with a non-traditional history that offers an insight into rural and urban accounts, and the place of popular culture, including music, cinema and literature, in the region.
- Mansfield (1992) and Sluglett and Farouk-Sluglett (1993) offer concise historical overviews and summaries of individual states and their histories; their accounts have not dated. Choueiri (2003) reflects on historical discourse of the nation-state in the region.
- For the debate on Orientalism, Said (1978) offers the platform from which many arguments and debates have been constructed. Other authors such as Turner (1994) must be included in any reading on the subject. These can be contrasted with Lewis (1968, 1976) and the debate in the *New York Review of Books* between Lewis and Said in 1982. Halliday (2003) offers a discussion of Orientalism and its critics which attempts an even-handed approach to the debate. In addition, wider aspects of the Orientalism controversy may be found in Butterworth (1980), Kerr (1980) and Hussain, Olson and Qureshi (1984). Further rebuttals can be found in Lewis (1993a). Lockman (2004) offers a survey of western knowledge of the Middle East or the 'Orient' from its earliest engagements with the region to the present. He examines Said's contributions and the debates they have provoked. This can be contrasted with Karsh and Miller's searing critique of Edward Said's *Orientalism* in their article of 2008.
- Contemporary perspectives on the state can be found in a variety of texts which examine the Middle East. It may be best to start with Owen (2004) who establishes a sophisticated level of analysis, as discussed above. Guazzone and Pioppi's edited text (2009) provides strong coverage of the state and its vagaries in the contemporary era. Fawcett's edited text (2016) is strong on the international relations of the region, including linkages to globalization, regional alliances, and a historical over-the-shoulder view that includes chapters on the Cold War and the emergence of the modern state system.
- State and its dynamic in the contemporary Middle East is powerfully conveyed in Hudson (2015) and other authors, such as the work of Heydemann and Leenders (2014) in exploring authoritarian state resilience in the wake of the Arab Spring.

CHAPTER ONE

Colonial Rule: Shaping the Destiny of a Region

Introduction

Direct colonial rule in the Middle East in the twentieth century was relatively short-lived, yet its impact on the political systems of the region was
immense and persists to the present day. The interest of various European
powers, and of the British and the French in particular, can be dated to the
end of the eighteenth and beginning of the nineteenth century, but it was
in the period between the First and Second World Wars that the potent
force of the West made its lasting mark. Foreign interest in the region was
nothing new and, when the European powers of the time became involved,
the shadow of earlier Crusades fell over them, arming them with biblical
and religious justification for their thinly veiled economic and strategic
enterprises in the area. In addition, European interference in the Middle
East was always competitive, with the French, Italians and British struggling with each other to secure their own national interests in the area.
The more benign explanation for this colonial enterprise was that Europe
was helping the Middle East fulfil its potential after centuries of backward-
ness and stagnation. This experience was not unique to the Middle East;
rather, it was just one other area of the globe alongside Africa and South
East Asia that was exploited as the Industrial Age created new demands for
profit at its European base. Today, multinational corporations compete for
markets in the region, but in those early days it was state power bolstered
by emerging market capitalism that advanced into economically uncon-
quered territory. Indeed, 'today's globalization and yesterday's colonialism'
are perceived as really not so very different by authors such as Henry and
Springborg in examining the nature of power and economy in the Middle
East (2010, p. xiii).

   The advent of European political as well as economic control over the
region began in earnest in the 1880s with Britain's occupation of Egypt, and
reached an apex after the First World War when Britain and France were

awarded mandates and protectorates and the right to redraw boundaries and create new nation-states in the region. The record of colonialism, however, was poor. From 1918 onwards, the Middle East was plunged into political turmoil as the colonial powers struggled to exert their power and influence over their subject populations. A way of life that had evolved over many centuries of Ottoman rule was disrupted, fractured and shattered by the colonial powers keen to expropriate traditions and customs, make their mark and shape the region in the European mould of political, economic and social relations. The process of modernization introduced by the colonial powers resulted in social dislocation, with traditional tribal powers under-mined by a new class of urban notables, a decline of the rural in favour of the urban, and the creation of new states such as Iraq and Jordan where boundaries took little account of pre-existing ethnic, religious and tribal configurations. Cities did not become more urban but more ruralized (Hudson, 1977, p. 143), and the state failed to meet the demands of the new urban mass, leading to political mobilization. The end product of all this was a political landscape that was first imposed on the region and then adapted by local elites, creating tensions that it has spent more than a century coming to terms with.

The impact of foreign intervention in the economy, politics and social fabric of the Middle East is subject to some considerable debate, led by scholars such as Charles Issawi and Roger Owen. Issawi (1982) outlined the matter in a plain fashion when he declares that 'for every single [colonial] country the direct economic costs of empire [in the Middle East] far out-weighed the direct economic benefits' (p. 214). If there were no direct economic benefits to be derived from the colonial exploitation of the Middle East, what then of the legacy the colonizers left behind when they eventually withdrew, or were ousted from the region? Mainstream thinking typically ascribes a colonial legacy that has scarred the region, frustrated political as well as economic development, and that supports the continu-ing hostility, suspicion and distrust that still disfigures relations between this particular East and West. Yet, while authors like Owen (2004) also acknowledge this legacy, they factor in other dimensions such as the new political space which the creation of the colonially inspired nation-state produced in the Middle East. The secularizing nature of the state is also brought into the equation when measuring the degree to which colonial-ism was able to transform the pre-existing social, religious, economic and political structures of the region. Building up a black-and-white vision of colonizers and colonized in the Middle East, of economic and political winners and losers, as both Issawi and Owen argue, is highly problematic and does not truly represent the reality of the experience in the region. In this respect, one is reminded of the scene in Monty Python's *Life of Brian* when the local rebels ask 'What have the Romans ever done for us?' The dialogue is worth repeating:

Box 1.1 Monty Python: 'What have the Romans ever done for us?'

The scene is set inside Matthias' house. The room is dark and the plotters are gathered. Reg and Stan and Francis address their masked comrades.

Reg: They've bled us white, the bastards. They've taken everything we had, not just from us, from our fathers and from our fathers' fathers.

Stan: And from our fathers' fathers' fathers.

Reg: Yes.

Stan: And from our fathers' fathers' fathers' fathers.

Reg: All right, Stan. Don't labour the point. And what have they ever given us in return?

Xerxes: The aqueduct.

Reg: Oh yeah, yeah they gave us that. Yeah. That's true.

Masked Activist: And the sanitation!

Stan: Oh yes ... sanitation, Reg, you remember what the city used to be like.

Reg: All right, I'll grant you that the aqueduct and the sanitation are two things that the Romans have done ...

Matthias: And the roads ...

Reg: *(sharply)* Well yes, obviously the roads ... the roads go without saying. But apart from the aqueduct, the sanitation and the roads ...

Another Masked Activist: Irrigation ...

Other Masked Voices: Medicine ... Education ... Health ...

Reg: Yes ... all right, fair enough ...

Activist near Front: And the wine ...

Omnes: Oh yes! True!

Francis: Yeah. That's something we'd really miss if the Romans left, Reg.

Masked Activist at Back: Public baths!

Stan: And it's safe to walk in the streets at night now.

Francis: Yes, they certainly know how to keep order ... *(general nodding)* ... let's face it, they're the only ones who could in a place like this. *(More general murmurs of agreement)*

Reg: All right ... all right ... but apart from better sanitation and medicine and education and irrigation and public health and roads and a freshwater system and baths and public order ... what have the Romans done for us?

Xerxes: Brought peace!

Peace, yes ... shut up!

Reg: *(very angry, he's not having a good meeting at all)* what!? Oh ... *(scornfully)*

(*Monty Python's Life of Brian*, 1979, transcript)

When Britain, France, Spain and Italy relinquished their claims and authority in the Middle East, other foreign forces attempted to fill their shoes. From 1945, for example, the USA became an increasingly important influence in the region, heralding an era of what some refer to as 'neo-imperialism' or 'pax Americana' (Zunes, 2009). Despite the decline of Cold War politics in the Middle East theatre, the American influence in the area persisted in the absence of a Soviet foe. This influence, however, began to dwindle in the wake of bruising interventions in Iraq, the NATO-led imposition in Libya in 2011, and the military showdown in support of local armed and allied forces in conflict theatres such as Syria. The American appetite for the neo-imperial project under the Obama administration waned markedly, leading to its declining influence and in turn the re-assertion of local regional power and that of states such as Putin's Russia (Pollack, 2016).

Merchants and missionaries

European interest in the Middle East was always part of the economic enterprise that started during the Industrial Revolution. As Europe expanded, its populations grew, industrial techniques were refined, transport and trade routes were developed, and it was inevitable that the impact of all this would wash up on the shores of the eastern Mediterranean and extend its influence throughout Arabia and Africa. In addition, the economic expansion was accompanied by the growing political, cultural and social interest in what became known as the Orient. As the historian Albert Hourani (1991) points out, 'behind the merchants and ship-owners of Europe stood the ambassadors and consuls of the great powers, supported in the last resort by the armed might of their governments' (p. 268). The great powers engaged in eager competition for the markets of the Middle East, and throughout the century the British, Russians, Germans, French and Italians struggled with each other to gain an influence over the Ottoman provinces and their governors. In this respect, as Owen (1981) argues, throughout the nineteenth century, 'the major force or group of forces behind the restructuring of Middle Eastern economic life can be shown to have come from Europe and from the world economy' (p. 292). While local or internally driven reforms undertaken by Ottoman or Egyptian rulers played their part in the great economic transformation of the century, the European imprint had been rapidly established and its effects would reverberate over the whole region.

The vanguard nature of the capitalist adventure in the Middle East should not be forgotten, as it predates the more formal intervention of European governments in the region. By the beginning of the nineteenth century, European businesses, investors and merchants had long-established strong economic ties with the region. Their ambition was to turn the markets of the East towards the West, create levels of dependency, establish a local bourgeoisie ready to support the capitalist venture, and encourage the religious and political rulers of the Ottoman Empire to opt into western-based capital markets. The financial adventure in the region paid off in a number of ways, the most important of which was the increasing dependency of the Arab and Turkish markets on Europe. As Ayubi (1995) remarks, 'The ever-increasing need not only for European expertise but also for European trade and finance eventually led to serious financial and economic difficulties everywhere as well as Ottoman and Egyptian bankruptcy, while Egypt's indebtedness actually brought British occupation to the country' (p. 87). Thus, when Gladstone ordered British troops into Egypt in 1882 he did so to preserve British imperial, economic and financial interests against French competition and Egyptian nationalism, rather than, as was claimed at the time, to promote political independence for the Egyptian people (Harrison, 1995).

It would take some seventy years before Britain's so-called temporary occupation of the country could be ended and, perhaps more importantly, Britain's financial hold released. Arab independence would never again be a purely political issue. British colonial policy was designed to encourage economic development in Egypt and the generation of wealth that Europeans, not the native Egyptians, would enjoy. The economic and political system was developed in support of this function. The Suez Canal, for example, was an excellent source of income for the Europeans, as Issawi points out:

Box 1.2 Suez, source of riches

By 1881 Britain accounted for over 80 per cent of canal traffic and nearly two-thirds of its trade east of Suez passed through the canal, as did half of India's total trade … Moreover, as a holder of 44 per cent of the canal stock after purchase, the British government drew a substantial income.

(1982, p. 51)

In North Africa, the French succeeded in extending their political and economic power over Algeria in particular; by the 1830s, they had established themselves in the country and were busy promoting themselves through local leaders such as Abd al-Khadar. By the 1840s, the French occupation of Algeria was complete and a policy of settling a community of French rulers and bureaucrats in the country was officially adopted. Throughout the 1870s and 1880s, thousands of French settlers arrived in Algeria to colonize land given to them for free by the French state. The end of the century saw the European population of the country rise to 578,000, with settlers living in European style, planning cities and spreading throughout rural areas in large landholdings. The colonization of the country would last for more than a century and would remain until the late 1940s. France was also influential in Morocco, competing with the Spanish for power, and in Tunisia, which became a French protectorate in 1881. The French colonization policy there did not succeed to the extent it had done in Algeria. As Lustick points out: 'As early as 1848, Algeria was officially declared an integral part of France. In 1871 Algeria was divided into metropolitan-style departments, shifting primary administrative control of the territory from the Ministry of Colonial Affairs to the Ministry of the Interior' (1993, p. 81). In addition, Algeria's rulers were not drawn from the indigenous Muslim population but from the French settler community.

In other North African countries during this period, it was the British and French competition over Egypt which was most significant. French interests were evident with Napoleon's conquest of the country in the 1790s and the Suez Canal project; however, it was Britain that succeeded in occupying the country in 1882. Of course, Britain was not acting altruistically but occupied Egypt to secure the Suez Canal as a passage to India – a strategic defence to the East, a market for British exports and a ready supply of cotton for the Lancashire mills.

The rest of the region was subject to various attempts at incursion and foreign domination by the Russians, Spanish, Germans, French, British and Italians. To a greater or lesser degree, the rulers of the Ottoman Empire were unable to resist the foreign encroachment and were increasingly compelled to relinquish economic and strategic rights in paper agreements with the governments of Russia, France and Britain. By the end of the nineteenth century, the imperial forces of Europe were dominating the region, while the leaders of the Ottoman Empire were perceived as nothing more than 'paper tigers'. Europe was in the region and the region was subsequently defined by Europe, as Edward Said remarks: 'For despite their differences, the British and French saw the Orient as a geographical and cultural, political, demographic, sociological and historical entity over whose destiny they believed themselves to have traditional entitlement' (1978, p. 221).

The merchants and, subsequently, the governments that engaged in this great escapade were supported morally, religiously and culturally in their 'traditional entitlement' by a growing corps of missionaries, artists, writers, and gentlemen and lady travellers who began to venture into the region to (re-)discover its people, its archaeological riches and culture. As empire expanded, so too did Orientalism as a legitimating ideology of oppression of the native people of the region. Missionary societies were active in the area from the early nineteenth century, with Protestant, Catholic, Anglican, Quaker, American Protestant, Presbyterian and others establishing missions throughout the region with the express purpose of converting Muslims and Jews to Christianity. The priests of the West were zealous in their efforts to convert the 'barbarians' of the East and were largely insensitive to the traditions of Islam as a faith and system of government.

Many believed that the colonial task could only be achieved if Christianity was resurrected, the humiliations of the Crusader kingdoms erased and the biblical obligation fulfilled. This obligation manifested itself in a variety of ways. It would result in the revival of evangelical activity, missions, schools, libraries, charities, churches, religious colonies in cities such as Jerusalem, Damascus, Beirut and Cairo, and growing support for the notion of the restoration of Zion as a homeland for the Jewish people. In the Ottoman province of Syria, which at that time included Beirut and Damascus, Christian religious orders were responsible for establishing hundreds of schools to educate thousands of local students. In Damascus, for example, an Irish Presbyterian school was established as early as the 1860s as part of an ongoing mission programme, that, in the words of its founding minister, would mean that everyone 'will know where to find a Bible, a Protestant minister and Christian worship'.

Writers, artists, travellers, poets, archaeologists and surveyors flocked to the Middle East. By the late 1870s, tour companies offered trips to areas within the Middle East including Egypt, Istanbul and the Holy Land (Lyth, 2013). Consulates and diplomatic missions were established, land was purchased and European society flourished in the cities of the Orient. Thousands of travellers returned and recorded their impressions in print, in poetry or on canvas, thereby feeding the image that the Middle East was a divine gift with a supine population of lazy natives grateful for Europe's role in their countries.

William Blake, Robert Browning, David Roberts, George Eliot, Walter Scott and Byron, along with many others from France, Italy, Germany and other European countries, produced a body of arts in the form of music, film, paintings, literature, poetry and theatre that actualized the Orient for western consumption (Teo, 2014). The native population – Arabs or others – were largely invisible, but when noticed were described in hostile terms. The following extract symbolizes such hostility to the 'inferior' locals:

Box 1.3 An Englishman and the Yemenite

'As ... a personal servant I had a Yemenite named Na'man Mohammed', writes one Englishman in his personal account of time in Arabia. 'He was useless at his job ... He was ugly and dirty and slow on the uptake ...', but he later commends the man for becoming 'adept with a tin opener' and cooking the best 'chipped potatoes' the Englishman had ever tasted. Describing another Arab worker he says, 'Official government guides were obligatory ... I had a repulsive specimen called Salim. He had a large Semitic nose, close set eyes and a harsh croak for a voice. Physically inferior, he achieved his ends in life by deceit and intrigue ...' Even 'good' men were regarded with suspicion though. The Englishman feared his Arab 'Moslems' of plotting to rob him, 'stealing from the Infidel', and they were described also as 'fanatically religious' only because they prayed 'at all the prescribed times'.

(Walford, 1963, pp. 30–7)

Such views were also popularly reinforced by the new 'pilgrims' from the West to the Holy Land who engaged with a wider shaping of an understanding of the region (Bar and Cohen-Hattab, 2003, p. 133). These contributions would help determine and support the dominant relationship based on the philosophy of colonial expansion in the Middle East that would endure well into the contemporary era.

By the end of the nineteenth century, British and French primacy in the Middle East seemed assured. Local elites supported the role of foreign forces in their countries, colonial and imperial development policies continued apace, and the notion of empire reached its apex. The social fabric of the region had been constantly refashioned or manipulated to suit, in part, western rather than indigenous political or economic agendas. Westernization continued and was evident in the politics, literature, art, political thought, dress, social pastimes and culture of the region. Westernization also meant secularization, and the impact of these forces was most obviously apparent among the urban elites of cities such as Algiers, Tunis, Beirut, Cairo and Damascus, where an audience receptive to the ideas of the West was found. Some of the indigenous bonds of identity in the region, whether based on tribe, ethnic loyalty, religion or other factors, were slowly eroded or rearticulated within a western framework. This transformation of society would have class-based features; indeed, the process created new classes and social groupings, and touched the lives of some groups far more deeply than others. In this way the colonial encounter brought benefit and privilege for the peoples of the region, but, as Issawi reminds us:

Box 1.4 Robber barons

per capita incomes … [had] … certainly risen; however, since a large part of the increment was absorbed by the privileged sections of society – foreigners, minorities, wealthy Muslims, army and bureaucrats – this does not necessarily imply that the levels of living of the mass rose correspondingly.

(1982, p. 103)

New forms of identity, in particular the rise of nationalist aspirations, were also a response to the colonial domination of the region and the increasing sense of powerlessness and loss of authority within the Ottoman Empire as it stood on the brink of its final decade.

The First World War and the death of the Ottoman Empire

The Ottoman Empire survived for over 400 years but ultimately it was unable to withstand the impact of Europe bolstered by the Industrial Revolution and post-Enlightenment thinking. Little by little, the Ottoman rulers of Constantinople first lost control over their eastern European provinces, then over Algeria and Egypt (to France and Britain). In 1908, in the heart of the Empire, the Young Turks took political control and openly promoted a secular Turkish nationalism (Kedourie, 1992, pp. 72–4). By 1911, Italy had succeeded in occupying Tripoli and Benghazi in what is present-day Libya. Ottomanism, as government, culture, politics and religious rule, was dying, and a struggle took place within the Middle East to establish alternatives. The unity of the Empire could no longer be counted on through appeals either to the Ottoman source of authority, to Islam or to newly emergent Turkish nationalism (Eligur, 2010, p. 29). There was no shortage of alternatives: Arab, pan-Arab, pan-Islamic, Wahabi, Turkish and Kurdish responses began to emanate from the region, many in reaction or response to the impact of colonialism. Apart from in Turkey, no indigenous nationalist movement was able to succeed against European competition for power in the region. The European defeat of the Ottomans, who had sided with Germany in the First World War, assured Britain and France the territorial prize of the Middle East. Since the war had been waged in the Middle East as much as in Europe, the European powers found themselves again in the position of enemies, forming strategic alliances between themselves but at the same time pursuing single-mindedly national rather than allied interests. Thus, while Britain and France were allied against the Germans and their Ottoman supporters, they also competed against each other for territorial control of as much land in the Middle East as possible. Behind closed doors, Britain and France operated in an atmosphere of mutual suspicion, conspiracy, competition and control, while maintaining a public face of alliance and benign patronage towards the incipient nationalist movements and their leaders.

Militarily, British successes on the battlefields of the Middle East assumed greater strategic, as well as emblematic, importance than French victories. In 1917, in Palestine, British General Edmund Allenby had marched into the city of Jerusalem to accept the Turkish surrender, a victory that was important symbolically as well as for the morale of the British war effort.

Box 1.5 Allenby's account

I entered the city officially at noon, December 11th, with a few of my staff, the commanders of the French and Italian detachments, the heads of the political missions, and the Military Attachés of France, Italy, and America.

The procession was all afoot, and at Jaffa gate I was received by the guards representing England, Scotland, Ireland, Wales, Australia, New Zealand, India, France, and Italy. The population received me well.

Guards have been placed over the holy places. My Military Governor is in contact with the acting custodians and the Latin and Greek representatives. The Governor has detailed an officer to supervise the holy places.

Box 1.5 *(Continued)*

The Mosque of Omar and the area around it have been placed under Moslem control, and a military cordon of Mohammedan officers and soldiers has been established around the mosque.

Orders have been issued that no non-Moslem is to pass within the cordon without permission of the Military Governor and the Moslem in charge.

(Source Records of the Great War, vol. V, ed. Charles F. Horne, 'National Alumni 1923': www.firstworldwar.com/source/jerusalem_allenby1.htm)

Strategic and political interests, however, were better served by British success in securing the Palestinian port of Haifa, and towns like Nazareth and Nablus. The Europeans did not fight the war in the Middle East alone. Through a web of intrigue and double diplomacy, the Arabs and the newly established Zionist movement were included in support of the allied effort. In particular, the Hashemites of Mecca and Hijaz, led by Sharif Hussein, became subverted to British interest (Tell, 2013). By 1916, the British had succeeded in persuading Sharif Hussein to raise an Arab army to lead a revolt against their Ottoman rulers. The British, in return for Arab assistance, had promised that Arab independence would be supported, an assurance that was made official in the McMahon–Hussein Correspondence.

Box 1.6 Letter from Sir H. McMahon to the Sharif of Mecca, 30 August 1915

We have the honour to thank you for your frank expressions of the sincerity of your feeling towards England. We rejoice, moreover, that your Highness and your people are of one opinion that Arab interests are English interests and English Arab. To this intent we confirm to you the terms of Lord Kitchener's message, which reached you by the hand of Ali Effendi, and in which was stated clearly our desire for the independence of Arabia and its inhabitants, together with our approval of the Arab Khalifate when it should be proclaimed. We declare once more that His Majesty's Government would welcome the resumption of the Khalifate by an Arab of true race ...

Friendly reassurances. Salutations!

(Signed)   A. H. McMAHON

(McMahon, 1939)

Yet the interpretation of so-called 'promises' made in the correspondence was later questioned: 'Whether anything was actually promised, and if so what, and whether the Sharif's revolt played a significant part in the allied victory, are matters in dispute, but what is clear is that for the first time the claim that those who spoke Arabic constituted a nation and should have a state had been to some extent accepted by a great power', remarks Hourani (1991, p. 317).

The Arab Revolt of 1916–18 which resulted in the capture of Damascus also involved the legendary Lawrence of Arabia on the Hashemite side. As figure 1.1 demonstrates, Arab interests were, however, constrained – Britain remaining literally at the shoulder of the new leaders. Believed to be pro-Arab, but ultimately controlled by British national interest, T. E. Lawrence and his Arab colleague Prince Faisal, son of Sharif Hussein, would play an important part in the post-war settlement of the Middle East at the Paris and San Remo peace conferences.

Following the end of the First World War, Britain and France engaged in what is described as an embarrassing squabble for control of territory in the Middle East. At the Paris and San Remo peace conferences, Arab hopes and demands for a new world order, where the Arabs' right to self-determination would be honoured, were dashed on the altar of British and French ambition. Secret agreements and double promises made during the desperate times of war were now made public, as the new generation of Arab leaders, who had led the Arab Revolt along with T. E. Lawrence as part of the war effort, realized they had been cruelly deceived by the Europeans. Little regard was paid

Figure 1.1 *Spoils of war? Arabs and T. E. Lawrence at the Paris Peace Conference 1919.* © CORBIS

to promises made in the now infamous McMahon–Hussein Correspondence. Sharif Hussein and three of his sons, Princes Abdullah, Faisal and Ali, were thwarted by the British and the French at the international conferences as they tried to achieve the goal of full independence. Instead, they were appointed as the puppet heads of new nation-states – Iraq, Syria and Trans-jordan – which were placed under the mandate and control of either Britain or France. Arab independence in these states would not be immediately forthcoming and a further world war would be waged before de jure or de facto independence was achieved.

The Sykes–Picot Agreement of 1916, in which Britain, France and imperial Russia agreed to partition the Middle East between them, did little to bolster Arab confidence in the promises of independence that they believed the allied powers had held out to them during the war.

Box 1.7 The Sykes–Picot Agreement

It is accordingly understood between the French and British Governments;
1. That France and Great Britain are prepared to recognize and protect an independ-ent Arab State or a Confederation of Arab States in the areas (A) and (B) marked on the annexed map, under the suzerainty of an Arab chief. That in area (A) France, and in area (B) Great Britain, shall have priority of right of enterprise and local loans. That in area (A) France, and in area (B) Great Britain, shall alone supply advisers or foreign functionaries at the request of the Arab State or Confederation of Arab States … (The Sykes–Picot Agreement, 15–16 May 1916)

Almost a hundred years later, the spectre of Sykes–Picot was raised by ISIS, who declared it redundant. Western commentators also viewed the agree-ment as redolent of a past age rather than the 'realities' of the present day.

In many respects the Arabs regarded the *coup de grâce* as the Balfour Dec-laration of 1917, in which the British government gave its support for the establishment of a Jewish homeland in Palestine. British policy fell in favour of supporting the Zionist cause:

Box 1.8 The Balfour Declaration, 1917

His Majesty's government view with favour the establishment in Palestine of a national home for the Jewish people, and will use their best endeavours to facilitate the achievement of this object, it being clearly understood that nothing shall be done which may prejudice the civil and religious rights of existing non-Jewish communities in Palestine, or the rights and political status enjoyed by Jews in any other country.

(Balfour Declaration, 2 November 1917)

Britain and France engaged in a 'disgusting scramble for the Middle East', described by Elizabeth Monroe as: 'pieces of unabashed self-interest, suggesting to onlookers that all talk of liberating small nations from oppression was so much cant' (1963, p. 66).

It was not only that Arab hopes of self-determination were let down. The European powers also succeeded in redrawing the boundaries of the region, creating new nation-states and imposing rulers principally to act as local agents for them. Before 1918, the inhabitants of the Middle East, the majority of whom were Muslim, had lived as subjects of the Ottoman powers of Constantinople, and the borders and boundaries of the region had encompassed provinces in which peoples of various ethnic and religious backgrounds co-existed in relative harmony. The map that emerged resulted in the artificial creation of new states to which the region's citizens felt little or no sense of loyalty or identity and in which European political control appeared assured. As Bromley notes:

Box 1.9 British dismemberment

Britain thus came to favour the dismemberment of the Ottoman Empire and the independence of the Arab provinces. Of course, by this British officials meant 'independence' from Ottoman suzerainty; since the Arabs were unfit for self-government.

(1994, p. 74)

Appearances, however, could be deceptive. Europe's role in and impact on state-formation in the modern Middle East was as much about perception as reality, something that is currently reflected in the ongoing academic controversy over the extent to which colonialism promoted state-formation in the region and the extent to which the western- or European-inspired model was also rooted there. Both Zubaida and Owen note that while modern states in the Middle East are born out of the western model, they are 'for the most part ... not modern Western states' (Zubaida, 1993, p. 145). Indeed, the rootedness of the western model may be challenged from this perspective as it would appear that the success or otherwise of the 'compulsory form of the western model' depends very much on the inclusion of the indigenous political field, pre-existing political institutions, religious influences and socio-economic order. This approach contrasts starkly with the claims of authors like Brown, who believe that the politics and state-formation of the region have not just been 'shaped by intrusive western influences in modern times', but rather that 'the Middle East has become so continuously interlocked politically with the West as to have become almost an appendage of the western power system' (1984, p. 5). Bromley sums up the debate in his criticism of Brown and Fromkin's thesis in which they argue that the Middle East is inherently hostile to the nation-state system, when he declares that, after the European dismemberment of the Ottoman Empire, the 'politics of tribe, Islam and Arabism were all shaped by this context [the modern nation-state], rather than constituting impregnable barriers to modernity' (1994, p. 84).

1918 and after: mandates, protectorates and colonial power

Between 1918 and 1922, when the French and British were awarded their protectorates and mandates and maintained their colonies, the indigenous populations of the Middle East struggled to assert their national rights, their identity and desire for independence. All of them – Arabs, Kurds and Armenians – failed, as the Europeans met behind closed doors in Paris and San Remo to decide the fate of the region. The end product, the new Middle East, was almost unrecognizable from the old empire where rule was Muslim and land was not occupied and settled by strangers from Europe. The region, before and after, highlights the startling changes that the Europeans had wrought in the area. Under the Ottoman Empire, the Arabs had co-existed with their ethnic and religious neighbours without boldly demarcated borders. Under the new order, entirely new political entities were created.

By 1922, the new Middle East was emerging. Modern states were subsequently created, for example, by the British and the French, in Transjordan (which later became the Hashemite Kingdom of Jordan), Syria, Lebanon and Iraq. States were created regardless of the multitudinous ethnic or tribal make-up of the territories. In Lebanon alone, six distinct communities – Maronite Christians, Druze, Sunni Muslim, Shi'a Muslim, Armenians and Greek-Orthodox Christians – were now part of one territorial entity that France governed as a mandated territory. Syria also became a French mandate. Its 'ruler' Faisal – the son of Sharif Hussein, the Hashemite leader of Mecca who, along with his friend Lawrence of Arabia, had occupied Syria during the First World War – was forced by the French to flee his new capital. As a consolation he was 'gifted' the throne of the new state of Iraq when it was created by the British in 1920. However, the consolation of Iraq for Faisal was bitter, and in Baghdad everyone appeared to know that the power behind the throne still lay with the British. 'Well obviously there were riches in Iraq', remarked Iraqi novelist Khaled Khistainy, 'there was oil and so they wanted to secure it and so the British thought it was a good award for them out of the war' (Khistainy, 2002). In Transjordan, Faisal's brother Abdullah sat upon another British-backed throne (Milton-Edwards and Hinchcliffe, 2009, p. 19).

As in other parts of the Third World, rule by the West and from the West took a variety of forms and resulted in a range of state types emerging in the region. Foreign political authority varied from direct to limited control with autonomy for specially selected elites or local agents, including an increasing dependency on the newly established military not just for state coercion but for stability in the modernization process.

It is worth making a distinction, at this point, between the three types of political control undertaken by the British and French in the inter-war period: mandates, protectorates and colonies all imply different types of political rule and expectations. Mandates were a creation of the ill-fated League of Nations. This permitted its member states to take administrative control of other territory on the condition that it was formerly governed by a defeated, or 'backward', enemy. Article 22 of the League's Covenant provided for the mandates system in the Middle East and parts of Africa in those countries that were judged 'incapable yet of national independence', and placed them under the tutelage of a member state perceived as an 'advanced nation'. Today, the very notion of describing states as 'backward' in terms of self-government seems anachronistic and outdated. Mandated territory was divided into three categories, A, B and C, with the former Ottoman Empire falling into category A, which included countries described as having 'peoples not able to stand by themselves under the strenuous conditions of the modern world', and where 'the tutelage of such peoples should be entrusted to advanced nations' (League of Nations, 1919, Article 22). Article 22 also stated that the wishes of the communities in such mandated territories should be a 'principal consideration in the selection of the Mandatory', although in practice there was little evidence of this stricture being adhered to. The territories classed as category A were: Lebanon and Syria, under the mandate of France; Iraq, Palestine and Transjordan, under the mandate of Britain.

Protectorates were territories governed, but not formally annexed, by a stronger state. However, as the example of Egypt highlights, the declaration of a protectorate by Britain in December 1914 was perceived as a 'precedent for other expansionist bookings-in-advance' of British interests in the rest of the Middle East (Monroe, 1963, p. 26). As a British protectorate, the fate of Egypt was no less and no more closely entwined with this particular colonial power than if it had been declared a colony – appearance was the only motive behind this declaration by the British government.

Finally, colonies were semi-independent settlements of emigrants and their descendants, usually in relatively undeveloped areas distant from the homeland. The French colonization of Algeria illustrates this particular European strategy in the Middle East. From as early as 1848, Lustick argues, the French 'officially declared' Algeria 'an integral part of France', treating it as nothing more than another *département* of the country geographically removed from the European frontier (1993, p. 81). Throughout the nineteenth century, the French encountered local resistance in Algeria and defeated it through military encounter and the policy of official colonization adopted by Napoleon III, which encouraged French settlement of land. Whether it is true, as Ageron suggests, that 'Muslim society did not resist the progress of colonization; with its framework broken, it collapsed' (1991, p. 65), has been open to debate. The relative success of local resistance to European intervention and colonialism in the Middle East in the nineteenth and early twentieth centuries is being reassessed by historians currently producing work based on archival research within the region rather than outside it. Moreover, Halliday contended that the tensions generated across the region as a result of western state domination did lead to 'recurrent waves of popular unrest and mobilization' (Halliday, 2003, p. 29).

Inter-war European decline

The inter-war period in the Middle East was dominated by the attempts of the European powers to establish their authority over almost the entire area. The task they faced was impossible more or less from the start. They faced a region-wide movement of political discontent based on the notion of the right to self-determination, a massive social and economic upheaval triggered by the modernization and development process and growing anti-European feeling that reached fever pitch by the late 1940s. The entire period was characterized by rebellion, tension and conflict, rather than stability. Even countries where Britain and France enjoyed a relatively stable colonial past, such as Egypt or Algeria, were caught up in the struggle.

Nevertheless, the British and the French went some considerable way towards shaping and moulding the political features of the new nation-states and existing protectorates and colonies. Very few escaped the impact of the Europeanization of politics, economy, culture and society in the region. As Mitchell highlights in the example of Egypt,

> ### Box 1.10 British penetration in Egypt
> The power of colonialism was itself a power that sought to colonize: to penetrate locally, spreading and establishing settlements not only in the shape of cities and barracks, but in the form of classrooms, journals and works of scholarship. Colonialism – and modern politics generally – distinguished itself in this colonizing power. It was able at the most local level to reproduce theatres of its order and truth.
>
> (1988, p. 171)

The degree to which the colonizing project succeeded in the twentieth century, however, was soon affected by factors such as local resistance, economic issues, global political patterns and the degree to which the traditional state system was altered or reshaped by western forms and institutions of government. In the new states, such as Transjordan and Iraq, the British set about imposing a system of government and politics that attempted the maintenance of British control rather than helping new states towards independence. The rulers of Transjordan and Iraq, Hashemite brothers Kings Abdullah and Faisal, were generally treated with mistrust, suspicion and, ultimately, as puppets of British policy. Any attempt by either of these men to assert their independence from their British overlords resulted in difficulties. In both countries, the British maintained power and influence not only by controlling the purse strings of these infant states and sending out advisers to 'guide' the kings, but also through policies of establishing and maintaining internal security structures, controlling foreign affairs and granting incremental privileges and powers to the Arab rulers only when it suited their interests.

For the British, the inherent weakness of such policies was never acknowledged until it was too late. By promoting puppet rulers, imposing an artificial leadership on people, creating subjects in a new state, establishing new boundaries under a new flag, oath of allegiance and anthem, the British were sowing the seeds for conflict and internal instability. Underneath their benign attitude towards the Arabs, British finance – often of extremely limited means – was forwarded to pay for the new Arab armies and police of these young states.

The intentions of the Arab Hashemite rulers of these political entities were honourable: they dreamt of uniting the Arab people under the same banner that had been raised during the successful Arab Revolt. They saw themselves as leaders of the Arab nation, united by the Muslim faith and common language – Arabic. In reality, the situation could not have been further from the truth, as the Hashemites were compelled to adopt a British-inspired agenda for rule and hegemony over the region. In addition, the most common indicators of identity among the Arab people – the tribe and clan – were identified by the new state bureaucrats as the biggest obstacles to national unity under new rulers and new flags. Tribal sheikhs were often perceived as a significant hindrance to the difficult task of state-building in the new states of Arabia (Bagot-Glubb, 1948).

Sunset empire

Despite the Allied victory in the Second World War, the balance of external, European power in the Middle East began to change in the post-war period. Although Britain appeared to emerge triumphant there, with the French marginalized and weak, policy-makers in London, while continuing to give the impression they were strong players in the region, quickly realized that the war-induced indebtedness and the rise of nationalism at a global level would hinder the pursuance of their interests in the region. From 1945 onwards, Britain descended a slippery slope in the Middle East, one that would lead them to relinquish their mandate in Palestine, weaken their grip on Transjordan and abandon Iraq to the forces of Arab nationalism. British officials were compelled to admit that their time was past and new gods inspired the people of the region.

In Egypt, the jewel in the British crown, the Free Officers coup of 1952 and the Suez Crisis of 1956 put an end to British power there (Kyle, 1991). Only in the Gulf countries would British influence – of sorts – endure for several more decades. In the rest of the Middle East, British prestige went into surprisingly rapid decline. New forces challenged both British and French dominance.

The path of disengagement that took place can be easily traced (see table 1.1). It is not easy to identify a pattern – breaking away from British, French or Italian subordination manifested itself in a variety of ways. Through coups, deposed monarchies, wars of independence, peaceful transition and the ending of protectorate relationships, regional leaders brought about a change of rule. The internal dimensions of change within the region were, of course, also reflected in other parts of the globe, where the process of independence and decolonization dominated the politics of the Third World.

TABLE 1.1 European disengagement from the Middle East, 1945–1971

Date	Event
1943–6	French mandates come to an end in Lebanon and Syria
1946	Transjordan granted independence, becoming the Hashemite Kingdom of Jordan
1947	UN agrees to partition of Palestine
1948	Israel declares independence
1951	Libya granted independence, after the UN rejects British and French petitions for 'trusteeship'
1952	Military coup in Egypt, led by Gamal Abdel Nasser, deposing King Farouk
1953	Egypt declares independence
1956	Egypt nationalizes the Suez Canal
1956	Morocco declares independence
1956	Tunisia declares independence
1957	Formal British–Jordanian Treaty terminated by Jordan; British forces removed from the country
1958	Military coup in Iraq: monarchy overthrown and independence established
1961	Kuwait declares independence
1962	Yemen Arab Republic declares independence
1962	Algeria declares independence
1967	People's Democratic Republic of Yemen declares independence
1971	Bahrain, Qatar, United Arab Emirates declare independence

A characteristic that may be identified in the process in the Middle East is the reluctance with which Britain and France relinquished their hold. This was sometimes combined with their failure to anticipate change in the political environment and, as a result, their questionable approaches and policies to enable political transition whilst protecting their own interests. This is all the more ironic given the fact that the original idea behind the mandate system was that the stronger powers would 'assist' the mandated states to independence. In reality, their presence, politically and militarily, hindered the smooth transition to independence. In addition, with Britain and France no longer in the frame, other external powers stepped into the region with the express desire of building spheres of influence and alliances. Thus, where once France and Britain competed for power in, for example, Egypt, as a means of securing strategic as well as economic interests, there now stood the new superpowers: the USA and the Soviet Union.

Independence subsequently came to mean many things in the Middle East. The nature of the state system, for instance, was not always reconfigured at a local level, nor was there always a complete rejection of the colonial model of government. Indeed, in some cases, new, local, western-educated elites from the military, bureaucracy or urban upper classes merely represented the colonial model as being somehow indigenous, while at the same time declaring their independence and rejection of 'all things western' on the international stage. Political independence in Iran, for example, did not necessarily mean economic independence, as the increasingly oil-based economy of the country remained under western control. Power over the sale of oil and its exploration in Iran became a foreign affair involving first the British and then the Americans. State-formation, therefore, was as much the interest of foreign capital as of the local ruling elite. As Halliday asserted, 'Iran is a country whose recent development has been to a considerable degree shaped by the international ties it has had with the more advanced capitalist economies' (1979, p. 21).

From 1945 to the early 1950s, the movement towards Arab, Iranian and other forms of independence gained momentum, as more and more nationalist groups and young leaders emerged in countries such as Algeria, Egypt, Iran, Iraq, Jordan, Syria, Lebanon and Libya. While the British position in the region following the war may have appeared 'unshaken and in some ways strengthened', less than a decade later this hold appeared increasingly untenable. In this respect, the same was true of France, which was weakened by the war and which found it increasingly difficult to re-establish the control over its colony, protectorates and mandated territory that it had enjoyed before the war. It is asserted that there was a change in British policy towards the Middle East during this post-war period, in which there was support for 'Arab independence and a greater degree of unity, while preserving essential strategic interests by friendly agreement', but British strategic and national interests were always placed above Arab calls for independence (Hourani,

1991, p. 357). While the British may have believed that the Arabs would wait uncomplainingly for independence, they failed to recognize the signs of growing impatience.

The impact and legacy of European domination are varied and complex. Nevertheless, economic and strategic motives were usually the prime drivers. As such, the relationship between Europe and much of the Middle East was antagonistic with one side perceived as permanently strong, the other permanently weak. The relationship between faiths was also emphasized in the Middle East, between the so-called 'Christian West' and the 'Muslim East'. Yet the degree to which religious character really defined relations between these two regions has been grossly overemphasized and utilized consistently to create a perception of difference which damagingly persists to the present.

Independence from European rule was rarely achieved without conflict, and this legacy would mar British–Arab and French–Arab relations for decades. In addition, it is argued that the roots of much of the instability of the present-day Middle East can be found in the colonial era. Colonial rule, and by extension western intervention, is still 'experienced' in one form or another in the present. The culture, economy and politics of the region are affected by the legacy of this experience and this in turn has played its part in creating the sense of crisis and instability that characterizes the region. It is ironic that European states such as France rail against the American assault on their culture, literature, language and mass media, while at the same time appearing to ignore the far greater assault mounted by the colonial European powers, the French included, on the Middle East, which led to a cultural crisis of identity.

The debate about the impact of colonial rule in the Middle East is still ongoing. Some analysts believe that the nature of the relationship between colonizers and colonized can best be explained by looking at economic issues, while others focus on the social structures to inform this debate. But political, social and economic issues, as well as cultural and other effects of colonialism, have all influenced the overall experience. While some believe a uniform picture can be drawn of the degrees of influence the process has had on country-specific economies, political systems and society, others concentrate on the uneven patterns of development and modernization. What remains consistent, however, is the way in which, through the colonial relationship, the nature of the links between the Middle East and the West has been irrevocably altered, creating dynamics of conflict and cooperation.

Case study

Egypt – cotton colony and gateway to riches

Although at the beginning of the twentieth century the Middle East was still under Ottoman rule, in Egypt a European foothold in the country had been established as early as 1798, when French forces led by Napoleon occupied the country. The first decades of the nineteenth century heralded great change in Egypt, encouraged by its Arab ruler Mohammed Ali and his successors. The Egyptian economy was oriented to the European market, and cotton, in particular, became a prime export. The building of railways and other transport routes such as the Suez Canal, which was opened in 1869, however, led Egypt into increasing financial over-extension. Large sums of money were borrowed from European governments and private finance. Indebtedness and the prospects of political instability prompted the British to move against the Egyptians in 1882 to restore order, at which point their military occupation began. From 1882 to 1956, British influence and control over Egypt would dictate the development of the country.

The British occupation of Egypt by more than 24,000 troops was supposed to be short-lived, designed to quell a local nationalist-inspired rebellion led against Mohammed Ali's successor Khedive Ismail. Yet it became rapidly apparent that the 'rebellion' was a pretext by which Britain could assert itself over the most important country in the region. For the next seven decades, real power and control over the affairs of the Egyptian state rested in British hands. This in turn gave Britain economic, strategic and political control over the Suez Canal, which had been described in Whitehall as the 'Gateway to India'. From 1882 to 1914, during the first phase of British rule over Egyptian political life, control of the state and its institutions and the economy remained a largely British affair, with nominal and symbolic power placed in the hands of the Khedive and later the king (Fuad 1922–36 and Farouk 1936–52). Britain certainly preferred to promote monarchy rather than republicanism in the country, and the region as a whole. This was because, as Owen (2004) points out, a 'king constrained by a constitution was seen as a vital support for the British position, since he provided an important element of continuity and could always be used to dismiss any popularly elected government of nationalists that threatened to tear up or amend the arrangements defining Britain's rights' (p. 21).

The development of the country was geared to economic exploitation, and to this end certain developments in Egypt's infrastructure were initiated by Britain. In particular, the cotton industry, which ultimately represented Egypt's entire foreign trade, led to the establishment of an agriculturally based and capital-driven infrastructure. Such developments included large-scale irrigation works (which profoundly affected Egypt's social structure), roads, railways and a trading system which sent basic food prices up and created new levels of poverty for ordinary Egyptians – the peasants (*fellahin*) involved in growing and cropping cotton for export. Wealth derived from the production of cotton and its export was largely enjoyed by the Europeans and a small class of Egyptian landowners. In 1821, the export of Egyptian cotton was just 1,000 quantars; in 1823, this rose to 259,000, and by the 1880s 2.5 million quantars of cotton were being exported from Egypt for the

cotton mills of Lancashire and beyond. By 1910–14, cotton accounted for over
90 per cent of Egypt's exports, and the growth of other crops, such as wheat,
went into decline, as more and more acreage around the fertile Nile River
was given over to the production of cotton. Colonial control over Egypt did
bring some benefits to the Arab population, but these benefits were never
distributed evenly and the British deliberately pursued a policy of 'divide and
rule'. Some classes or groups of Egyptians were always more privileged than
others even in the distribution of benefits such as improved transportation,
health care and education. But at the bottom of the social and economic pile
lay Egypt's largest social group or class, the Muslim rural peasant population
who toiled the land generating the profit that Britain enjoyed.

The First World War added a new dimension to colonial politics in the
Middle East, and in Britain the strategic importance of the Suez Canal was
emphasized. In an attempt to shore up its interests further, Britain declared
Egypt a 'protectorate' in December 1914. As such, Egypt was placed under
the tighter grip of British rule, which was augmented by a large and powerful military and security system. Opposition to the British grew among
Egyptians and intensified during the war, and by 1918 an emerging nationalist movement had developed. It was encouraged further by regional successes
of the Arab nationalist movement during the war and its goal was to put an
end to British occupation, and to establish self-determination and independence for Egypt. This desire was apparent in the formation of a new political
movement or party known as the Wafd, under the leadership of Saad Zaghlul
and Nahas Pasha. The British, however, were implacably opposed to Egyptian
calls for independence, a reaction that served only to deepen Egyptian opposition and hostility.

From 1918 to 1922, Egyptian pressure on the British for greater political
freedom grew, and in February 1922 the British terminated the protectorate
and declared the country a 'constitutional monarchy' under Egyptian kings
Fuad and Farouk. In theory, the Egyptians may well have been free, but in
practice the new political order was a façade for the maintenance of British
control. While a constitution was written and promulgated in 1923, a parliament elected, a government formed and King Fuad declared head of state,
Egyptians, despite many differences, remained united around one issue –
that Britain should relinquish its political and military control over their
country. But instead Britain persuaded the King to dissolve his government,
and maintained its political and military presence in the country. Negotiations between the two sides took place sporadically and resulted in the 1936
Anglo-Egyptian Treaty which further shored up British interests.

During the Second World War, Egypt served as an important base for
Britain, and military rule prevailed once more. When the war ended, nationalist and Islamic groups, like the Muslim Brotherhood that had been founded
in 1928, agitated for independence. For the next five years, Egyptian pressure
for independence grew in all quarters of society and political stability was

increasingly hard to maintain, despite the coercive powers of the British-controlled state and a malleable monarchy. The British found it increasingly difficult to resist the tide of change that by this stage had gripped the rest of the Third World. In 1950 they eventually agreed to enter into negotiations with Egyptian nationalists. A deadlock in the talks by 1951 led the nationalists to abrogate the Anglo-Egyptian Treaty unilaterally. Widespread violence and attacks against the British soon broke out and by January 1952 martial law was declared over the entire country. In July 1952, Egyptian nationalist officers mounted a coup d'état, King Farouk abdicated, the 1923 constitution was abolished, and political parties were dissolved. The Free Officers, led by Muhammad Naguib and Gamal Abdel Nasser, had finally succeeded in ousting the British. The new military government quickly sought a settlement with Britain to get it to withdraw its forces, and in October 1954 an agreement was signed between the two, declaring the termination of the 1936 Anglo-Egyptian Treaty and withdrawal within twenty months. Nasser's ultimate blow against the British was his announcement in July 1956 of a decision to nationalize the Suez Canal and thus wrest control of it and the majority of its revenues from British hands. The import of this decision lay not just around the issue of Suez as a strategic waterway and the revenues that now accrued to Egyptian national coffers, but the ability of leaders in newly independent countries to assert their control over the superpowers. After the Suez Crisis, in which Egypt defeated the combined military might of Britain, France and Israel, colonial rule in the region would never be the same again.

Case study
The Palestine *débâcle*

The prospects for British rule over Palestine were never very good. When Allenby conquered Jerusalem in 1917, however, the British government envisaged a new era of rule in the Holy Land. But what it failed to realize, even from the earliest times, was that it would never be able to reconcile the demands made on it by Zionist Jews, keen to hold Britain to the promises implicit in the Balfour Declaration, and the rights of the indigenous Palestinian Arab population to self-determination and independence (Milton-Edwards, 2008). Britain's failure to reconcile these demands and its inability to govern the mandate territory of Palestine left a lasting mark on the region.

Following Allenby's occupation in 1917, the area was placed under military administration (or occupation) until 1920. Palestine was divided into districts and, as far as they were compatible with the military nature of the occupation, Ottoman codes of law were applied. From 1920 onwards the British, in receipt of their League of Nations mandate, governed the country under civil administration. The indigenous inhabitants of the country, the

Palestinian Arabs and Jews and the newly established Zionist Jewish community, were given no political powers by the British. A curious aspect of
the mandate was the extent to which it safeguarded the interests of the
Zionists, obliging Britain to 'be responsible for placing the country under
such political, administrative and economic conditions as will secure the
establishment of a Jewish national home', while Palestinian Arab political
rights to self-determination were neglected.

The inability of the British authorities to address the dual issue of Zionist
aspirations and Palestinian rights over the same piece of territory ensured that
the period of the mandate (1920–48) was characterized by almost continual
communal conflict, revolt and political upheaval. The British allowed both
sides to believe – at one time or another, or to a greater or lesser degree – that
self-determination and statehood would be fulfilled. Britain had promised
support to the Zionists and the Palestinian Arabs during the war, and in the
post-war era both sides expected Britain to maintain its side of the bargain.

The notion of a return to Zion was always present in the Jewish Diaspora,
but it was on the heels of the Russian pogroms and a revival of European
hostility to Jews and anti-Semitism that a Jewish man named Theodor Herzl
formulated a political vision of an in-gathering of the exiles to Zion. In 1896,
Herzl wrote and published a book entitled *Der Judenstatt* in which he argued
that Jewish assimilation in Europe was a pipe dream. He presented an alternative vision of a return to Zion that at this point consisted of an idea rather
than a place. In the years that followed, Herzl's supporters began to propose
a number of locations for the new Zion, amongst which Palestine featured.
Herzl was a secularist; his vision was a political solution to the growing tide
of anti-Semitism sweeping Europe in the latter half of the nineteenth century.

In 1897, Herzl held the first Zionist Congress in Basle in Switzerland and
his ideas found support. Validation was not universal, however, and many
Jews complained that Herzl's endeavour to establish a new homeland undermined assimilationist Jews. Herzl needed to find assistance not only from the
Jewish community. For twenty years, he and his followers, including the
British Jewish figure Chaim Weizmann, advocated for their project around
the capitals of Europe. At various points it looked as if first the Ottomans,
then the Germans and finally the Russians would support the Zionists. In
the end, it was the British government that helped. Lord Arthur Balfour, a
conservative politician and former Prime Minister, befriended Weizmann
and became a keen supporter of the scheme.

In November 1917, in his capacity as Foreign Secretary, Balfour issued his
eponymous declaration (see box 1.8). To what extent the British government
intended to keep its promise, or whether the Declaration was just another
wartime expediency in the bid to win support for the British war effort, has
been open to contention. Nevertheless, the Zionists held the British government to its word and when the war had ended and the peace conferences
were held they quickly mobilized to ensure that the British followed through.

One obstacle stood in the way of Jewish aspirations: Palestine's Arab population. Yet, from a Zionist perspective, writes Gerner, 'that Palestine had an existing population, with its own history and aspirations, was no more relevant ... than was Kenyan history to the British or Algerian society to the French' (1994, p. 15). The above quote is a generalization that overlooks the varying political and ideological dispositions emerging within the Zionist movement. Nevertheless, we can see that the Arabs believed that they had been promised Palestine in return for their support against the Turks during the war. They increasingly felt betrayed at news of Balfour's declaration in support of the Zionists. The Arabs of Palestine were not consulted, and their national rights went largely unrecognized. Throughout the period of the mandate, the British mostly supported and allowed for the rapid migration of Jews to Palestine. British attempts at supporting the rights of Palestinian Arabs failed. Plans for a legislative assembly were never fulfilled, land sales to Jews increased, and thousands of Arabs were dispossessed.

The mandate authorities heralded their rule not by establishing power-sharing institutions to prepare the path for Palestinian independence, but rather by adopting the classic colonial policy of divide and rule between Jews and Arabs. By the end of the first decade of the mandate it was obvious to all concerned that this policy was failing miserably. The security situation had deteriorated and Jewish immigration accelerated. In 1930, only 4,000 entered Palestine, yet three years later the British granted 30,000 entry in one year alone. The immigrants were also granted special privileges that were denied to the Palestinian Arab community. Societal upheaval grew in scale and tension between the Jews and Arabs – with Britain in the middle and reviled by both – increased to a violent level. In 1921, 1922 and 1929, Arab-perpetrated violence and revolt led to horrific massacres against Jews in Jerusalem and Hebron (Segev, 2000). From 1936 to 1939, notions of public order evaporated. The Palestinians, led by religious figures, the young leaders of notable families who had founded as many as six nationalist-based political parties, staged revolts, strikes and demonstrations in a desperate bid to halt Jewish immigration, land sales and the illegal shipment of arms.

The British responded in a typically 'colonial' fashion, ordering one commission of inquiry after another with little meaningful political strategy in-between. By 1936, British policy-makers in London were advising that the government relinquish its mandate on Palestine and that territory be partitioned between the Jews and the Arabs. They also proposed a quota system to be imposed on Jewish immigration into the country in order to slow its flow. These proposals were contained in two documents: the Peel Commission of 1937, and the 1939 White Paper. Both proposals were rejected by the Arabs, and Britain was unable to undo the web of deceit it had spun through its promises made during the war. By the end of the Palestinian Revolt in 1939, the British had to recognize the mandate would never succeed. All they could hope to achieve was the re-establishment of public order and security in this strife-torn land, and even this was ultimately an impossible task.

The recommendations of Peel and the 1939 White Paper left no party satisfied. The Palestinian community, weakened by years of revolt, strikes and hardships and the forcible dissolution of its religious and political leadership by the British, were still denied the right to self-determination in a land which they had lived in for centuries (Gerner, 1994, p. 28). The Zionists were now forced, by the British, to slow the rate of immigration, to 15,000 a year instead of the 60,000-a-year peak that had been reached in 1935. This had been at a time when Hitler's rise in Europe had signalled a public and open campaign of anti-Semitism.

British policy was characterized by containment, but from 1939 to 1945 the political situation continued to deteriorate at an alarming rate. The Zionists, led by David Ben Gurion, responded by organizing a campaign against the British deemed as terroristic. The now infamous Stern Gang, Haganah and Irgun Zvai Leumi militant groups were headed by young Zionist immigrants from Europe like Yitzhak Shamir and Menachem Begin, who would both later become Prime Ministers of Israel. The political violence of some of these groups was initially directed against the Palestinians, but the British authorities were soon targeted. Bombings, assassinations and other attacks increasingly marked the period, as the Zionists attempted to hasten Britain's departure and their own independence.

By 1945, the British knew that continued rule in Palestine was no longer tenable. The Labour government elected after the war, struggling to reconstruct Britain, quickly realized that colonial obligations could no longer be met. Palestine, along with Burma and India, was the first to be released. The chief beneficiaries would be the Zionists, and the stability of the region as a whole would subsequently be undermined by decades of conflict. Within Palestine the British authorities were already admitting to themselves that hatred and lawlessness had reached such a pitch that partition seemed the only solution. This decision was hastened in July 1946 by the Irgun's bombing of the King David Hotel (acting headquarters of the mandatory government), killing ninety-one people.

Britain was also under pressure from the Americans to give further support to Jewish immigration to Palestine (some 100,000 were waiting to be admitted). The response was to order yet another commission of inquiry – this time a British and American body deliberated over the future of the country. The commission's conclusions were of little help to anyone, recommending the continuation of the mandate. But by 1947 Britain was in no position to maintain the mandate on anyone's recommendation, and it announced its intention to relinquish it and to leave Palestine on 15 May 1948. The fate of Palestine was put into the hands of the newly formed United Nations.

In time-honoured tradition, the UN dealt with the problem by forming a committee of inquiry to investigate the competing claims to self-determination by the Palestinians and the Zionists. In August 1947, this committee recommended the partition of the country into two states, with Jerusalem under international jurisdiction. The proposal was debated and then put to the vote on 29 November 1947. The General Assembly voted to accept the partition plan. When the mandate ended, the Zionists would be granted independence over 55 per cent of the territory of Palestine (previously, they had only managed to secure 6 per cent through land purchases), and the UN partition implied that Palestinians would have to relinquish land that they had owned, farmed and lived on for generations. It was not a voluntary, but a forcible partition: the Palestinians would be compelled to relinquish their right to statehood in their coastal cities along with hundreds of small towns, villages and hamlets. Of course, they could remain, but only as citizens of the burgeoning ethnic democracy, the Jewish state of Israel (Yiftachel, 1993). While the Zionists begrudgingly accepted the partition plan, working on the principle that half a loaf was better than no loaf at all, the Palestinians and their Arab allies refused to recognize it at all.

From November 1947 to May 1948, the conflict between the Palestinians and Zionists deepened. Jews and Arabs were literally at each other's throats and the British authorities were increasingly impotent in the face of yet another situation where public order could not be enforced through a British-imposed security presence. The prelude to independence was bitter and tense. Even before the British had pulled out of the country, terrible deeds were perpetrated by one community against the other, and vice versa. The Zionists, now with a highly organized, well-equipped and disciplined paramilitary, prepared forcibly to wrest further territory, including Jerusalem, from the Palestinians before the mandate ended. Indeed, historiography by writers such as Benny Morris (1988) hint at a Zionist agenda on which ethnic cleansing of the Arab population was considered as a strategy.

By April 1948, the battle for Jerusalem had begun and the Zionists inched their way from the coastal plain of Tel Aviv up the mountainous slopes to Jerusalem, capturing, securing and subsequently demolishing Palestinian villages. The Zionists faced a constant barrage of attacks from the Arabs, including the forces of the Iraqi and Jordanian armies. The British were still obliged to maintain internal security and protect the Palestinian inhabitants of the country, but they had given up the ghost a long time back.

The events at the Palestinian village of Deir Yassin were a focal point in the conflict. When the Irgun arrived in the village, they massacred more than 200 Palestinians, mostly women and children (Hogan, 2001). The impact of this event and the widespread feeling of fear that permeated the Palestinian community of the day led to an exodus, and Palestinians either voluntarily or forcibly fled their homes, fearing for their lives. Whether the exodus was voluntary or forcible, the result of Zionist massacre or Arab urging, has been the subject of academic and national debate in Israel and the Arab world ever since. However, what really mattered was the fact that, when the war of 1948 was over, Israel prevented those Palestinian refugees from exercising their rights to return to their homes, lands, farms, shops, schools, churches, mosques and the graves of their forefathers. The right of return, however, was extended by the state of Israel to all Jews across the globe and they could be citizens of the new state, but not to those Palestinians who had fled or been expelled from their homes in 1948. The refugee issue was created and remains unresolved for the millions of Palestinians who today still call for their right to return.

The British terminated their mandate in Palestine on 15 May 1948, as planned. Britain failed in Palestine but the costs would largely be borne by other parties. British foreign policy in the Middle East during this period was highly charged and turbulent, buffeted as it was by the importance to London of maintaining control of assets like the Suez Canal. 'The British had come with good intentions and had set the country on a course for the twentieth century', so one official claimed (Segev, 2000, p. 514). The course, however, a century later and well into the twenty-first, was one characterized by conflict.

Case study

Algeria – a colony or *province outre mer*?

The prospects for French colonial rule in the North African state of Algeria were quite different from those of the British in either Egypt or Palestine. When the French first established their foothold in Algeria in the late 1820s through military invasion, the political objective in Paris was to form a settled colony that would, through annexation, form part of the French state. This political objective was achieved as a result of widespread colonization of Algeria and its native population by French settlers: *colons*. For some 1 million of these *colons* and their descendants, Algeria became home. Political legitimacy was ceded to this process when French policy-makers in Paris declared that Algeria was not a colony but simply a *province outre mer*. Algeria was not considered a territory subject to the policies of the French Ministry for Foreign Affairs but instead was placed under the authority of the Ministry of the Interior. Algeria did have a strategic importance for the French as well. It served as a foothold in North Africa and allowed France to pursue its rivalry with Britain as a competing colonial power. The later discovery of oil and gas reserves in Algeria's southern deserts was also a further economic incentive to hold on to this particular piece of North African territory.

The annexation of Algeria by the French in the 1840s, however, was not passively accepted by Algeria's indigenous Arab and Amazigh population. Throughout the mid to latter part of the nineteenth century, local resistance was apparent. In 1871, a local uprising against the further extension of French *colon* authority over Arab lands gripped the country. The French authorities exacted a high price upon the rebels. The French had exploited Algeria's lands in a variety of ways: to own and develop for French settlers and to harness in terms of agricultural production for French, rather than local, consumption and demands. Like other colonial powers, the economic imperative also meant that the French authorities and local colons set about a process of incipient modernization that included economic modes of production, infrastructure, industry and education. Moreover, the cultural dimensions of Algerian life were subject to the *colon* and Francophone imprint. In this way, Algeria and all its inhabitants became part of the French collective consciousness.

The ruling elite developed a particular attitude towards the local Muslim population, tribes and leaders. This attitude was informed by superiority common to the metropolitan centre in any colonial enterprise, as well as the romanticism associated with classic Orientalism of the nineteenth century. Hence, the majority of local peoples – with the exception of particular tribal favourites and 'pets' – were regarded with suspicion and as part of a subsect in society to which there was little obligation or responsibility. Muslims were considered French subjects in the *province outre mer* but were not entitled to citizenship unless they converted to Christianity. Such a conversion automatically divested them of their Muslim heritage and identity. It was clear that the French state left little room for the admittance of the 'other'. Attempts by local Muslim and tribal leaders to assert rights for their own communities were brutally suppressed, and political organization among such elements was prohibited and subject to severe punishment. Patronage of local elements through the well-tried colonial incentive of education and employment in the state enterprise largely failed in terms of bridging the disconnection that emerged in Algerian society in the late nineteenth century between the French-inspired ruling elite and the local Muslim population.

The Algerian national movement arose in the early decades of the twentieth century but real freedom and independence would not be won until 1962 when the war of independence finally delivered Algeria from French rule. Like those of other national movements across the Middle East at the time, the demands of the Algerians were initially modest and centred on rights and freedoms under French rule, rather than autonomy or independence. Such demands were, however, largely resisted by French power-holders wary of granting 'equality and liberty' to the Muslim. By 1939, the Algerian response was apparent in the formation of a nationalist anti-French political party called Amis du Manifeste et de la Liberté (Friends of the Manifesto and Liberty), whose members included both Muslims and communists. During the Second World War, other local political groupings arose, including the Parti du Peuple Algérien (Party of the Algerian People), who, along with others, waged a growing campaign for independence.

Attempts by the French government after 1945 to incorporate local elements of the Algerian community into structures of indigenous governance failed largely because they were viewed with suspicion and as a means of stifling or even halting the growing demands for independence. Such demands were also being expressed through an increasingly well-organized and armed structure of Algerians who were able to transcend religious, political and class differences to unite in their desire for freedom from France. The French responded by seeking to severely repress such demands, but by 1954 exiled nationalists and revolutionaries formed the Front de Libération Nationale (National Liberation Front) – or FLN, as it became known – from their base in Egypt.

In the latter part of 1954, the FLN and other revolutionary elements launched a series of guerrilla attacks that would ignite the peoples of Algeria to embark on a war of independence. The French government was caught on the back foot and rushed its troops to Algeria in a desperate attempt to put down the rising populist push for independence. In the war, over 1 million Algerians out of a population of 9 million would lose their lives. Despite the increasing French troop presence, the war spiralled into a bitter conflict that pitched entire populations into resistance to the French presence. The French authorities resorted to increasingly repressive and brutal measures in their desperate attempts to put down the Algerian rebellion. Thousands were arrested, placed in detention camps, tortured and even executed. The struggle and colonial response to it is tellingly captured in Gillo Pontecorvo's 1964 film *The Battle of Algiers*. Shot in black-and-white and capturing a 'real-time' approach, it portrays the guerrilla struggle waged against the French forces in the streets and alleys of the Algerian casbah. The film depicts the enduring battle that waged for years as the Algerian freedom fighters took on and conquered the seemingly superior French forces. The film draws in and centres on ordinary people caught in a trap of power which is resisted and defeated. The film portrayed scenes of torture as the French sought to quell and put down the guerrilla resistance. Banned in France, the film held up a mirror to the country as an example of its worst excesses in terms of power and control.

As the crisis peaked in 1958, the colonels of the French army brought down the government in Paris, and Charles de Gaulle came out of retirement to lead the country as it faced the demands of the warring Algerians. A political solution to the impasse seemed an outright impossibility. De Gaulle promised that he would face down the Algerian 'terrorist' threat and restore French pride and prestige in Algeria. His method of resolution, however, angered many of his supporters on the right. He proposed a referendum on the destiny of Algeria in which Algerians themselves would decide their fate.

The *colons* knew that the referendum would not deliver them from the hands of the revolutionaries and their demands for independence. In alliance with some military and right-wing elements, they formed an organization to launch attacks not only on the FLN but on the French government as well. They were determined to topple de Gaulle.

By March 1962, however, the FLN and the French government had reached terms on a ceasefire in Algeria. De Gaulle's referendum was held the following July and the outcome was a foregone conclusion: independence for Algeria. Following the result, the *colons* began a process of mass exodus from their positions of power, as well as the lands that they had settled. The French dream that Algeria serve as the *province outre mer* had turned into a bloody nightmare and colonial disaster.

Questions for discussion

- Explain the major motives behind British and French intervention in the Middle East in the late nineteenth century.
- Was the post-First World War mandate system a case of ill-disguised colonialism?
- What is the most significant legacy of European colonialism in the Middle East?

Recommended reading

- For a deeper general understanding of colonialism in the Middle East, the edited reader by Hourani, Khoury and Wilson (2009) provides a broad-based account for first-time students of the Ottoman and colonial periods. There are some excellent essays by historians such as André Raymond on Cairo, C. Ernest Dawn on Ottomanism to Arabism, and Hanna Batatu on Iraqis.
- Further reading of authors such as Franz Fanon (2001) and Pierre Bourdieu et al. (2014) will move you beyond strictly academic literature but aid in understanding the processes of subjugation, domination and – eventually – emancipation of the peoples of the region, particularly in the Algerian context.
- For a more economic perspective, Issawi (1982) is a superb introduction to the economic dimensions of European expansion in the Middle East – well written and engaging for a student specifically interested in the economic drag created through the colonial enterprise.
- On France in Algeria and Syria, accounts by Khoury (1987), Ageron (1991) and Martin Evans (2012) are excellent. Moore (1970) provides an in-depth account of French colonialism in North Africa. Monroe (1963), Nevakivi (1969) and Marlowe (1971) review and analyse the tensions behind Anglo-French relations in the Middle East. Fieldhouse (2004) and Méouchy and Sluglett (2004) provide interesting narratives around the mandate system established by the British and French. Through his analysis of newly declassified papers, Barr (2012) revitalizes the discussion of Anglo-French tension and its effect upon the relationship between the Arabs and the Jews.

- For the Egyptian case study, Owen (1969) outlines a strong account of the Egyptian economy under colonial rule. Historical perspectives on Egypt under British rule can also be found in Marlowe (1954 and 1970), Woodhouse (1959) and Darwin (1981). Tignor (1984) relates state and economic development in Egypt under British rule until the Free Officers' revolution. Kyle's history (2002) and McNamara (2003) highlight the tensions between Nasser and the British that precipitated the Suez Crisis. Noorani's book (2010) is very good in terms of examining responses to and impacts of colonialism, especially in Egypt and among the works of Egyptian thinkers, writers and intellectuals.
- On Palestine, for an introduction to the impacts of the mandate on the genesis of conflict, read Milton-Edwards (2008). Abboushi (1985) presents a critical account of Britain's mandate, while Antonius (1969) is credited with authoring a nationalist-inspired account of the mandate period. Morris (1988), Pappe (1994) and Tessler (1994) all provide accounts of the birth of the conflict between Israel and the Palestinians and Britain's rule over Palestine.

CHAPTER TWO

Nationalism: the Quest for Identity and Power

Introduction

According to a variety of writers, nationalism in the Middle East – and, more specifically, Arab nationalism – is very much a twentieth-century phenomenon associated with a variety of factors including anti-colonialism, romanticism, state-building, self-determination, socialism and religion (Tibi, 1997). To be blunt, there is no one phenomenon that may easily be described as nationalism that can be applied to the region as a whole. Instead, as much recent academic work has begun to highlight, nationalism in the Middle East has taken many forms and guises, including state nationalism, patriotism, pan-Arabism, pan-Islamism, Zionism, Islamic nationalism, Arab nationalism, Ba'thism, Nasserism, Maronite nationalism, Kurdish ethno-nationalism and so on.

In addition, the very applicability of nationalism within the region was questioned after the Six Day War of 1967 when pan-Arabism was declared dead by Ajami (1978), and writers such as Zubaida (1993) began to question the saliency and utility of the concept of the nation-state and nationalism in the region. In 2014, this debate was resurrected when ISIS declared a caliphate and denounced Arab nationalism and nation-states as false. The discussion about nationalism, therefore, embraces a variety of perspectives and explanations. Some of these explanations focus on socio-economic issues, including fringe economies, the politics of ideology, national liberation movements, state-building, national identity, Islam, principles of self-determination, international human rights and the ethnic cleansing tendencies of some nationalist leaders. Certainly, in the twenty-first century, ethno-nationalism is still considered salient. The leaders of ethno-national movements still call for their rights to autonomy or self-determination (Storm, 2005). In 2017, for example, solutions to the Syrian conflict increasingly have to reflect the ethnic rights and demands of the Kurds.

Before examining the specific manifestations of nationalism in the Middle East, it is important to outline some of the most important definitions of the term in this context. More specifically, it is helpful to pose a number of questions, such as, what does nationalism mean in the context of the modern Middle East? Is it relevant and applicable, can it be historically located or associated with particular events, figures or personalities? Is it as relevant today as it was two or three decades ago? What can general theories of nationalism outlined by authors such as Kedourie, Gellner, Smith and Anderson tell us about the Middle East?

First, it is worth noting that the debate about nationalism in the region, and more specifically Arab nationalism, is strongly linked to issues and analysis of political Islam and ethnicity. Christie and Masad, writing in 2013, remind us that this has been a much overlooked phenomenon, especially as it relates to the state (Christie and Masad, 2013). While these issues will be remarked upon in this chapter, it is also worth reflecting on the correlating debates that will be reviewed in chapters 5 and 8 on political Islam and ethnicity, respectively. Second, there are disagreements amongst those who define nationalism in the contemporary era, disagreements that are extended to the Middle East when authors try to explain aspects of politics that they believe are associated with this tendency. Arab nationalism has been declared extinct in the region on more than one occasion. For example, in the wake of the Arab Spring, Dawisha contended that 'the demand for instantaneous and drastic change was evoked through a number of lofty values and ideals. Yet the observer is hard put to find Arab nationalism among them' (2016, p. 320).

Second, the debate among theorists of nationalism can be divided into a number of perspectives, including the theories of scholars such as Rousseau, Fichte, Herder and Hegel, who outlined a relationship between nationalism and doctrines of liberty, self-determination and statehood. Kedourie expanded on this concept, outlining nationalism as a form of 'secular millenarianism' in a modern age, in which religion has gone into decline and the individual enjoys greater independence. As Hutchinson and Smith (1994) argue, 'Kedourie regards nationalism as an extremely powerful, if destructive force. Its appeal is explained by social breakdown occasioned by a collapse in the transmission of traditional values, and the rise of a restless, secular, educated generation, ambitious for power but excluded from its proper estate' (p. 47).

Third, there are theorists associated with the modernization thesis, and in particular the work of Ernest Gellner, who argued that nationalism is a modern phenomenon and that pre-existing nations 'can be defined only in terms of the age of nationalism, rather than, as you might expect, the other way round' (1994, p. 64). Gellner contended that the Industrial Revolution and the subsequent reconfiguration of social and economic forces breathed new life into nations, whose relationships to political units such as the state, family, tribal and clan ties create new bonds and loyalties. Thus, modernization theorists, including Marxist writers such as Tom Nairn, associate the phenomenon with economic transformation and the impact this has on social and political arrangements in modern societies. Gellner also identified factors such as culture and language as important signifiers of twentieth-century nationalism and nation identity, but this approach has its critics, including Anthony Smith (1986), who gives greater emphasis to pre-existing

ethnic bonds than to the modernization process in explaining the phenomenon of nationalism in the twentieth century. Smith argues for a more
nuanced approach to explanations of nationalism than Gellner. While he
often concurs with Gellner's explanations, he is unhappy with the emphasis
on the modern character of nationalism, arguing that 'ethnie' (the ethnic
group) provides the foundation-stone on which 'modern nations simply
extend, deepen and streamline the ways in which members of the ethnie
associated and communicated. They do not introduce startlingly novel elements, or change the goals of human association and communication' (1986,
p. 215). Smith encourages a wider, more embracing explanation of nationalism as a product of the modern and the traditional in which ethnic bonds
play a significant role.

The extent to which the ethnic bonds that Smith emphasizes are real or
imagined are explored in the work of Benedict Anderson. While Anderson
agrees with Gellner that nationalism is a product of modernity, he is, according to Kellas (1998), 'concerned to explore the psychological appeal of nationalism which is close to the primordial approach' which Smith acknowledges
(p. 56). Anderson (1983) contends that modern-day nationalism and nations
are an imagined product, 'cultural artefacts of a particular kind'. He has
also argued that from the decline of old bonding elements such as Church,
Mosque and monarchical hierarchy in society, it was 'no surprise then that
the search [in the modern age] was on … for a new way of linking frater-
nity, power and time meaningfully together' (in Guibernau and Rex, 1997,
p. 43). As society, according to Anderson, transits from a religiously based
to a secular order, the composition of nation-states must be articulated in a
new way. The primary way in which identity and nationalism are now communicated is a product of the industrial age and print capitalism: 'the convergence of capitalism and print technology on the fatal diversity of human
language created the possibility of a new form of imagined community, which
in its basic morphology set the stage for the modern nation' (p. 51). Lebanese
writer and novelist Amin Maalouf sums this up in terms of his personal quest
for identity:

Box 2.1 An identity-defining gaze

What makes me myself rather than anyone else is the very fact that I am poised
between two countries, two or three languages, and several cultural traditions. It is
precisely this that defines my identity. Would I exist more authentically if I cut off a
part of myself … Every individual is a meeting ground for many different allegiances,
and sometimes these loyalties conflict with one another and confront the person who
harbours them with difficult choices … For it is often the way we look at other
people that imprisons them within their own narrowest allegiances. And it is also the
way we look at them that may set them free.

(Maalouf, 2001)

More recently, the ethno-national dimension of theorizing about the Middle East has emerged and dominated. Here the boundary is set by ethnic markers (including religion) and translated into the politics of a minority quest for autonomy, increased rights as citizens and even self-determination or secession from larger 'national' state structures. Such discourses are emergent in the politics of ethno-nationalism across the region.

Nationalism as theory turned into practice

The theories of nationalism outlined above tend to identify its features from a Eurocentric viewpoint. With the exception, perhaps, of Anderson, the ties that bind nations outside Europe are viewed from afar and not from within, and are explained from a monolithic cultural background that is purely western or European in character. Theories of nationalism, therefore, have emerged with a particularly European hue, associated as they are with other traditions in western political thought, including the debate about liberty, democracy, individual sovereignty and secularization. As Hutchinson and Smith (1994) admit, 'the earliest nations and national states may be European but nationalism is a truly global movement and cultural system' (p. 196). Nevertheless, as we shall see in the examples below, the embrace of nationalist ideas, thinking, political institutions and economic models primarily associated with this approach, in the contemporary Middle East, often occurred as a result of a specific political relationships of domination and subordination between Europe and the peoples of the region. The so-called export of nationalism – described by Brown as a form of virus from the West (1988, p. 46) – and associated ideas to the Middle East impacted on religion, the social bonds of tribe and clan, ethnic identities and bonds and traditional agricultural modes of production in predominantly rural rather than urbanized societies. The region, therefore, highlights the many modern forms of nationalism, exhibited in ethnic and territorial nationalisms, state nationalism, religious-nationalist thinking evident in turn-of-the-century pan-Islamism and the anti-colonial nationalism of political leaders such as Gamal Abdel Nasser of Egypt.

In the context of the Middle East, the concept of nationalism or nation – or *watan* as it is called in Arabic – was explained in two ways. The first bore a strong relationship to the western notion of nation identified through the nation-state, which by the second decade of the twentieth century had been established in many parts of the region. The second concept is more indigenous in origin, drawing on Arab and Muslim notions of community (*umma*) and belonging through tribe, clan, religious or ethnic affiliation. For example, the Jordanian monarchy still refers to the people of Jordan as Banu Hashem, meaning 'from the tribe of the Hashemites', a group predating the establishment of the state of Transjordan by the British in the 1920s. The Jordanian people, however, also include among their number Circassians, Palestinians, Bedouins, Muslims, Christians and Turkic peoples. Jordanian national identity assumed growing political importance in a delicate demographic balance of power that witnessed Palestinians in the state reaching a majority. The 'Jordan First' campaign was thus the state's response to this challenge, demanding loyalty to the Hashemite throne and state first and foremost (Culcasi, 2016).

Nationalism in the Middle East is associated with a number of meanings. The first is state-based, anti-colonial and dependent on western notions of state, class and ideology. This conceptualization of nationalism is described by Breuilly as 'governmental nationalism', which embraces 'policies aimed at extending the territory of the state into areas that the state claims as belonging to its nation ... [and] internally ... as nationalist actions taken against specific groups or individuals and justified on the grounds of the anti- or non-national character of the groups or individuals' (Breuilly, 1993, p. 8). Indeed, writers such as Tibi outline three stages in the emergence of this phenomenon, from a 'literary and linguistic revival, to a transformation into political nationalism with a demand for a unified state to a form of Arab germanophilia' (Tibi, 1997, p. xiii). In the context of governmental nationalism, the project was usually elite-driven, part of the homogenizing task of the state, nationalism from above imposed on the masses, rigid and narrow.

The second expression of nationalism, as we shall see below, is found in the post-colonial anti-Zionist, socialist liberation movements and state elites of the 1950s and 1960s. The third expression of nationalist sentiment may be referred to as theo-nationalism or pan-Islamism, and is a product of the uneasy marriage between Islam and the West occurring both at the beginning of the twentieth century and towards the end of the century as a sustainable and politically meaningful phenomenon. Nationalism and nationalist movements have grown from elite-based secret societies in the 1920s and 1930s through popular mass movements in the 1950s and 1960s to the realm of state-based nationalism by the 1990s. National self-consciousness has become a firmly entrenched feature of the political landscape in the Middle East, one which even the Islamists have had considerable difficulty in overcoming. National self-consciousness is expressed through many mechanisms, at both a state and regional level, and national identity is expressed at a number of levels: within the boundary of the nation-state, as an imagined community, across the region as Arabs, and in the liberation struggles of the Palestinians. In this context, the vision of the Arab nation allows the development of a code of inter-state manoeuvre between population groups within the region.

Looking more specifically at Arab nationalism, it can be argued that it remains an expression of nation and nationalism through the state and in individual countries as well as at a wider level of the Arab world. As Matar contends, 'a majority, if not all, Arab states used, and continue to use "national" imagery and nationalist, as well as pan-Arab nationalist, discourse as frames of references to make sense of experiences, to make claims about power and agency' (2012: 130). At the wider level, it relates to attempts at greater regional harmony and uniformity of political institutions or forms of government. Arabs, then, have both embraced and repulsed the notions of nation and nationalism. I will now review the emergence of the intellectual development of Arab nationalism, its bourgeois and elite roots, and its importance during the First World War, and the articulation of nationalism through independence from the colonial powers in the 1940s, 1950s and 1960s.

The birth pangs of Arab nationalism

The emergence of nationalist sentiment in the Middle East preceded colonial government in the region, but did, in part, reflect growing foreign influence from the 1880s onwards in the areas of trade, education, religion, travel and culture. One argument that may be forwarded is that the first stirrings of national consciousness, and more specifically of an Arab identity, grew out of centuries-old tensions between the Arab people and their Turkish overlords. Although the Ottoman Empire was Muslim, it required its Arab subjects to learn Turkish, swear allegiance to Turkish governors and rulers and to carry the coin of Turkish rulers. Resentment, despite reforms in Ottoman rule, grew, particularly amongst the newly educated urban Christian and Muslim elite of cities such as Cairo, Damascus and Beirut. In addition, this elite acted as an important conduit for western ideas and philosophies of democracy, modernity and nation. The role of this elite in formulating Arab nationalism is recognized by Breuilly, who notes that 'such intellectuals have played a prominent part in Arab nationalist politics ... [T]he importance of nationalist intellectuals in Arab nationalism' cannot, therefore, from Breuilly's perspective, be underestimated (1993, p. 149). Aziz al-Azmeh, however, asks us to read history a little differently, arguing that Arab nationalism was the product of neither the Arab Revolt of 1917 (discussed below) nor direct western influence. Instead he explains a more indirect root, giving credit for Arab nationalism proper to the 'product of the Ottoman reforms (*tanzimat*) of the nineteenth century ... the incipient regime of modernity [and] ... small elite class intellectuals' (1995, p. 7). Breuilly and al-Azmeh concur that the intellectual base of this movement was extremely important, and, in turn, would have significant bearing on the subsequent nature of nationalist ideologies within the region. As al-Azmeh ominously sounds off,

Box 2.2 Born from the books of the bourgeoisie

Thus was Arab nationalism born and constituted. It was the political culture, initially of a political class which was acculturated to it and deployed it in struggles for independence, later of the entire population, through the state educational and cultural systems. It was the animating idea of a whole range of large-scale political and social forces ... also the expression of a social fact articulating various levels of social structuration and interaction.

(1995, p. 11)

In the coffee houses and salons of the urban bourgeoisie, a generation of young men, educated in Constantinople, in church schools and in Europe, raised the idea of a renaissance of Arab identity. Like so many before and after them, they shared a collective and often invented memory of a golden age of the Arabs or Islam, when the world – or at least large parts of it – was ruled by Arab leaders, when poets and artists were revered, when the Arabs achieved their greatest contributions to subjects such as astronomy and mathematics. The renaissance of the Arabs (Muslim or Christian) would embody these greater eras and result in the resurgence of the Arab nation, its people and its leaders, its arts, culture, poetry, science and philosophy. With respect to Arab arts and literature, poetry came to serve as a major cultural vehicle for the revived sense of Arab nationalism. Major literary figures such as Khalil Hawi, Nizar Qabbani, Adonis, and Naguib Mahfouz crafted poems, prose and novels that reflected this Arab identity. In addition, this notion of Arab identity would engage with Muslim identity, and many of the leading scholars of the time were Muslim intellectuals. In this context, nationalism was not always envisaged as embodying religion, and a role was created, by some Arab intellectuals, for the faith of Islam. As Kellas argues,

Box 2.3 Finding a place for faith

It is difficult, therefore, to relate the rise of nationalism to the decline of religion, except perhaps in some mainly secular societies. In some cases, religion and nationalism thrive together, in others, where a church is strongly supranational (as ... Islam), there may be a tension ... However, even supranational [religions] can underpin nationalist movements against oppressive states which deny nationalism its free expression.

(1998, p. 59)

Vatikiotis, however, does not perceive such an easy relationship between Islam and nationalism, arguing that the sheer incompatibility of these two terms made things difficult from the outset. Nationalism, imported from the outside, he argued, had to compete against the pre-existing ideology of Islam and 'when nationalism was linked to Islam, it failed to accommodate the different, or other, the non-Muslims, and thus accelerated the inappropriate-ness and the decline of non-Islamic nationalism as an acceptable political ideology' (1987, p. 74). Yet, for Vatikiotis the 'exceptionalist' nature of Muslim political culture in the Middle East meant that an imported western ideology of nationalism would never thrive.

The Arab intellectuals, however, debated and attempted to spread their ideas of Arab nation and nationalism by taking advantage of the modern processes of print and publication. Small literary and cultural societies pub-lished books, pamphlets, gazettes, newspapers, journal articles and constitu-tions, and revived old texts and literature for re-publication. Here, as Anderson (1983) argues, nationality or nation-ness (Arab) was constructed as a specific cultural creation emerging from print capitalism in a new era of modernity in the Middle East. The revival of the Arabic language played an important part in shaping the 'imagined community' that these urban intellectuals hoped to share with the rest of the Arab world. Language is not a prerequisite of nationalism and al-Azmeh (1995) has a point when he states it is 'not itself the most crucial factor'. Arabic and its renaissance in the written and literary form, however, was a significant thread in the generation of an ideology which could be 'sold', at a later date, as authentic to a mass audience (p. 10). As a language of communication, Arabic served the region well and played its part in promoting a notion of unity, whether at the level of political rhetoric or of humour.

The vision and aspirations that these turn-of-the-century intellectuals pro-moted can be divided into two themes or strands – Arab nationalism and pan-Islamism. Within these strands, authors such as Antonius have identi-fied nationalist movements, personalities or approaches, including Arabism, the Lebanese revival, the Young Arab Society (al-Fatat), Syrianism, Egyptian-ism, Butrus al-Bustani, Jamal ad-din al-Afghani and Abdul Raham al-Kawak-ibi. The two strands are representations of the types of nationalism that theorists such as Gellner, Anderson and Smith have outlined. Some were anti-colonial in nature, others embraced a western secular outlook to nation and nationhood that grew out of a particular Eurocentric perspective on these issues.

Others, as I have pointed out, reflected a literary base to the revival of Arab identity, following Anderson's 'imagined community', through poetry, the publication of classical Arabic works, newspapers, novels, music and other arts. Geographically associated with Lebanon and Syria, the intellectuals and theologians associated with this particular approach to Arab nationalism included, for example, Christian western-educated teachers such as Nasif Yaziji (1800–71) and Butrus al-Bustani (1819–83), founders of the Beirut-based Society of Arts and Sciences. They, along with their Muslim compatriots, including people like Amir Mohammed Arslan and Hussein Baihum, pro-moted an 'incitement to Arab insurgence ... the achievements of the Arab race, of the glories of Arabic literature, and of a future that the Arabs might fashion for themselves by going to their own past for inspiration' (Antonius, 1969, p. 54). The call was based on a desire to overthrow the mantle of Ottoman rule and to fashion a secular and non-sectarian future for the Arab peoples of the region based on the principle of self-determination.

While the importance of these first intellectual stirrings of Arab nationalist identity and nationalism have waxed and waned according to historical interpretation, they are consistently credited with playing a salient part in consciousness-raising and encouraging the growth of a secularized Arab identity that would, in theory, transcend the competing loyalties of class, tribe, religion and clan. This strand encouraged the emergence of state-centred patriotic – and, we might argue, patriarchal – nationalism, *wataniyya*, that would feature so strongly in the national homogenizing agenda of the new states established in the Middle East after the end of the First World War.

The pan-Islamist movement is associated with intellectuals such as Jamal ad-din al-Afghani, Mohammed Abduh and Rashid Rida, all of whom were scholars at the Islamic university, al-Azhar, in Cairo, Egypt. They reflected the association between religion and nationalism, anti-colonialism and religious resurgence that are common in other Third World contexts such as Asia and Latin America, where the Catholic Church and its priests were closely involved with nationalism. In addition, as Esposito argues, 'the development of modern Muslim nationalism was indebted to Islamic modernists as well as secular nationalist leaders' (1984, p. 60).

In Egypt, the emergence and prominence of such Islamic modernist-reformist thinkers were part of this new post-First World War intellectual response to the collapse of the Ottoman Empire and the Caliphate, the nation-state-building project pioneered by Britain and France, and the anti-colonial sentiment palpable by this point in history throughout the region. This response to nationalist sentiment had, however, first to deal with the issue of continuing Muslim identity in an era of global change and socio-economic transformation of society. It was this marriage of ideas that resulted in pan-Islamism.

The idea that Islam could rise to the challenge of unity presented in nationalism and at the same time provide a sense of identity that transcended national boundaries and protected its adherents was promoted by these modernists. The seeds of reformist thinking, the attempt to modernize Islam in the fields of politics, economy and society, while preserving the religious traditions established by the Prophet Mohammed himself, presented them with a formidable task. As the relationship between Islam and the West, nationalism and secularism became entrenched, this group of thinkers and writers emerged to challenge the dominance of the western-inspired secular project, with its accompanying notions of nationalism, modernization and liberalization that so many indigenous rulers of the colonized Muslim world were adopting for their own political systems. The westernization of the

Muslim political project was a significant factor, propelling the modernists to formulate a response to the political and cultural challenges posed by nationalist theories during this period. Not only was the West engaged in an economic project in the colonized lands of the Muslim world, but it sought to transform the very nature of political power, system of government and rule that had characterized the world of Islam for so many centuries.

Jamal ad-din al-Afghani

The founder of this pan-Islamic trend was an Iranian-born Muslim thinker Jamal ad-din al-Afghani (1838–97) who called upon fellow Muslims throughout the region, and beyond, to reassess the role of Islam in their lives, examine the causes of its increasing marginalization and question the benefits to all Muslims offered by the western secularist approach. Ayubi (1991) credits al-Afghani with reviving the process of *ijtihad* (interpretation) and thereby initiating 'a renaissance of Muslim philosophy, encouraging the direct study of the works themselves rather than the study, then customary, of the usually sterile commentaries or supercommentaries' (p. 57).

The fragility of the 'renaissance project' dogged its thinkers, with some critics, such as Kamal Abd al-Latif, arguing that the reformers had not really accepted modernism as an integrated philosophical outlook – related to such concepts as nationalism, liberty, individualism, social contracts, etc. – but had borrowed eclectically as it suited them, always extracting the 'modern' concepts out of their (European) intellectual and social context and trying to subsume them instead under familiar Islamic concepts (Ayubi, 1991, p. 58). Abd al-Latif's criticism seems harsh given the hegemonic nature of the European project at the time and the saturation of the Muslim body politic with western norms and values with little attempt to acknowledge Islam at the level of politics, government or leadership. As Ayubi (1991) reminds us, 'there is little doubt that the attempts by people such as al-Afghani and Abduh to initiate reform were mainly prompted by external stimuli, by confrontation with a technologically superior and politically dominant western presence' (p. 58).

Al-Afghani and his successor Mohammed Abduh (1849–1905) were modernists, however, in their own right, who wanted to formulate a response within Islam to the challenges and changes triggered by increasing western hegemony in the Middle East (Keddie, 2007). They were not just responsible for promoting a call to all Muslims to return to their faith, to the 'straight path' advocated by God in the Koran and the Prophet Mohammed through example, but for recognizing the eternal and inextricable links between the regeneration of faith and the particular brand of politics that has emerged from the practice of the religion.

These men sought to reacquaint Islam with the immense political, social and economic changes that were taking place around them as a direct result

of the colonial experience. As the fabric of society strained under secularizing influences, al-Afghani, Abduh and Rashid Rida formulated a response
that embraced modernization – of Islam – and advocated the primacy of
Muslim belief, asserting that an irrelevant and outdated interpretation of
Islam, promoted by backward and old-fashioned clergy (*ulama*), was actually
playing a large part, alongside colonialism, in undermining the unity of the
Muslim community itself.

Rashid Rida

Rida's contribution to the renaissance of political Islam and linkage or
engagement with the debate about nationalism was to develop a fundamentalist (*salafi*) approach to the modernization of Islam and its political regeneration. Throughout his life, Rashid Rida led the modernist movement in
Cairo and continued to win supporters for his ideas throughout the region.
Through the publication of a journal-cum-newspaper entitled *al-Manar* (The
Lighthouse), and his involvement with a religious school close to the tradi-
tionalist religious university, al-Azhar, Rida played his part in maintaining
the momentum for reform initiated by his mentors al-Afghani and Abduh.
Rida, however, was a conservative rather than a liberal reformer, rejecting
the argument for liberalization of Islam through westernization of the religion. For him, there would be no Islamic reformation where the forces of
religion and the state were unleashed to depart on separate paths. For Rida,
the answer to modernization lay in strengthening and further forging the
ties within Islam that marry the spiritual and the political together.

As Egypt modernized under British influence, Rida increasingly advocated
a rejection of the West and a return to the roots of Islam. He became the first
advocate in the Arab world of a modernized Islamic state and its need to
respond through inner renewal to these secularist pressures before it was
too late. By the late 1920s and early 1930s, Rida had become an influential
figure throughout the Muslim world; his journal and associated publications
were read by young people who were thus encouraged to explore and put
into practice the ideas of Rida and his predecessors. In this way, the reformers planted the seed that encouraged the regeneration and defence of Islam
from within.

The extent to which this revival of Islam took place is hard to measure.
Although not broadly populist in appeal, al-Afghani, Abduh and Rida
managed to inspire a new generation of educated Muslims to rethink the
role that Islam could play in their lives and the unifying nationalist role it
could maintain. Whether this new generation of thinkers would actually
lead peasants in rural revolts, organize new societies based on Islam or join
arms with their nationalist brethren in anti-colonial struggle, they were all
in one way or another touched or influenced by the reformers. The implications of the political message they conveyed were not lost on them.

New identities and hopes

According to the modernists, the future of the entire Muslim community (*umma*) lay in the ability of each member to profess a new Muslim identity based on notions of communal unity, solidarity and strength. Fear of the West or modern economic, political and social changes, the modernists argued, should be replaced with challenge and the ability of the Muslim community to offer a viable alternative to the dominance of the West and western secularized identities such as nationalism. The modernization of Islam should acknowledge and pay homage to its own important history, civilization, science, economics, art, poetry, social mores and architecture. Islam, they asserted, was capable, as a political as well as a religious force, of addressing the issues raised by western modernization processes in the Middle East and their impact at all levels of society. Of course, in recent years, the debate about the authenticity of this particular reconstruction of the Islamic past has been questioned at length. But, in the context of the time, this political response was inevitably anti-colonial and anti-western, while at the same time pro-Arab and pro-Islam. It embraced a nationalist pan-Islamist philosophy which promoted liberation from colonial rule through localized and regional political agitation.

This pan-Islamist emphasis on unity and reform encouraged many supporters throughout the region. Revolution or jihad against illegitimate rule, no matter what form it was manifested in, the modernists argued, must be undertaken. If the ruler of a country was corrupt and a westernized enemy, then his rule must be resisted. It was with these beliefs that al-Afghani supported attempts to end the rule of the Khedive in Egypt. The jihad against unjust and corrupt Ottoman rule and domination was launched in Arabia by Sharif Hussein of Mecca in the early years of the First World War. In other Arab capitals, young Muslims formed secret societies based on the new dream of pan-Islamic thinking which put the unity of the Muslim Arab peoples before loyalty to territory, nation-state or ruler. If such unity could be achieved, the liberation of Muslim lands from corrupt rule and foreign usurpation would naturally follow.

Throughout the first decades of the twentieth century, the Arab nationalists and pan-Islamists formed groups, societies and literary circles to promote their message. The first Arab Congress of nationalist groups was convened, however, outside the region, in Paris in June 1913. The Turkish authorities had been alerted to the threat latent in Arab nationalism to their authority to rule over the region and had tried to stop the Congress. In addition, by this point the Ottoman powers were admitting to themselves that the earlier policy of Turkification of the region, through changes in school syllabi, language and business, had failed. In their failure, the Ottoman authorities resorted to violence to quell the new force of nationalism. In the province of Syria, for example, the Ottoman ruler of Damascus, Jamal Pasha, ordered the imprisonment, exile and public execution of Arab nationalists. Throughout the region, the intellectual swing away from Ottomanism to Arab national-ism and pan-Islamism of a particularly Arab nature was perceptible.

The first Arab Revolt: the Arab princes at the helm of British imperial ambition

An important watershed or turning point in the movement for Arab nation-alism and, in particular, in the linkage to a form of territoriality or the nation-state (al-Azmeh's criticisms notwithstanding) was the First World War. Following the decision by the Ottoman rulers in Constantinople to side with the Germans against the British and the French, the Middle East became an important arena for battle during the conflict. Colonial aspirations towards the region by this point were intense and, as highlighted in chapter 1, a significant feature of the war was the rivalry between Britain and France to gain influence over local Arab leaders in the region and to secure a foot-hold over particular territories.

During the war, the greatest symbol of Arab nationalist aspirations was the Arab Revolt. The revolt was organized by Sharif Hussein, and the libera-tion of Damascus was led by his son Prince Faisal of the Hashemites, assisted by T. E. Lawrence: 'Lawrence of Arabia'. Although not a mass movement, the revolt was the clearest sign that the Arabs – and, more specifically, their leaders – wanted both political and territorial independence after the war, no matter who won. As Antonius (1969) remarks, 'after the revolt the Allied cause had become identical with the cause of Arab independence; and ... the triumph of Allied arms would bring freedom to the Arab people' (p. 225).

The ruthlessness of Ottoman governors like Jamal Pasha in Damascus helped to fire Arab nationalist fervour and turn them against their Turkish overlords. The deployment of Turkish troops commanded by the Germans in southern Arabia also alarmed Arab leaders. It was Sharif Hussein who subse-quently lent his support and that of his sons, Ali, Faisal and Abdullah, to the allies, in their military campaign against the Germans in the deserts of Arabia. The particular ally that became embroiled with the Hashemites was Britain, which, as part of war policy, was keen to establish local Arab support. The British assured Hussein of their support for Arab nationalist claims in return for Arab assistance during the war. In a letter dated 24 October 1915, Sir Henry McMahon, High Commissioner in Egypt, had declared to Arab leader Sharif Hussein that Britain was 'prepared to recognize and support the independence of the Arabs in all the regions lying within the frontiers proposed by the Sharif of Mecca'.

In June 1916, following the British assurances, Hussein and his sons led a revolt against the Ottoman rulers and raised the first Arab force for independ-ence. Military success, although limited, was forthcoming, and Hussein was able to oust the Turkish garrison force from Mecca and other surrounding settlements. By November, Hussein was declared 'King of Arabia'. The British and French, however, who were engaged in further negotiations to secure their own, rather than the Arabs', interests over the area, only agreed to recognize him as King of Mecca. As discussed in chapter 1, the secret Sykes–Picot Agreement already contained an arrangement between the French, British and imperial Russia, for the territorial carve-up of the region after the war. The agreement would have remained secret had the Bolsheviks not released the papers to the Turks following the Russian Revolution in November 1917. For the Arabs, the implications of the agreement were plain: the document was a direct contradiction of nationalist aspirations. As Antonius remarks,

Box 2.4 Sykes–Picot greed?

The … Agreement is a shocking document. It is not only a product of greed at its worst, that is to say, of greed allied to suspicion and so leading to stupidity: it also stands out as a startling piece of double-dealing.

(1969, p. 248)

Throughout 1917–18, however, Hussein and his sons continued with their plan to unite the Arabs of Arabia, Transjordan and Syria under the banner of Arab independence and nationalism. They organized their supporters around certain themes or concepts that Hudson (1977) identifies as 'hallmarks of modern Arab identity … Arabic language and culture and Islam' (p. 38). They plotted the conquest of Aqaba on the coast of the Red Sea, and outposts in Transjordan and Damascus, which were still under the rule of Jamal Pasha.

Following the Turkish defeat in Arabia, Jamal Pasha had ordered a bloody crackdown on the secret nationalist groups that had flourished in Damascus and Beirut, and throughout the early spring, public executions were stepped up. Hussein, by this point, had charged his son Faisal with the task of liberating the north, including Damascus. Faisal faced a formidable challenge and it has been argued that victory would have eluded the Arabs under Faisal's leadership had they not been supported by the British through arms, money and the legendary Lawrence of Arabia. Nevertheless, Faisal succeeded in uniting the tribes of Arabia against the Turks, while Lawrence managed to secure British military approval of the revolt against Damascus.

Box 2.5 Arab Revolt timeline

1915–1916 July to January. McMahon–Hussein Correspondence.

1916 June Sharif Hussein of Mecca enters into alliance with the British and French against Ottoman-Turkish rulers of Arab territories in the Middle East.

(Continued)

Box 2.5 *(Continued)*

1916 June–December Series of attacks by Arab forces and British allies on Ottoman positions in Jidda, Rabegh, Yenbo, Qunfida, Medina, as well as the Hejaz railway.

1917 January Attack on Ottoman position at Wejh, Saudi Arabia.

1917 July Battle of Aqaba, Jordan – victory secured by Arab forces closes Red Sea supply-lines to the Turks. Further attacks by the Arab forces, commanded by British officer T. E. Lawrence, launched on the Hejaz railway.

1918 January–February Arab forces under Lawrence's command have now moved inexorably northward from Arabia through territories that would become Transjordan and later the Hashemite Kingdom of Jordan. Battle of Tafileh is one of the largest set-piece encounters between Arab and Turkish forces. Lawrence and his Arab allies defeated the Turks. In his report, he states of the Turks that 'They lost many men, and our left flank was finally able by a sudden burst of fire to wipe out the Turkish machine-gunners and rush the guns. The mounted men then charged the retreating Turks from our right flank, while we sent forward the infantry and the banners in the centre. They occupied the Turkish line at sunset, and chased the enemy back' (http://telawrence.net/telawrencenet/works/articles_essays/1918_battle_of_seil_el-Hasa.Html).

1918 September–October Hashemite cavalry forces led by Prince Faisal, the son of Sharif Hussein, enter Damascus to secure a Turkish surrender of the city.

1918 1 October T. E. Lawrence reports:

> In Damascus, Shukri el-Ayubi and the town council had proclaimed the King of the Arabs and hoisted the Arab flag as soon as Mustafa Kemal and Jemal had gone. The Turk and German morale was so low that they had marched out beneath the Arab flag without protest: and so good was the civil control that little or no looting took place … Nasir, old Nuri, Major Stirling and myself, entered the morning of October 1, receiving a tremendous but impromptu greeting from the Moslems of the town.
>
> (http://telawrence.net/telawrencenet/works/articles_essays/1918_destruction_of_the_fourth_army.htm)

1919–1920 Post-war peace conferences. Arab claims for independence are promoted.

1920 March Faisal crowned King of Syria in a ceremony in Damascus.

Notably, however, the British were not prepared to deploy their own troops to Alexandretta to support the Arab effort, for fear of a rift in relations with their French allies.

On 1 October 1918 Damascus fell to the Arabs. Although a contingent of Australian troops had occupied the city, it was Faisal, with Lawrence at his side, who entered popular myth as the liberator of the city that had for so long quivered under the grip of Jamal Pasha's iron fist. The conquest of Damascus was important to Hussein and his sons in the quest for Arab nationalism, and independence. Their claims to the leadership of the Arab world were bolstered by the victory and acted as an important counterbalance to the growing perception that the allies, whether British or French, were untrustworthy partners. The British triumph in Palestine, with the fall of Jerusalem to Allenby in November 1917, and the revelations surrounding the Sykes–Picot Agreement that soon followed, alerted the Arabs to the possibly duplicitous character of the British in particular. The conquest of Palestine was also coupled with the revelation that the British had announced their support of the fledgling Zionist movement. The Balfour Declaration, as discussed in chapter 1, sealed Britain's role in Palestine and sowed the seeds of double promise and betrayal for a long time to come. This commitment to support the Zionists in their quest to settle Palestine would create significant political and strategic problems throughout the mandate period. Although authors such as Mansfield (1992, p. 159) maintain that the declaration was 'apparently unsensational' at the time, the ripples in Arab nationalist circles at the news of Balfour's promise were immediately evident. While the Arab peoples celebrated their liberation from the Ottoman authorities and savoured the very real prospect of independence, the Arab leadership was already facing up to the prospect that their European allies would not live up to their promises.

Arab independence in the territory was short-lived. Faisal ruled Damascus until 1920 when the British supported prior French claims over Syria and stood by as Faisal was expelled. The shamefaced British offered Faisal the leadership of Iraq, while his brother Abdullah claimed control over the newly created state of Transjordan with its capital in Amman. The Arabs received the minimum when they had demanded the maximum. New nation-states under the mandated authority of either the British or the French – puppet kingdoms – were created for the Hashemites in Iraq, Syria and Transjordan. As a British official maintained, 'London's support for Arab claims should not be pushed to the point of conflict with France' (Dockrill and Goold, 1981, p. 153). The import of this Arab autonomy over territory in Iraq in particular cannot be underestimated, as Kedourie (1992) argues:

Box 2.6 Iraq, where the crown sits uneasy on the head

Like its short-lived predecessor in Damascus, the Kingdom of Iraq would become the base whence Arab nationalism would be spread over the Arab world … attempting to create a unified Arab state: as Arab nationalists repeatedly reaffirmed in the 1930s, Iraq was to be the Prussia or the Piedmont of an Arab world … It was in Iraq that a fully-fledged doctrine of Arab nationalism was articulated.

(p. 295)

Arab autonomy under the mandate system instituted after the war, however, was not enough to satisfy the growing and increasingly mass-based identity of Arabism which emerged throughout the region. From this point onwards, Arab nationalist demands increased and political change placing more power in Arab hands was inevitable.

Taking state power

In 1932, Hans Kohn, one of the founders of the study of nationalism, noted that the Middle East was entering an 'epoch in which nationalism is the highest and most symbolic social and intellectual form and sets its stamp upon the whole era' (1932, p. 32). Yet, less than twenty years earlier, religion had been the determining factor in the region. Nationalism was not ousting religion, but was more or less rapidly taking a place beside it, frequently fortifying it, beginning to transform and impair it. National symbols acquired religious authority and sacred inviolability. As Kohn again noted, 'the truth which men will defend with their lives is no longer exclusively religious, on occasion it is no longer religious at all, but in increasing measure national' (p. 35). The Arab Revolt had fuelled the popular imagination and helped shape national consciousness throughout the region. The single most significant factor, however, that accounted for the ascendance of Arab nationalism was the perceived betrayal by the colonial powers, in particular Britain and France. During this period Arab nationalism became, in Breuilly's words, symbolic of 'one sort of modern anti-colonial nationalism', whereby Arab identity was forged in opposition to the colonial West (1993, p. 149).

The effect of the post-war settlement of the Middle East between the colonial powers on Arab nationalist ideology and sentiment was perceptible throughout the inter-war period. As western interests in the region expanded, the Arabs gained a new sense of unity and direction, this time against the West rather than the Ottomans. They were increasingly hostile, and populist agitation for change became a major feature of the region. They still maintained their claims to independence and agitated for change under the mandate system run by the British and the French. The European powers responded by trying to split the Arab nationalist movement, weaken it and discredit it. They were not successful. By the late 1920s and early 1930s, public order in Palestine, Transjordan, Iraq, Syria and Lebanon had been severely undermined by localized revolts, demonstrations, strikes and disturbances.

Throughout this period, however, it can be argued that the movement for Arab nationalism was characterized by the emergence of two strands: pan-Arabism or unification nationalism, and Arab nationalism or patriotic/state nationalism. The first was based on grand visions for Arab unity across the region, transcending the new boundaries of nation-states, which were viewed as a temporary measure or step towards the creation of one whole Arab nation that did not recognize state boundaries. Indeed, one governing factor in the fight for independence based on pan-Arab aspirations during this period was that this approach could make most regimes 'look small and petty, just disembodied structures headed by selfish rulers who resisted the sweeping mission of Arabism and who were sustained by outside powers that supposedly feared the one idea that could indeed resurrect the golden age of the Arabs' (Ajami, 1978, p. 361).

The emergence of thinkers such as Sati al-Husri, first in Iraq and then in Syria, described by Kedourie (1992) as the 'first ideologue of Arab nationalism' (p. 296), and Salah ad-din al-Bitar and Michel Aflaq, founders of the Ba'th Party, promoted the idea of anti-colonial resistance that involved pan-Arab unity. Inherent, however, in the appeal of unification nationalism was patriotic or state nationalism, which Owen (2004) describes as presenting or creating the paradox of 'the contradictory necessities of state-building versus Arabism' which was reflected in the region from the 1920s onwards as the struggle for independence grew (p. 86).

The second strand reflected the difficulties that would be associated with state-building and creating new national identities within certain boundaries during the inter-war period, and which in turn would propel revolutionary movements throughout the Middle East. In this context, a new generation of Arab leaders repeatedly made an appeal for unity within the boundaries of the new states, playing their part in shaping the national agenda – in school curricula, radio, television, arts, literature and so on – which would combine to construct, as Anderson has highlighted, 'imagined' Syrian, Iraqi, Egyptian, Tunisian 'communities' and identities. The success, therefore, of patriotic/state nationalism is inextricably linked to more than a decade of revolution and independence which befell the region after the Second World War (see table 2.1).

With revolution, a coup d'état or independence achieved in countries like Egypt, Lebanon, Syria, Iraq, Libya, Tunisia, Morocco, Transjordan, Algeria and Yemen by the early 1970s, a new era had been proclaimed in the region. With independence, however, the new political elite of the states of the region were forced to address the pressing issue of creating new bonds in old boundaries, while at the same time balancing the demands of old bonds in new boundaries.

The extent to which this delicate balancing act resulted in the emergence of stable democratic nation-states is largely found wanting. In addition, other factors need to be addressed, including the swing within the Third World as a whole to revolutionary regimes, and the emergence of Arab / African / Latin American Marxist, socialist and revolutionary movements. The impact of global capitalism on emerging oil economies in the Arabian Gulf must also be factored into any assessment of the nationalism issue within the region as a whole. In Iran, for example, the apparent failure of Mossadeq's nationalist government of the early 1950s can partly be explained by internal factors and failure to appeal to the masses, but the coup of 1953 in which Mossadeq was ousted from government can only fully be explained by highlighting the role of the CIA in supporting the coup as a means to protect their oil interests and overall regional security strategy (Halliday, 1979, p. 25) (see figure 2.1).

A final factor that has been identified in the attempt to explain the competing pulls and pushes of nationalism within the region is the Palestine issue. As Owen (2004) explains it, the 'Palestine issue also possessed the same

TABLE 2.1 Coups, revolts and revolutions: post-war Arab nationalist impulse and regime change in the Middle East 1952–1970

1952	Coup d'état led by the Free Officers Movement in Egypt deposed British-backed monarch. Gamal Abdel Nasser became President of the new Arab republic of Egypt.
1953	CIA- and MI6-backed coup d'état against democratically elected Iranian Prime Minister Mohammed Mossadeq. Shah Reza Pahlavi installed as monarch. Deposed in 1979 during the Iranian revolution.
1956	Morocco regained independence from France and Spain.
1958	Coup d'état led by the Free Officers Movement in Iraq led to the overthrow of the Hashemite monarchy. The coup overthrew King Faisal II, the regent and Crown Prince 'Abdallah, and Prime Minister Nuri al-Said. The coup established an Iraqi Republic. Lebanon Crisis involved a US military intervention.
1960	Coup d'état in Turkey organized by Turkish army officers against the democratically elected government of the Democratic Party. The military junta returned power to civilian rulers 17 months later in October 1961.
1961	Coup d'état in Yemen (Mutawakkilite area) led to North Yemen Civil War fought between royalists of the Mutawakkilite Kingdom of Yemen and factions of the Yemen Arab Republic. The coup was carried out by the republican leader, Abdullah as-Sallal, which ousted Imam Al-Badr.
1962	Algerians won war of independence against the French.
1963	Coup d'état in Syria. Ba'th Party took power. Attempted coup d'état in Turkey failed. Iraqi coup d'état overthrew the regime of Brigadier General Abdul-Karim Qassem. The Ba'th Party took power under the leadership of General Ahmed Hassan al-Bakr (Prime Minister) and Colonel Abdul Salam Arif (President).
1965	Coup d'état in Algeria led by Colonel Houari Boumedienne, President Ben Bella ousted in the process.
1966	Coup d'état in Syria led by neo-Ba'th Party members against the country's first Ba'thist government. Bloodless family coup d'état in Abu Dhabi when Sheikh Bin-Sultan Al Nahyan, the ruler of the Emirate, was replaced by his brother Sheikh Zayed bin Sultan Al Nahyan.
1968	Coup d'état in Iraq. The 2nd Ba'thist regime took over. A bloodless coup by senior Arab Nationalist officers and retired Ba'thist officers overthrew the regime of President Arif. Saddam Hussein, though the Deputy Secretary-General of the Ba'th Party at the time, played a minor role in the coup.
1969	Coup d'état in Libya, led by a young army officer Muammar Gaddafi, established the Libyan Revolution.
1970 August	A bloodless family coup d'état in Oman saw Qaboos bin Said oust his father Said bin Taimur to become Sultan.
November	Coup d'état in Syria. Minister of Defence Hafez al-Assad led the coup, ousting the civilian party leadership and assuming the role of President.

Source: Iranian Historical Photographs Gallery.

Figure 2.1 *Futile politics, Pro-Mossadeq demonstration, Iran 1953*

ability both to unite Arabs and divide them' (p. 88). Evidence of the degree to which this issue united the Arab people is easy to find in the annals of official organizations, like the Arab League, and in the financial pledges made by wealthy Gulf states. The countless petitions of Arab states in international organizations such as the UN and the military encounters between the Arab states and Israel that had locked the region into a cycle of conflict also attest to forms of unity in this issue. All this, however, has to be contrasted, as we shall see, with the national, rather than regional, agendas of individual states such as Jordan, Libya, Syria, Iraq, Tunisia or Egypt – with the animosity between Arab states that has led to conflicts and even wars. There can be no doubt, therefore, that the emerging force of nationalism in the Middle East that would characterize the politics of the region in the 1960s was a double-edged sword on which so many ideals and principles that had assisted the people of the region to independence would flounder.

Unification nationalism: the United Arab Republic and beyond

Following the successes of the various movements for Arab independence in the 1940s and 1950s, one might have expected to witness the decline of Arab nationalism and the rhetoric that supported such aspirations. Instead, Arab nationalism was further strengthened as the new regimes of the Arab world used the ideology of nationalism to pursue the unification agenda more strongly. It could be argued that the success of Arab nationalist movements in achieving independence at the level of nation-states encouraged some tendencies to promote the nationalist agenda to supranational levels. As Breuilly (1993) argues, 'one would have expected Arab nationalism to recede in the face of increasingly important territorial nationalist movements, especially once these had acquired independence' (p. 283). Breuilly and others have pointed out that, alongside the Palestinian issue that unified the Arab nation, the emergence of Egyptian leader Gamal Abdel Nasser was the other significant force explaining the durability of pan-Arabism.

In Egypt, after the 1952 Free Officers coup, a programme of pan-Arabism and the unification of states was pursued. In the context of the Cold War and superpower rivalry in the Middle East, any form of co-operation between Arab states under the banner of pan-Arabism was perceived within the region as positive. During the years following Egypt's nationalization of the Suez Canal, Arab nationalism became increasingly popular in the Middle East and pan-Arab ideas were at the base of political mergers between states. It was believed that pan-Arabism would allow the leaders of the Arab world to transcend state boundaries, many of which had been artificially imposed during the colonial period, to obtain the ideal of Arab unity. The Arab state system became defined as 'first and foremost a Pan system. It postulates the existence of a single Arab nation behind the façade of a multiplicity of sovereign states. In pan-Arab ideology, this nation is actual, not potential' (Khalidi, 1997, p. 181).

Although initially proposed by Syrian communists, such a political, economic and social dream was pursued by President Gamal Abdel Nasser of Egypt in two ways, from 1958 to 1961. Following Egypt's union with Syria, they formed the United Arab Republic (UAR). Ironically, the UAR is often understood as the classic example of the Arab Cold War rather than pan-Arab unity. It was characterized by two central themes: the centrality of Egypt in the region for strategic and political reasons, and the flexibility of alliance based upon existing core Arab concerns. Pan-Arabism was identified as possessing six attributes that combined to make it an evocative ideology with mass appeal. The six features were: universalism; Arab nationalism as an intellectual force; the decline of the colonial powers; a mobile trans-state Arab elite; the 1948 Palestine débâcle, which 'forced Arabs to unite against Israel'; and the 'power of pan-Arabism [from 1956 to 1970] derived from Nasser's charismatic leadership of the movement' (Ajami, 1978, p. 368). As Drysdale and Blake (1985) point out, however, 'the discrepancy between hope and reality is immense and a source of anguish to all Arabs' (p. 224).

The growth of Nasser's power base in the region was simultaneous with the rise of Arab nationalist Ba'thism. In Syria, it was the communists and later the Ba'thists who first raised the issue of union with Egypt. In spite of his pan-Arab rhetoric, Nasser was initially cautious about the Ba'thists' proposal, fearing the immense differences between the Egyptian military authoritarian regime and the Syrian system of parties, parliament and a free press. Nasser met his fears by announcing that he wanted 'internal union of the countries' citizens', and that Syria should dissolve its parties to make way for a unitary state. The Ba'thists accepted these conditions, believing that they could still dominate Syrian political life. Thus, on 1 February 1958, the UAR was proclaimed.

However, the new Republic was almost strangled at birth and proved to be both a political and economic disaster in the making. This historically important attempt at Arab unity based on pan-Arabism failed for three principal reasons. First, because Nasser was not prepared to share power with the Syrians, the UAR became an experiment in Egyptian imperialism. Second, the union strengthened the Egyptian state but only by weakening the Syrian state at an institutional level, and as a result there was no parity of political power. Finally, the most significant weakness of the UAR lay in Nasser's attempt to introduce rapid social and economic change and his failure to find a suitable political framework to support this process.

The experiment in Arab unity illustrated by the UAR outlines a depressing picture in which Egypt remains central to the region and eschews relationships of parity with other Arab states. The centrality of Egypt in the region throughout the period 1958–70 was ultimately instrumental in the conduct of inter-Arab politics and attempts at unity or integration. A number of factors strengthened Egypt and Nasser's position during this period, including Egypt's strategic location, its national identity, its pre-existing military and social infrastructure and its modernized economy. Egypt and its leaders, however, failed to establish the 'superstate' that would threaten the dominance of the superpowers. The demise of the UAR, the establishment of the Baghdad Pact resulting in conservative versus radical Arab states and the defeat of the Arabs in the Six Day War of 1967 were all factors that played a part in what Ajami (1978) refers to as the 'end of pan-Arabism'.

Ajami and others exposed the myth of unification nationalism or pan-Arabism, arguing that by the end of the 1970s it had been replaced by local nationalisms, patriotism and the resurgence of Islam. This coincides with the argument that, by the 1970s and 1980s, there was a triumph of state over nation in the region. In the past, it had been possible to examine the Arab nation as a 'unit of analysis' (Hudson, 1977, p. 83), and authors like Esposito had regarded the Arab nation as a fairly homogeneous unit (1983, p. 59). In the modern-day Middle East, however, it became increasingly apparent that unification nationalism was not enough on its own to sustain the power of any Arab regime. The loads on the hypothetical system of the Arab nation were far too great and, as Hudson contends, 'the rapid modernization of the state as a unit of analysis has been at the cost of the nation' (1977, p. 83). State and territorial nationalism is no longer regarded as a transitory phenomenon on the path to unification nationalism; today it is regarded as a permanent feature of politics in the region. However, as Hudson reminds us, 'if the Arab state is stronger than it used to be, it is not just because their populations are more harmonious and supportive of the system. More important is the fact that the system itself can exert increasingly pervasive influence (both positive and negative) over individuals and society' (1977, p. 83).

The defeat of the Arabs in the Six Day War of 1967 against Israel, and the further loss of Palestinian territory, were also considered by most writers on the Middle East to be the watershed or turning point in pan-Arabism and Arab nationalism. The rout of Nasserite Egypt and Ba'thist Syria in the war shattered the image of radical power in the region, as revolutionary Arab politics suffered its most crushing defeat (Dessouki, 1982, p. 322). Arab unity around the Palestinian issue did enjoy a brief revival during and shortly after the war with Israel of 1973. A new sense of triumph emerged, but triumph was not associated with the lofty ideals of pan-Arabism but with the economic strength of the oil-producing economies of the region. From this point onwards, a threshold was crossed: the radical nationalist regimes had failed to unite, but the clout of the petro-dollar had increased regional interdependency. Oil and its multiplier effects led to a greater interdependency among the Arab states as a new order turned previous positions of regional leadership on their heads. As money from the Gulf states, and migrant labour from Egypt, Syria and Jordan flowed in more or less opposite directions, relations changed. The end result of this new order was an Arab Cold War in which the radical and conservative states of the region found themselves locked in the most bitter of disputes.

The rhetoric of Arabism was still broadcast across the region by radical states like Iraq, Syria and Libya, but their calls largely fell on deaf ears and were discredited by recent experience. The mask of Arab nationalism could no longer conceal the personalized political agendas of Arab leaders throughout the region. Clearly, the system of regional relations that rose from the ashes of the 1967 defeat, known as the 'new Arab order', was no bright new dawn for politics in the Middle East. In the era of crisis that followed 1967, the field of politics was open to the appeals of other forces, in particular political Islam and Islamist movements. The contested ground of ideology grew, with many declaring nationalism the loser and Islam the victor. Yet the picture that has emerged is far more complicated than this. As Tibi reminds us:

Box 2.7 New era

Now the claim of Islamic fundamentalists is universal, but the realities they are operating within are related, among others, to ethnic, sectarian and national strife. Thus, in Islamic fundamentalism we can observe a mix of ethnicity, nationalism, and sectarian rivalry.

(1997, p. 220)

In addition, there are no strict differences to be found between Islam as Islamic state and nationalism as nation-state. As Piscatori (1986) observes, in some respects there is no tension between the nation-state and modern political Islam – the nation-state is a fact of life in the current global order and Islam has learnt to live with and accommodate it.

The interdependency and co-operation, however, that Islamic fundamentalism fostered until August 1990, when Iraq invaded Kuwait, stood in stark contrast to the adversarial and ideologically pan-Arab and Arab nationalist politics of the Cold War period that preceded it. Despite the distinct lack of rhetoric surrounding the changes, the inter-Arab links forged by millions of migrant workers and the millions more who depend on their earnings adds up to an interdependence and integrating force far in excess in real terms of anything that was enacted between the formation of the Arab League in 1945 and the defeat in the Six Day War of 1967. Importantly, the two myths upon which Arab nationalism, pan-Arabism and the Cold War relied became irrelevant. The first myth stated that the Arabs constitute one nation; the second that the needs and desires of millions of people could be neatly summarized in slogans such as 'unity, liberation and revolution' (Kerr, 1971, p. 3). If it appeared that Islamism had eclipsed nationalism, this was, in part, true. The events of the Arab Spring in 2011, however, revived distinctly civic, national ideals and beliefs that had more in common with conceptions of Arab identity than Islamism – even in its post-Islamist mode – by that point. In the period of instability that has proceeded from the momentous Arab awakening of 2011, nationalist sentiments, ethics and values remain in significant contention.

Case study
Nationalism defined by a man – Nasserism

The rise of Egyptian nationalism at the turn of the twentieth century was associated with an urbanized, anti-colonial, educated elite which was determined to end Britain's hold over the largest country in the region. During the First World War, London proclaimed Egypt a British protectorate and the country was subordinated to British strategic, military and political interests. Opposition to the British among Egyptians centred on mobilizing opinion and developing strategies to oust the British from their country. Egyptian consciousness-raising centred on the belief in the unity of the Arab people in the face of damaging foreign interference.

The goal of the national movement was an end to British control, independence and self-determination. This vision was articulated by the leaders of a new political group led by prominent Egyptians and named the Wafd. The British basically refused to legitimate the call for independence and instead pursued policies of suppression. This refusal to allow greater political freedom for Egyptians only served to intensify hostility towards the British in the aftermath of the war. From 1918 to 1922, Egyptian opposition increased, through Arab nationalist and pan-Islamic political platforms. Pressure was so great that eventually the British were forced to concede some ground for fear of full-scale national revolt. In February 1922, the protectorate was terminated and the British decreed that Egypt was a 'constitutional monarchy'. Technical independence may well have been declared but Britain remained firmly in control.

This technical and titular Egyptian head of state did not satisfy nationalist demands. While many differences existed within Egyptian society, for example between the peasant population and land-owning classes, all were agreed on one thing – that Britain should relinquish its political power over the country and let the Egyptians rule. Negotiations did take place, but by and large the position on key issues changed little and British influence remained significant. A new Anglo-Egyptian Treaty signed in 1936 shored up Britain's interests.

The Second World War proved a turning point in Anglo-Egyptian relations. Britain used the war situation to impose its security apparatus over the Egyptians, and military rule was supported by press censorship, and suspension of the Egyptian legislature and government, as well as the further imposition of martial law. All this took place in a country acting as an important base and ally for the British. In post-war Egypt the nationalists and their Islamic counterparts took advantage of the relaxation of various war restrictions to push their agenda into the public arena. Indeed, during the period from 1945 to 1950, mass-based demands for independence from the British were articulated throughout the country, ultimately making British rule increasingly untenable. The movement for independence in Egypt was difficult to withstand, and public protest and demonstration became an almost daily occurrence. Although Britain extended its coercive powers, it was compelled to enter into talks with Egyptian nationalists to determine the country's future. By 1951, however, the talks had stalled and the Egyptians broke the treaty with Britain. Public demonstrations and disorder became the rule of the day, as ordinary Egyptians took to the streets in cities and towns throughout the country. In early 1952, even the Egyptian police, who were employed by the British, had turned against their overlords and, once again, the British announced martial law across the whole country. In July 1952, the military coup d'état took place. King Farouk abdicated, the constitution of 1923 was abolished and political parties were dissolved and banned. British days were numbered.

Gamal Abdel Nasser, the Egyptian nationalist leader, ranks as one of the most significant political figures in the Middle East in the twentieth century. His sustained vision of a united Arab world was rapidly translated into populist support which spread throughout the region in the 1950s and 1960s. For better or for worse, Nasser and his supporters shaped the future of Arab nationalism both within the region and in the international arena. Indeed, the ideology of nationalism that became associated with this era was known as 'Nasserism'. It was largely an expression of the marriage between revolutionary socialism and pan-Arabism on Egyptian – or, rather, Nasser's – terms. The Suez Crisis of 1956, despite the military defeat of Egypt, projected Nasser's vision of pan-Arab unity and nationalism throughout the region and encouraged him to promote further his agenda for Arab unity. It can be asserted that, from this point, 'Nasser himself made nationalism his personal message, especially in the sense that he was its natural leader and Egypt the nucleus state of the Arab world' (Hopwood, 1985, p. 98).

The reality of promoting the Egyptian state as the 'nucleus' of the pan-Arab model was somewhat different from the ideas developed by Nasser and his supporters. While it is true that Nasser did enjoy widespread popular Arab support, the same could not be said of levels of support for Nasser's pan-Arab ideals among the political elite and leaders of a variety of Arab states. Indeed, while on one hand Nasser promoted unity, on the other hand his unwilling-ness to compromise and his quest for Egyptian supremacy in any regionally integrated order created new tensions and fissures between the leaders of Arab states. This would ultimately kill the unity dream from within and leave the Arabs, post-1967, in a state of disarray. Nasser's successors, Presidents Sadat and Mubarak only succeeded in burying the dream of Egyptian nation-alism further, making the state and its people increasingly subordinate to authoritarian and thieving agendas. They succeeded in turning the country from a high-ranking Arab power to one widely perceived as a puppet of American whim and preference.

That agenda was disrupted in 2011 by the emergence of new popu-list nationalist symbols and heroes that galvanized Egyptians (see figure 2.2). Khaled Saeed, for example, was a young Egyptian from Alexandria killed while in police custody in June 2010. Those who highlighted his death helped ignite the Egyptian Revolution of 2011. When images of his tortured body were circulated on social media, in particular on the Facebook group 'We are all Khaled Saeed', moderated by online activist Wael Ghonim, widespread outrage at the Egyptian state grew (Alaimo, 2015). These new nationalist heroes were victims of the Egyptian state, which mobilized millions to rise up and call for Mubarak's resignation. They proved, however, transient symbols. First they were replaced by the symbols of the Muslim Brotherhood and the Morsi Presidency. After 2013 they were supplanted by counter-revolutionary rhetoric and authoritar-ian-nationalism symbolized by General – soon-to-be President – el-Sisi. This is a form of Egyptian nationalism that is tied intimately to Egypt's military and security architecture as the mainstay of a regime governed by 'strong' leaders in uniform.

Figure 2.2 *Khaled Saeed*

Case study

Ba'thism – the Arab socialist future unveiled

From the 1970s to the end of the 1990s, Ba'thism (Renaissance) played a pivotal ideological role in the states of Syria and Iraq. Ba'thism has subsequently become associated with one-party rule, a lack of democracy, militarized society and dictatorship. It was not just an expression of an Arab nationalist identity, but called for a wider unity among the Arab people under a socialist agenda.

The Ba'th Party was founded by two Syrian intellectuals, Michel Aflaq and Salah ad-din al-Bitar, in the early 1940s. Aflaq, a Christian, and al-Bitar, a Muslim, drew up an agenda based on the principles of secular, nationalist socialism which would unite all Arabs throughout the region, irrespective of religion, nation or class. Their ideas were crystallized in the establishment of the Ba'th Party when it held its first congress in Damascus in 1947. In addition to the party establishing itself in Syria, branches soon followed in

Iraq, Jordan and Lebanon by the early 1950s. The objectives of the party were based around the theme of pan-Arab unity under the banner of 'one nation' with a policy of socialism and national revival. This call found a large audience in a period following the decline of the colonial powers, which included the departure of the French from Syria and Lebanon, the British from Iraq, Egypt, Palestine and Jordan, the phenomenon of pan-Arabism and pan-Islamism that had been established in other parts of the region, and the example of other post-colonial socialist movements in the Third World. Ba'thism would promise the liberation and subsequent freedom of the Arab people from communal, religious and ethnic loyalties as well as loyalties to artificially created nation-states, which had been the product of western interference in the region. Aflaq enshrined these aspirations in the slogan 'unity, liberation and socialism'. Freedom was envisioned in a personal as well as a national sense.

Socialism was the ideological facilitator for the aspiration for freedom and Arab unity, outlining a social and political order designed to eliminate confessional and class difference. The problem that the Ba'th Party faced, however, was how to achieve the necessary political change to reach its objectives. The solution presented itself in the form of a coup d'état rather than reformist change, along the path advocated by many other national liberation movements throughout the region and the Third World in general.

A coup d'état rather than society-wide revolution was the path that eventually allowed the Ba'thists to obtain power in both Iraq and Syria. Thus, the link between Ba'thism and militarism was established and some of the earlier ideas advocated by Aflaq were abandoned. In Syria, the Ba'thists had been significant political actors throughout the 1950s and by 1963 were major players in the military coup. However, it was not until the second coup of 1966 that the Ba'thists were able to consolidate their power over the state and its political institutions. By 1966, the Ba'th Party was firmly in the hands of the young military Alawites – an Islamic sect, in the minority in Syria – and Aflaq and al-Bitar had become marginalized figures (Hinnebusch 2015a, p. 112). Although leadership of the country changed again in 1970, when General Salah Jadid was defeated in a third coup led by Hafiz al-Assad, an Alawite, Ba'thist ambitions for Arab unity and socialism were maintained.

After 1970, President Hafiz al-Assad established an authoritarian presidency. Pluralism in politics almost vanished, Alawite sectarianism came to dominate the ethnic and religious mosaic of the country, a socialist state-planned economy failed and intransigence over the conflict with Israel was maintained. Politics became meaningless unless played out under the rubric of the party through recruitment, membership, policy, the military, elections and participation. The death of Hafiz al-Assad in June 2000 led to the succession of his youngest son, Bashar.

Since 2000, Bashar al-Assad has presided over a state engulfed in the ever tightening grip of its military, its party and its minority Alawi rule. The outbreak of the uprising in the southern Syrian town of Derra in March 2011 and subsequent civil war across the country has resulted in the collapse of the state into a devastating conflict (Glass, 2016). By 2017 that conflict had devolved into a sectarian fight that had drawn in regional and international players supporting multitudinous warring factions and proxy armies. The brutal face of Ba'thism and the regime led by al-Assad was exposed by its policies of siege, bombardment, helicopter gunships, barrel bombs, and chlorine attacks on its own defenceless citizens (Yassin-Kassab and al-Shami, 2016).

The same defeat of the principles of Ba'thism became largely true of Iraq where, following the Ba'thist coup of 1968 and the rule of Saddam Hussein (figure 2.3), who became President in 1979, one-party rule and authoritarian presidency were prevalent. In Iraq, however, the pretence of party leadership, according to Owen, was soon dropped by Hussein, who 'made it clear he was no longer interested in an image of collective leadership but one of personal power' (Owen, 2004, p. 263). The Ba'th Party was eclipsed by this drive for dictatorship, and the military/security apparatus, rather than the party – despite its million-plus membership – was the vehicle employed by Saddam Hussein to maintain power. The call to Arab unity was merely a foil for his personal ambitions in territorial conflict with Iran and Kuwait, or Jordan and Syria. Arab unity in Hussein's lexicon implied his personal dictatorship through military control and fear. The visionary calls of Aflaq and al-Bitar for a pluralist socialist state were brutally dissipated.

Figure 2.3 *Hail the tyrant, Iraqi leader Saddam Hussein.* © *Stephen Farrell*

Iraq's economy was ravaged by a combination of war and UN sanctions, its population living in the apocalyptically named 'Republic of Fear'. Unity, liberation and socialism were largely lost in both Syria and Iraq, replaced by a slogan for the twenty-first century, 'fragmentation, subjugation and authoritarianism'. These three factors represent not just the failures of those who claimed to harness the ideas of Ba'thism as an expression of Arab nationalism, but the profound political and economic changes in the global environment and the fall of the former Soviet Union, the resurgence of Islamist movements and ethnic conflict. These wider global changes compounded the paradox of the Ba'thist tendency to authoritarianism, the primacy of continued dictatorship being more desirable than further ethnic or religious fragmentation and political change in these two countries.

In Iraq, Ba'thism was put to death as Saddam Hussein was toppled from power in April 2003, and the country fell under the military and civil occupation of allied forces led by the USA. The immediate collapse and dismantlement of the Ba'thist state – including the political party, its various committees, military, police and security apparatus – plunged post-war Iraq into a security vacuum. US and UK de-Ba'thification approaches have been recognized as contributing to the problems from which Iraq has yet to recover. Among the myriad findings of the UK Iraq War Inquiry, otherwise known as the Chilcot Report, was that the government of Tony Blair was aware that the USA had 'inadequate' plans for the dismantling of the Ba'th party and its control over the institutions of the Iraqi state (Chilcot, 2016). Some contend that from the ashes of Ba'thism, the terror and tyranny of ISIS arose (Reuter, 2015).

Box 2.8 Chilcot judgement: You f***ed it up Mr Blair

Mr Blair told the inquiry that the difficulties encountered in Iraq after the invasion could not have been known in advance. We do not agree that hindsight is required. The risks of internal strife in Iraq, active Iranian pursuit of its interests, regional instability and Al-Qaeda activity in Iraq were each explicitly identified before the invasion.

(Chilcot, 2016)

It cannot be argued that nationalism epitomized by the Ba'th Party in either Syria or Iraq represented or expressed an inclusive sense of nation. In this respect, if Ba'thism represented a nationalist ideology, it had truly, to paraphrase Gellner, 'come before a nation'. It also failed to unite or create a sense of nation among a disparate group of peoples divided by tribal, ethnic and sectarian difference. In these cases, nationalism failed in its unification function and its success lay only in allowing minority interest (Tikrit – the clan within Iraq from which Saddam Hussein came – or the Alawites of the al-Assads) to be promoted and consolidated.

In post-war Iraq, nation-building and the discourse on Iraqi nationalism had to begin all over again. The state remains susceptible to new debates and divisions over what it means to be an Iraqi national in the twenty-first century. Indeed, since 2003, national identity has fissured into ethno-sectarian dimensions of Kurd, Shi'a, Sunni and other minorities. The western vision of a new nationalism binding the Iraqi state post-Saddam has encountered significant difficulty (Milton-Edwards, 2010). In Syria, such a discourse seems jarringly out of place. The enmities on the ground and the opposing agendas of the region's actors and patrons are too intense to make the situation look anything other than impenetrable. The complexities of the conflict are no longer limited to how a people define themselves as a nation. Instead, it has become a contested prize for a variety of foreign powers who seek to shape Syria beyond a national mould.

Case study

Stateless nation – the Kurds

It is important to discuss an example of nationalism within the region that lies outside the dominant discussion thus far of Arab and Islamic nationalism and its associated variants. A discussion of Kurdish nationalism allows the reader the opportunity to examine and analyse a nationalist movement, national identity and discourse rooted in its ethnic variant. Nevertheless, it is important to highlight that the manifestation of Kurdish nationalism had much in common with Arab and other expressions of the late nineteenth and early twentieth centuries in the region.

The origins of Kurdish nationalism lie with the same nationalist stirrings and sentiments evident in Arab nationalism in the second half of the nineteenth century. Kurds were a 'nation' characterized by distinct cultural, ethnic, linguistic and geographical markers (Jwaideh, 2006). These markers were historically rooted to contiguous territories but, within those, there were dimensions of tribal, linguistic, religious and class differences that most Kurdish nationalists would claim are primordial (Gunter, 2013).

Yet at the heart of the matter is the fact that the Kurds are one of the largest ethnic groups in the Middle East, following the Arabs, the Turks and the Persians. For over 2,000 years, they have retained a distinct ethnic identity. Essentially, they have been described as a tribal people, even though nomadic mountain lifestyles are a thing of the past (McDowall, 2007). In the Middle East, Kurds live in the areas occupying a large triangular-shaped region currently divided up among four states in Turkey, Iraq, Iran and Syria. They form a minority population in all four states: Kurds make up about 10 per cent of the population in Syria, 18 per cent of the population in Turkey, 15–20 per cent of the population of Iraq, and nearly 10 per cent of Iran. Although they are dispersed over many countries, they inhabit areas that often border each other.

The Kurdish nationalist struggle for self-determination and independence had remained, until the late twentieth century, one of the untold stories of the region (McKiernan, 2006). Like the Palestinians and other minority groups, when the Ottoman Empire dissolved in the early part of the twentieth century, the Kurds and their leaders believed they would be granted their rights by the international community and the colonial powers who held sway over the region. Kurdish nationalist claims, however, were sacrificed in the 'undignified' colonial scramble for control, their land vital to British claims to Iran and Hashemite Iraq, and French claims in Syria (Entessar, 1992). In Turkey, Kemal Atatürk's era of Turkish nationalism allowed no room for competing identities – religious, ethnic or otherwise – and in the Soviet Union the spread of communism put an end to any hopes that the ethnic minorities of Kurdistan or Armenia had of national independence.

The Kurdish nationalist cause has been beset by a variety of problems (Jabar and Dawod, 2006). Internal Kurdish conflicts, for example, have been long-standing and Kurdish unity has been an ideal rather than an enduring reality. This lack of unity has exacerbated the physical divisions that exist.

The Kurdish nationalists have largely rejected assimilation into their host states and, although some factions have colluded with the state against their fellow Kurds, they have successfully resisted attempts by, for example, Turkey to reshape their identity into 'Mountain Turks' while denying their Kurdish roots. The Kurdish cause, then, has been a long-standing one and, while it is easy to identify their main objective, which is a nationalist call for self-determination and independence from central government, their successes have been limited to autonomous territories rather than statehood.

From the 1920s onwards, the Kurdish minorities of Iran, Iraq, Syria and Turkey formed themselves into political movements to put pressure on their governments for independence. However, it must be noted that the struggle for independence has not been just political but has embraced the strategy of armed resistance as well. As Van Bruinessen points out, 'it is easy to portray the Kurdish problem as essentially a conflict between a liberation movement and a central government that tries to enforce its rule over them' (1986, p. 4). There exists a distinct lack of incorporation of the Kurdish minority into the state in the Middle East. Historically, Kurds have been excluded from power. In Iraq, Iran, Syria and Turkey, the minority population of the Kurds was perceived as a threat to national unity, a group that could agitate and threaten state legitimacy. In Iraq, state-building in the wake of the fall of the regime of Saddam Hussein led to a new political dispensation. This included Iraqi Kurds such as Jalal Talabani and Fuad Masum successively serving as Presidents of the country. Moreover, the new Iraqi constitution allowed Kurds forms of self-governance in the Kurdistan Regional Government (KRG). Nevertheless, tensions endure between the governing elites of Erbil and Baghdad. The Kurdish leadership of Erbil have criticized Iraqi

Prime Ministers for their failure to respect constitutional rights. By 2017, the Kurds had called a 'symbolic' referendum for independence.

In Syria, where before 2011 Kurds accounted for an estimated 2 million of the population, the al-Assad regime was accused of systematic discrimination and repression. Since the outbreak of the civil war in Syria, Kurds in the north of the country – in areas like Kobane, Afrin and Rojava – have established armed rebel units to fight the forces of the al-Assad regime, ISIS and others. They have seized control of Rojava, and declared an autonomous federation. The Rojava federation encompasses three Kurdish-majority territories: Afrin, Cizire and Kobane. Sheppard in 2016 asserted the following.

Box 2.9 Rojava Declaration: 'Jin, Jiyan, Azadi'

[Rojava] was defined by the principles of democratic confederalism … Power is as decentralized as possible, rising up from village assemblies and communes to the legislative councils and commissions that run the economy, defense, and justice ministries. At all levels, the ethnic and gender balance is zealously asserted. Arabs, Yazidis, and Turkmen participate in the public sphere alongside the Kurdish majority, while the mantra of Rojava as a whole is 'Jin, Jiyan, Azadi' ('Woman, Life, Freedom').

(Sheppard, 2016)

These factors help explain the nature of the Kurdish issue and the strategies adopted by states like Iraq and Turkey. The experiences of Iraq's Kurds during the 1991 Gulf crisis emphasized the nature of this ethnic issue within Iraq's borders that threatened both the legitimacy and stability of Saddam Hussein's regime. Even before the Kurdish uprising of 1991, Saddam Hussein had conducted a ruthless campaign against the Kurdish population of northern Iraq. His 'Anfal' campaign led to the ethnic cleansing of as many as 100,000 Kurds.

In 1988, he had attacked the Kurds using chemical weapons – nerve gas had been used against a defenceless civilian population. At that time, however, the international community did not come to the aid of the Kurds or support their cause. In March 1991, the situation was quite different. The Kurdish population was encouraged by the international community to rise up against Saddam Hussein at the same time that the Shi'a community in the south of the country was also staging a revolt. The revolt was short-lived; Iraqi forces quickly gained control of Kurdish cities and bombing raids resulted in a mass exodus to the borders with Turkey and Iran. The leaders of two main Kurdish resistance groups, the Iraq Kurdistan Front and the Kurdistan Workers' Party, entered into autonomy negotiations with Baghdad.

The refugee problem grew, forcing the international community to take action – by May 1991, a safety zone in northern Iraq had been established.

The US administration rapidly abandoned the Kurds, one White House analyst summing the situation up: 'It probably sounds callous, but we did the best thing not to get near [the Kurdish revolt]. They're nice people, and they're cute, but they're really just bandits. They spend as much time fighting each other as central authority. They're losers' (Entessar, 1992, p. 155). The message was clear: even the tyranny of central government was better than ceding to the minorities of the region; the stability of the nation-state had to be preserved, no matter how high the price. Of course, that price was exacted by the governments of the USA and UK in 2003 when they launched a war on Iraq. The participation of the Kurds of Iraq in the post-war elections for the Iraqi parliament in January 2005 also allayed fears that the Kurds would press ahead with secessionist demands. The election of Kurds to the new Iraqi legislature signalled an intent to maintain autonomy through a federal approach in post-war Iraq (Anderson and Stansfield, 2005). As discussed above, the decision to make the Kurdish leader Jalal Talabani the President of Iraq in April 2005 was momentous in terms of the campaign by Kurds to assure their future in the modern state. Such ambitions have been viewed with interest in Iraq's neighbouring states where so many more of the region's Kurdish population still reside – without rights or recognition for the foreseeable future. Today, as noted above, the Iraqi Kurdish region is highly autonomous and is, in many realms, as detached from the central government of Baghdad as is possible. This 'Other Iraq' maintains its own armed forces, legislative assembly and trappings of a state – it is ultimately defined by its ethnic ambition. In recent years this has led to significant investment in the international system, seeking to achieve statehood through institutions that secure international recognition and legitimacy. This, as Voller argues, is part of a successful transition by the Kurds from rebel movement to de facto statehood (2014).

Questions for discussion

- Define the fundamental tenets of Arab nationalism.
- Is Kurdish nationalism sufficiently distinct from Arab nationalism to explain why the Kurds remain stateless?
- What, if anything, do the events of the Arab Spring tell us about the future of nationalism in the Middle East?

Recommended reading

- General theoretical accounts of nationalism can be found in Smith (1979), Gellner (1983) and Breuilly (1993). Eric Hobsbawm's (1990) account of nation and nationalism is also particularly useful for a general overview of debates, and Benedict Anderson (1983) pays particular attention to the construction of national identities.

- On Arab nationalism, historical overviews from Provence (2005) and Abdul-Jabar and Dawod (2003) are helpful. Tibi (1994 and 1997) provides a comprehensive account of contemporary theories and approaches associated with thinking on the subject. Dawisha (2016) provides a significant overview of Arab nationalism and pan-Arabism in terms of both its historical origins and its apex and eclipse by other ideologies in the region. His epilogue examines the phenomenon in relation to the stability of the region following the Arab Spring.
- Choueiri (1989) presents a critical analysis of Arab nationalism and related debates of historiography. He further extends his analysis in his work of 2001. Suleiman (2004) reflects on issues of nationalism, national identity and language in the Middle East.
- Debate on the import of Arab nationalism and historiography is covered by Khalidi et al. (1991), AbuKhalil (1992), Firro (2003) and al-Azmeh (1995) and should be contrasted against more traditional accounts such as those of Antonius (1969), Brown (1984) and Fromkin (1989).
- The nationalism and Islam matrix is reviewed in texts such as Moaddel (2005), Piscatori (1986), Vatikiotis (1987) and Tibi (1987), and further reading on this subject can also be found in chapter 5.
- On early Egyptian nationalism and Nasserism, books abound. Coverage of early Egyptian nationalism can be discovered in Coury (1982), Khoury (1983), Warburg and Kupferschmidt's edited collection of historical insights (1983), Wilson (1983) and Dawn (1988). Stephens' (1971) biography of Nasser is extensive in its account and adds detail to the more general records found in Mansfield (1969) or Hopwood (1985). Gordon (1992) and Abdel Magid (1994) have both produced cogent and interesting books on the Nasser era.
- Regarding Ba'thism in Iraq, Devlin (1976), Batatu (1979), Farouk-Sluglett and Sluglett (1990) and Baram (1991) examine the impact of this philosophy on state-formation and political life. Khalil (1989) outlines an account of life in Ba'thist Iraq with chilling clarity. Tripp (2002) and Dodge (2003) both demonstrate the problems inherent to nation- and state-building in Iraq and the impact of Ba'thist ideology and rule under Saddam Hussein. Moreover, they highlight the many problems that lay in the colonial roots of this newly forged nation and state created in the early part of the twentieth century. Kienle (1990) achieves a similar feat in his text on Ba'thism, which takes a comparative approach to the Syrian and Iraqi examples. Hopwood (1988) provides a good overview of politics and society in Syria from 1945 to 1986, and Seale (1988) offers the most comprehensive and in-depth account of the country under Hafiz al-Assad. Perthes (2004) has produced a new work on Syrian politics under the new President Bashar al-Assad that demonstrates the issues besetting this President of the Arab republic.

- The essays in the collection edited by Lawson (2009) highlight the legacies of Ba'thism and Arab nationalism as Syria redefines its role in the region in the wake of 9/11, the collapse of the Ba'thist state in neighbouring Iraq, and Syria's own disengagement from neighbouring Lebanon.
- On more specific examples of ethnic nationalism, such as the Kurds, see McDowall's (2007) comprehensive historical account and the contributions of Gunter (2016). Both examine the Kurds in Iran, Iraq and Turkey as well as broader issues of the international context of the Kurdish question.
- A book by Gunter (2007) examines the so-called Kurdish issue against the backdrop of federalism, arguing that this form of power-sharing may constitute the solution to the historic Kurdish struggle for self-determination. The book also outlines the structure of the KRG.
- Texts by Stansfield (2007) and Aziz (2014) reflect events and debates as they impact on the Kurds of Iraq. Jongerden (2007) and Ozcan (2010) specifically focus on Turkey and its Kurdish population. Allsopp (2015) provides an important contribution to the dynamic of Kurds in Syria and the establishment of self-rule projects. Natali (2005) offers a detailed account of Kurdish nationalism and the differences between Kurdish national movements in Iraq, Iran and Turkey. It dismembers the socio-political, tribal and cultural differences of the Kurdish communities while also looking at their integration into their respective local societies. An edited text by Romano and Gurses (2014) offers insight into the Kurds in the four main localities of the Middle East.

CHAPTER THREE

A Very Political Economy

Introduction

It is tempting to believe that the issues affecting contemporary economics and politics (or the political economy) in the Middle East revolve solely around oil and gas and the revenues, including rents, derived from their production. While oil and gas are important to any understanding of political economy in the region, there are a number of other issues which are worth examining, including debates about market-based systems, structural economic issues, middle-class defection, rising inequalities, retreat of the state from service provision and welfare, corruption, aid dependency, urbanization and the region's economic competitiveness in global markets.

Nevertheless, our popular conception of the region and its wealth is dominated by the discussion of oil and gas. Cheap caricatures of an oil-rich region populated by wealthy Arab sheikhs who gamble away millions at the casinos in Cannes or Monaco feed our perception of the area. The region has significant proven oil reserves. The Organization of Petroleum Exporting Countries (OPEC) estimated in 2015 that they could account for 81 per cent of the world total, of which more than 65 per cent was in the Middle East. This has resulted in the rapid creation of wealth for some states and an often near-total dependency on oil revenues (OPEC, 2015b). Nevertheless, these proven reserves are shrinking. The Middle East, including the North African oil-producing states, makes a major difference to production gluts and shortages with significant impacts on domestic economies. Syria, for example, witnessed a rapid decline in oil production in the decade 2005–15, from 448,000 barrels produced per day to 27,000. In one year alone, from 2014–15, a reported 18.2 per cent decline in production from Syria was recorded by BP (BP, 2016).

The region's relations with the West (as well as other global actors) have also been significantly affected by the oil and gas factor. It has eased integration into the world trading system and papered over some inherent economic weaknesses. But in the twenty-first century, such oil- and gas-producing states must also grapple with the prospect of 'oil/gas peak', as well as, conversely, overproduction creating surpluses and price drops and their implications for their economies. These are complex issues of economies of production of available resources and their implications for politics in the region should not be under-estimated. There is an intricate inter-linking of such issues. In Kuwait in the spring of 2016, for example, oil-sector workers staged a general strike in protest at proposals by the government to cut public sector payrolls leading to a drop in oil prices on the global market, which only rallied after the strike was called off.

Is there a 'pan-Arab' economy internal to the region which is united by the above factors? The group of countries that the term seeks to cover are disparate entities and separate economic units with diverging economic policies and different historical and political foundations. Can we speak of an oil or gas economy? Here, as this chapter illustrates, the ripples in the oil/gas pool are easy to discern. Irrespective of economic policy, political orientation or historical antecedents, there are very few – if any – economies in the region that are not altered or affected by oil and gas, their production and their revenues.

Other issues evolve out of these debates, including the impact on economies of other natural resources in the region, and related questions about excessive energy use, climate change and the global debate about carbon-dependent societies and transitions to alternative energy sources. Political and economic development in Algeria, for example, could never be adequately understood without first analysing the impact of the gas industry and the wealth associated with it. The success of the Algerian FLN (Front de Libération Nationale) in state-building and consolidation was significantly bolstered by the wealth created by gas. Mismanagement, the constriction of state control of the industry and declining prices in the world market all played their part in the economic crisis of the late 1980s and early 1990s. This, in turn, provoked political instability that played a part in the civil war that devastated the country for most of the 1990s. In Libya, post-Gaddafi, oil and gas fields have become subject to the contesting rivalries of the myriad militias seeking to control the country. For example, by 2016 an armed group established to protect the country's oil assets had been accused of becoming a 'private army' accruing resources to itself and controlling their export to foreign markets. The Petroleum Facilities Guard (PFG) (which even had its own Facebook group) was able to leverage power over the conflict-riven state and its economy, effectively giving them the ability to hold the political leaders of the UN-backed government to ransom. Furthermore, from 2014 onwards, ISIS control of Syrian and Iraqi territories, including most of Syria's oil fields, gave the group a major revenue boost. This underscored fears that the jihadist group would use such revenues not only to consolidate its power in those areas under its control but to expand exponentially across the Middle East and beyond. Such concerns have been realized, despite concerted air strikes against ISIS oil fields where – beyond Syria and Iraq – ISIS had sought and gained footholds in other oil-rich states, such as Libya.

Regional wealth and extremes of inequality

Economic inequality is a major feature of the Middle East. Located in the region are some of the world's poorest and richest states. In 2016, Qatar, according to Global Finance data garnered from the World Bank, the Organisation for Economic Co-operation and Development (OECD) and the International Monetary Fund (IMF), was the richest country in the world, while Yemen, however, was among the poorest, ranked at 161 (Global Finance, 2017). Such facts raise important questions relating to development and development studies. Is the Middle East part of the developing or global South? If countries such as Yemen or Egypt are cited from such diverse perspectives as gross domestic product (GDP), gross national product (GNP), infant mortality, literacy rates, national debt and IMF loans, it might lead us to conclude that it is. Since the late 1990s, as a percentage of GDP, agriculture in Egypt has been in decline. With so much of Egypt's population being rurally based and dependent on agriculture, this is a major issue that the state has to struggle with.

In Yemen, the economic situation has been on a downward spiral since unification of the country in 1990. The country is beset with high inflation, food prices and unemployment. By 2016, approximately 43 per cent of the population were living below the poverty line. Yemen was ranked by the World Food Programme (WFP) as the 11th most food-insecure state globally. 'Overall', the WFP concluded, 'one in three Yemenis are acutely hungry; they do not have sufficient resources to access nutritious food necessary for a healthy and productive life' (World Food Programme, 2015). Yemen remained poorest within the region with little prospect of such a trend being reversed in the short to medium term. The dire economic situation was linked to rising political instability in the country, including al-Qaeda's increasing hold and the protests that swept the country in 2011 during the Arab Spring and the subsequent ouster of President Saleh. Economic crisis has been further exacerbated by the consequences of the Houthi rebel takeover of Yemen in 2014. These consequences have included the formation of a Saudi-led military alliance waging war against the country since 2015.

Poverty, development crises, disease and economic stagnation are, therefore, not unknown in the region. Such factors played a significant part in fuelling the protests against incumbent regimes in Tunisia, Yemen, Egypt and Jordan in 2011, and the political crises they led to. We must be wary here though. Cammett et al. remind us that, on the eve of the Arab Spring, the region was relatively stable economically and that 'discontent on the economic front interacted with a broader socio-political context to ignite the risings' (2016, p. 4). Other characteristics of colonial and post-colonial society, proximity to other developing regions, the former Cold War theatre and polarized development strategies, all support inclusion in the developing-world category. The mega-wealthy states of the region, however, would, one might imagine, make it harder to generalize and apply the 'developing world' label. But there are a number of ways in which even those wealthy states are somehow still denied membership of the developed nations club. Here, all the economic clout in the world can still be ignored in favour of ascribing predominantly developing-world characteristics – especially around freedom and democracy indicators – to political systems, governments, institutions and the law. Structure and rule still condemn the nations to developing status in popular and global perception.

There is still merit in exploring the patterns of economic similarity within the region that characterize states as either rich or poor. What kind of wealth one is talking about is also worth reflecting on. Is wealth distributed equally among citizens, or is it the privilege of the few, and what is the nature of state and class relations in the rich and poor states of the region? How relevant, for example, are other indicators of economic development, such as expansion of industry, a strong agricultural sector or the access to essential natural resources such as water, in telling the story of economic development in the region? Wealth, then, becomes a relative term depending on which perspective one takes. For example, Saudi Arabia may be able to afford an agricultural sector that grows its own wheat and breeds its own cattle for milk and beef, but at what cost and level of sustainability? In Egypt, agricultural diversification in the Nile delta has evolved over centuries and currently includes more than half of the cultivated land in the country, yet it has struggled with import dependency issues for decades and its cotton industry, once providing a key national export, continues to decline (Held, 1994, p. 261). These issues assume as much importance in the eastern states of the region as the preoccupation with oil does in the western states of the area. The issue of water, for example, has become increasingly important in assessing the relative wealth of states in the region and their capacity for future economic development. Water wealth, then, will become vital in the economic, political and territorial future of the region, as well as a source of conflict (Dolatyar and Gray, 2016).

Economic development has been affected by the rapid population growth witnessed across the region – the Middle East has some of the highest rates of population growth in the world, combined in states like Yemen with some of the highest rates for infant mortality. The consolidation of post-colonial economies through programmes of national development, diversification and sustainability has not always been successful. National debt and public spending deficits, for example, in countries like Egypt, Syria and Jordan, have economically enslaved them to the dictates of foreign government aid programmes, such as those from America to Egypt. The US has granted Egypt more than $75 billion in US aid since 1948. In addition, planning and economic policy are also dependent on international lending organizations like the IMF and World Bank, on which, for example, in the 1990s, Yemen was dependent for $80 million as part of the economic recovery programme of the International Development Association (IDA) and an IMF 'stand-by arrangement'.

The political implications of such relationships are not difficult to discern. They explain, for example, Egypt's role in the American-sponsored Arab–Israeli peace process, Jordan's path to political liberalization, and Syria's past military alliances with the Soviet Union and present-day relations with President Putin's Russia. Real economic independence, then, whether in rich or poor states in the Middle East, remains somewhat elusive. In the so-called sanction country of Syria, the same problems of wealth creation, distribution and sustainability occupy policy-makers, economists and citizens alike. Under President Obama, sanctions against Syria were renewed and deepened as the crisis turned into a prolonged civil war and aid pit. Indeed, the emergence of a war economy in Syria was described in 2016, in an IMF report, as having 'set the country back decades in terms of economic, social and human development' (Gobat and Kostial, 2016). Economic crisis or instability of any sort can be identified in any state in the region – irrespective of relative wealth – as potentially explosive. Explosive, because citizens remain consistently weakened by the vagaries of their economies and marginalized or excluded from the political leaders who decide policies of resource allocation within their societies. This is particularly true in the case of those Arab states, such as Egypt, Syria, Algeria or Tunisia, where nationalist single-party regimes instituted classic developing-world policies of import-substitution industrialization (ISI) in the modernization and development of state and national economies. The policy of ISI implied a decline in dependence on the export of raw materials and basic commodities, and in dependence on imported goods. Previously imported goods would be produced by the economy at home and raw materials, such as cotton, which had formerly been exported, would be manufactured into cloth in the domestic economy. The economic benefits of ISI were a reduced dependence on the world market and independence from costly foreign imports.

The associated state model of corporatism has created new class interests associated with the state elite (industrial bourgeoisie) and widened the very gap, between the state, its middle classes – which were until 2010 generally characterized as state-vested – and working classes, that the populist appeals of such regimes initially attempted to narrow. Such exclusion, as noted in other chapters, has led to growing economic discontent, food riots and price rise demonstrations in an increasing number of economies, consequently emphasizing the vulnerability of claims to legitimacy by political leaders.

This particular phenomenon has been highlighted by the failure of the corporatist model throughout the single-party states in the region in the mid to late 1980s and the concurrent waves of popular protest which accompanied programmes of economic liberalization that these states were encouraged to adopt. Indeed, the very failure of ISI by the 1970s led to an era of recession and economic adjustment throughout the region. In Tunisia, for example, the direction of the economy under socialist principles had already failed by 1970, and the state began an inexorable path towards decentralization, liberalization and a reduced role in the economy. By the mid 1970s, a similar economic path had been adopted in Egypt, as illustrated in one of this chapter's case studies. The process highlighted the paradox for state elites who, on the one hand, knew that their very survival depended on policies of liberalization, but, on the other, were unwilling to relinquish control over the economy (Ayubi, 1995).

In addition, as for many nationalized industries across the globe, the process of privatization did not always guarantee economic success. The pressures of economic events regionally and globally, especially by the 1980s when oil prices reached an all-time low and recession gripped the advanced industrialized economies, inhibited the momentum for adjustment and expanded capitalism. Thus, conversely, the further the economy was restructured to promote profit, deregulation and a reduced role for the state, the more indebtedness grew. Political movement did not occur in a broad-based liberalized form and opposition to these economic changes continued to grow. Global recession from 2008 onwards also impacted on the economies of states in the Middle East, particularly in terms of investment and incomes. In 2009, for example, Dubai hit a major financial crisis and the rulers of the state were forced into a major debt restructuring programme. One explanation for lack of agility by the state across the Middle East and North Africa was its function both in the social contract with its citizens and as a major employer of labour across the region (Hertog, 2016b).

Endemic corruption, poor planning of resource allocation and misappropriation of state funds in Middle Eastern economies also reflect the chasm between state and citizens and opaque mechanisms of state control over the economy (Schwarz, 2008). While this may have contributed to the resilience of some authoritarian regimes, such factors would also perform a function both as slogan and as key demand in the protests that characterized the Arab Spring across the Middle East in 2011 (Bellin, 2012). Attempts at economic adjustment appear to have succeeded only in widening the gap between rich and poor in nearly every country throughout the region. Yet this need not be the case, as Stewart (1995) argued: 'while increasing poverty is the norm for countries undergoing adjustment, this is not necessary; poverty can be reduced during adjustment ... governments can make choices ... which offset, or accentuate any ill-effects of adjustment on the poor' (p. 193). In addition, the state elites which redistribute national wealth, revenue and funds to their own pockets are found in nearly every capital city in the region. Irrespective of whether they are Arab, Israeli, Wahabi, Maronite, Ba'thist, Alawite or Tikriti, their 'theft' of national wealth has severely undermined economic confidence in the region. In the Gulf states, business people are wary of trading with Arab governments, given the vast level of bribes needed to secure contracts. Debt is becoming a common feature of these wealthy regimes and, as in the case of Saudi Arabia, budget cuts of around 20 per cent in 1994 did 'not affect the royal family' but only the rest of Saudi society, leading to dangerous political antagonisms (Aburish, 1994, p. 304).

Business development in most states in the region is beset with bribery and corruption, thus further inhibiting the economy and politics (Greenwood, 2008). In the autonomous Palestinian West Bank and Gaza Strip, corruption became a currency as a form of reward for Fatah loyalists who supported the Palestinian National Authority (PNA), whose $326 million in foreign aid was subject to persistent allegations of misuse amid accusations of poor mechanisms for financial accountability and rumours of extortion by Palestinian public officials. The same stories are repeated in Damascus, Riyadh, Kuwait City, Tunis, Algiers, Cairo, Baghdad, Tripoli, Beirut and Manama – while the Arab world burns, their leaders dance, eat and make merry on profits from state industries, revenues from state assets and investments, bribes from the business community and loans secured in the name of poor and destitute populations (Henry and Springborg, 2010).

The remedy is linked to the political argument for increased democracy: open government and an end to the authoritarianism – both economic and political – that currently characterizes the region (Greenwood, 2008). This particular assessment of the Middle East economy is highlighted in the work of Richards and Waterbury and later developed by Cammett et al., who stress the symbiotic nature of the relationship between politics, state development, modernization and the transformation of societies from traditional agricultural modes of production to the ISI-corporatist and authoritarian models of rule and economic planning. These authors want to refocus the lenses of analysis onto the allocation of resources by the state. This particular lens, looking at the economy and its impact on the political, is especially useful in explaining the growth and nature of the rentier economies in the contemporary Middle East (Luciani, 2009). The durability of these complex forms of economic governance in explaining the resilience of authoritarian regimes across the region is evident in the staying power of Assad's Syria post- 2011 (Heydemann and Leenders, 2013).

Many models make poor work

A variety of economic systems and interpretations of economy have been practised in the Middle East with varying degrees of success, and there has been no single uniform pattern of economic relations across the region (Schwarz, 2008). Too often the nature of economic systems and practices has been affected by political, religious and cultural considerations which impact at the same time. Talk of a 'nonaligned' form of economy (devoid of cultural persuasion) in the Middle East, therefore, is difficult; even in those rare attempts to develop 'pure type', ideology-based economies, other factors have soon muddied the waters. In addition, Gran (1990) highlighted that in the past the way in which political economists perceived the Middle East was still blurred by orientalist assumptions and the unique supremacy of western-inspired liberal trade theory:

Box 3.1 Economically blinkered by Orientalism

They argue that when British industrial goods reached the Middle East in the nineteenth century, people bought them because they were cheaper. But why should pricing, taste and access to market have been such simple matters in the Middle East when studies of working class culture elsewhere suggest how complicated such matters were?

(p. 231)

Indeed, the way in which most economies of the region were distinguished, identified and differentiated was along western lines of analysis, taking limited account of traditional or indigenous patterns of commerce, trade, ownership, religious belief (Muslim, Christian or Jewish) or gender relations. What becomes clear, however, is that, while a particular economy may be described in broadly, say, liberal, or market-based terms, for comparison's sake, the local patterns of economic relations must be reflected in the discussion of specific economic indicators.

Capital economies in the region have flourished with limited success and there are few notable examples. In Lebanon, however, the economy has always been market- rather than state-led. Indeed, Lebanon is a notable example of a free market economy and its resulting impact on the state and political system. Here the state is weak in a variety of ways including in terms of corruption, but particularly in terms of directing the national economy. A lack of natural resources in Lebanon, fifteen years of civil war (1975–90) which cost the country more than $25 billion in damage to infrastructure alone, a small, largely urbanized population of 4.1 million and a significant refugee and migrant population have all contributed to the development of economic practice based on a large service sector (that used to serve the whole of the region) and commercial interests. Yet, as a result of a weak state and the perennial problem of corruption in the 1970s, the government wrought its own downfall and the commencement of the civil war that would last for fifteen years. The revival of the capitalist economy throughout the 1990s and into the twenty-first century has been characterized by many of the features from the 1970s, and attempts to introduce a mixed approach to the economy are few and far between. This leaves the country facing the same political fallout from economic policies as it did in the 1970s, with anti-government protest focusing on demands that Lebanon's leaders change their economic policy (Leenders, 2012). In May 2004, protestors filled the streets of Beirut in dispute over rising fuel prices and five were killed by

Lebanese armed forces. In 2010, the IMF warned that the Lebanese government would have to be much more robust in addressing structural economic weakness and fiscal crisis which were contributing to the country having one of the highest national debts in the world. The state and its local municipalities have been in constant retreat ever since. This was symbolized in 2015 in the eruption of protest at the government's inability to provide even a basic general waste collection service in cities like Beirut in the #YouStink protests. Popular mobilization, protest and a 78-hour demand on the government to stop in-fighting and provide services highlighted Lebanon's economic woes amidst an unprecedented refugee crisis prompted by having to host millions of Syrians fleeing from war over Lebanon's eastern border.

Examples of socialist- or Marxist-based economies in the region had included Egypt, Syria, Iraq, Yemen, Libya and Algeria. The political linkage between these economic types and the emergence of one-party states in the 1950s, 1960s and 1970s was strong. The socialist economies of the region, based on the ideological agenda of Arab nationalist and state-led development, had included land reform, industrialization, nationalization (e.g. the Suez Canal in 1956), planned economies, state-centred development policies and limits on private capital and commercial interests or land ownership. The success of such economies, however, particularly by the late 1970s, was called into question. Since that point, crisis precipitated a move towards liberalization or *infitah* (open door policy). In the case of Syria this led to economic reform which included a greater role for the private sector, cuts in public expenditure, reduction of foreign trade imbalances, but avoidance of large-scale privatization or major expansion of the merchant sector in Syria's economy. Syria actually side-stepped incurring debt or seeking loans from the World Bank or IMF, but much of its economy still remained highly dependent on income derived from oil. Further economic reform, however, was dependent on the willingness of the regime to engage in political liberalization at the same time. The government avoided this particular issue and, by taking an incremental and selective approach to reform, delayed the political impact of the widespread alienation and legitimacy crisis which accompanied the problems of the 1980s in other states of the region (Perthes, 1995, p. 251).

Syria, like the other primarily socialist economies of the region, engaged in a delicate balancing act between economic reform and the maintenance of state power amid pressures from external players like the USA that resulted in the imposition of trade sanctions. Central to this balancing act was the ability of the state elite to manipulate the process of change rather than allow the masses to determine the pace and extent of political empowerment. While still an 'inclusionary, populist and redistributive state' (Heydemann and Leenders, 2013), Syria's regime under Bashar al-Assad remained resilient. But it was a break from this social contract, and a move to 'exclusionary-repressive' state practices with their impacts on normally loyal segments of the population, which begin to explain the economic discontents as linked to the political, giving rise to the protests which broke out across the country in 2011 (Heydemann and Leenders, 2013).

Principles of Islamic economic practice are found in multiple locations in the region, from the Islamic banking systems of Cairo to the levy of a charity tax (*zakat*) by government in Saudi Arabia. Islamic economics is a growing area of activity within the region (10–15 per cent annual growth) and in its relations across the globe. The Islamic finance sector, including banking, manages assets running at over US$1 trillion. In the Gulf region there have been growing expectations that Islamic finance will dominate economic activities. Islamic economic principles include the following measures: 'approval of certain aspects of capitalism, including private ownership of the means of production, profit maximization as a motor force in economic behaviour and free market competition in products, service and labour' (Pfeifer, 1997, p. 157). In addition, the religion prohibits usury – interest on money loaned – and applies Islamic law in banking, business and finance sectors.

Following the 1979 revolution in Iran, the theocracy established by Ayatollah Khomeini attempted to Islamize the economy in a number of ways, including state confiscation of privately owned businesses and industries and the introduction of Islamic banking, involving the abolition of interest. For most of the 1980s, the creation of an Islamic economy in Iran was hindered by the war with Iraq, sanctions levied by the international community and a decline in oil prices. In the 1990s, however, the advent of a pragmatic government led by Rafsanjani encouraged economic development, including a free trade zone in Qeshm, re-privatization of some industry and a more stable oil economy and production. Moreover, a slow but gradual rehabilitation in international economic markets had encouraged some foreign investment with prospects for strong acceleration in terms of future investment once international sanctions were lifted in January 2016.

Iran, like other Islamic states or economies, has acknowledged the power of the international market and faces the challenge of achieving economic arrangements that meet religious as well as international economic requirements. Islamic economic principles, therefore, are neither wholly capitalist nor socialist/Marxist – rather, they reflect a unique marriage of economic principles and ideas that are familiar to economic theorists across the globe.

In the case of Iran, developments in the 1990s and early twenty-first century highlight the advent of a certain approach to economic policy in the contemporary Middle East that is associated with liberalization. Specific aspects of this approach are examined in the case study of Egypt at the end of this chapter, but at this point a few general remarks are required. Economic liberalization occurred in the region from the 1970s onwards and was further entrenched in the early 1980s as many states there faced vast foreign debts, the collapse of their own currency, rampant inflation and crisis in their economies. While modernization and ISI policies had encouraged a rapid population boom and demands for higher living standards from the newly urbanized population of the region, the economy could no longer deliver. While it was true that the region enjoyed varying degrees of wealth generated from oil reserves, the plummeting price of oil and recession in the world economy began seriously to affect the amount of rent enjoyed from this source. As has already been noted, the region could no longer feed itself, had become increasingly aid-dependent and had a poor record in global export markets. There were few diversified economies and even so-called stable democratic Israel was suffering severe economic problems with survival dependent on huge American loans and aid and other forms of financial support from the diaspora community.

One path out of this economic meltdown, for both energy-rich and energy-poor states, was a policy of structural adjustment and liberalization of aspects of the economy. Liberalization eventually occurred, in one form or another, in most countries of the region as a response to increasing poverty rates and growing international pressure from institutions like the IMF and World Bank. It is also important to remember that this state-led planning of the economy was a way in which the elite could remain resilient in their authoritarian regimes, preserve power and continue to maximize their share of the national profit. In many respects, structural adjustment and liberalization was a compulsory 'no option' trend which would characterize the region from the 1980s onwards.

The aim of such an approach in Algeria, Syria, Tunisia and Egypt was to create a new base for sustainable growth, even though this meant a cut in state provision in terms of social expenditure (it is worth noting that defence expenditure often remained stable), thus exacerbating the problems of poverty which economic crisis had created. Macro-economic liberalization resulted in a negative effect on the distribution of income and issues of social equity and welfare leading to an ever-increasing gap between the expectations of citizens, especially the expanding and increasingly well-educated middle classes, and the capacity of the state. Indeed, when the leaders of Egypt, Syria or Jordan announced price rises or cuts in welfare spending in the name of reforming the economy, the effects not only hit the poor and working classes but began to impoverish the middle classes too.

Nevertheless, the forced agenda of economic liberalization, relinquishing state control over the welfare economy, encouraging new economic actors, foreign investment and capital, and diversification of industry resulted in limited economic improvement in some states of the region. For example, Egypt's economy was recognized as holding real promise, with macro-stabilization efforts which Egypt undertook in the early 1990s a success, and longer-term structural reforms under way (Global Agenda, 2005, p. 13). The political consequences of even such faltering and minor improvements in disparate economies of the region have been serious and are characterized, as discussed at length in the chapter on democratization, by an increasing tendency to reassert state authority through coercion. Ultimately, economic liberalization in the region, unlike in other areas of the developing world, did not usher in democracy; rather, as Ehteshami and Murphy (1996) argued, 'economic liberalization creates a restructuring' of interests which only consolidates and benefits the power-holders rather than the powerless (p. 768).

Evolution of oil-based economies

For as long as the Middle East is home to the world's largest oil reserves, the fascination of economists, politicians and policy-makers with the region will remain. The presence of large oil reserves in countries like Saudi Arabia, Kuwait, the United Arab Emirates, Iraq and Iran have ensured the past domination of the Middle East in the world oil market and producer organizations such as OPEC. As far back as the 1970s, Hudson (1977) recognized that oil was 'beginning to transform the Arab economy in fundamental ways ... oil is certain to be increasingly linked with politics – internal, regional and international – as Arabs debate who shall control the oil and how the revenues should be used' (p. 140).

Since the discovery in the 1920s of major oil reserves and the establishment of oil-producing fields in the Gulf area, the clamber to cash in on Arab and Persian oil has carried on. The oil epoch is littered with alarming episodes, among which are the European and American exploitation of reserves, price-fixing through the 1973 oil boycott, the Iranian revolution, and the *débâcle* of three wars in the Gulf. Oil features in abundant conspiracy theories to explain myriad dimensions of political perspectives connected to the region (Stokes, 2007; Zambelis, 2008). It is these episodes of conflict over oil – as figure 3.1 illustrates – and conspiracy over fuel, as much as the startling but rather dry economic calculations of wealth, price per barrel, production costs, sales, production capacity and OPEC quotas, that illustrate the impact of oil on the economy, and politics in the region.

Oil production, then, has shaped and influenced the nature of most states in the region, in particular the Gulf states that include the largest oil producers in the world – Saudi Arabia, Iran, Iraq and Kuwait. It does this through the impact on state revenue of income derived at home and abroad (Luciani, 2009). Hence the revenue earned from oil, and the rising and lowering of oil prices through the OPEC mechanism on global markets plays a fundamental part in the operation of the levers of power by the ruling elite in such states over their citizens. Price control and the role of OPEC was illustrated in 2016 when a price agreement was reached to help producers (particularly in the Middle East) try and address fiscal imbalances wrought by major price drops and their impacts in the years before. Nevertheless, oil producing states still have to contend with the growing assertion of states like Canada and the USA in shale gas production. Countries like Iraq, if they are to win and

Source: Wikimedia.

Figure 3.1 *Oil fields afire, Operation Desert Storm 1991*

consolidate victory over groups like ISIS through re-building the economy, see oil revenue as essential.

The story of oil, its discovery and production within the region is inevitably rooted in the colonial era. The role played by British companies, particularly in Iran and other parts of the Gulf, in the exploration of oil resources coincided with British government attempts to strengthen its foothold in the region – as an old joke illustrates, 'BP' stood for 'Bugger Persia' not 'British Petroleum'. The first decades of the twentieth century witnessed the discovery and exploitation of the region's oil resources by various foreign powers. In Iran, for example, from 1920, British influence in and control of the country were consistently linked, until the 1950s, to the production of oil and monopolized by the Anglo-Iranian oil company later known as British Petroleum (BP). By the 1930s, however, BP became a force in the region, playing their part (alongside the Anglo-Dutch company Shell) in the oil consortium called the 'Seven Sisters'. This ensured a complete foreign monopoly over oil. The impact on the political systems of the region at this time was significant. The oil companies worked in co-operation with each other and resisted demands from local leaders and rulers for greater royalty payments or control over their own oil fields. Control of the oil business by the Seven Sisters extended from reserves, through exploration and production, to the petrochemical industry and oil refineries (Almulhim, 1991, p. 14). The Seven Sisters encouraged political development and governance only in so far as foreign patronage would allow, and more often than not the Arab and Iranian rulers of the region were surrounded by external advisers on military, foreign, economic and political affairs.

By the 1950s and early 1960s, increasing resentment over the ratio of royalty payments (50/50), the impact of political radicalism and the rise of nationalism and pan-Arabism in the region provided an impetus for the first Iranian and Arab challenges to the monopoly on economic (and, therefore, political) power that the Seven Sisters enjoyed. Iran was the first to undermine the status quo when it announced the nationalization of its oil resources in 1951. The government seized BP's installations, and oil production was halted for three years. The Americans gained a vital interest in the country by brokering the agreement in 1954 that allowed the resumption of production, and licences to work in Iran were granted to a consortium of oil companies.

The Iranian dispute was the first of many that would characterize the period. Nationalization was the goal of most Arab oil-producing states at that time. Some wanted to nationalize so as to direct their revenue from natural resources to their radical, socialist agendas, while others wanted to resist the pressure for change and preserve traditional dynastic rule and conservatism. The Seven Sisters, however, were not passive bystanders to these events and did their utmost to stem the tide of change. Iraqi nationalization of its oil industry in 1961, for example, led the major players to strike back and tighten their stranglehold on the oil market (Halliday, 1974, p. 397).

The ultimate expression of localized resistance to the domination of the oil market and price-fixing by the Seven Sisters came in 1960 with the formation of OPEC (OPEC's seven original members included Iran, Iraq, Kuwait, Saudi Arabia and Venezuela). Within the decade, the power of this newly founded organization became apparent, as further nationalization combined with the OPEC agreement to take more control over fixing the price of oil per barrel and greater control over the running of the members' oil industries. Collective action had bolstered the Middle East oil-exporting countries, along with states like Venezuela, which discovered that their unified rather than individual weight could be brought to bear to win bigger and better concessions for themselves over their natural resources. By 1972, despite nationalization, the formation of OPEC and concessions over control, the price per barrel of oil was still low, at only $1.40, and the Seven Sisters continued to dominate the market. The political changes in the region and the new-found confidence of the oil-producing countries would, however, precipitate the energy crisis of 1973, the oil weapon, and the growth of the petro-dollar and the political clout wielded by the region.

Sheikhdoms and petro-power

The energy crisis of 1973 was the result of a number of factors, including the preceding pattern of nationalization, the internal battle between radical and conservative elements in the Arab world, foreign involvement in the region and the Arab–Israeli conflict. Indeed, it was the 1973 war between Israel and the Arabs that prompted the oil-producing states to announce production cuts which would send oil prices sky high. The Arab oil producers, with the exception of Iraq, and led by Saudi Arabia, asserted their power by punishing America and Holland, as well as other European countries, for supporting Israel during the war. The impact of this decision was profound. The American economy, for example, was rocked by the 'oil weapon'. America had felt secure in its supply of Arab oil, as companies like ARAMCO in Saudi Arabia had spent decades discovering and exploiting some of the largest oil fields in the world and so believed that they had the support of Saudi Arabia. In addition, the US economy, despite its own oil resources, was increasingly dependent on the profitable exploitation of Saudi oil fields. Low production costs, the post-war economic and manufacturing boom and domestic oil price quotas all propelled the Americans into a relationship of weakness which the Saudis and other Arab oil producers both exploited and exposed in 1973–4.

The production cuts announced in 1973 as a result of the Arab boycott led to a series of startling oil price increases. First, in October, the price per barrel shifted from $1.40 per barrel to $5.90. By December 1973, the price had risen again to $11.60 per barrel, heralding an energy crisis in Western Europe and America. Petrol in Britain, for example, was suddenly subject to rationing, and power cuts became a frequent reminder of the impact of the 'oil weapon' in the Middle East on the distant lives of ordinary people. By 1971, oil had replaced coal as the most important source of energy and the crisis of 1973 made the economy vulnerable. However, it did prompt British politicians and policy-makers to exploit fully their country's own reserves in the North Sea oil fields so as to decrease the dependence on oil from the Middle East (Odell, 1981, p. 222). In the Middle East, the effects of the production cuts and subsequent price rises were staggering: revenues derived from the sale of oil quadrupled and the power of the petro-dollar was felt throughout the world economy. In Saudi Arabia, the production cost per barrel of oil was just 1 cent while, as already noted, the price at sale was $11.60, leaving the Saudis to make huge profits (Wilson, 1979, p. 41). Countries like Saudi Arabia and Kuwait were transformed almost overnight into major players in the world economy, and their rulers gained greater authority within their own countries to pursue their own conservative and anti-democratic agendas without requiring the political fealty of their citizens. Indeed, the tax-free economies of rentier states showed little inclination towards expanding or even establishing a democratic base in their societies (Luciani, 1990, p. xxiv).

The oil price bubble was burst by the Arabs themselves, again led by Saudi Arabia, which moved in 1974 to end production cuts and restore some sense of stability to the oil market. After all, the long-term interests of the Arab oil producers would not be served by the perpetuation of high oil prices associated with the oil weapon.

Nevertheless, five years later the oil industry was shaken again following the events in Iran which brought about the fall of the Shah and the rise of Ayatollah Khomeini and the establishment of the Islamic Republic of Iran. Economic growth in Iran under the Shah had largely been dependent on the revenue from the country's oil fields. Much of the politics of the country under the Shah and his father before him had been shaped by first British and then American interest in exploiting these resources. Indeed, the Shah's quest for power had been supported by the Americans and the CIA on a number of occasions. The 1979 revolution and its political stand of intense hostility to foreign power, and the USA in particular, gave rise to fears that Iran's oil production would cease, and as a result some 2 million barrels a day disappeared from the international market (Richards, 1993, p. 69).

These fears of further price rises as a result of political instability in the region were further compounded by the war which broke out in 1980 between the revolutionary Islamic Republic of Iran and Ba'thist Iraq. Not only were both countries oil producers, but their strategic location, in and around vital Gulf shipping lanes, alarmed the oil market once again. This time, however, although price rises occurred, the market soon stabilized as a result of the pragmatic outlook by all parties involved.

The economic fortunes and the political clout of the oil-producing states were maintained in the early 1980s. However, by the end of the decade, the effects of the world recession were hard to ignore, particularly in the rentier economies of the Gulf that were dependent on income from oil revenues and their substantial investments in a number of by now recession-ridden western economies. This decline in revenue coincided with the rise of political and economic discontent within a variety of oil-producing states. Political protest and opposition to the spending policies and rampant corruption apparent in Saudi Arabia, for example, were manifest in a series of workers' protests throughout the decade, which were brutally suppressed by the Saudi military (Aburish, 1994).

While international human rights organizations and exiled dissident groups tried to highlight the poor political and human rights enjoyed by citizens in the oil-rich Gulf, the majority of western governments, including the Americans, were prepared to turn a blind eye as long as the flow of oil remained unhindered and prices remained stable. Any threat to that precious stability was worth opposing. The political nature of such states, whether progressive nationalist socialist, or conservative religious-dynastic, was immaterial to the equation in which oil prices and production were kept stable. Yet this preoccupation with authoritarianism, in whatever shade it was expressed, as a form of protection in the capital-led market of the world economy, would ultimately have its price in the Middle East.

That price was the Gulf crisis of 1990–1. Debates about oil and its revenues have also been key in the toppling of the regime of Saddam Hussein in Iraq and the costs of reconstruction in post-war Iraq. Before the war, US Deputy

Secretary of Defence Paul Wolfowitz had confidently asserted to the US Congress that oil production, post-war, would derive revenue for Iraq of between $50 and $100 billion in a three-year period. Post-war, the reality was a little different. Despite US protection, oil production has been subject to persistent sabotage by Iraqi insurgents and production has declined, leaving a major shortfall of promises for the national budget. In January 2017, Iraq's Oil Minister, Jabbar al-Luaibi, reminded an international audience of the continuing importance of oil to the country.

Box 3.2 Oil and the very future of the Iraqi state

I must emphasise and be crystal clear that the prosperity of Iraq depends on its energy sector. It has almost become the sole source for the Iraqi economy. 83–85% of its revenues come from its oil and gas sectors. So, the sector is very very vital not only for Iraq's prosperity and development but also for the entire country to emerge as strong and united.

(23 January 2017, Chatham House MENA Energy Conference, 'On the record' remarks)

Rentier futures, profit in decline?

Since the emergence of the argument that oil is the single most important factor in determining the nature of the economy in the Middle East, a variety of writers have contributed to the reassessment of appropriate economic models and their impact on the political systems and nature of the state. As Beblawi (1990) has argued, 'the whole of the Arab world, oil rich as well as oil poor, is becoming a sort of oil economy with various undertones of rentier mentalities. This development has affected the role of the state in the whole Arab world' (p. 88). In turn, the nature of relations between the economy and the state can best be understood in association with a number of other themes, including rentier economies, distortion of agriculture and raw material uses, the problems of urbanization and excessive energy use, dependent development and the relatively poor economic performance of the region in global markets. These themes will be examined in the rest of this section.

The emergence of oil economies dominating the region has encouraged certain political economists to engage with the rentier model. In particular, both Luciani and Beblawi use this approach to explain the nature of state and politics in the region. The primary argument put forward by these scholars is that, unlike other states which derive income from taxation or internally generated sources, many states in the Middle East derive their revenues from rent and more specifically from external rent. This rent is defined as the wealth generated from ownership of natural resources such as oil or gas, and, as Beblawi highlights, 'in rentier states only the few are engaged in the generation of this rent (wealth), the majority being only involved in the distribution or utilization of it' (1990, p. 87).

In a rentier economy, the state has a monopoly on rents and employs a policy of expenditure around this revenue. Benefits are distributed to citizens, and the state demands nothing in return in terms of economic revenue. As Luciani (1990) remarks, 'allocation is the only relationship that they [the state elite] need have with their domestic economy' (p. 76). The outcome of this situation politically is a relationship between state and citizen that takes a new perspective on legitimacy, citizenship and loyalty to the state, which in this case becomes the 'crucial mover of economic activity' for a whole country (p. 79).

In addition, the extension of rentier logic is not confined to those countries within the region which possess oil reserves, export it and live off the rents derived from this resource. Peripheral states (so-called semi-rentiers) have also been identified, with the claim that in countries like Jordan, Syria, Egypt and Yemen external rent has bred 'a chain of second-order' rentiers. Luciani (2015) highlights the extent to which rentier states impacted, through grant giving, on governments elsewhere in the region where there were no rents to derive from oil or gas.

There can be no doubt – despite the criticisms of the approach by some authors that the rentier model ignores 'history' and differences in the political features of oil-producing states themselves, and that 'too much emphasis is placed upon the role of oil' – that the model has proved durable. In the 1990s, following the decline of oil prices on global markets, the Gulf crisis, the growth of internal opposition in many rentier states, budget cuts and decreasing rents due to world recession, rentier explanations prevailed. In the wake of the Arab Spring Luciani again provided a compelling argument by stating: 'faced with region turmoil, the Gulf rentier regimes dusted off the old tools of government-to-government largesse, and staked their bets in the revolutionary process', this is well evidenced in Egypt, Yemen and even with non-state actors such as the Muslim Brotherhood (2015, p. 199). Yet, by 2014–15, Gulf regimes were experiencing the impacts of drastic falls in the price of oil and compelled into restructuring dynamics in their own economies, retrenching from external aid, investment and development projects (*The Economist*, 2016).

One aspect of economic activity that has been severely dented in the contemporary Middle East by the decline of hydro-based and emergence of hydrocarbon societies has been the agricultural sector and production of raw materials. Until the advent of oil production in the region, the net export of raw materials derived from agriculture had accounted for the largest part of economic activity in the majority of countries there. Today, the 'food gap', whereby the region cannot produce enough from agriculture to feed its population, has made the area 'the least food self-sufficient region in the world' (Richards and Waterbury, 1990, p. 139). Indeed, Held claimed that, by the 1990s, at least fifteen countries in the region were importing more than 50 per cent of their food (Held, 1994, p. 99). In 2015, the majority of countries in the region were dependent on food imports of the most significant staple of the Middle Eastern diet: wheat. In 2017, food dependence in the Gulf state of Qatar hit the headlines following a land, air and maritime blockade imposed by Saudi Arabia, UAE, Bahrain and Egypt. The blockade initially impacted the import of food needed to meet the basic needs of Qatar's population and highlighted import versus domestic production issues. Additionally, in countries like Yemen the majority of the population were declared food-insecure (FAO, 2016).

The agricultural sector and production of raw materials have also gone into decline in terms of GDP and, understandably in the Gulf states, their contribution to GDP has become insignificant. Yet even in states like Syria or Egypt, where the agricultural sector remains significant, providing employment for 30 and 42 per cent of the economically active population respectively, these figures represent a decline on earlier decades, particularly the 1950s and 1960s when the agricultural sector of these countries was significantly altered by the respective populist policies of Nasserism and Ba'thism.

Despite initial optimism in Egypt, for example, that land reform might increase the wealth of the agricultural sector, Nasser quickly ran into problems, including rapid population growth, expansion of per capita income, increasing defence expenditure and ISI policies. Indeed, by the 1970s, the government was forced to introduce a scheme of generous food subsidies on basic commodities such as flour and bread, amounting to 10–15 per cent of government expenditure and contributing to the large budget deficit the country had generated (Stewart, 1995, p. 88).

Agrarian change, therefore, has become a significant feature of the region, contributing to the economic decline or crisis of many countries, particularly from the 1980s onwards, and leaving certain states increasingly prone to a number of features: externally earned remittances from a workforce which in the past had been employed in domestic agriculture; indebtedness and austerity programmes requiring intervention from the IMF and World Bank; increasing unemployment, particularly in the newly urbanized areas, following migration from rural areas; and concurrent episodes of political protest, food riots, demonstrations and pressure on government from its people. As a percentage of GDP, agriculture in Egypt has declined from 19.6 per cent in 1983 to 16.1 per cent in 2003 and as low as 11.2 per cent in 2015 (Bank Audi, 2016). Additionally, issues of food security have been seen as key in triggering conflicts across the region, especially in relation to fragile states such as Yemen.

These debt-ridden economies remain in a perpetual process of adjustment, management and limited change. Nevertheless, the prospects are not overwhelmingly favourable, particularly given the comparatively poor performance of the region in terms of economic recovery following the exogenous shock of the 2007–8 global recession and financial crisis. The Middle East, despite its huge wealth, has not shown the same potential to integrate with the world economy at a variety of levels or sectors. Transition from the Arab Spring has only heightened the region's economic problems. A 2016 World Bank report called economic prospects for the region 'grim', noting slow growth, increasing debt and poor GDP.

Box 3.3 Arab April showers

Syria, Iraq, Libya and Yemen are in civil war, causing untold damage to human lives and physical infrastructure. Fifteen million people have fled their homes, many to fragile or economically strapped countries such as Jordan, Lebanon, Djibouti and Tunisia, giving rise to the biggest refugee crisis since World War II. The current turmoil in Yemen has set that country's development back several years. Blockades and repeated cycles of violence have made Gaza's unemployment rate the highest in the world and with Gross Domestic Product at only 40 percent of its potential. Countries undergoing political transitions, such as Egypt, Tunisia, Morocco and Jordan, are having to address security concerns over growth-promoting policies. The relatively peaceful oil exporters, such as Algeria, Iran and the GCC, are grappling with low oil prices alongside chronic youth unemployment and undiversified economies.

(World Bank 2016a)

Labour mobility and employment

In many ways, the phenomenon of labour mobility within the Middle East is linked to a number of economic factors. These include the development of the oil- and gas-based rentier economies, the patterns of distribution of wealth and other issues such as the increasingly high rates of birth and population growth, refugee flows, migration pushes and the poor natural resources of some states in the region. The impact of Arab and other migrant labour on the economic well-being of the region reflects a complex system of economics that has reigned over the region for decades.

These issues of migrant labour also highlight the economic relationships of dependency, dependent development and interdependency that exist in the contemporary Middle East. These relationships are sometimes voluntary, but at other times they reflect the internal balance of power within the region, whereby – and perhaps uncharacteristically – both geographically and demographically larger states are dependent on smaller states. It reflects the inability of some domestic economies to develop and sustain their populations and the concurrent political problems of legitimacy that this bestows. In Egypt, for example, Dessouki noted that workers abroad had become a significant foreign income source: 'their remittance constituted a major source of Egypt's hard currency' (1991, p. 162). With low levels of regional trade and capital flows (particularly when compared with flows outside the region), migrant labour from capital-poor to capital-rich states represents one of the most significant indicators of intra-regional, and specifically inter-Arab, economic relations. According to the World Bank, in 2015 the top ten remittance recipients in the Middle East and North Africa were: the Arab Republic of Egypt ($20.4bn), Lebanon ($7.5bn), Morocco ($6.7bn), Jordan ($3.8bn), the Republic of Yemen ($3.4bn), Tunisia ($2.3bn), the West Bank and Gaza ($2.3bn), Algeria ($2.0bn), the Syrian Arab Republic ($1.6bn) and the Islamic Republic of Iran ($1.3bn) (World Bank, 2016c).

The import of this should not be ignored, and whether this represents a positive or negative development in the region should also be questioned. What is certain is the vulnerability not only of migrant populations but of the states to and from which they move, according to the vagaries of regional political and economic events. This can be seen to be particularly true in relation to the case of Yemen and Saudi Arabia. During the Gulf crisis of 1990–1, some 700,000 Yemenis were repatriated from their jobs in the area, and the government of Saudi Arabia suspended aid programmes to the country. This resulted in serious economic crisis and mounting political instability. Throughout the 1990s, as a result of this rapid decline in relations, Saudi Arabia has experienced a wide variety of problems with its Yemeni neighbours and the relationship between the two countries has been significantly altered, adversely affecting the stability of both states.

Saudi Arabia, however, still pays more of its workers as migrants (80 per cent of the workforce) than any other country in the world. In the early 2000s, Saudi Arabia and other Gulf states had been urged to reconsider hiring Yemeni expatriate workers as a way of helping its near neighbour tackle high unemployment (40 per cent) and the vulnerable economic conditions of the country which, it was believed, would provide a fertile breeding ground for support of al-Qaeda and popular protest. The instability in Yemen and concerns about the resilience of Gulf monarchies to the protests of the Arab Spring, however, gave rise to a major clamp-down on foreign labour from 2011 onwards. This has had particularly adverse effects on Yemeni migrant workers, who have been deported from states like Saudi Arabia in their tens of thousands back to a civil war and a crisis economy which is still classed as dependent on Gulf remittances for important shares of GDP (World Bank, 2016c).

Labour shortages, particularly although not exclusively in the oil-producing states of the Arab Gulf, became a significant developmental issue from the 1940s onwards. These shortages arose for a variety of reasons, including the small size of indigenous populations in oil-producing states like Kuwait and a lack of skilled and educated labour among the existing population.

This has created significant imbalances in such states between local and expatriate populations. In Qatar, for example, according to the Gulf Labour Markets and Migration (GLMM) programme, as many as 89 per cent of the population were, by 2016, foreign nationals, and in the United Arab Emirates the figure similarly sat at as many as 88 per cent foreign nationals (GLMM, 2016).

Thus, from the earliest development of the oil-producing states, a pattern of dependence on migrant labour emerged. During the early periods of development, labour was imported not just from within the region. The first wave of Palestinian skilled workers arrived in the early 1950s in Kuwait, Saudi Arabia, Abu Dhabi, Dubai, etc., and was accompanied by American and European workers associated with the major foreign-owned oil companies which were exploiting the oil fields of the region. The patterns of dependency which emerged during this period were not only broadened but also strengthened following the 1973 oil crisis and the quadrupled revenues that the oil-producing states enjoyed.

Now the energy-rich states could pay the costs of importing skilled workers, and states like Iraq, which was labour-rich, could even afford the luxury of importing labour for a variety of unskilled and menial jobs. By 1975, Arab labour was a significant factor in the economic development of a variety of Gulf countries. In Saudi Arabia, for example, the native population was significantly smaller than the migrant population of more than 1 million, the majority of whom were drawn from Yemen to the south, Jordan (including Palestinians) to the north, and Egypt to the west (Findlay, 1994, p. 106). Even the economic recession of the 1980s failed to curb the appetite for imported labour, and the problem of encouraging native labour into the domestic economy was recognized. The Gulf crisis, in the early 1990s, however, did alter these patterns significantly, resulting in the wholesale deportation of some labour groups, including Palestinians, Jordanians, Egyptians and Yemenis. Arab migrant labour to the Gulf states has never recovered to such pre-war levels but has remained significant in terms of remittances to their home countries.

Box 3.4 Diaspora-te times

- In 2015, there were 32 million international migrants in the Arab states region.
- The number of refugees hosted by countries such as Jordan and Lebanon has grown rapidly, to a combined total of 5 million migrant workers and refugees in 2015.
- The Arab states hosted 17.8 million migrant workers in 2013, and the majority are from Asia, with a sizeable number also coming from Africa, especially Egypt.
- Migrants in the six Gulf states account for over 10 per cent of all migrants globally, while Saudi Arabia and the United Arab Emirates host, respectively, the fourth- and fifth-largest migrant populations in the world.

(Continued)

Box 3.4 *(Continued)*

- Migrant workers make up the majority of the population in Bahrain, Oman, Qatar and the United Arab Emirates (and more than 80 per cent of the population in the latter two); while in construction and domestic work in the Gulf states, migrant workers make up over 95 per cent of the work force.
- Migrants in the Arab states remitted over US$109 billion in 2014, with Saudi Arabia and the United Arab Emirates ranking second and third globally in terms of remittance outflow (after the USA).
- It is estimated that some 600,000 migrants are victims of forced labour in the region. (ILO, 2017)

For the labour exporters, including those mentioned above, the impact of this pattern of economic relations was manifest in a number of ways. There was a variety of negative factors that were never really considered. Among these were the cost of educating a population and then facilitating the export of its brightest and most talented workers. The Arab brain drain to the Gulf states has been identified as a serious socio-economic consequence of governments like Egypt encouraging migration.

Furthermore, in the wake of the Arab Spring, the UN estimated that the Arab 'brain drain' from the region had accelerated by as much as 20–25 per cent (Reinl, 2015). In addition, migrant labour from Jordan, Yemen and Egypt has left many households without a male head for prolonged periods of time, significantly altering social relations within society.

Thus, patterns of birth, marriage and education of children have all been altered by migrant-led economies. Family resources were often collectively directed to the education and subsequent professional employment of one child, who in turn would support others in the family through remittances sent from the Gulf.

Remittances in themselves have been a mixed blessing. They have promoted consumer booms and private capital projects such as house-building, and funded large dowries for weddings, but they have not necessarily increased the health of national economies in countries such as Egypt, Yemen or Jordan. In addition, the abrupt loss of remittances plus the forced and wide-scale return of labour, as witnessed to Yemen from Saudi Arabia in the wake of the Arab Spring, can have a severe dislocating effect on the economy and lead to further social unrest and political mobilization. Remittance economies, then, are not to be encouraged in the Arab world.

The political and economic implications of these arrangements in the region are clear, leading to new patterns of economic development and dependency, with exploitative relationships between receiving and sending economies, and affecting political issues of democratization, citizenship and Gulf-based aid packages to the rest of the region.

Patterns of migration have been altered within the Arab world, with a switch by Gulf economies from Arab- to Asian-based labour, which was accelerated by (amongst other things) the fallout of the Gulf crisis in 1990–1 and subsequently the Arab Spring. Those Arab migrant labour groups which have endured enjoy few if any political or labour rights within the host country. Labour unions are prohibited, and working conditions, rates of pay, etc., remain largely unregulated internally. Integration of long-term migrant communities is not particularly apparent and, again, those communities – such as the Palestinians in Kuwait – who had perceived their migrant status as long term, permanent and economically viable, discovered the opposite when 100,000 of them were ejected from the country in 1991. In 2014, the Saudi government announced it would crack down and deport as many as 1 million 'illegal' migrant workers from the Kingdom, many thousands of whom came from the Arab world.

As far as settlement is concerned, hopes for naturalization or even citizenship are largely illusory and have proved costly for all sides – the migrants, the receiving state and the sending state. Such illusions, for example, have inhibited migrant workers from investing their remittances and capital in home-based industrial, commercial or agricultural enterprises. Future prospects for migrant labour remain unpredictable and uncertain, to say the least. As oil economies face the task of economic diversification, demands for increased political participation and the threat of further conflict with their neighbours, internal security threats and dissension, the issue of labour mobility within the region must be balanced against these factors. Within the labour-rich states of the region, the balance between the quest for foreign earnings and the actual developmental impact these have on national economies must be reassessed, patterns of dependence must be questioned and inter-Arab relations, integration and economic development need to absorb the economic changes.

Case study

Saudi Arabia – Vision 2030 or bust

Even the most resource-rich states of the Middle East understand that there will be a post-oil era and that if the political systems which they preside over are to survive then reform must be undertaken. Saudi Arabia is one such state. Like other oil-producing states in the region, however, it was compelled to respond in the wake of unprecedented oil price drops beginning in 2014. News that the country was running a budget deficit of US$98 billion and was dipping into its reserves to stay afloat was exceedingly worrisome (Nereim and Carey, 2015). Additionally, state spending was frequently deemed 'inefficient' with a worsening impact on the wider economy and its development (Waldman, 2016).

Saudi Arabia, like many other Gulf states, is highly dependent on remittances from oil. To this extent, the economy – but also, as discussed above, the political structure of the state – had become dependent on rentier bargains with the population that the state could afford to make when revenues were strong. With revenues drastically reduced, Saudi rulers were forced to rethink the social contract with their own citizens. Indeed, in the wake of the Arab Spring and fearful of a rebellious and revolutionary contagion effect impacting their own country the Saudi government increased public expenditures but, as Hertog highlights, 'the Saudi wealth sharing regime has bolstered political stability since the 1970s, but has created deep dependencies and distortions that have become a threat to the kingdom's economic sustainability' (Hertog, 2016a).

There were also warnings from the IMF, as well as Saudi sources themselves, that the economic outlook was grim (IMF, 2015). As the new King – Salman – succeeded the throne in 2015 he was greeted with the fact that oil remittances to state coffers had dropped by as much as 23 per cent. Moreover, Saudi Arabia faced economic problems at home associated with poor performance and was engaged in costly conflicts abroad as well. The state responded to the oil price crisis through a number of austerity measures that also included accessing foreign reserves, cutting government spending, issuing government and semi-government bonds, and engaging – in 2016 – in international debt issuance (Coates Ulrichsen, 2016).

Not all have, or would have, chosen substantive economic reform of their economy, otherwise. In April 2016, the Kingdom's then Deputy Crown Prince Mohammed bin Salman al Saud publicly offered details of the 'Saudi Vision 2030' as the plan to overhaul and reorient the economy (see figure 3.2). This was a plan that spoke of 'different dreams for a generation in a post-carbon future' for the country (Waldman, 2016). The state-owned ARAMCO Company would be privatized to reform and re-position Saudi Arabia globally. ARAMCO is believed to have a market valuation of $1 trillion, making it the richest company in the world. Any IPO would mean huge revenues accrued to the state. Government ministries would also be restructured to reflect the primary importance of energy, industry and natural resources. By June 2016, further indications of reform were apparent in the launch of the 'National Transformation Program' (NTP). At the root of the NTP is a plan to move government income away from its crippling dependence on oil revenues and concurrently to boost economic activity in Saudi Arabia's private sector and generate tax revenues for the state. Such plans, however, require Saudis also to employ each other in the private sector as a means of tackling high-level unemployment. This is problematic when incentives are much lower than those of the past (El-Katiri, 2016).

It is interesting to note that much has been made of the fact that the Saudi Vision 2030 has emerged at a time of generational leadership changes in Saudi Arabia and that the champion of this initiative is himself a 'thirty-something'

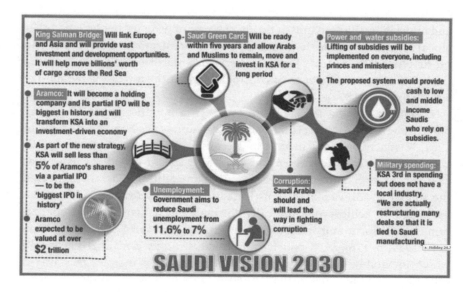

Source: www.arabnews.com/news/vision-2030-may-lead-saudi-ratings-boost.

Figure 3.2 *Saudi Vision 2030*

who represents, and appears to be in tune and step with, young Saudis who constitute the majority of the indigenous population.

Nevertheless, youth does not necessarily trump experience as the Kingdom is being forced, rather than choosing, to make significant trade-offs economically in the face of unprecedented domestic and regional political challenges. The current generation of Saudis, for example, are equally as affected by a deeply ingrained entitlement culture as their predecessors but live in an economic climate that simply will not permit it. Hence the words of economic rightsizing have to be matched by sustained and sustainable deeds to move the country away from its hydrocarbon dependence forever. Saudi Arabia cannot undertake this task in isolation from the regional environment in which it is located nor ignore the deeply rooted and complex economic and political dependencies with its neighbours in the Middle East. This means that no state actor in the region can afford to ignore the current Saudi experiment in reform and transformation.

Case study

Egypt – too big to fail or succeed

This profile of Egypt's economy will date from 1952 following the Free Officers coup d'état and the advent of Gamal Abdel Nasser as leader of the country. Until this time, the Egyptian economy had been largely governed and directed by the demands of the British economy, in particular, and other global forces. Economic development and modernization in the country in the first half of the century had been directed by the British, who had secured the political system under their control and sat at the top of the pyramid of wealth (Issawi, 1982, p. 8).

Nasser's revolution took time to establish a populist base and appeal, but through a socialist economic agenda, announced in the decrees of 1961, Nasser hoped to achieve a new economic dawn for the country. His policy of economic reform was influenced by socialist ideology as well as elements of Arab nationalist interpretation. In addition, Nasser engineered the slogan 'al-adl wa-l-kifaya' (justice and sufficiency for everyone), which he hoped to achieve economically through mechanisms of nationalization, land reform and industrial as well as agricultural expansion (Richards, 1982, p. 176). Such policies required a strongly centralized economy which inevitably moved away from strict socialist principles to state-led capitalism. The first five-year plan led to only partial economic successes and the second five-year plan was never implemented. Nasser's commitment to the social contract – including rights to basic provision of food, health care, education and housing – would also require large amounts of capital. By the early 1960s, Nasser's populist-driven economic policies had run into trouble, exacerbated by the military defeat of 1967 and a leadership crisis that led many to question the viability of the socialist Arab nationalist experiment.

When, following Nasser's death, Anwar Sadat assumed power in 1970, the nature of Egypt's economy changed dramatically. Indeed, Ayubi (1995) goes as far as to state that 'Egypt can be said in a certain sense to be the "mother of Arab liberalization". Just as she was the first Arab country to champion a leading public sector ... she also became the first ... to experiment with economic liberalization and privatization, from the mid-1970s onwards' (p. 339). As part of his programme of 'de-Nasserization', Sadat was to reshape Egypt's ailing economy, address indebtedness and depart from the socialist-led pre-planned economy developed by Nasser and the Revolutionary Command Council. In one respect, it might be argued that Sadat was hoping to bring a new era of prosperity to the country. Nevertheless, the programme of economic restructuring known as *infitah* or liberalization, announced by Sadat in April 1974, would prove to be hasty and ill conceived. In addition, *infitah* was as much about politics as about economics and, although Sadat announced political reforms to accompany economic change, they were largely empty of real political import and left the executive authority of the President untouched.

Sadat's policy, however, would also have to address a series of major problems affecting the Egyptian economy by the early 1970s, including 'stagnant productivity in the (overwhelmingly public) industrial sector, lagging agricultural growth and growing food imports, a serious imbalance of trade and a large resource gap' (Richards and Waterbury, 1990, p. 240). A policy of economic liberalization was designed to affect the Egyptian economy in a number of ways. First, it was believed that state-approved liberalization would attract foreign investment capital into Egypt – capital which came from the West as well as oil-rich Gulf states. Billions of dollars of Arab, European and American capital flowed into the country throughout the 1970s, eventually totalling $4.4 billion. Second, liberalization also encouraged increased rates of bilateral aid to the country, with the Arab Gulf states contributing $5 billion between 1973 and 1976. The state introduced legislation which protected new investors from nationalization and confiscation and which bestowed favourable tax benefits as well. Third, the public sector, the largest employer of labour, would be reorganized to increase productivity and set prices for utilities at a profitable level. Finally, the region-wide oil boom promoted an era of prosperity leading to a high level of remittances being received from Egypt's army of workers in the Gulf states. By 1985, for example, remittances from Egypt's migrant workers contributed $3.3 billion to the country's foreign exchange earnings, making them the top contributor in this field.

Has liberalization profited the Egyptian economy? In the 1970s, there was no question that the policies associated with *infitah* increased the wealth of the country and contributed to economic growth. For example, per capita GDP grew by 8–9 per cent per annum. By the 1980s, however, with the advent of Sadat's successor Hosni Mubarak, growth had slowed down and economic crisis still prevailed over the economy. Mubarak introduced only limited economic reforms and, as the economic crisis worsened, the government instituted wide-scale austerity measures to try to address issues such as its foreign debt, which by the mid 1980s had reached more than $30 billion.

Foreign debt has left Egypt increasingly dependent on US aid, the IMF and World Bank strictures vis-à-vis economic planning. This relationship was emphasized during the 1990–1 Gulf crisis, which brought both negative and positive aspects to the economy: 'On the negative side it [the Crisis] exacerbated financial and economic problems ... On the positive side external aid (mainly grants) worth about $3.9 billion was rushed to Egypt' (Ayubi, 1991, p. 346). Some foreign debt was cancelled and new agreements favourable to Egypt were negotiated with the IMF. What seems certain is that the process of economic recovery in Egypt will always be slow in coming, given that indebtedness and dependency on foreign imports, even for basic foodstuffs, will be a long time in declining or even disappearing altogether. Wealth creation as a result of liberalization has not been evenly spread and the emergence of the wealthy elite only serves to heighten economic and political tensions in the country. In addition, 'the state retains a dominant role in the economy, and the basic problems of providing food, jobs, and basic consumer goods for the mass of the population continue to cast a shadow over the Valley of the Nile' (Richards and Waterbury, 1990, p. 244).

Economic uncertainty was apparent in the calls for protest and national demonstration that took place all over Egypt in January and February 2011, culminating in the ouster of President Mubarak from power. Protest calls concerning corruption and the economy were the culmination of decades of under-development, faulty economic policies and increasing inequality which hit the middle classes and working families of Egypt (Dunne and Revkin, 2011). Egyptian protest also centred on issues of food insecurity, poor labour rights and unemployment, highlighting the extent to which economic factors, combined with limited political rights, contributed to the widening gap and the lack of legitimacy attributed to the Egyptian state by its citizens (Chekir and Diwan, 2012). There were hopes that, with the change in power, free elections and the rise of the Muslim Brotherhood, post-revolutionary Egypt would reorient its economy towards a more equally prosperous horizon for many more of its citizens. Yet political events would transpire to create more economic uncertainty, and perpetuate the elite hold, particularly of the Egyptian military, over society and its economy.

The problems of the economy have remained a driver of transition under the government of President el-Sisi. By 2017, growth in the economy had stalled, and the foreign debt burden accounted for 12 per cent of GDP. There was an evident lack of foreign investment in the country, vital revenues from tourism had declined drastically, the Egyptian pound was over-valued, there was a dollar shortage, Egypt was a net importer and there was a rise in the black market for hard currency. President el-Sisi was forced to return to the IMF for lending to keep the country afloat. These severe problems reflected the culmination of decades of financial mismanagement, corruption and the ever-deepening role of the military in the Egyptian economy, which in turn has inhibited other investors from stepping forward. The return of the IMF to Egypt reflects a cycle of macro-economic performance that keeps its economy the right side of the brink of collapse amidst concerns that, if it fell, the subsequent de-stabilization of the state would be catastrophic domestically as well as within the wider Middle East region. In this respect, many consider Egypt too big to fail.

Case study

Collapsing globalization and its regional consequences

The global financial crisis of 2008 dealt a deathly blow to the economies of the Middle East affected by the drivers of globalization. Indeed, the economic and developmental woes of the Middle East in the twenty-first century are intimately connected to the drivers inherent to the neo-liberal agenda advocated for the region. Growth had occurred but, as much of the statistical evidence from UN reports began to highlight, it was not contributing to development. Indicators such as illiteracy – particularly among women – youth employment rates, unemployment rates, poor GDP performance, growing poverty rates, mediocre access to technology, risible participation of women in legislative systems and the articulation of a desire by the majority of Arab youth to work in economies other than their own, highlighted the formidable challenges facing the state system in the Middle East, and its populations, in relation to building economies for prosperous societies.

An emergent explanation for this state of affairs indicated that globalization – the process of economic (and other forms of) integration across the globe as a result of free trade policies – was impacting negatively on the Middle East (with a few notable exceptions) and in fact making it harder for the region's populations to keep up with the new global tempo set by multinational enterprises. This critique of globalization in the Middle East emerged both inside and outside the region. It formed part of the discourse of the anti-globalization movement – particularly concerning the effects of neo-liberal economic agendas – as well as of some Islamist popular movements.

As the sections above have indicated, the impact of a changing global economy has already been significant in the various states of the Middle East for more than several decades. The accelerating push for free trade, liberalization, and investment and capital flows has not only impacted on the economies of the region but has been accompanied by expectations of change within political systems as well. Yet the emergent economic conditions and the responses of state elites in many countries in the region have resulted in lagging economic and political reform. In the AHDR (Arab Human Development Report) of 2009, twenty-two Arab countries were criticized for failing to meet local aspirations for development and political freedom. The authors warned that:

Box 3.5 Failing the people

The region faces growing challenges to the security of its population from environmental stresses

Stressed groundwater systems are often the only source of fresh water in the region

Desert has swallowed up more than two-thirds of total land area of the region

Large and frequent shortfalls can turn the state into a threat to human security

Most states failed to introduce institutions of representation

Ethnic, religious, sectarian, and linguistic differences can be associated with persistent group struggles

Many Arab countries allow freedoms and individual rights to be violated

(Continued)

Box 3.5 *(Continued)*

Anti-terror laws have given government security agencies sweeping powers
Many Arabs live under various 'un-freedoms'
The relationship between the state and human security in the region is not straightforward
It is difficult to gauge the prevalence of violence against women in Arab societies
Arab countries are the site of both the world's longest-standing refugee question and its latest such problem
The fabled oil wealth of the Arab countries presents a misleading picture of their economic situation
Overall, the Arab countries were less industrialized in 2007 than in 1970
The Report projects that the estimated numbers of Arabs living in poverty could be as high as 65 million
Inequality in wealth has worsened significantly more than the deterioration in income.

(UNDP, 2009)

In terms of development and economic profiles, UNDP statistics indicate that the population birth rates in the Middle East are higher than in other parts of the globe – the demographic time bomb becomes an increasing reality. In some cases, this high birth rate has led some states in the region to attempt to hide such rates as they expose greater not fewer numbers living in abject poverty. Despite the perception that many Arab countries are wealthy, development reports highlight that economic growth is generally weak throughout the region.

Other economic indicators are also far from healthy. The clear linkage between economic development, human security and political reform has been established in debates about globalization and the Middle East by world organizations such as the IMF, World Bank, the United Nations and the European Union. The issue often at stake, however, is whose definition of globalization the peoples of the Middle East should be working with.

Although globalization is commonly understood as a term for the economic integration of the contemporary world, its meanings have been interpreted as having significance in the fields of technology, society and politics. Nevertheless, the term does imply connection and integration across 'borders' and 'barriers' that have previously existed. Globalization can have both negative and positive connotations. As Noam Chomsky has argued, ' "globalization" used in a neutral sense just means "international integration" … The term has come to be used in recent years as a kind of a technical term which doesn't refer to globalization, but refers to a very specific form of international economic integration namely based on the priority given to investor rights, not rights of people' (Danilo, 2005, p. 1). Globalization cannot be rolled back or easily resisted for it is a complex process with a number of dimensions to it that involve such factors as good governance, migration, ethnic integration, the removal of trade barriers, popular protest, and the centrality of issues such as the knowledge economy. The limits of integration inherent to the definition of globalization are contested and challenged.

As an economic experience, the process of globalization optimizes profit making in the free-market economy. For the proponents of economic globalization, the larger that market, the fewer barriers to trade and the greater the efficiency of the process, the better the profits. Market competitiveness, low inflation, foreign investment and new technologies spur this economic process. It is reported that economies with these features grow quicker than others (Lukas, 2000, p. 2). But for the majority of economies in the Middle East there has been a state-led resistance to such changes, and globalization penetration by actors from outside the region has impacted negatively. Moreover, it is argued that 'the drama of globalization is a continuation of the colonial dialectic played out by earlier generations of the indigenous elite' (Henry and Springborg, 2010, p. 15). Many contend that in fact the problem of resistance lies with the elites of the region and the dominant cultural trend of Islam. Authoritarian elites are persistently blamed for failing to allow the state to relinquish control of the economy and, ergo, the rest of society, including the political system.

Outside agencies are variously accused of double standards in calling for reform but standing by or propping up states like Tunisia or Egypt that resisted such changes. During the Arab Spring, it was argued that the repository of the globalized lay with the tech-savvy young protestors – creating and reinforcing networks of resistance in the anti-globalization campaign. They were symbolized by the Facebook posting, Twitter-feeding activists that much of the western media seized upon in their search for 'heroes and heroines' to communicate back to home audiences. Nevertheless, such 'globalized' symbolism was short-lived. The region, post-Arab Spring, has proved resilient to such critiques. The economic 'precarity' of life in the region remains the dominant feature, evidenced in unemployment, poverty, low life expectancy, poor education and inequalities – especially as they relate to women (Achcar 2013). Alas, 'the two decades of rapid globalization in the Middle East did not produce a new MENA liberal age', argues Springborg (2016).

Questions for discussion

- Explain the development of oil economies in the region.
- What is meant by a rentier economy?
- Why is globalization problematic for the Middle East?

Recommended reading

- Cammett et al. (2016), which incorporates Richards and Waterbury (1990), is a solid introduction to the political economy of the region.
- An edited text by Kheir-El-Din (2008) has some interesting in-depth chapters on issues such as youth employment/unemployment and macro-economic issues such as poverty and growth. Bina (2013) highlights oil and conflict as issues essential to the study of this topic.
- Farah's text (2009) examines the political-economy dimension with contemporary detail. Henry and Springborg's (2010), alongside Dodge and Higgott's (2002), texts on globalization and the politics of development in the Middle East region are worth looking at for an insight into the continuing issues that beset economic development there in the twenty-first century. Stetter (2012) links the issues in the economies of the Middle East to the wider global system.
- Kuran (2004) takes a wider perspective on the debate about Islam and the economy, but it is one worth pursuing for further reading.
- Galpern (2013), Mitchell (2011) and Gilbar (2013) all address the pressing issue of carbon economies in the region and future prospects for oil-producing rentier states. Herb (2014) links the specifics of the oil-producing debate to politics in the Gulf states of Kuwait and the UAE. Bazoobandi (2013) also examines Gulf economies such as Iran, Kuwait, Saudi Arabia and the UAE, framed by the theme of sovereign wealth funds. Crystal (2016) focuses on the challenge of transforming the 'oil state' of Kuwait, while Pesaran (2013) tackles such issues with a specific focus on Iran and its drive to develop its economy.
- E. G. Young (2014) incorporates essential gendered analysis of the economy of the region. This is useful in understanding the important economic drivers behind political change in the region. Galal and Diwan (2016) also extend this debate in terms of the transition and uncertainty impacting the Middle East in the wake of the Arab Spring, crises of the global economy and oil price crises that had a particular effect on the region.

CHAPTER FOUR

Conflict and Lack of Peace

Introduction

The Middle East has been characterized as a battleground. From this region – more than any other – opinion in the West has crystallized around the issue of conflict, terrorism and war. In the twenty-first century, the region has become synonymous with conflict and terror. Conflict in the region has taken place at a number of levels: first, long-standing regional conflicts; second, short-lived conflagrations within the region; third, localized disputes; fourth, the rising terrorism phenomenon; and, finally, wars waged by external actors. There have been conflicts between states as well as between ethnic groups at all levels. Regional conflict has been primarily shaped by the Arab–Israeli conflict, while conflict between actors within the region and outside it is illustrated by the Suez Crisis of 1956, when Nasser of Egypt challenged both the French and the British, or the allied attack on Iraq in 2003. Intra-state conflict is currently epitomized by the sectarian conflict that has scarred Syria since 2011 and in the past dispute in Lebanon that led to fifteen years of civil war from 1975 to 1990. Today, terrorism within and from the region is commonly associated with ISIS and al-Qaeda.

Debates about conflicts in the region have examined such factors as traditional state-to-state rivalries, conflicts over natural resources such as oil or water, sectarian and ethno-national disputes and the role of external factors such as international actors, particularly in proxy wars. In addition, academics have raised questions over the legitimacy of certain regimes whose leaders have attempted to create a sense of cohesion by playing the nationalist card in times of crisis – an example of this was President Saddam Hussein of Iraq in the 1990s. Although this chapter is not specifically about the military but about conflict in more general terms, the prevalence of the military in the politics of the region helps to explain the apparent and widespread phenomenon of conflict across the Middle East.

Wars have broken out between Arabs and Israelis, Palestinians and Israelis, Arabs and the states of Europe, Arabs and Arabs, Arabs and Iranians, Sunni and Shi'a Muslims, Muslims and Christians, Kurds and Arabs. There have been civil conflicts in Iraq, Syria, Algeria, Yemen and Lebanon, and further tensions centred on these dynamics in Gulf states such as Bahrain and Saudi

Arabia. Because authoritarian regimes are 'concerned with the internal paci-fication and repression of domestic populations', they increase the likelihood of conflict (Bromley, 1994, p. 116).

Border conflicts have also been evident in the region and have occurred between countries such as Egypt and Libya, Morocco and Algeria, Jordan and Syria, Israel and Lebanon, Iraq and Kuwait, and Iran and Iraq. Such conflicts reflect the ongoing contested nature of boundaries in the contemporary Middle East – a certain legacy of the nature of colonially inspired state-for-mation from the turn of the twentieth century.

The arms race has also played a substantial part in perpetuating conflict. Arab states, Iran and Israel, as well as a variety of non-state armed actors, have all sought to build up significant arsenals, including conventional weaponry, chemical weapons and nuclear capability – hence the real fear, particularly in the late 1970s, of a nuclear Armageddon in the area. Inter-national support for the arms race has been ill disguised and has also been used to maintain vital relationships within the region. The nuclear issue arose once again in the twenty-first century as Iran continued to develop nuclear capability. It has been limited by the 2015 Iran nuclear deal frame-work agreement between Iran and the permanent members of the UN Secu-rity Council, Germany and the EU. Iran agreed, as part of the deal, to redesign, convert and reduce its nuclear facilities. In return, economic sanctions against the country would be lifted and this would allow access to important oil revenues and other assets (Tarock, 2016).

National spending on arms and the military in the Middle East and North Africa region is higher than in any other developing area or even conflict-affected locations in the world. In some Middle East states, spending on arms and the military as a percentage of national income is as high as 14 per cent, particularly in the Arab Gulf states such as Oman, and Saudi Arabia. In 2015, Saudi Arabia was considered to be the third-largest military spend-ing nation in the world, behind the USA and China (SIPRI, 2016). Hence, the Middle East also remains one of the world's largest markets for weapons. The rise of the civil conflict in Syria, for example, has contributed to a significant upswing in arms traded to the regime and the variety of armed rebel forces by a number of regional and international state actors. As well as seeking profit in such exchanges, regional and international state actors are also seeking to shore up important political and diplomatic, strategic and economic ambitions in Syria as well as the wider region. This is evident, for example, in Russia's ever-deepening role in support of the regime of President Assad against rebel forces that have battled against him since 2011 (Bagdonas, 2016).

The role of the military in the political systems of the area should not be underestimated. Firstly, as discussed in chapter 2, military coups, revolutions and counter-revolutions have been a feature of the Middle East and North Africa for decades. It can be convincingly argued that the military in Egypt determined the outcome of both the people's revolt of 2011 against then-President Hosni Mubarak and the counter-revolution of August 2013 against a democratically elected President Mohammed Morsi and his Muslim Brotherhood-dominated government and legislature. Moreover, in countries like Egypt, the military-industrial complex significantly allows for the power of the military institution and its autonomy from other arms of the state, including civil control. The tentacles of the military-industrial complex spread wide. As Bassiouni demonstrates:

Box 4.1 The Egyptian military from bombs to pasta

Over time, military-industrial production has become roughly 25 percent to 30 percent of Egypt's $256 billion economy. This includes military production ... but has expanded into the civilian sector as well, producing construction machinery, refrigerators, furniture, pasta and bottled water. It also is involved in agriculture, and associated industries.

(Bassiouni, 2016, pp. 155–6)

Military-based regimes have been characteristic of states such as Syria, Algeria, Libya and Egypt. There can be no doubt that close political and economic links between the military, power and politics help to explain the nature of some of the conflicts within the region. As both Picard (1990) and Owen (2004) highlight in their own debates about the role of the military forces in state-building, these armed state actors have been increasingly independent politically and an important force in the region in their own right.

While Picard went on to discuss the stable nature of the military regimes in the region, it is still important to remember that regimes posited on such power will depend on the military to support the state and this can often only be done through war. In addition, while in the 1960s, as Richards and Waterbury (1990) suggest, the role of the military in the politics of the region was perceived as a positive development heralding progress, technological efficiency, modernization and the promotion of the nationalist agenda, a dramatic volte-face had occurred two decades later. The true nature of conflict and the military in society has convinced many that the negative effects of this feature of politics in the region has a significant consequence for freedoms and prosperity. The pervasive nature of factionalism and internal strife within the officer class, the lack of economic development, economic crises, widespread corruption, coercion and lack of democracy convinced many that military insertion or influence in the politics and economies of the Middle East has been far from helpful in promoting peace and prosperity and avoiding conflict (Grawert and Abdul-Magd, 2017).

While the role of the military has been debated extensively, other explanations of conflict also need to be highlighted. In this sense, the phenomenon of terrorism within the region also needs to be acknowledged. This is highly contentious given the explicit link in the past between such acts and the goals of national liberation movements and the present-day concerns with the kinds of terrorism associated with the radical extremist ideology of groups like ISIS and al-Qaeda, as well as their many off-shoots. Political violence is perceived as characterizing the region (Piazza, 2007). This is why the Middle East has mattered so much of late to global political players like the USA and Russia. The region appears to play host, and naturally ally itself, to extreme manifestations of violence: anti-American terrorism of the 'Why-We-Hate-America' variety; suicide terrorism carried out both within the region and outside it; and Islamic–Muslim terrorism.

State-sponsored terrorism is also apparent in the dark and twisted power-plays that have embroiled a variety of political leaders and their regimes across the decades. Ethno-terrorism has become associated with the armed manoeuvres made by groups in conflict with powerful states. Today, there is also talk of manifestations of narco-terrorism, sectarian terrorism and oil-threat-terrorism plots linked to groups such as ISIS and al-Qaeda. The victims of this terrorism are preponderantly people from the region, going about their daily business. Such terrorism has had the capacity to paralyse such everyday activities and has led to an inexorable securitization of the region as a whole. This is apparent in airports, at borders, in police and military presences, blast walls, security cameras, X-ray scanners and barbed-wire fences. This has literally altered the landscape of the Middle East, its sense of contiguity is lost. Barriers and suspicion prevail amidst rising security concerns.

Ideology, religion, resources, socio-economic crisis, state-formation and nation-building are all factors that have been cited to one degree or another in explanation of conflict in the region. In the past, especially before the end of the Cold War and during particular historical epochs such as the decade of Arab nationalism during the 1960s, it was argued that most disputes were the result of ideological differences. Such disputes between pan-Arabism and Zionism were given added impetus by the role of other actors in the international community, particularly the extension of superpower rivalry between the USA and the Soviet Union to the shores of the Middle East.

These factors have been explored and examined extensively in works by Taylor (1991), Efrat and Bercovitch (1991) and Freedman (1991), all of whom have highlighted the impact that these particular actors had on the nature of conflict, the military and the perpetuation of arms in the region. The end of the Cold War in 1989–91 and the apparent resurgence of Islam were identified by authors such as Huntington (1993) as a new source for conflict both within the region and with the West. Moreover, the declaration by the government of the USA in the wake of the 9/11 attacks of a 'war on terrorism' and the naming of such Middle Eastern states as Iraq and Iran as part of an 'axis of evil' then led to increased confrontation and war (Adib-Moghaddam, 2008). In addition, the rise of competing ethnic identities in states such as Iraq, Syria and Turkey has created a new axis for tension and conflict and undermined the apparently stable edifice of the nation-state. In sum, then, a variety of conflicts characterize the region in the contemporary era and hamper the maintenance of stability and development, create further dependency and encourage forms of authoritarianism in an age in which other regions of the globe have slowly evolved away from these negative political, social and economic forces.

The bigger battle: Arab–Israeli hostility

The conflict between the state of Israel and the Arab states dominated the political life of the Middle East for decades. As Sahliyeh claimed, 'the Palestinian–Arab–Israeli conflict is potentially the most lethal and volatile … and the most difficult to resolve' (1992, p. 381). Although the conflict originally centred on the establishment of a Jewish state in Palestine and the subsequent dispossession of the Palestinian Arab population, over the decades the dynamics of the conflict resulted in a character often far removed from the original Palestinian issue.

At a wider level, the Arab–Israeli conflict has come to symbolize the internal competition for leadership of the region, the phenomenon of Arab nationalism, solidarity and power-balances with external powers. It is also about the legacy of colonialism and independence, East versus West, the nation-state versus the boundaryless aspirations of Arabness or Islam, and the limits of diplomatic efforts in resolving conflict.

The origins of the conflict, the explanation for its longevity, its history, its seeming intractability and difficulty to resolve have all been subject to a variety of explanations and often fierce political discourse. Particular events, such as the war of 1948 or the role of the USA in the conflict and its resolution, are subjected to controversy, interpretation, reinterpretation, revisionism and accusations of fabrication. For sure, there can be little else in the realm of contemporary Middle Eastern politics that is more hotly contested than the explanation of this particular conflict, for in any explanation there is also, explicitly or implicitly, an accusation of blame and responsibility, an 'auditing of antagonism', which is mutual and often inflexible.

Some have crudely limited the explanation of these interpretations as either pro-Arab or pro- Israel with no other residual category. Like any other deep conflict, there is always pressure to be on 'one side or another'. Such reductionism, however, does not help to explain the dynamics of the conflict or the multitude of factors involved, including important debates about the nation-state, self-determination, the arms race, and the international community, forms of political violence, genocide, partition, civil disobedience, negotiations and economics. Suffice it to say, any 'reading' of the conflict must be placed in this wider context of politics in the Middle East and North Africa throughout the last half-century. For example, even the ambitions of the Iranians (who are not Arab) post-1979 cannot be understood without reference to the Arab–Israeli conflict, which resulted in the 1982 Israeli invasion of Lebanon to oust the Palestine Liberation Organization (PLO), which in turn led to the formation of a radical Shi'a pro-Iranian militia Hizb Allah, the kidnap of Americans, the US Irangate scandal, arms to Nicaragua, and support extended by the Iranians to the Palestinian cause and later to specific Palestinian factions.

The Palestinian issue, then, has done more both to unite and to divide the Arabs, Israelis, Iranians and Turks than any other issue. The conflict pitting the Arab and Muslim states against Israel has been dominated by war rather than reconciliation. Since the establishment of the state of Israel in May 1948, there have been six major wars, and every state from Morocco to Iran has been engaged at some point in an economic, political and diplomatic boycott of the country, designed to deny its existence in the region. Only two Arab countries have made peace with Israel. The first was Egypt under the Presidency of Anwar Sadat in 1978 (which we discuss as a case study); the second in November 1994 when King Hussein of Jordan signed a peace treaty with Yitzhak Rabin, the Prime Minister of Israel. Jordan has yet to experience the real dividends of peace concluded with Israel more than twenty years ago or, despite the historical references to the Hashemite–Yishuv pact, warm relations with its peace partner (Milton-Edwards, 2016c).

The wars of 1948, 1956, 1967, 1973, 1982 and 2006 have resulted in both Arab defeats and Israeli victories, and Arab victories and Israeli defeats. They have perpetuated the arms race which has characterized the region, the superior role of the military in politics, the politics of attrition, authoritarianism, national unity and emergency – often providing the excuse for the praetorian politicians of the region to practise dictatorial measures at home by promoting states of emergency, national service, perpetuation of the 'uniform' culture, obsession with internal and national security threats, censorship of the press, extended police powers and a culture of hostility to the 'other', that is disseminated in the national media and educational curricula.

Territory – its acquisition or loss – has also been a major feature of the hostility between these state actors. The land of the region is subject to competing claims, battles and disputes. Antagonism over rights to territory, self-determination and sovereignty has led the Israelis and the Arabs into a seemingly intractable conflict. While at a state-to-state level there have been attempts and limited successes, as noted above, between Israel, Egypt and Jordan, at resolving conflict, region-wide resolution of the Arab–Israeli dispute remains an elusive goal, even given the relative strides in peacemaking achieved at the beginning of the 1990s.

There had been hope that the 2002 Arab Peace Initiative that was adopted at the Beirut Arab Summit might offer a route out of conflict for Israel but to date it has floundered on mutual mistrust and a lack of leveraged international support (Podeh, 2014). The territorial claims of one side over another have been alternately bolstered by the instrumental construction of political, historical, economic and even religious claims. For example, the constructivist Zionist claim to Eretz (Greater) Israel, supported by a notion of being 'Chosen People', is countered by the instrumentalization of Muslim claims of custodianship of the Holy Places and the covenant of *waqf* maintaining eternal Muslim ownership of land for future generations of the Muslim faithful.

The first war between Israel and the Arabs broke out on 15 May 1948, the day after Israel announced its independence. The armies of Egypt, Jordan and Syria, backed by those of Lebanon, Saudi Arabia and Iraq, attempted to regain Palestine for the Arabs by force. In theory, the combined military might of the Arab armies should have made short work of the poorly equipped Israeli Defence Force (IDF). In practice, the Arab armies lacked a united command or unity of war aims, and proved weak in combat. By the end of the summer of 1948 the Arabs were facing a defeat, and by July 1949 they had signed an armistice with Israel.

One direct outcome of the conflict was a mass of Palestinian refugees and the creation of a new factor in this dispute: a dispossessed population with an internationally recognized (UN Resolution 194) right of return and right to self-determination. By 1949, some 700–800,000 Palestinian Arabs had either fled or been forced to leave their homes. Whether the mass movement of Palestinians out of Israeli territory was part of a Zionist policy of transfer has recently been the subject of passionate debate among Israeli and Jewish historians, with some, such as Karsh (1997), claiming that his colleagues, including Benny Morris and Avi Shlaim, have 'fabricated' Israeli history, coining it a 'new Israeli distortiography'. Whether or not the Zionist leadership, including David Ben Gurion, was 'predisposed to nudge the process along, occasionally with the help of expulsions', these refugees ended up in the Jordanian-controlled West Bank, Egyptian-supervised Gaza Strip, Egypt, Lebanon, Jordan, Syria, the Arab Gulf states and elsewhere across the globe (Morris, 1998, p. 81).

The effects of the war and the increasingly long-term nature of the Palestinian refugee sojourn in other Arab states were palpable throughout the region, largely radicalizing Arab leaders and the masses around the symbol of Palestine, a symbol that would persist as a motif for wars between Israel and the Arabs in 1956, 1967, 1973 and 1982. For sure, the presence of large numbers of Palestinian refugees and successive generations in countries like Jordan, Lebanon, Syria, Kuwait and Saudi Arabia irreparably altered the dynamics of internal and regional politics in those states. In Jordan, for example, by 1970 the large Palestinian population represented a very real threat to the Hashemite monarchy, leading to civil war and the expulsion of the PLO. Today, Palestinians in Jordan are a major demographic grouping in this pivot kingdom, and face an undetermined future. Regionally, the Arab advocacy of the Palestinian cause was a double-edged sword, encouraging both inter-Arab rivalry and unity, as demonstrated during the 1973 war when the Arab oil boycott brought the international community to its knees.

Israel was declared the enemy of the Arabs, and an agent of the widely despised western powers – in particular, the USA. Israel's strategic and military alliance with the West during the Suez Crisis of 1956 confirmed Arab perceptions. The Six Day War of 1967, which resulted in a massive military defeat, again, for the Arab states of Egypt, Syria and Jordan, only served to consolidate a cycle of conflict between Israel and the Arabs which often lost sight of the Palestinian issue and assumed its own specific Arab–Israeli character. The careers of statesmen like Gamal Abdel Nasser, Hafiz al-Assad and Saddam Hussein were often dominated by the Arab conflict with Israel, while in their own countries they persecuted their own Palestinian populations, imprisoning, torturing, expelling and even executing them.

Even the defeat and despair which followed the *débâcle* of 1967 did not release the Israelis or Arabs from further battles. Sadat's attempt to recover Arab pride – the October War of 1973 – assisted by Syria, resulted in temporary and small-scale Arab victories. The recovery of Arab pride, however, was not enough to promote peace, and Israeli belligerency also intensified. American brokerage in the region, born out of superpower rivalry with the Soviets, the oil embargo and western fears about the 'oil weapon', resulted in the signing of a peace treaty between Israel and Egypt in 1978. In the same year, Israel invaded south Lebanon. Again, in 1982, Israel launched another offensive and, under the codename 'Peace for the Galilee', declared war on the PLO in Lebanon. The Palestinian refugee community and the Lebanese citizens of the country and Syrian military forces present in Lebanon were inexorably tied into the war; even those sectors of the Lebanese community (the Shi'a in the south) that initially welcomed Israel's invasion turned against them as the truth of the civilian casualty and death tolls emerged.

The wars in Lebanon had now become another episode in the Arab–Israeli conflict. This time, however, Israel began to flounder when, following the PLO's departure, its continued occupation of the country enraged the Shi'a community of the south. The war aims of the government were questioned by the Israeli people, Israeli casualties grew, the PLO had gone but the conflict with the Arabs remained (Schiff and Ya'ari, 1984). In 2006, the conflict between Israel and Lebanon was reprised with both sides forced to contend with the significant impacts on the nations that such violence leads to.

It can be confidently asserted, therefore, that the Arab–Israeli conflict established a dynamic of its own that was often explicable, not by reference to the status of the Palestinian issue, but by the individual ambitions of certain regional political leaders at home, the relative success or otherwise of their domestic policies, the concurrent nature and status of superpower rivalry, the common agenda of Third World states, the price of oil on the world market, the current status of arms contracts, strategic developments and nuclear capability, and the ability of diplomats to win concessions in international forums such as the United Nations or World Bank. This was clearly epitomized in the 2006 war between Israel and the Lebanese Shi'a group Hizb Allah.

In sum, the Arab–Israeli conflict has created pockets of profit for the Arab elite, built on the maintenance of authoritarian power, the wealth derived from arms and the military industry and associated economies, as well as the political prestige associated with any form of victory (real or otherwise) over Israel. In turn, Israel in its defence of itself, has established a state consistently concerned with its security, the poor relations with its neighbours and the maintenance of further territorial claims as a result of past conflicts, begging the question: 'What price for peace in Israel?'

Israel and its Arab neighbours still face an uphill struggle in the search for peace treaties and enduring peace-building between their peoples. Normalization between Israel and its neighbours is piecemeal and highly limited. For example, in 2016 Israel and Turkey agreed to restore normal diplomatic relations six years after they had broken down in the wake of an Israeli raid on a Turkish-supported solidarity flotilla to Gaza in which eight Turks were killed. The 2016 deal was underscored by Israeli compensation payments, economic trade deals and approval of Turkish humanitarian aid to Palestinians in Israeli-blockaded Gaza. Before 2010, Turkey had proved to be friendlier to Israel than others in the region and the restoration of 2016, though significant for the two states, could hardly be categorized as a turning point or signal for Israel's other neighbours in the region. Even normalization remains incipient and highly problematic. The increasingly preferred and soft route, however, for Israel is based on economic factors, especially as it relates to energy supplies and, in particular, gas deals.

Killing dreams: the Israeli–Palestinian dimension

In early 2017, amidst his huge domestic plans and frequently communicated tweets about making America 'great again', President Donald Trump found time to say something important about the Middle East. He announced his intention to move the US Embassy from Tel Aviv to Jerusalem. Since 1967 when, in the Six Day War, Israel occupied East Jerusalem and announced the city the undivided capital of the Israeli state, the international community has refused to recognize such claims and located their embassies in Tel Aviv instead. The announcement of Trump's intention was welcomed by Israel and condemned as a provocation by France and other international actors. Once again the Palestinian–Israeli conflict dominated the global headlines and chatter of social media.

The Israeli–Palestinian conflict has assumed a nature and dynamic all of its own, particularly from the late 1960s when aspects of the pan-Arab dimension diminished and a culturally and politically specific Palestinian nationalism was ascendant. While the roots of nationalist conflict between Palestinian and Jewish nationalists lay in the Yishuv and Zionist colonization of Palestine at the turn of the twentieth century, the transformation of Palestinian national consciousness, translated into their own political movements for liberation, emerged after the *débâcle* of 1967 and Israel's occupation of East Jerusalem and the Palestinian-populated territories of the West Bank and Gaza Strip. Indeed, from this point onwards, the conflict between the Palestinians and the Israelis changed, altering the political objectives and strategies of both parties and leading to the Palestinian terror campaigns of the 1970s, Israel's illegal settlement building and a further entrenchment of views on both sides which would remain unaltered until the Palestinian uprising (Intifada) in 1987. The dimensions of this conflict reflect political, ethno-national, class, colonial, religious and economic antagonisms that have proved difficult to resolve. This conflict, however, is primarily one between two peoples over one territory, of competing nation visions used by both sides to support their case in the domestic, regional and global theatre of politics.

It is apparent how quickly the lines of conflict between the Palestinians and the Israelis had become seemingly intractable during the period of the British mandate (1920–48). From 1948 to 1967, political solutions to this conflict were limited. Conflict characterized relations as Israel embarked on a period of successful state-building, creating an ethnically Jewish state in which its Arab citizens were not treated equally. The Palestinians, meanwhile, formed national resistance movements and, through the strategy of armed struggle, sought self-determination and statehood.

In addition, after 1967, the Palestinians realized they could no longer depend on their Arab brethren for liberation and that their fate now rested on their own shoulders. The two communities could not be completely segregated and the conflict was characterized at a day-to-day level by the way in which individuals related to one another. As Israel's occupation continued throughout the 1970s, the rate of illegal Israeli settlement in the West Bank, East Jerusalem and Gaza Strip increased in one direction.

In 2017, fifty years after Israel occupied Palestinian territories, over 500,000 Israelis were living in an estimated 125 Israeli settlements in the West Bank and 12 neighbourhoods in Jerusalem, and approximately an additional 100 'settlement outposts' on Palestinian land (B'tselem, 2017). Cheek by jowl, Israeli settler and Palestinian were forced to reside in the same small densely populated areas, which, in the case of the West Bank, led to significant loss of geographical contiguity so vital to hopes of statehood post peace agreement. Israeli settlements are considered by the international community illegal, and as a significant obstacle to peace.

Although Israelis may have shopped in Arab towns like Bethlehem, and Palestinian labourers worked on building sites in Tel Aviv, true integration never occurred, mixed marriages were and remain almost unheard of, and a mentality of distrust and mutual antagonism characterized both sides (Milton-Edwards, 2008). For decades, Palestinians and Israelis sought ways to distinguish themselves from each other. Difference was created – whether religious (Muslim, Christian, Jew), ethnic (Jew and Arab), social, linguistic or cultural, through cuisine, dress code, social values, art, literature, media and any number of social rites – rather than mutual bonds to promote compromise.

The Palestinian–Israeli conflict was not just confined to the occupied territories. The culture of hostility spread to all corners of the globe, wherever Israelis and Palestinians resided. In Lebanon, Cyprus, Munich, Entebbe, Rome, London, Algiers, Amman and Dubai, the battle between Palestinian factions and Israel's Mossad wore on for decades. The 1960s, 1970s and early 1980s, while characterized by creeping annexation and political violence within the West Bank, Gaza Strip and Israel, were also marked by acts of terrorism such as bombings, hijackings and assassinations abroad. Following Israel's rout of the PLO from Lebanon in 1982, the Palestinian nationalist movement was weakened and an era of internal dispute and fissure beckoned as the factions of the PLO squabbled among themselves and blamed each other for the Lebanon *débâcle* (Sahliyeh, 1988). In addition, within the West Bank and Gaza Strip a new political force, the Palestinian Islamists – including the Muslim Brotherhood, Islamic Jihad and the Mujama – waged a campaign for political power in Palestinian universities and professional associations, against the nationalists. They quickly established themselves, particularly in the Gaza Strip, as contenders for local power (Abu Amr, 1994; Milton-Edwards, 1996a).

By the mid-1980s, there was growing resentment within the Palestinian community against the Israeli occupation authorities. Any form of political activity was criminalized, the PLO was outlawed, membership of political organizations was punishable by long prison sentences, people were banned from free assembly and public meetings were forbidden. Within Israel, Labour or Likud hegemony in government, which had been established by the 1984 elections, was often immobilized through squabbles between these two sides, while the leftist peace movement which had become so strong during the Lebanon war tried to maintain momentum on the Palestinian issue. The government, however, led by Yitzhak Shamir, remained implacably opposed to the idea of any peace moves towards the Palestinians and remained content with the status quo (Arian, 1989). The settlement by right-wing Likud-voting Israelis continued almost unabated and international censure was ignored. The outbreak of the Intifada on 9 December 1987 was, therefore, inevitable. Throughout the Gaza Strip, the West Bank and Jerusalem, the residents of refugee camps, villages, hamlets, towns and cities rose up in a spontaneous protest against the occupation. The Palestinian community was gripped by one of the most significant social and political revolutions in its history (Peretz, 1990).

The long-term goals of the Intifada were articulated as a desire to end the Israeli occupation of the West Bank and Gaza Strip, and the establishment of an independent Palestinian state (Lockman and Beinin, 1989). In the short term, hundreds of thousands engaged in activities designed to disengage in any way possible from the structures which supported the occupation and to achieve a much greater level of Palestinian self-reliance and independence from Israel. Separation would take a variety of forms, from resignations from employment with the Israeli authorities, to boycotting Israeli-produced goods, displaying the Palestinian flag, organizing marches and demonstrations, sit-ins at human rights organizations, alternative education committees which drew up Palestinian rather than Israeli teaching curricula, and any form of popular culture that celebrated the existence of Palestine as a nation (Nassar and Heacock, 1991).

The Intifada was the most significant indicator of the depth of malaise that had set in during the Palestinian–Israeli conflict. Palestinians, through the framework of the Intifada, indicated that they were rejecting anything that represented Israeli rule or domination over their lives; they were no longer willing to pay taxes without representation, to fund the military occupation of land which they perceived as their own. Until the Intifada, there was every indication that Israel might annex the occupied territories. There is no doubt that the Intifada led Israel to question its hold over the West Bank and Gaza Strip. In 1993, Israel and the Palestinians signed the Declaration of Principles; a timetable for negotiations and interim limited autonomy for the Palestinians ensued.

The Oslo, Cairo and Wye Accords did not guarantee peace, nor were they a peace treaty in themselves, but they irrevocably altered the dynamics of conflict and peace-making between Israel and the Palestinians forever. By 2000, the momentum for peace was halted as a result of both Israeli actions and the outbreak of the second Palestinian uprising – which became known as the al-Aqsa Intifada. Hopes for peace diminished throughout the next decade. The passing of time did nothing to moderate enmity, and in both Israel and the Palestinian territories voters supported more right-wing and extreme elements who were opposed to peace talks. In 2006, Hamas, the Islamic movement, won a majority (Milton-Edwards and Farrell, 2010), and in Israel successive coalition governments have become more and more right-wing. In 2008, 2012, and 2014, Israel and Palestinians in the Gaza Strip were embroiled in violent conflict again and the attempts to broker peace by the international community through forums such as the Quartet for peace seemed futile. As other conflicts and instability increasingly gripped the wider region, the desire to take the steps necessary to promote a resolution to intractable conflict was lacking.

East against West in the Suez Crisis

More than sixty years after the Suez Crisis of November 1956, following the decision of President Nasser of Egypt to nationalize the Suez Canal on 26 July, this conflict may seem irrelevant. Yet it was an important conflict in terms of illuminating the still-enduring relations and involvement of western state actors in the region today. Involving Egypt, Britain, France and Israel, it irrevocably altered regional and international relations. A number of factors have to be borne in mind when reviewing the crisis, including the impact of political personalities such as the Egyptian President Gamal Abdel Nasser, the British Prime Minister Anthony Eden, and President Eisenhower of the USA. The particular personalities of all three men were largely at odds with each other. Other factors include the international nature of this particular Middle East dispute, which brought an Arab state into direct conflict with former colonial superpowers Britain and France. In addition, the Cold War climate in which the war occurred inevitably drew, directly and indirectly, both the USA and the former Soviet Union into this 'local conflict', which in turn had implications for the Hungarian crisis of 1956 (Thomas, 1986, p. 12). Within the region, Nasser's decision to challenge the previous hegemony of the West – or, more specifically, Britain (and France) – changed the pattern of Arab politics, bolstered notions of pan-Arabism and encouraged the nascent movement for Arab independence in states such as Iraq and Algeria.

The prelude to the war over Suez was characterized by Nasser's increasingly belligerent attitude towards the West, and Britain in particular. The special relationship between Britain and Egypt had been under severe strain since the Free Officers coup led by Nasser in 1952. Until that time, the politics and government of Egypt had been dominated by Britain, not Cairo. Under Nasser, however, a quest for neutrality, followed by a challenge to Europe and the rest of the world, would occur. That challenge resulted in the departure of one set of players from the Middle East (Britain and France) but further encouraged superpower rivalry over the region. The challenge to Britain also became personalized, as Nasser attempted finally to sever the knot between Cairo and London, and the British Prime Minister Eden perceived Nasser as 'the new Mussolini or Hitler whose ambitions needed to be curbed, just as Hitler's should have been at the time of the Rhineland crisis in 1936' (Fraser, 2015, p. 68). Yet Egypt, Nasser had determined, was carving a new role for itself on both the regional and the international stage.

Whether Nasser was able to formulate a clear policy on Egypt's regional and international role is disputed, but he was determined to make an impact on the international stage by promoting his leadership of the largest Arab state in the Middle East and his quest for leadership of the Arab world, and by forwarding Egypt as a lead state in the collective and burgeoning non-aligned movement. He was particularly influenced by the Third World context, and impressed by Tito of Yugoslavia's concept of non-alignment – a policy which avoided anti-Russian or pro-western pacts, but did not debar them from receiving aid or purchasing arms from either side. Nasser embraced the concept, found himself a celebrated hero at the 1955 Bandung conference of newly independent Third World states and was encouraged to undertake his next step – the nationalization of the Suez Canal, the final step in Egypt's liberation from British colonial rule.

The Suez Crisis, however, was not just about nationalization, a policy deci-sion taken in light of the funding crisis caused by American refusal to support loans for the building of the Aswan Dam. The decision to nationalize the Suez Canal, which potently symbolized the West (Britain and France) in Egypt, also reflected Nasser's attempt to carve out a fully independent non-aligned role for Egypt on the international stage. As the Egyptian govern-ment faced the tripartite alliance between Britain, France and Israel, the rest of the world waited with bated breath for the outcome of this first direct challenge by a Third World state to the great powers. As a result of a secret agreement between the tripartite alliance, known as the Protocol of Sèvres, it had been decided that, under the pretext of an Israeli invasion and occupa-tion of the Sinai and Suez region, British and French air strikes would be launched against Egypt on 31 October 1956 (figure 4.1), with a land offensive planned for 5 November (Kyle, 1991, pp. 314–31). British and French incom-petence and deception, however, had resulted in the isolation of the USA and the Eisenhower government, which was up for re-election. Eisenhower was outraged at the British and French deception and the attention it was divert-ing from the revolution taking place in Hungary. He urged Eden to act with moderation, stating in a letter to the British Prime Minister, 'you are making of Nasser a much more important figure than he is ... and where we appar-ently do not agree is on the probable effects in the Arab world of the various possible reactions by the western world' (Thomas, 1986, p. 77). Britain ignored the USA and paid a high price, its future as a major power in the Middle East effectively halted by the Suez débâcle.

The Egyptian victory, however, was largely due to the intervention of three external parties: the United Nations, the USA and the Soviet Union. American pressure on British currency reserves, for example, compelled the Chancellor of the Exchequer to advise an end to the British war against Egypt. The United Nations, meanwhile, played an important part in brokering ceasefire agreements and the subsequent deployment of UN forces in the Sinai region. In effect, while Nasser rid himself of one superpower, he saddled himself with another. US policy in the Middle East following the Suez Crisis resulted in an ascendant role, while Britain and France engaged in a bloody departure from the region in Iraq and Algeria.

The Suez Crisis, however, still left Nasser in a fairly strong position inter-nationally and proved extremely useful in his pursuit of domestic and

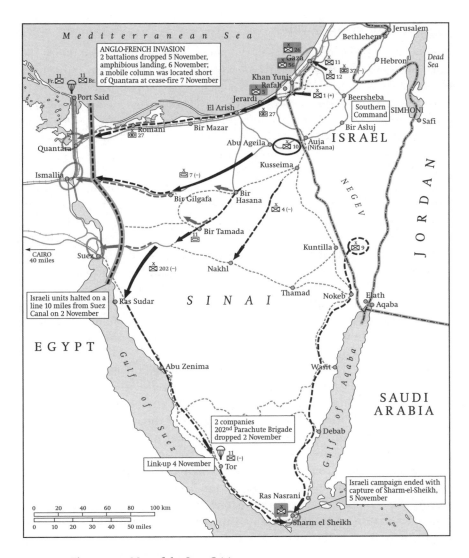

ANGLO-FRENCH INVASION
2 battalions dropped 5 November,
amphibious landing, 6 November;
a mobile column was located short
of Quantara at cease-fire 7 November

Southern
Command

Israeli units halted on a
line 10 miles from Suez
Canal on 2 November

2 companies
202nd Parachute Brigade
dropped 2 November

Link-up 4 November

Israeli campaign ended with
capture of Sharm-el-Sheikh,
5 November

Figure 4.1 *Map of the Suez Crisis*

regional policies. The ideology of Nasserism turned out to be highly popular at home, and across the region radical nationalist Nasserist groups sprang up to challenge the hegemony of British-supported rulers in Iraq and Jordan, as well as elsewhere. Irrespective of his failures in the coming decades, the apogee of Egyptian power under Nasser during the Suez Crisis was never forgotten. As Hopwood remarks, following Suez, Nasser 'stood as a man who had successfully defied the two old colonial powers on behalf of Egypt and the Arab world' (1985, p. 49).

Arab versus Arab

Inter-Arab rivalry is no stranger to the politics of the Middle East. Since the turn of the twentieth century, the leaders of a variety of Arab states have found themselves in competition with each other for political power, territory and control of the region's vital natural resources, including oil and, just as importantly, water. Even in the heyday of Arab unity in the 1950s and early 1960s, when Nasser of Egypt championed the Arab cause and urged his 'brothers' across the region to unite, rivalry characterized relations between most Arab states and even resulted in war in the case of Yemen.

While political rivalry within a region is not unusual or unique to the Middle East, the occurrence of conflict between Arab states has allowed an insight into the regional balance of power. Over the decades, the illusion of unity in the face of a common enemy – Israel – has been used to mask the individual ambitions of political leaders. Behind the façade of unity, a usually more personal or national ambition may be discerned, as Hourani remarks about Nasser: 'the events of 1956 and subsequent years turned Abd al-Nasir into the symbolic figure of Arab nationalism, but behind that there lay a certain line of Egyptian policy: to make Egypt the leader of an Arab bloc so closely united that the outside world could deal with it only by way of an agreement with Cairo' (1991, p. 411).

While it is true that much has united and promoted the integration of the Arab world, two factors in particular have led to divisiveness and even conflict. The first has already been alluded to: the competition for regional rather than just national leadership. The helm of the region, or even a significant coalition of states, has been a prize that many Arab leaders have fought over and, to a greater or lesser degree, continue to dream of. This was the case in Yemen from 1962 to 1967, when the competition for power within the region embroiled both Egypt and Saudi Arabia on opposing sides during the civil dispute. Furthermore, one might argue that this rivalry has played its part in terms of Arab state support and intervention for rebel elements in Syria since the outbreak of the conflict there in 2011 (Glass, 2016). The second factor is linked with the decline of pan-Arab unity and the emergence of greater economic ambitions among Arabs, as demonstrated by the Iraqi invasion of Kuwait in 1990. Indeed, this event could truly be dubbed the 'Mother of all Economic Wars' in the region.

When President George Bush of America opposed Iraq's invasion of Kuwait, he declared that the economic stakes were high. Iraq already possessed the world's second-largest reserves of oil and had more than 1 million men under arms, making it the fourth- largest military force in the world. With the USA dependent on imports for half its oil, it literally could not afford to let an authoritarian leader of a Third World state monopolize control of the world's oil supply. Despite the many other factors cited for the invasion, Iraq's sole goal was economic. Production exceeding the OPEC quota, Kuwait's decision to recall loans to Iraq which had been extended to the country during the war with Iran, accusations of oil-stealing and border disputes all contributed to a list of grievances which Khalidi (1991b) argued 'indicate[d] the existence of a three-decades long background of tension in Iraqi–Kuwaiti relations constituting an extended prologue to the invasion' (p. 64).

Within the region the war ended any illusion of Arab unity as, for the first time in a century, the conservative regimes of the Gulf found themselves supported by radical states such as Syria against their brethren in Iraq. Indeed, the war confounded so-called normal patterns of inter-Arab politics, with, for example, the normally conservative monarchy of Jordan compelled by its own population to side with Iraq. Such short-term decisions had profound long-term consequences for Jordan and its relations with the Gulf Arab states, affecting aid and employment issues, creating a refugee problem and putting pressure on an already weak infrastructure and new domestic political issues at home (Milton-Edwards, 1991). To this day, Jordan has only managed limited repair of relations with Gulf states such as Saudi Arabia. The Arab world appeared to be split fifty-fifty down the middle, in either siding with or opposing Saddam Hussein, and, as Khalidi (1991a) noted, the invasion 'retard[ed] the prospects for the progress and advancement of the Arab world. It squander[ed] the patrimony of the Arab world and divert[ed] attention from the real challenges facing it' (p. 162).

The allied military operation in the early months of 1991, known as Desert Storm, ousted Saddam Hussein's troops from Kuwait, encouraged Shi'a and Kurdish uprisings in both the north and south of Iraq, freed the Kuwaiti oil fields, restored the al-Sabah monarchy and led to UN sanctions against Iraq and to war being waged for the first time ever in the organization's name. The war changed the status quo, with mixed effects felt throughout the region. For the Gulf states, stability was only achieved by the intervention of foreign military support evidenced by US military bases in Saudi Arabia, Kuwait, Qatar, Oman and Bahrain to the present day. In Egypt and Syria the financial rewards were immediate. Yet, more than anything, as Owen notes, the fundamental result of the war was fissure and division within the Arab world, a gap not just between states but within states, with elites and leaders holding different views from those of the Arab masses (Owen, 1991).

Since the 1990s, the effects of the Gulf *débâcle* have remained palpable throughout the region: Saddam Hussein remained in government in Iraq; inter-Arab relations were still soured by the events of 1991 and by the pressures for peace, driven by US ambitions for stability to protect oil in the region; and there was little movement for democratizing forces in the Gulf or Egypt, Jordan, Tunisia or Algeria.

Memories of unfinished business between Iraq and the USA were revived after 9/11 when the neo-conservatives of the earlier Bush administration began to press his President-successor son to set his sights on Iraq. By the spring of 2002, George W. Bush openly declared that regime change in Iraq was now a priority for his administration. When Iraq was invaded in 2003 and Saddam Hussein deposed by the US-led western alliance, there can hardly have been a tear shed in the Gulf capitals of Kuwait City or Riyadh. It was not until 2009 that Iraq appointed an ambassador to Saudi Arabia, and it would be 2012 before Riyadh would reciprocate by appointing an ambassador to Baghdad, who would be the first there since 1990.

The lion and the peacock: Arab–Iranian relations

There is a history of Arab–Iranian conflict in the region that dates back to the power struggles which took place between the Persian and Arab empires of Islam's Golden Age. Through conquest by the Arabs, the Persians adopted Islam. From that point in the eighth century to the rise of the Ottoman Empire in the sixteenth century, the Persians played a minor political and major cultural and religious role in the region. From the sixteenth century, however, the first Persian challenge to Arab authority emerged under the leadership of Ismail Safavi. Not only was Safavi successful in challenging the rule of Constantinople in Persia (Safavid rule 1501–1732) but he associated his rule with sectarian Shi'ism to forge a sense of identity different from Sunni Arab Ottomanism. Islam, then, has acted as a paradoxical force between the Arab and Persian empires, serving on the one hand to unite and on the other to result in important doctrinal splits, such as the Sunni/Shi'a split that has led to enduring tensions over the centuries and open sectarianism in the twenty-first (Abdo, 2016).

In the contemporary era, the Iranians and the Arabs fell under the authority of the colonial powers after the collapse of the Ottoman Empire. However, the colonial experience was not uniform and resulted in further tensions. Under the influence of the Russians, the British and, later, the Americans, Iran became identified with the West, as an agent of imperialism in the region, harbouring expansionist ambitions which were a threat to Arab and other states. The rule of the Pahlavis, from 1925 onwards, was largely perceived as anti-Arab, as the Pahlavi dictatorship increasingly depended on the promotion of a Persian rather than a Muslim sense of national identity to legitimate its rule over an ethnically and religiously diverse population. In addition, the political independence of the Shah was consistently called into question. Yet, as Halliday (1979) remarked, 'the Shah has been neither as independent as he himself claims, nor as reliant on foreign [mainly American] assistance as most of his enemies allege' (p. 21).

In the neighbouring Arab state of Iraq, the experience of rule through a British mandate served to radicalize the minority Sunni population and lead to rejection of colonial interference. Following the first Ba'thist coup, which overthrew the pro-British monarchy in 1958, Iraq promoted itself as a major regional player and secular Arab nationalist state. Holding at bay its majority Shi'a population, as Zubaida (1993) highlighted, for the Sunni minority 'whose traditionally dominant position is threatened by the entry into national politics of Shi'is and

Kurds ... the appeal of Arab nationalism is that it relates the Sunnis to an Arab world in which Sunnis are the predominant majority' (p. 92).

Significant political change in both Iran and Iraq in 1979 led, almost inevitably, to a major war between the two states that would last for nearly a decade (Karsh, 2014). In Iran, the Pahlavi regime, headed by Reza Shah Pahlavi, was brought to a sudden end during the revolution of 1978. By early January 1979, the Shah had fled Iran and in his place the Shi'a clergy of the country, led by the charismatic Ayatollah Khomeini, announced the establishment of the Islamic Republic of Iran. The world was shaken by this revolutionary change and the USA bemoaned the loss of one of its most important client states in the region. The threat of an Islamic revolution washing up on the shores of other states in the area, and the instability and threat to Gulf oil states were deliberated in the West as Iran declared its anti-western and anti-imperialist credentials. In Iraq, Saddam Hussein became President following the unceremonial ousting of Ahmed Hassan al-Bakr who had led the coup of 1968. Saddam Hussein's imprint on politics was immediate: rivals and opposition were immediately imprisoned and executed as rule by dictatorship was almost established. Within a year, the hard-won treaties between Iraq and Iran over sovereignty in the Shatt al-Arab waterway and mutual borders and boundaries would disappear, as Saddam Hussein set his sights on neighbouring Iran.

Conflict seemed the only option between these neighbouring states. Ba'thist Iraq represented the antithesis of Islamic Iran. Politically, economically, religiously and culturally, the breach between the two states appeared insurmountable. Bolstered by western, including American, support, Saddam Hussein ridiculed Iran, and on 20 September 1980 sent his troops to invade the country.

Box 4.2 Ambitious war-aims

Saddam Hussein's war aims were ambitious: first, the battle with Iran was promoted as ideological, the forces of Arab nationalist secularism against Iranian Shi'a Islam; second, there were economic benefits to be derived from wresting control of the Shatt al-Arab waterways from the Iranians and placing them in Iraqi hands, and acquisition of territory in the Khuzistan province of Iran to Iraq's south-eastern border would guarantee additional oil reserves; third, Saddam's actions were supported by the West, which hoped that Iraq could defeat Iran and thus kill the expansionist plans which Iran was perceived as harbouring.

Whatever Saddam Hussein's ambitions, the defeat of Iran would not be achieved as easily or as swiftly as he and the West imagined. The war, as one journalist wrote in the *Guardian* newspaper, became the 'most expensive and futile' in the contemporary Middle East. The statistics were frighteningly eloquent: it was estimated that the two countries were responsible for more than 1 million civilian and military deaths. According to the most realistic estimates, the two belligerents had spent between a third and a half of their national budgets on the war. In all, additional military expenditure, losses in GDP and non-invested capital would reach $500 billion between the two countries. For all that, was this war as futile as the *Guardian* journalist claimed? The absurdity of it did became apparent following a ceasefire accepted in August 1988, and the dramatic 1990 volte-face of Saddam Hussein when he announced that he would return Iranian territory seized in the war of 1980–8 and respect previous agreements over Shatt al-Arab. This grand gesture made a mockery of one of the region's most destructive conflicts, nullifying the loss of life, prosperity and peace.

In March 2015, Saudi Arabia led a military coalition of mostly Gulf Arab states in attacks on Yemen to oust Iranian-allied Houthi rebels who had captured the capital Sana'a and other parts of the country (Laub, 2016). The Houthi rebels had forced the serving President Mansour to flee to exile in Saudi Arabia. Two years on and the Saudi alliance had yet to declare 'mission accomplished' and Yemen was looking more and more like a Shi'a (Iranian) versus Sunni (Saudi-led) proxy battleground. Saudi efforts to restore President Mansour to power had all but failed. In March 2017, Houthi rebels in northern Yemen remained as firmly entrenched as ever. Saudi Arabia's credentials as a Sunni regional powerhouse were looking sorely dented.

The conflict had prompted a worsening humanitarian crisis affecting what is the Middle East region's poorest country. Humanitarian and human rights organizations have censured both the Saudi alliance and Iranian-supported rebels. Saudi Arabia has yet to find a face-saving exit point from the conflict. UN attempts to obtain and maintain ceasefires have resulted in frequent failure. Iran's political and military leadership perceive Saudi Arabia as an increasingly weakened foe in Yemen and are certain that their support will help the Houthis to maintain the strategic upper hand. The notion of a Sunni counterweight in Saudi Arabia to Iran's growing influence has been increasingly questioned as the Gulf and other parts of the region appear to fall under worsening sectarian tension and conflict.

Sectarian politics

Sectarian tension and conflict occur throughout the Middle East. By making reference to conflict as sectarian, we mean that there is a form of communal tension and violence between the sects of a religious grouping. All too often in the Middle East, episodes of religious or confessional violence, in which one faith group engages in attacks against another or targets it, are also conflated with sectarianism. Sectarian dispute between Alawites and Sunni Muslims in Syria, Shi'a and Sunni Muslims in Iraq and Sunni and Shi'a in Gulf states like Bahrain is evident in recent years. Religious conflicts between Christian Copts and Sunni Muslims in Egypt, Jews and Sunni Muslims in

Israel, may all, to a greater or lesser degree, be characterized as sectarian. Indeed, given the importance of the region to the three great monotheistic religions, Judaism, Christianity and Islam, it should not be surprising that an element of sectarian conflict or rivalry has always existed.

Religious minorities of all types have long existed in communities scattered throughout the Middle East, but in the twentieth and twenty-first centuries there has been a tendency to believe that the secularization of the state system and society has diminished the associated tensions. This belief, however, has always been challenged by the politics of confession and sectarianism that has re-emerged as a defining feature in states such as Lebanon, Syria and Iraq.

In the case of Lebanon, it resulted in significant conflict in 1958 and from 1975 to 1990. Civil war in Lebanon was the product of the failure of confessional and consociational arrangements in state and politics to account accurately and fairly for all its religious groups.

The confessional state system established in countries like Lebanon, under the French mandate in the 1920s, privileged one religious grouping over another. This system incorporated the principal religious groups of the country into a state that, in matters of personal status, allowed individual communities to decide, but maintained an artificial Christian political majority position and in the pact of 1943 allotted government posts according to religious group, with a Maronite President presiding over government.

As Gresh and Vidal highlight, the drawbacks to this system of politics are significant, while the 'presidential nature of the regime has accentuated the large hegemony of the Maronites. The country has thus been divided into virtually homogeneous cantons, each cosily withdrawn into its own communal solidarity' (1990, p. 30).

The political system was designed to take account of difference, but some enjoyed more power than others. This assemblage of power made the state weak and created rivalry and competition to advance the interests of one minority over, or at the expense of, another. From 1975 to 1990, this rivalry led to outright civil war in Lebanon. Furthermore the war engaged and drew in outside actors, such as Israel and Syria, that took positions and sided with opposing forces. Attempts at peace-making were then thwarted by internal as much as external factors, and the ceasefire phenomenon was always short-lived (Hiro, 1993).

Since 1990, however, Lebanon has lived under a fragile peace. The 1989 Taif Accords, set up under the auspices of the Arab League (initiated by Saudi Arabia, Algeria and Morocco), formulated an agreement whereby limited reforms to Lebanon's political system were designed to weaken the Maronite monopoly of power and increase Sunni Muslim representation in the National Assembly. The Taif Accords, however, have not solved Lebanon's problems. The state remains weak and the politics of

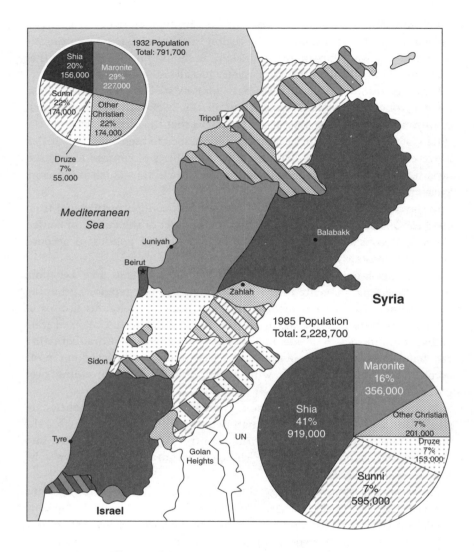

Source: Library of Congress, Geography and Map Division.

Figure 4.2 *Distribution of Lebanon's main religious groups*

confessionalism – which played such a large part in the conflicts and wars of the past – have remained enshrined in a system of government and politics. The new Lebanon has a long way to go before the reconstruction of a national identity which all citizens feel they can share is achieved. In Iraq, too, identity has been subject to tenuous constructions.

With respect to Iraq, Sunni–Shi'a sectarian difference, combined with a Kurdish minority element, has defined the country since its establishment and construction by the British in the early 1920s. Here we see evidence of a privileging of a Sunni minority in power over the Shi'a majority. The majority of Iraqis are Shi'a Muslims (55–60 per cent); Sunni Muslims (30–35 per cent) are the second-largest grouping. Under the Ba'th state led by Saddam Hussein, sectarian difference should have been subsumed under broader national identities and ideological attachment to the Arab socialist project. The constitution should have protected rights equally, but in practice the Shi'a majority (along with others) was subject to systematic persecution by the regime of Saddam Hussein.

In the wake of the US-led 2003 invasion, sectarian violence between Shi'as and Sunnis spiralled. Shi'a politicians took power and revenge cycles of violence occurred across the country. By 2007, sectarian violence had escalated into a civil war. The death toll is estimated in the hundreds of thousands, entire neighbourhoods have been subjected to sectarian cleansing by rival militias. This has led to the internal displacement and creation of an Iraqi refugee population in the millions. Post-2003 elections have led to the installation and monopoly of Shi'a power in Baghdad, with strong leanings to Iran. One response from the Sunni heartlands was an escalation of insurgency and attacks – led by Abu Musab al-Zarqawi in Iraq – against Shi'a targets across the country. The post-war power-sharing mechanism has not contributed to a sense of equality and stake-holding for Iraq's Sunnis. This was clearly apparent in 2014 when the extremist Islamic State group a.k.a. Islamic State Iraq and Levant (ISIL), an al-Qaeda splinter group led by Abu Bakr al-Baghdadi, captured large swathes of Iraqi territory and declared open war on the Shi'a. Iraq remains a deeply fragile sectarian state.

Case study

Egypt and Israel – this is what peace looks like

There is peace in the Middle East. There is evidence that within the framework of the most significant regional conflict – the Arab–Israeli conflict – state actors have negotiated and achieved formal peace treaties. Yet the regional context limits the effects of such peace and has done little if anything to establish a model or momentum for further peace efforts. Nevertheless, it is important to examine one such case study in this chapter.

The Camp David Peace Treaty signed by the leaders of Israel and Egypt on 29 March 1979 marked a significant turning point in the Arab–Israeli conflict and for peace-making in the Middle East in general. Of equal importance was the fact that the world community heralded the treaty as the first sign of peace in the conflict between Israel and the Arabs that, to that point, had lasted more than thirty years. The consequences of the treaty would be momentous, and some declared the 'end of adversary relationships in the Middle East'.

More than thirty years after the treaty was signed, it is apparent that it did not produce a comprehensive peace settlement to the Arab–Israeli conflict. By 2017, only one other Arab state had concluded a formal peace treaty with Israel (Jordan in 1994); other states in the region, such as Algeria, Bahrain, Iran, Iraq, Lebanon, Libya, Morocco, Oman, Qatar, Saudi Arabia, Syria, Tunisia, UAE and Yemen, still refused to recognize the state of Israel.

The peace treaty of 1979 – which America had negotiated – was a document mapping out the future of negotiation between Israel and the Egyptians and provided a timetable for part of them. Issues that were deliberately avoided were to be addressed in the future. Little wonder, then, that fourteen years later, commentators would remark on the resemblance between Camp David and the Oslo Accords signed between Israel and the Palestinians. Obviously, strategies for peace-making between Israel and the Arabs would have a particular character and pattern, choosing the most minor concessions as a starting-block for a protracted, difficult and oft-stalled negotiated settlement. Common security should be the goal that all sides seek in negotiations, but this definition of security between Israel and its allies has been fiercely contested, making any form of negotiation difficult.

The three parties involved in the evolution of this particular treaty, America, Israel and Egypt, each had their own idea of how negotiations should be conducted and what issues should be placed on the agenda. In particular, Israel and Egypt saw the aim of the peace-making process in very different lights. It was the self-appointed job of the Americans, under President Carter's leadership, to seek a workable compromise. Indeed, the Camp David Treaty was described as 'the only case so far in the Middle East in which successful crisis management and resolution ultimately led to conflict resolution' (Yariv, 1992, p. 144). So, the Israel–Egypt peace process highlighted the importance of negotiation and the role of the USA as a Middle East peace broker. From 1973 to 1976, under US Secretary of State Henry Kissinger, a process of 'step-by-step' diplomacy resulted in disengagement agreements between Egypt and Israel. The US administration, fearing the resumption of general hostilities between Israel and the Arabs and the continuation of the oil embargo, was aiming to create a role for itself, while at the same time excluding Soviet influence. The US had vital oil interests in the region – by the 1970s, a third of its oil consumption had to be imported. Kissinger promoted himself as an 'honest broker', but there was considerable criticism of his role in pressurizing Sadat into what were considered concessions in Israel's favour. The American agenda, however, lay in getting Israel and Egypt to make peace without getting mired in the issue of a 'comprehensive' agreement that would have to take account of the Palestinian issue as well. In many respects, America would attempt to replicate this 'broker' role in conflicts and disputes in the region for decades to come, with limited degrees of success. We see the 'broker' model, including attempts to diplomatically manoeuvre Russia out, in US peace efforts under the Obama administration and Secretary of State John Kerry's role in mediating the Syria conflict (Crocker et al., 2015).

Egyptian President Sadat's decision to enter into peace negotiations was influenced by the impact of the military defeat against Israel in the war of 1973. Although Egypt had scored early military successes, President Sadat still had to face up to the loss of Egyptian territory to Israel and the fact that at one point during the war Israeli tanks had reached the suburbs of Cairo. In addition, Sadat believed that Egypt's regional role would be better served with support from the Americans. He knew that, in terms of diplomatic settlement, only the Americans could deliver Israel to him, only America had enough influence over the Israelis to pressurize concessions out of them. Sadat wanted to lure the Americans into a more active role in resolving the dispute. Luckily for him, the pressure of the oil embargo and the orchestrations and moderation of his stated goals were conducive to the realization of at least some of his American-orientated aspirations.

President Sadat's objectives were twofold: first, he wanted a rapid peace settlement because Egypt was becoming increasingly unstable and opposition was mounting from all sectors of society. Second, he wanted to cement an alliance with the USA and was willing to turn all of his predecessor President Nasser's policies on their head in pursuit of this goal. This was demonstrated when in November 1977, against the advice of his fellow Arab political leaders, Sadat travelled to Jerusalem and addressed the Israeli Knesset and declared his objectives for peace. Among the Arab states, Sadat's gesture was treated as one of betrayal. For them, every step taken towards Israel was a step further away from the Arab regimes and their economic and diplomatic support. Nevertheless, Sadat pursued his peace agenda and, in August, President Carter invited him and Israeli Prime Minister Begin to Camp David to discuss a peace settlement.

In contrast to Egypt, the Israeli position from 1973 to 1979 grew from one of low morale to one of power, with Israel eventually holding the predominant position in negotiations. A large part of this achievement was due to the political and diplomatic skills of Israeli premier Menachem Begin and three of his cabinet colleagues – Moshe Dyan in particular. The Begin–Dyan plan was premised on time: they were willing to draw out the peace process, negotiate each point separately, avoiding so-called comprehensive packages and would not countenance, under any circumstances, a Palestinian state in the West Bank and Gaza Strip. There would be a complete diffusion of the peace process, splitting it into three parts: territory, the nature of peace and the Palestinians. For the most part, the plan succeeded, although the Israeli government was placed under US pressure to make certain concessions. Israel, nevertheless, sought American-guaranteed compensation including supplies of oil, an increase in economic and military aid and guarantees that Egypt would not break a peace treaty.

Source: Wikimedia.

Figure 4.3 *Brotherly love*

The peace treaty was a limited success. A state of war between Egypt and Israel halted, territory was relinquished and Israeli settlements in the Egyptian territory of the Sinai dismantled. Diplomatic relations, including embassy and consular representation for each country, were established and limited trade agreements signed. President Sadat paid dearly for the peace agreement, assassinated in 1981 by Islamist extremists opposed to the treaty. Egypt also spent many years regionally isolated by its Arab neighbours, and it was only by the 1990s that Sadat's successor Hosni Mubarak was able successfully to embark on a process of reintegration into the Arab world. For Israel, the treaty did not lead to peace with other Arab states; the domino effect did not take place. Instead, Israel became embroiled in conflict in Lebanon (invading in 1982 and occupying south Lebanon until May 2000), and later faced a full-scale Palestinian revolt – the first Intifada. Since 1979, however, the Egyptian–Israeli relationship is best defined as a 'cold peace'. Relations between the two states and their citizens have rarely been warm. There has been little by way of a peace dividend. In 2011, for example, hundreds of protestors attacked the Israeli embassy in Cairo and diplomatic staff were evacuated by air to Tel Aviv. More recently, only one issue – at the level of state-to-state interaction – has encouraged the two states together and that is mutual security concerns over the threat posed by jihadists in the Sinai. Israel recently granted Egypt an increased security presence in the Sinai to help to combat the mutual threat. However, despite the recent uptick in Egyptian–Israeli security cooperation, progress on other fronts remains almost non-existent, and mutual animosity persists.

Case study

Iraq – enduring conflict

The war in Iraq in 2003 that led to the toppling of the regime of Saddam Hussein has been mired in international controversy and once again placed the politics of the Middle East centre stage in international affairs. The reasons for the war, as cited by the USA and UK governments, hinged on a belief that Saddam Hussein possessed weapons of mass destruction (WMD) that were a direct threat to the West. It was also believed that Iraq had links to al-Qaeda, which in turn had been responsible for 9/11; that Saddam Hussein presided over a regime in which the majority of Iraqis lived in a permanent state of fear; and that, with western support, Iraq could turn itself into a model of democracy that the rest of the region could emulate.

The prospect of waging a war on Iraq animated the whole of the international community in ways that were previously unheard of. Millions demonstrated against the western plan to intervene in Iraq, and certain European governments publicly opposed the USA–UK plan; the work of the western intelligence services, the mission of the UN arms inspectors in Iraq, the legality of such actions all appeared to throw the international community into temporary turmoil.

The war in Iraq is also understood by many commentators as an arena in the American-led and defined war on terrorism that was formulated as a response by the administration of George W. Bush in the wake of 9/11 (Halliday, 2005). According to this thesis, Iraq was quickly identified by American policy-makers and politicians as part of a threat defined by President Bush as 'the axis of evil'. Iraq represented a threat because of the aforementioned links with WMD and al-Qaeda. Moreover, others argued that economic factors also had their part to play as Iraqi oil resources were important to the US energy agenda and hence they remained vulnerable in Saddam Hussein's hands.

This view re-surfaced in January 2017 when President Trump caused foreign policy controversy by suggesting the USA should have kept Iraqi oil after its drawdown from the Iraq war, and stating 'maybe we'll have another chance' at accessing that natural resource. He also claimed Iraqi oil was responsible for the rise of ISIS. 'If we kept the oil, you probably wouldn't have ISIS because that's where they made their money in the first place, so we should have kept the oil, but, OK, maybe we'll have another chance,' he said (@realDonaldTrump, 2017).

Back in 2002–3, the wider geostrategic import for the USA lay in the message that a military success in Iraq would convey to other states and actors that they considered a threat. As Hersh noted in reflecting the view of one US intelligence official, 'This is a war against terrorism, and Iraq is just one campaign. The Bush Administration is looking at this as a huge war zone' (Hersh, 2005, p. 3).

Figure 4.4 *Conflict in a region, British troops and Iraqi civilians.* © *Stephen Farrell*

In the Middle East itself, the prospect of the western intervention in Iraq to topple Saddam Hussein was greeted with almost universal hostility at a popular level, and with some mistrust and suspicion by the leaders of many regimes in the region. A year after the 2003 war, Muslim opinion surveyed highlighted that 'opposition to the war remains nearly universal' (Pew Global Attitudes Project, 2004). The war itself was a relatively short-lived affair. The Ba'th regime was easily defeated by the combined military prowess of the USA and UK but there was a sense of disappointment that the western liberators were not greeted with open arms by the people of Iraq. In the wake of the war, the extent of Saddam Hussein's crimes against his own people was revealed; the reality of western occupation and the scale of reconstruction made themselves felt; security for ordinary citizens diminished; and the political wrangling over the future of the state commenced.

The official mandate of occupation for the American-led Coalition Provisional Authority was short-lived, and its head, Paul Bremer, departed from Iraq in June 2004, leaving power in the hands of a transitional government headed by Iyad Allawi. During the one year of official occupation, however, the security situation, despite the presence of over 100,000 western troops, spiralled out of the control of the governing authorities. Significant parts of the country fell into a security vacuum, and ungoverned spaces appeared over which the western military authorities had no power. Sabotage, looting, kidnappings, suicide bomb attacks on crowded streets, religious shrines and ceremonies, gun attacks on occupation and local police and military forces quickly became the reality of post-war Iraq and hampered reconstruction efforts. Not only did resistance against western occupation quickly manifest but so too, as discussed in chaper 8, did ethnic hatreds and sectarianism.

Allawi's power, however, remained dependent on the continuing military presence of thousands of western forces stationed throughout the country. They, in turn, were viewed as the real tools of power in Iraq and insurgency quickly marred the post-war landscape. For more than a decade, insurgency has expanded and intensified in many forms, including among both Sunni and Shi'a elements in Iraq. Surges have come and gone, American and British troop draw-downs and withdrawals have occurred. The costs of the conflict have been high. Debates in America focus on the costs to the US taxpayer – estimated at more than US$2 trillion. There is also the human cost to Iraqis, along with the regressive effect on Iraq's post-war economic recovery programme.

Initially, the prevailing environment of insecurity did not decrease Iraqi demands for free elections. Free elections for all Iraqis were seen as an important mechanism for increased sovereignty and independence. In particular, the prospect for elections was viewed positively in both the majority Shi'a community and among the sizeable minority of Kurds living in the north of Iraq. When the first elections were held in January 2005, the majority of Iraqis participated in the poll. Only in the Sunni areas, where security fears were at their highest and the greatest antipathy to the western presence has been expressed, was turnout poor. The elections were an achievement in themselves, but they would not be sufficient for political or other forms of stability to emerge in Iraq, nor to serve as a much-touted model for democracy for other states enduring authoritarian regimes elsewhere in the Middle East. It took many months of negotiation among the winning parties to agree on the formula and balance of power among Iraq's many ethnic and religious elements before the formation of the new Iraqi government and legislature was announced in late spring 2005. Ahead of the new government lay the task of agreeing on a new constitution that would be ratified in a referendum to the Iraqi people.

From 2003 to 2010 the continuing presence of western troops in the country, with little indication initially of the exit strategy proposed by the UK and US governments, also led many sceptics to conclude that the war in Iraq had more to do with the wider agenda of the US war on terrorism and the military tactics employed to pursue that war. In June 2003, a senior American official argued that 'the liberation of Iraq is a triumph for American forces' and went on to outline the US commitment to the country in the wake of the war. He noted that the majority of the burden for reshaping, building and redefining Iraq as a modern democratic state lay with the Iraqi people themselves, and affirmed that 'the long-term future of Iraq depends on the establishment of rule of law, representative government, and sustainable economic development' (Larson, 2003).

As noted above, within a few short years, the country was embroiled in major sectarian conflict, and an insurgency against the foreign occupiers had also been mounted by Sunni rebels, including Abu Musab al-Zarqawi, with al-Qaeda in Iraq (AQI) (Kubba, 2010). Successive elections, including those held in 2010 and 2014, have done little to bring much-needed stability to the country. British and American combat troops were withdrawn but conflict and violence still dominates, with the threat that this brings to the wider region, including neighbouring Iran, Saudi Arabia, Jordan and other Gulf states. This was apparent as regional and international actors marshalled to join the alliance against AQI's successors ISIS when it took control of Iraqi territory in 2014 and declared a caliphate. In America, there were fears that once again the USA would be inexorably drawn into the Iraqi maelstrom. Certainly, their role, alongside Iran's, has been decisive in the push by Iraqi government troops against ISIS in Mosul, which commenced in October 2016. The conflict endures.

Case study
Al-Qaeda – the recurrent threat

The existence of a violent radical Islamic group called al-Qaeda, which emanated from the Middle East, only really entered into global public consciousness in the wake of the attacks on major American targets such as the Pentagon in Washington and the World Trade Center in New York on 11 September 2001. But it has remained in public consciousness ever since. In early 2017, for example, al-Qaeda in the Arabian Peninsula (AQAP) called President Trump 'the White House's new fool', following a raid in Yemen in which American military losses and injuries, along with the Yemeni death toll, were reported. The Trump administration have made no secret that it has a national security priority to fight Islamic radicalism in all its guises, including al-Qaeda in the Middle East.

The dimension of political Islam that al-Qaeda are rooted in has been experienced in many parts of the Middle East. What is frequently overlooked in the West is the war against Muslim society in the region conducted by al-Qaeda and their forerunners. In countries such as Syria, Iraq and Yemen where ungoverned spaces flourish, al-Qaeda have successfully rooted themselves. There they have carried out attacks against ordinary Muslim civilian populations, as well as agents of the state or state elites. Such events arise out of a political context that is often characterized by conflict and struggle against the state. Yet al-Qaeda's worldview and ideology are significantly different from other Islamist groups such as the Muslim Brotherhood, which eschews violence, or even groups like Hamas, because they recognize and compete in existing political systems. Indeed, al-Qaeda's leaders have vehemently rejected and harangued the Muslim Brotherhood and Hamas. Al-Qaeda are different because they hold a Manichean view of the local and global universe.

Some authors, such as Hafez, contend that this notion of radical rejection or 'exclusion' has much to do with the nature of the societies in which such groupings have emerged but this is somehow insufficient explanation in accounting for al-Qaeda and their ideology of hate and terror (Hafez, 2003). Al-Qaeda can be classified as a movement of transnational extremism and violence across the Middle East. Their expression of jihad is a violent symbol of the outright rejection of the contemporary Muslim order represented in the nation-states of the region. These nation-states are viewed as anti-Muslim repositories of authoritarian power oriented to the West.

Box 4.3 The advent of transnational terrorism

It is argued that 'al-Qaeda (modern in terms of educational profiles, knowledge and use of modern technology ...) represents a new form of terrorism, born out of transnationalism and globalization. It is transnational in its identity and recruitment and global in its ideology, strategy, targets, network of organizations, and economic transactions' (Esposito, 2002, p. 151).

The ideologues of al-Qaeda – and, in particular, Usama bin Laden and the Egyptian Ayman al-Zawahiri – premised their view of the contemporary context as un-Muslim or pre-pagan. They refer to this context as *jahilli*. They advocate withdrawal from this context and denounce others – including fellow Muslims – as apostates. This radical worldview has meant that the al-Qaeda target list is almost limitless and includes those regimes of the Middle East, such as Saudi Arabia and Egypt, whose leaders they accuse of being apostate supporters of the West. The ideologues of al-Qaeda then provide a theological justification (included in certain fatwa) for their particular brand of violence (Esposito, 2010a).

While it is true that al-Qaeda have been responsible for a great many acts of terrorism committed throughout the Middle East, there may be a danger post-9/11 of putting the blame on them for all such violence. The 'idea that a single man and a single group are behind the current threat is convenient and reassuring ... the creation of "al-Qaeda" as a traditional terrorist group constructs something that can be defeated using traditional counter-terrorist tactics' (Burke, 2004, p. 15). In some respects, traditional counter-terrorist tactics employed more recently in states such as Saudi Arabia, Egypt and Morocco have gone some way in dealing with and identifying al-Qaeda elements. But, conversely, in the wake of the dispersal of al-Qaeda from

TABLE 4.1 Major attacks attributed to al-Qaeda in the Middle East, 2000–2017

Algeria
- **December 2007**. Attacks in Algerian capital Algiers, in which more than 60 people are killed, including 11 UN staff members, when al-Qaeda terrorists detonate two car bombs near Algeria's Constitutional Council and the UN offices.
- **2010**. Al-Qaeda in the Islamic Maghreb (AQIM) launch a series of attacks throughout the year, including one in the Kabilye region that kills and injures more than 35. This affiliate group has launched attacks on targets from 2002 to the present including tourists, government officials, police officers, soldiers and security personnel.
- **January 2013**. AQIM behind attack and hostage crisis on a BP-operated gas plant. Death toll of at least 55 including hostages and militants.
- **July 2015**. AQIM ambush and kill at least 9 Algerian soldiers.
- **March 2016**. AQIM claim responsibility for an RPG attack on an Algerian gas plant.

Egypt
- **October 2004**. A truck bomb attack kills 34 people and wounds 120 in the Hilton Hotel at the Egyptian border resort of Taba and in two other explosions which hit the resort of Nuweiba, southwest of Taba.
- **July 2005**. Car bombs set off in Sharm el-Sheikh, killing 67 and wounding more than 200, including some foreigners.
- **April 2006**. Three bomb blasts in the resort of Dahab kill 20 people.
- **2011–present**. Ansar Beit al-Maqdis, an Egyptian inspired and al-Qaeda-influenced group, based in Northern Sinai, launches a series of attacks on Egyptian targets and claims responsibility.

Iraq
- **2003–present**. Al-Qaeda Iraq (AQI), founded in 2003 and active to the present, infiltrate and organize insurgency and attacks in the country. It is contended that, in addition to attacks on foreign targets, al-Qaeda foment sectarian tensions by attacking the Shi'a population. Major attacks including suicide bombings were organized and led by Abu Musab al-Zarqawi until his assassination by coalition forces in Iraq in 2006.
- **March 2012**. AQI attack on Haditha.
- **July, 2012**. AQI claim responsibility for a range of attacks across the country.
- **June 2013**. AQI 'breaking walls' campaign succeeds with attack on the infamous Abu Ghraib prison to break out militants from the group.
- **2014**. AQI affiliate Islamic State in Iraq (ISI) attacks and seizes Iraqi towns, including Mosul.
- **2014**. Al-Qaeda disassociate ISI – aka ISIS.

Jordan
- **November 2005**. Jordan capital Amman is bombed using suicide bombers targeting western hotels.
- **October 2012**. Jordanian authorities foil major terror plot by al-Qaeda.

Lebanon
- **2007**. Lebanese state forces battle with Fatah al-Islam in the Palestinian refugee camp of Nahr al Bared. Over 400 are killed. The group is believed to be linked to al-Qaeda.
- **February 2014**. Al-Qaeda linked Abdullah Azzam Brigades claim a twin bombing attack in Beirut.
- **January 2015**. In Tripoli, 9 are killed in an attack that Syrian-affiliated al-Qaeda claim responsibility for.
- **June 2016**. In Beirut, a series of suicide bomb attacks are attributed – in part – to claims of responsibility from al-Qaeda affiliate in Syria, Jabhat al-Nusra (Nusra Front).

TABLE 4.1 *Continued*

Libya
- **September 2012**. Al-Qaeda suspected of responsibility for an attack in which US Ambassador to Libya is killed.
- **2012–present**. Al-Qaeda gain a foothold in southern ungoverned spaces in Libya.

Morocco
- **May 2003**. Al-Qaeda attack in Casablanca on 16 May. Suicide bombers using cars or explosive belts set off at least five blasts in Morocco's biggest city Casablanca, killing 45 people, including 13 attackers, and wounding 60 others.
- **April 2011**. Al-Qaeda in the Islamic Maghreb (AQIM) are blamed for a bomb attack which kills 17 in the Moroccan city of Marrakesh.

Saudi Arabia
- **May 2003**. Riyadh: suicide bombers kill 34, including 8 Americans, at housing compounds for westerners. Al-Qaeda suspected.
- **2004**. Al-Qaeda attack on Saudi oil company at the Khobar complex. 22 people killed. Kidnappings and execution of foreigners, gun attacks on foreigners.
- **December 2004**. US consulate attacked in Jeddah.
- **February 2006**. Attack on the Abqaiq petroleum processing facility.
- **April 2015**. Al-Qaeda attack and kill Saudi officers at a border post close to Yemen.

Syria
- **2011–2016**. Al-Qaeda affiliate Jabhat al-Nusra launch a series of attacks against government forces and other armed elements in the civil insurrection and conflict which ensues. Jabhat al-Nusra recruit many foreign fighters from the Middle East and western Europe.
- **2012**. The USA designates Jabhat al-Nusra a terrorist organization.
- **2013**. The organization offers allegiance to al-Qaeda.
- **July 2016**. Announcement that Jabhat al-Nusra in Syria is no longer affiliated with al-Qaeda. This split is seen as nothing more than superficial, with evidence of al-Qaeda's continuing role in the re-branded Jabhat Fatah al-Sham.
- **January 2017**. Jabhat Fatah al-Sham merges with four other jihadist rebel groups in Syria to form Tahrir al-Sham.

Tunisia
- **2002 April**. Explosion of a fuel tanker outside a synagogue in Tunisia.
- **February 2015**. Four Tunisian police officers killed in an attack by al-Qaeda near the Algerian border.

Turkey
- **2003**. Istanbul bombings carried out on 15 and 20 November, leaving 57 people dead and 700 wounded.
- **2014**. Al-Qaeda attack the town of al-Reyhanli near Turkey's border with Syria, leaving 52 dead and 146 injured.

Yemen
- **October 2002**. Attack on a French tanker off the coast of Yemen.
- **May 2012**. Al-Qaeda in the Arab Peninsula (AQAP) kill 120 people during a suicide bombing attack at a military parade in Sana'a.
- **December 2013**. AQAP raid a military hospital and kill more than 56 people.
- **January 2015**. AQAP claim responsibility for deadly Paris attacks.
- **April 2015**. AQAP expand territorial control over the Abyan province.

Afghanistan in 2001, the movement has become more diffuse and difficult to identify across the Middle East. Arabic news media across the Middle East and North Africa regularly report the presence of al-Qaeda elements. Until his death at the hands of US Special Forces in May 2011, it is alleged, cells and branches across the region looked upon Usama bin Laden as 'a symbolic leader' even though they were not necessarily controlled by this powerful figurehead (Burke, 2004, p. 14). In this sense, the symbolic power of al-Qaeda stands in significant contradistinction to acts that are now perpetrated by operatives under the direct orders of the al-Qaeda leadership – wherever they may be. The legitimacy of such violence has been questioned widely within and among Muslim ranks. In Yemen, the proliferation of al-Qaeda, and their growing threat internally as well as internationally, were dramatically underscored in December 2009 when a Yemeni-trained al-Qaeda-affiliated terrorist tried to blow up a US airliner. AQAP claimed responsibility and warned of more attacks to come. In the spiral into civil conflict in Yemen and the Houthi rebel takeover of power, AQAP elements add to the growing collapse of political and civil order.

Al-Qaeda are accused by authors such as Wiktorowicz of having a *salafi* perspective that legitimates such acts of terrorism by relying on the 'Quran and authentic hadiths, citing pieces of evidence according to the Salafi manhaj and praising publications by other well-known Salafis' (2001, p. 22). While it is true that scholars associated with *salafi* thinking in Islam, such as Sayyid Qutb and Ibn Taymiyyah, are alleged to have influenced the ideological imprint of al-Qaeda, this accusation fails to account for the breadth of influence that these thinkers have across the canon of contemporary Islamist thinking. As Doran notes: 'when it comes to matters related to politics and war, al-Qaeda manoeuvres around its dogmas with alacrity' (Doran, 2002, p. 178). This manoeuvrability means that al-Qaeda have come to represent more than the sum of their parts. Much that represents political Islam in the Middle East is now interpreted – both within the region and outside it – within a paradigm over which al-Qaeda have dominated. The statements, actions, ambitions and inspirations of countless Islamic movements are now measured against al-Qaeda to determine the ways in which the governments of the region (and their allies across the globe) should now respond.

The issue here is whether this is the right yardstick for the political expression of a faith system which accounts for the identity of the majority of the region's citizens and the choices that face such citizens in fractured, authoritarian and broken states.

As such, al-Qaeda remain as a marker of violent and extreme conflict on the landscape of the contemporary Middle East. Through their actions in the form of terror attacks in vulnerable states across the region, through their ideas in influencing debates within Islam about the future of the faith in the Middle East, and in terms of a symbol of antipathy and hatred towards that which is considered un-Islamic and sympathetic to the West, al-Qaeda endure

(Esposito, 2010a). While the terrorist threat may be contained, it is in the realm of ideas and symbols that the biggest battle against al-Qaeda in the region may yet take place.

Questions for discussion

- Assess the centrality of the Palestinian–Israeli conflict in the wider Middle East region.
- Is civil war or inter-state war more likely in the Middle East?
- What are the five key ingredients for peace in the region?

Recommended reading

- Debate on the causes of conflict in the Middle East can be found in a variety of texts, many of which are written from a particular perspective – for example politics, international relations, peace studies, economics, history or anthropology.
- Many accounts of the Arab–Israeli conflict can be found. A number of introductory historical accounts are worth citing, including Milton-Edwards and Hinchcliffe (2008), Smith (2004) and Fraser (2015), which give concise overviews of the conflict between Israel and the Arabs since 1948. Schneer (2011) takes the Balfour declaration as a historical marker through which to examine the origins of the Arab–Israeli conflict. Monem (2013) examines the wider dimensions of the conflict between Israel and the Arabs to debate peace-making.
- Spangler (2015) examines the Palestinian–Israeli conflict from the perspective of race, nation and human rights, while Faris (2013) highlights the problems and limits of peace-making and the prospects for a two-state solution to the conflict.
- Turner (2012), Steed (2016) and Jackson (2016) offer some new appraisals and evaluations of the Suez conflict from the perspectives of energy, British political ambition and intelligence, as well as foreign intervention. All themes are apposite for examination in the contemporary Middle East.
- A significant number of texts were published in the wake of the Gulf crisis of 1991, including Gowan (1991), al-Gosaibi (1993) and Gow (1993); valuable readers include Bresheeth and Yuval-Davis (1991), Brittain (1991), Sifry and Cerf (1991) which includes texts of speeches, documents and opinion pieces, and Bennis and Moushabeck (1995).
- The war between Iran and Iraq is the subject of literature on the region, including Cordesman (1987 and 1988), in which the military/security dimensions of the conflict are examined. Michael Evans (1988) and Creighton (1992) examine the political implications of this conflict, with Creighton in particular comparing the war between Iran and Iraq with the 1990–1 Gulf crisis.

- The sectarian and civil dimensions of the conflict in Lebanon between 1975 and 1990 are examined in Shehadi (1988), Fisk (1992), Hiro (1993) and Salem (1995). The future of Lebanon after the conflict is discussed in Collings (1994), Hollis and Shehadi (1996), Young (2010), Llewellyn (2010) and Blanford (2008). Hirst (2010) overviews the implications of conflict in Lebanon for the rest of the Middle East region. Conflict and sectarianism are examined in Salloukh (2015) and Knudsen and Kerr (2012), in the context of post-war Lebanon and its vulnerability internally as well as to the reverberations of sectarian conflict in neighbouring states such as Syria.
- There have been a large number of books authored about the war, occupation and the future in Iraq, including Chomsky (2005) and Hoffman and Bozo (2004). They cover topics ranging from weapons of mass destruction to ethnic issues and governance (Paya and Esposito, 2010). Among the more thought-provoking and informative texts are Dodge (2003) and Tripp (2002), which should be read in conjunction with books such as Feldman (2004) which discusses the ethics of war and nation-building by the West in Iraq.
- On al-Qaeda, there is much material and analysis in Burke (2004) and Bergen (2001), and by extension the debate in Esposito (2002) and Gray (2004) places the issues in comparison to wider issues in modern society. A text by Esposito (2010a) explores the phenomenon of Islam in the post 9/11 al-Qaeda era. Jenkins (2012) examined al-Qaeda to debate its possible decline or the continued impact that the movement has had on the politics of the Middle East. Byman (2015) directs study of al-Qaeda alongside the rising phenomenon of ISIS. Lister (2015) examines the jihadist conflict proliferation in Syria to overview the growing number of groups and rivalries this has evidenced.

CHAPTER FIVE

Past, Present and Future Politics: Islam

Introduction

When the muezzin at the mosque call faithful Muslims to prayer five times a day, they do so in step with a tradition established in the seventh century by an Arabian merchant's son known as Mohammed. Islam is one of the three monotheistic religions founded in the Middle East. The politics of Islam constitute a myriad phenomenon, and are the product of varied social bases across the Middle East and North Africa.

Political Islams rather than political Islam best describes the different kinds of political movements which have emerged in the Middle East over the last century to contest politics in domestic, regional and international settings. Such movements manifest in the formal as well as in the informal worlds of politics. On the street, as figure 5.1 shows, across the Middle East – whether in Fallujah, Basra, Hreit Hreik, Cairo or Nablus – Islamic leaders have influenced responses to Middle East populism, problems of dependency, indebtedness and poverty. In addition, political Islams have consistently tussled with their political opposites – notions of secularized nationalism, which have held the ideological sway over the Middle East. Islam, in response, has gone some way both to accommodate – through notions of pan-Islamism and Islamic nationalism – and to reject this very real challenge.

The two sides to this particular argument are presented by Juergensmeyer, who contends that political Islam has been presented as a form of religious nationalism – 'many Muslim movements are indeed nationalist ... most Muslim activists seem happy to settle for Islamic nationalism' (1993, p. 47). Tibi, who argues the opposite, claims that the call of contemporary fundamentalists 'becomes a call for an Islamic order opposed to the order of the secular nation-state' (1992, p. 183). Al-Azmeh, however, points out that the distinctions are less than clear: 'Be that as it may, a number of conceptual features common to the ideologies of Arabism and Islamism rendered possible the association between them and their occasional power of mutual convertibility' (1993, p. 69).

It would be unthinkable to study the politics of the Middle East without examining or taking into account the impact that Islam has made on the

Figure 5.1 *Shi'a clerics through the ages.* © Stephen Farrell

dynamics and interchange of policy, politics and the state in the contemporary era. In almost every Middle Eastern state, the majority of the population is Muslim. In the twenty-first century, both state and non-state actors
recognize Islam as an increasingly important political force. Islam becomes
coterminous with politics in terms of issues such as the rights of women, the
mistreatment of religious minorities or terrorism. While Islam has always
acknowledged the political as well as the spiritual, many authors argue that
in the twentieth century – because of colonialism, the struggle for independence and establishment of the post-colonial nation-state – a resurgence of
Islam as a political force took place in response to secularization.

The resurgence of Islam, argues Esposito (1992), however, is about its
'higher profile' in political life rather than its absence during previous eras
(p. 11). The revival in political life has also been accompanied by a resurgence
of interest in all things Islamic, from the five pillars of the faith, to its literature, societal and social programmes, relations to folk and Sufi Islam, orthodox literature, law, economic practices and sectarian differences. Frequently
the focus has been on the emergent contest between political Islam and

secularism. In sum, political Islam is as much an internally as an externally driven dynamic force in the contemporary Middle East.

Political Islam, described by Dessouki as 'an increasing political activism in the name of Islam by governments and opposing groups alike' (1982, p. 4), then, is one part of the larger resurgence of Islam and other religions that many authors have argued has taken place in the Middle East and North Africa since the 1970s. The re-emergence of Islam as a potent political and social force came at a time of immense change in the Arab world, following the defeat of the Arabs in the war of 1967 and what has been termed by Fouad Ajami as the 'end of pan-Arabism' (1978). As the Arab secular nation-state and pan-Arabism were discredited and legitimacy undermined, the crisis which emerged 'contributed to the … the rise of an alternative: political Islam', claims Tibi (1997, p. 218). The subsequent relevancy of political Islam, the varying interpretations of its ideologues and thinkers and the formation of many new movements for change became increasingly salient and noticeable. The oft-quoted 'revival', 'resurgence', 'rebirth' or 'return' of Islam as a response to the crisis of identity and legitimacy in the face of the 'humiliating defeat in the war, the loss of Jerusalem, and the occupation of the West Bank, as the western secular model of government failed, was Muslims' only hope' (Esposito, 1984, p. 215). A new generation of political players emerged, challenging the legitimacy of the nation-state and its rulers.

Islam and politics

The participation of Muslims in the political life of a community is perceived as embedded in the religion itself. The Prophet Mohammed set the first example when, following his flight from Mecca in the seventh century, he directed his political energies to the governance of the city-state of Medina, establishing the rules for a political as well as religious community which would later extend its power over other parts of Arabia, and eventually beyond. The growth of Muslim rule in the seventh and eighth centuries promoted a principle to win not just the souls of converts to the faith, but also their hearts and minds. The political expansion of Islam was inextricably linked with the spread of the religion itself, encompassing not only the act of worship and the mosque but all aspects of life – political, legal, economic, cultural and social relations. Under this arrangement, it has been argued, religion and politics became fused, with no separation between the state and the mosque, in the same way that there was no separation between the state and church before the Reformation in Europe.

This view of the inextricable ties between faith and politics has, however, been challenged by Eickelman and Piscatori, who contend that, historically, such linkage was just not present. In addition, Muslim thinkers have always held a 'variety' of views about the relationship between Islam and politics.

Box 5.1 Indivisibility between Islam and politics

Nevertheless, 'the indivisibility of the two realms persists in the study of Islam', creating three significant obstacles, 'exaggerating the uniqueness of Muslim politics, inadvertently perpetuat[ing] "Orientalist" assumptions' and, finally, 'contribut[ing] to the view that Muslim politics is a seamless web'.

(Eickelman and Piscatori, 1996, p. 56)

The religion, however, has always accepted a tradition of interpretation (*ijtihad*) and innovation (*tajdid*), and doctrinal differences and schisms have resulted in differing political practices and approaches. The difference, for example, between Sunni and Shi'a Muslims is reflected in a variety of ways and includes political dispositions. The Sunni–Shi'a split emerged during the contest for succession and political authority following the death of the Prophet Mohammed (AD 632). One faction of the Muslim community was determined to follow the Prophet's most trusted companions, the 'rightly guided Caliphs', under the authority of Abu Bakr al-Siddiq, Umar ibn al-Khattab, Uthman ibn Affan and Ali ibn Abi Talib. Others followed rule by the Prophet's cousin and son-in-law, Ali. A battle between the two camps followed the power struggle that emerged after the death of Othman (AD 656). Ali's (Shi'a) supporters believed that authority should rest with the descendants of the Prophet, not with his companions. Ali's rule, however, met resistance and revolt, led by Muawiyah of Syria, and eventually resulted in Ali's assassination. Nevertheless, the split, which resulted in the first war between Muslims and further splits within Ali's camp (the Kharijites, for example), established modes of rule and political power which represented differing approaches to authority, leadership and the system of politics within the religion. It is claimed that the denominational differences have shaped Shi'a Islamic political thinking – particularly in areas of leadership, politics of opposition and the role of the *ulama* (clergy) in the political as well as the spiritual life of the community.

This period provided the example of many experiences and visions of the new religion, which would guide its followers for many centuries. It encouraged different paths to rule through the example of the Prophet himself (creating the *sunna* – accounts of his acts), the Medinan state, the development of Islamic rule through appropriate political and legal structures, and the success of the 'rightly guided Caliphs' in establishing the rule of Islam over vast territories in the region. Indeed, from the seventh century onwards, Islam was established through successive dynasties that ruled over the region until the 1900s. The Ummayads, Abbasids, Mamluks, Safavids and Ottomans assured the legacy of Islamic rule and incorporated many styles of leadership and systems of governance. The religion acted as a foundation stone for political systems that were widespread and varied. Islamic law remained the legal basis of many of these states, the ruler ruled in the name of Islam, and politics evolved under a system of consultation (*shura*) and councils (*majlis*) in which Muslims could claim representation. Above all, Allah, not the particular leader or sultan of a dynasty or community, remained sovereign.

The impact of the political on the religious and vice versa resulted in a complicated history in which the political hue of Islam assumed greater importance, often in response to a challenge or contest for authority, yet none of this was unusual. The history of Islam and, therefore, of political Islam is one of ebb and flow. Dynamic, turning and reaching out to respond to the passing of history, the followers of Islam have contributed to the development of political systems. Political Muslims have been rulers, the ruled, in government and in opposition, claiming legitimacy in the name of the faith, contesting and protesting against it. The utopian vision of Islam's thinkers, theologians and politicians has led to the development of schools of thought and practice that advocate particular paths or visions of Islam, while also challenging traditional orthodoxy.

At the dawn of the twentieth century, the Turkish Ottoman Empire reached over the territories of the present-day Middle East. The rule of the Ottomans had endured for more than four centuries, yet the impact of global political changes had weakened its defences and its grasp on the Islamic way of life and the example of the past. The security of Islam was weakened as western political ideas were imported almost wholesale, along with the colonial experience that had been established in the region. While the British and the French may have exported Egypt's cotton, in return they imported ideologies and ways of thinking that challenged the traditional orthodoxy of Islam. The traditions of western political thought encouraged the secularization of society, the breaking of bonds between religion and politics, and the notion of rule by the people for the people. In the realm of economics, western philosophical traditions promoted capitalist and other economic agendas, all of which clashed jarringly with the hitherto-held norms which had governed the Islamic world. Muslim thinkers responded by calling for reform, and set about the modernization of Islam with an increasing sense of urgency.

Thoroughly modern Muslims

The modernist trend within political Islam, led by Jamal ad-din al-Afghani, Mohammed Abduh and Rashid Rida, had an important impact on the emergence of a new generation of thinkers and activists who embraced many of the ideas and approaches advocated by these men. Indeed, the very notion of Islamic modernism, as opposed to traditionalism, was in itself revolutionary and acted as a catalyst for change in a number of political arenas. While the pan-Islamic import of the message promoted by the modernists has already been recognized, there are other areas of their work, in particular on the relationship between Islam and the state, theology and politics, modernism and the rights of women, that were also significant in altering or reshaping the political landscape. Indeed, as Esposito (1984) highlights, 'Unlike conservative Muslims, however, Islamic modernists asserted the need to revive the Muslim community through a process of a reinterpretation or reformulation of their Islamic heritage in light of the contemporary world' (p. 47). They created a new space within Islamic circles. As Ayubi (1991) contended, 'whereas the earlier "Islamic reformers" such as Afghani and Abduh were striving to modernize Islam, the following generation of Islamists such as al-Banna and the Muslim Brothers were striving to Islamise modernity' (p. 231).

Although al-Afghani, Abduh and Rida are linked together through brotherly bonds and a sense of sharing the same intellectual roots, the ideas and careers of the three men also reflect the differing approaches they took to the modernist project. In turn, their impact on the political establishment and emergence of a new Islamic project would change the face of Islamism in the region forever. Al-Afghani was a noted activist seeking to turn his ideas into deeds that would help to shape the approach of modern Muslims to the impact of modernization through the vehicle of colonialism. Al-Afghani called for the regeneration of the faith by returning directly to the text of the Koran and casting off the customs of tradition. He also promoted a confidence about the religion as a whole to meet the demands and challenges posed by the new western-based order in ascendance over the Middle East. Kedourie (1992), however, levels a bitter attack against al-Afghani, accusing him of being a charlatan, neither Sunni nor Afghani: 'he cultivated a reputation of Islamic zeal, while he was in fact a secret unbeliever' (p. 80). Yet Kedourie misses the essential point of al-Afghani's appeal; irrespective of whether such accusations were true, national identity, schism or sect were entirely irrelevant to al-Afghani's conceptualization of the modern Muslim project. For him, the politics of identity lay not in nation, state or tribe, or in the difference between Sunni and Shi'a Muslim. The route out of oppression, subjugation and dependence lay, in al-Afghani's opinion, in a rediscovery of a true and pure Muslim identity. The tainted past and decline of Islam was explicable only by acknowledging that the time had come for change, resistance and a return to the faith.

If al-Afghani represented a more activist approach, Abduh's scholarly demeanour and intent allowed the representation of modernist expressionism to filter through the hallowed halls of al-Azhar University. He is described as a 'rationalist who influenced and inspired not only a whole school of thinkers and reformers ... but a number of non-Egyptians and even non- Muslims as well' (Ayubi, 1991, p. 57). Abduh was never the political activist of the al-Afghani mould, and from the late 1880s onwards it is understood that he 'accepted the existing political framework [colonial Egypt] and channelled his energies into religious, educational, and social reform. Nevertheless, it would be disingenuous to assume that he was an apolitical creature without influence' (Esposito, 1984, p. 49). If, for example, politics is about power, and power can be represented at the level of state and society, then much can be made of Abduh's considerable contribution to the debate about the rights of women according to Islam. His work on women and Islam was predicated on reform of outdated practices. Hence, on the issue of polygamy, Abduh argued that, if Islam was a faith based on principles of justice, then 'the ban on polygamy becomes imperative to prevent any injustice towards the wives'. In addition, he argued that modern social, economic and political circumstances meant 'that the practice of polygamy is no longer a necessity or requirement' (Jawad, 1998, p. 45).

If a linkage between this reformist approach to Islam and the state was required, then the impact on legislation in Muslim countries from Abduh's new perspective on issues of arbitration during marriage breakdown and divorce is important. This is the case in Tunisia, which 'was one of the few Muslim countries which decided to introduce legal reform based on Abduh's view of judicial divorce ... Thus, all divorce actions were prohibited, henceforth, from taking place outside the domain of the court', and women were accorded greater legal representation than hitherto had been the case (Jawad, 1998, p. 77). Abduh's fresh approach was a direct result of the modernists' approach to the faith, making it relevant to a modern age, referring directly to the source (the Koran) and moving away from the ornamented traditions and mystique that surrounded the *ulama*, and over-dependence on the authority of the *hadith* rather than the word of God.

Abduh is credited with a contribution to updating the boundaries of modern Muslim scholarship and for a fresh approach to his faith that led his own disciple Rashid Rida to further work under the modernist rubric. Rida, however, can be categorized as a scripturalist modernist representing a trend called *salafi* Islam – meaning, or pertaining to, the good 'ancestral' example and tradition of Prophet Mohammed, his companions and the first four caliphs, rather than the centuries of Muslim rule which followed. Those who invoked *salafi* principles wanted a return to the fundamental tenets that underpinned the faith. In this respect, the *salafiyya* were not primarily political animals, as al-Azmeh (1993) argues: 'salafiyya reformism engaged in theorising the reconstitution of civil society in terms of itself rather than in terms of politics' (p. 65). Rida, as was noted in chapter 2, was the fundamentalist modernist who directly influenced young Muslim activists in Egypt and beyond, and who went on to play such important roles in the reformist wing of modern political Islam: 'Abduh is not normally identified as a fundamentalist but rather as a liberal reformer with a nineteenth-century faith in progress through enlightenment.' Rida, however, promoted a less liberal and more strict version of the modernist approach. Although the heir to the modernist throne, Rida 'developed his own distinctive position and legacy during the thirty-year period after Abduh's death' (Esposito, 1984, p. 62).

Rida's own work reflected more political matters and examined the decline of Islam in relation to the nature of the state and balance of power therein. He recognized that any regeneration of the faith had to be underpinned not only through a revitalized spiritual community but by the state and through the instrument of the legislative process as well. From this starting point, the logical outcome, according to Rida, was a call for a restoration of true Islamic government and the caliphate, as Esposito (1984) notes: 'for Rida the true Islamic political system is based upon consultation between the caliph and the *ulama*, who are the guardian interpreters of Islamic law' (p. 63).

At the time, the modernists failed to inspire a mass movement of Islamic reform, but it would be wrong to underestimate the influence of their ideas on future generations. It is also important to acknowledge the fundamentally important part they played in opening up new fields of debate within Islam at a time in the region when great changes were occurring. Here, Rida's analogy to the lighthouse, which he used in the title of his journal, proves useful. Modernist thinking, while reflecting diverse and individualist approaches, exposed the perilous path of unquestioning acceptance within Muslim societies of the modernization project and accompanying political principles, and revealed Islam as the guiding light for Muslims who were believed to have lost their faith and were out of touch with its true meaning.

Muslim Brotherhood

This organization founded by Hassan al-Banna in 1928 would have an immense impact on the revival of Islam and the resurgence of Muslim political thought. As Zubaida (1993) points out, 'This is the movement, which, in one form or another, has been the most prominent fundamentalist current in Sunni Islam' (p. 47). Hassan al-Banna and others, such as Sayyid Qutb, would help shape the political response of Muslims throughout the region (and beyond) to the forces of capitalism, materialism, colonialism, sovereignty and secular nationalism. The Muslim Brotherhood has faced successive attempts by such ruling regimes as those in Egypt and Syria to eradicate the force of political Islam that they represent (Milton-Edwards, 2016a). The movement persists to the present day and has continued to promote a message that has won many millions of supporters and the ire of many state actors (see table 5.1).

The idea behind the organization was very simple, and this may explain the endurance of its populist appeal for the better part of ninety years. Hassan al-Banna and his followers expounded a message that promoted Islam politically, religiously, economically, socially, legally and culturally as the only alternative to the forces of westernization, secularization and materialism that had penetrated Muslim society in the Middle East. They argued for the wholesale adoption of Islam.

TABLE 5.1 The Muslim Brotherhood in the Middle East

Egypt	Founded in 1928, has been subject to state repression and banning. In the wake of the Arab Spring in 2011, the Muslim Brotherhood contested and won legislative and presidential elections. President Mohammed Morsi was deposed from power in August 2013. In December 2013, the military-backed government declared the Muslim Brotherhood a terrorist organization.
Syria	Branches established in the 1930s. Played a limited part in parliamentary life until Ba'th coups of the 1960s. In 1982, the Assad regime perpetrated a massacre against activists in the Syrian town of Hama.
Jordan	Branches established in the 1940s. Loyal opposition throughout the 1950s to 1980s. Contested elections since 1989 with varying degrees of success under the Islamic Action Front (IAF). In 2016, authorities closed down the Muslim Brotherhood in Jordan but IAF contested legislative elections.
Palestine	Branches founded in the 1930s and 1940s. Hamas described itself as part of the Muslim Brotherhood. Hamas won the majority in the 2006 Palestinian legislative elections. Since 2007, Hamas has ruled the Gaza Strip.
Morocco	The Justice and Development Party (JDP) is considered an affiliate of the Muslim Brotherhood. The JDP supports Islam and democracy and has served in government since 2011.
Tunisia	The Muslim Brotherhood-inspired Ennahda has embraced democratic politics and played a significant part in the transition in the wake of the Arab Spring.
Libya	Branches established in the 1930s, with initial close ties with Egyptian neighbours. Forced underground by the regime of Gaddafi. Since the collapse of the Gaddafi regime in 2011, the Muslim Brotherhood has attempted to reconstitute its organization. In 2012, it announced the formation of a new political party called the Justice and Construction Party. It subsequently competed in and won seats to the Libyan legislature.
Algeria	Branches established in the 1950s. In the 1990s, following the announcement of elections, the Muslim Brotherhood organized as the Movement of Society for Peace (MSP). Remained an active Islamist presence and supported the ruling coalition. In 2015, the MSP engaged in preparations to re-position itself and create distance from the ruling regime.
Saudi Arabia	No formal branches permitted, but the Saudi regime had tolerated the presence of Muslim Brotherhood members since the 1950s, until, in 2014, it announced that the Muslim Brotherhood was a terrorist organization.
UAE	Al-Islah group considered an affiliate of the Muslim Brotherhood. In December 2014, the UAE declared the Muslim Brotherhood and its local affiliates a terrorist organization.
Kuwait	Muslim Brotherhood elected and acts as part of the parliamentary opposition.

(Continued)

TABLE 5.1 *Continued*

Bahrain	Contested and won elections to the legislature as the al-Minbar Islamic Society. Since 2011, the ruling regime has relied on al-Minbar and the *salafi* society, Asala, to counterbalance the Shi'a opposition. Despite pressure from Saudi Arabia and the UAE, rulers in Manama have not declared al-Minbar a terrorist organization.
Yemen	As the Islah Party, the Muslim Brotherhood in Yemen has contested elections and formed tactical alliances with populist leftist elements. After 2011, Islah pursued opportunities for political power, and joined the coalition government. Following the Houthi takeover in Yemen, Islah was targeted and its offices seized.
Iraq	Branches active from the 1940s to 1970s. The Brotherhood was revived post-1991. After the fall of Saddam Hussein, the party re-emerged as one of the main advocates of the country's Sunni community. It was sharply critical of the US-led occupation of Iraq, but participated in elections. In Kurdistan, too, affiliates of the Muslim Brotherhood are active.
Lebanon	Known as Al Jama'a Islamiyya, the Muslim Brotherhood in Lebanon first founded branches in the 1960s. After entering into electoral alliance with Saad Hariri's Future Movement, the party enjoyed limited polling success in local and national elections.

The strategy for promoting this message would be influenced by the hugely charismatic al-Banna until his death in 1949, and would change following the ideological split within the Egyptian movement. Under al-Banna's leadership, the Muslim Brothers' strategy focused on a gradualist-reformist approach which continued to emphasize the need, previously advocated by Rida, to return to the roots of the religion, to the Koran, the Prophet and the Golden Age of rule under the 'rightly guided caliphs'. The strategy was not modernist in the sense that Islam should embrace western political thought, innovation or technological expertise and reformulate itself. Rather, its response lay in the rejection of these alien tendencies and in the promotion of traditional Islam. The Muslim Brotherhood eventually incorporated politics into its strategy, as well as the option of jihad as an act of defence against aggression. Following al-Banna's assassination by Egyptian secret police, the strategy of the movement was reassessed.

Throughout the 1950s and 1960s, internal debate and dispute centred on these issues and resulted in a split, with one tendency supporting the radical agenda of Sayyid Qutb and another pursuing the gradualist approach promoted by al-Banna in the first years of the Brotherhood and carried on by his successor Hassan al-Hudaibi.

When Hassan al-Banna and his supporters established the movement, their aim was to create a mass-based populist organization that would encourage Egyptian Muslims to renew their interest in the faith of Islam. The principal aims of the society at this time were not political but religious, although politics could only help to influence and shape people's ideas. Thus, through a rapidly expanding network of mosques, clubs, reading and discussion groups, public prayer meetings and sermons, clinics, hospitals, schools and income-generating projects, the Brotherhood impacted on Egyptian society and its individuals; the politics would follow later.

This strategy, as Zubaida (1993) highlights, was innovative, looking to the populist base, 'the common people'. The networks established by the Muslim Brotherhood in the 1930s and 1940s earned the title 'state within a state', and in countries like Egypt they withstood the radical changes of government, persisting through many decades. As Kepel (1994) asserts, these networks (now apparent throughout the Middle East) 'play an essential part in assimilating those elements of the population who aspired to taste the fruits of modernity and prosperity but could not get them' (p. 24).

The first step taken by the Muslim Brotherhood was to persuade people to return to the practice of Islam and to educate them in its ways. Al-Banna started on the premise that Muslims must return to their faith in its fundamentalist context. Thus, his first message was one of preaching and education (*da'wa wa tabligh*) to encourage people back to Islam, to teach them how to appreciate its message and the alternative it promoted. For ten years, the Muslim Brotherhood established branches throughout Egypt, Palestine, Jordan and Syria, with the principal aim of educating people in the ways of Islam. The Muslim Brotherhood taught the illiterate to read, learning from the Koran. In each mosque where the Muslim Brotherhood was able to preach, its activities also included lessons in Islamic practice, the pillars of the faith and sometimes debates about politics, law, social issues and economics. The young were identified as an important target, especially those recently educated men who aspired to liberation from colonial rule. Little distinction was apparently made by class, background (urban or rural) or education, as the Muslim Brotherhood attracted new recruits to its movement.

The second step, later advocated by al-Banna and adopted by many but not all branches throughout the region, was to agitate for political change, to undermine the existing political order and contest the legitimacy of those who claimed to rule in the name of Islam. While the strategy of education and social reform was maintained, some within the movement, including radical thinkers like Sayyid Qutb, argued for a more politically proactive path to bring about the societal change which was needed to resurrect Islam. This step met with resistance from the post-colonial nationalist governments of the 1960s and 1970s that ruled over large parts of the Middle East. The potential of the movement to destabilize powerful Arab states like Egypt was precipitated by the Six Day War of 1967 and the crisis of identity that subsequently swept the Arab world.

Sayyid Qutb had promoted this approach within the Muslim Brotherhood. A prolific author, he was imprisoned by the Egyptian authorities in 1954 and executed in 1966. Influenced by Hassan al-Banna and the Pakistani Islamist Mawlana Mawdudi, Qutb made a major contribution to contemporary Islamic thinking and inspired a number of region-wide Islamist groups. As Ayubi (1991) notes, 'Qutbian discourse ... tends to influence people's thought and action in a psychologically tense way that creates in the individual not the ability to reconstruct reality but rather the dream of breaking with that reality' (p. 141). These groups fuelled an important change in the direction of Islamic politics, propelling it into an activist revolutionary realm based on change through jihad.

Qutb's analysis of Egyptian society focused on the nature of decline into a state of chaos, paganism and disorder known within Islam as *jahili*. The only route out of the decline, argued Qutb (1988), was revolutionary and some-times violent. He advocated jihad as the method of liberation: 'The truth of the faith is not fully established until a jihad is undertaken on its behalf among the people ... a struggle to remove them from this state (jahili)' (pp. 8–9). Qutb's call reflected a change in the ideology of political Islam. As Kedourie (1994) remarks, for Qutb it is Muslim rulers, above all, who are 'infected with the spirit of idolatry ... They are apostates from whose deadly clutch Muslim society has to be saved' (p. 333). While Hassan al-Banna had argued for gradual change from within society, Qutb called for disengage-ment and even the overthrow of power to establish the Islamic state. The Qutbian perspective proposed an Islamic order, established through struggle and the politicization of the religion.

There are many interpretations of Qutb's impact on Islamic politics. Sivan (1985) argues that his message contained 'violence of tone and urgency ... [addressed] to his fellow Muslims who were tempted and even brainwashed by western ideas' (p. 24). This particular liberation theology has been classi-fied as fundamentally violent. Yet Qutb himself is more circumspect, neither ruling violence out nor actively advocating it. The 'martyrdom' of Qutb, at the hands of the Egyptian state, only served to emphasize the durable nature of his message, which has persisted and inspired Islamic groups in the con-temporary era. The radical agenda that eventually characterized Qutb, its hostility to the West and fear of tyranny from within, became the starting point of many extremist groups. As Esposito (1992) points out, Qutb's influ-ence (along with others) can be seen in 'the two options – evolution, a process which emphasises revolutionary change from below, and revolution, the violent overthrow of established systems of government' (p. 129).

The Muslim Brotherhood endured in the wake of the death of these impor-tant leaders and ideologues. Today, in the region, it remains an important – if divisive – element of political Islam. Its leaders are convinced that they will continue to play a fundamental part in shaping political discourse in the twenty-first century. Yet events in the wake of the Arab Spring have not augured well for the Muslim Brotherhood. It was the best-organized opposi-tion element in states like Tunisia and Egypt. However, their ascension to power through the ballot box has been less than easy. In the case of Egypt, the startling reversal of fortunes brought about by the state forces of General al-Sisi against the Muslim Brotherhood in August 2013 has severely debilitated the movement not only in Egypt but elsewhere in the region too (Milton-Edwards, 2016). Today the Muslim Brotherhood's future is subject to the deep hostility that it tends to elicit from a range of states in the Middle East. This is only ameliorated by the degrees of popular support that it is still capable of commanding.

Fervour

From the 1970s onwards, the phenomenon of political Islam was perceived as veering to the path of revolution rather than evolution. Academic literature and popular media increasingly portrayed Islam as violently fundamentalist or radical. Sayyid identifies five issues that accounted for this so-called rising new phenomenon: the 'end of secular Arabism', an increasing tendency by governments towards authoritarianism, the impact of economic crisis in the region, the 'crisis of the petty bourgeoisie', and the culminating cultural effects of the West on Muslim societies. As Sayyid remarks, 'these five arguments are those most often deployed to account for the rise of Islamism', yet, as he continues, 'why have these problems met their response in the form of Islamism?' (1997, p. 26).

The answer was never going to be easy, and was made even more difficult by the emergence of a narrative in which

> **Box 5.2 Instigators and protagonists**
>
> Islam and Muslims are portrayed as the instigators and protagonists in fourteen centuries of warfare. Islam is the aggressor ... Islam and the acts of Muslims are described as aggressive – responsible for attacks, jihad and conquest – while the West is described as defensive, responding with counterattacks, crusades, and re-conquests.
>
> (Esposito, 1992, p. 178)

Fierce debate and controversy have also surrounded the process of labelling Islam in its contemporary condition. To date, a number of definitions have emerged which in turn indicate particular views of Islam. These perspectives are variously described as orientalist, neo-orientalist and apologist. There are a number of definitions which may support one particular perspective over another.

Fundamentalist Islam is defined by Beinin and Stork as a phenomenon that may be 'compared to politically activist, socially conservative movements mobilized by revivalist Christian, Jewish and Hindu identities'. In addition, they argue that it may be defined as representing 'the restoration of a pure unsullied, and authentic form of religion, cleansed of historical accretions, distortions and modernist deviations' (1997, p. 3). Despite this definition, Beinin and Stork reject it as unhelpful when looking at Islam. They prefer a definition of political Islam which writers like Ayubi (1991) suggest 'tend[s] to emphasize the political nature of Islam and to engage … in direct anti-state activities' (p. 69).

Other authors, however, prefer to ascribe the following explanation.

Box 5.3 Cutting edge

… the radical end of the spectrum [of Islamic revivalism] (which encompasses more than just 'extreme radicals' or terrorists) … is only a part of a whole, but being the cutting edge of the Islamic resurgence – its most creative and consistent expression – it may also tell us something about the revival movement as a whole.

(Sivan, 1985, p. xi)

This view sees all Islamic politics as being radical, associated with violence and terror. As Miller claims, 'in Islam's war the end justifies the means. Radical political Islam placed atop these societies in the Middle East has created a combustible mixture' (1993, p. 33). An Islamic state, meanwhile, represents theocratic, conservative, radical, anti-democratic and violent politics. Islam, from this perspective, became commonly associated with a threat to the international order. Bernard Lewis echoes this perspective, declaring that 'the Muslim world is again seized by an intense – and violent – resentment of the West. Suddenly America has become the arch-enemy, the incarnation of evil, the diabolic opponent of all that is good, and specifically for Muslims, of Islam' (1990, p. 53).

This is a view that, under the administration of President Donald Trump, has been apparent in extreme form. A hostility to Islam and a designation of the faith that equates its believers with violence and terrorism became a central platform of the populist agenda of politicians like Donald Trump, and European populist leaders such as Marine Le Pen and Geert Wilders. In February 2017, de Bellaigue summed up the new mood in the following way:

Box 5.4 Ya-boo sucks to Muslims

Naming the enemy, calling a spade a spade; yah-boo-sucks candour is the special pride of those leading the anti-Muslim charge. These also include Trump's chief strategist Steve Bannon, … as well as Wilders, who has compared Islam to a 'totalitarian ideology aimed at establishing tyrannical power'.

(2017).

To suggest, therefore, that something called Islamic fundamentalism exists is both right and wrong. It is right, in the context of a literal sense, that, as authors such as Zubaida argue, any Muslim who is a believer is a fundamentalist because by believing they accept the fundamental tenets or principles of their faith. However, is it right to categorize all politically active Muslims as fundamentalist in the sense that it is commonly understood in the West? Since the early 1980s, thousands of articles, news items and books have appeared in Europe and the USA describing a phenomenon known as fundamentalist Islam. This fundamentalism is manifest in the news pictures of self-flagellating Shi'a in Lebanon and Iran, and is associated with the violent atrocities carried out by groups such as ISIS and al-Qaeda. Bearded fanatics, wielding guns, punching the air with their fists populate this particular fundamentalist landscape. Syria, Iraq, Iran, Afghanistan, Algeria and Sudan are the backdrop for a supposed tidal wave of fundamentalism washing up on the shores of the Middle East since 1979. Some authors, such as Halliday, remind us, however, that it has also suited some Islamists – such as those in ISIS or al-Qaeda – to encourage such fear, doing much to create and perpetuate mutual suspicion and hostility between, to quote Anderson, two 'imagined communities': the neo-Crusader West and the Muslim fundamentalist East (Halliday, 1996, p. 110).

The current populist stereotype has been constructed with little acknowledgement of the true breadth of activity and opinion in a movement for political change which has spread throughout the Middle East and North Africa. While stereotypes do have their uses, in this instance they only serve to reinforce Islamophobic discourse, representing the 'other' as completely negative. As Said (1981) angrily declares, 'All discourse on Islam has an interest in some authority or power' (p. xvii). While Said alerted people to the dangers of Orientalism, the resurgence of Islam and the interest in this phenomenon expressed in the West serves to remind us that the debate is far from over. Indeed, Said argued that *Homo islamicus* does not exist, that it is nothing more than a western invention, in an era in which 'Islam is defined negatively as that with which the West is radically at odds and this tension establishes a framework radically limiting knowledge of Islam' (Said, 1981, p. 155).

Islam – or, more specifically, political Islam – is thus consistently portrayed as a negative 'signifier' (Laclau, 1996). Political Islam and Islamism have become 'bad', argues Hamid and Ruekert:

Box 5.5 Bad Islamism

[b]ecause the Islamists we hear about most often are those of ISIS and al-Qaeda. Most Islamists, however, are not jihadists or extremists; they are members of mainstream Islamist movements like the Muslim Brotherhood whose distinguishing feature is their gradualism (historically eschewing revolution), acceptance of parliamentary politics, and willingness to work within existing state structures, even secular ones. Contrary to popular imagination, Islamists do not necessarily harken back to seventh century Arabia.

(Hamid, 2015)

Equally significant about this debate is the impact that this has on general perceptions of political Islam, and the specific impact that these views have on the policies of governments involved with the Middle East.

The debate about political Islam, therefore, has an extremely important bearing on trade policy, arms sales, counter-terrorist strategies, diplomatic relations and the balance of power in the global order. The West, far from appearing indomitable, is vulnerable to a perceived threat from the funda-mentalist Arab heartland and this weakness is exploited on all sides. Islamo-phobia is fuelled by western governments, the media – particularly in the USA – and popular culture. This in turn makes the Middle East – birthplace of Islam – the locus of Islamophobic discourse. For example, in the 2016 American presidential election campaign, Beydoun contends that Islamo-phobia played its part in the victory of President Trump. 'From start to finish, the 2016 presidential election vividly revealed that Islamophobia is alive, and potent and politically resonant as ever. Scapegoating Islam and vilifying Muslims was far more than merely campaign messaging; for Donald Trump it was a winning strategy' (2016).

As a body of post-orientalist writers emerges, so too does a difficulty in accepting 'fundamentalism' as a useful label for describing a political phe-nomenon manifest in the Middle East. Aware of the diverse nature of the current Islamic revival, authors like Guazzone, Ayubi, Esposito and Piscatori embrace the more narrowly defined terms to describe the movement of political Islam, whether referring to the Wahabi state of Saudi Arabia, the Muslim Brotherhood in Jordan or the government of Iran. These terms aid us all in more accurately representing other polities, cultures and traditions, while going some way to avoiding the trap of neo-Orientalism.

To date, the debate remains as current as it ever was and has led scholars into fierce combat with each other. Islam has been and remains, in its politi-cal dimension, a widely varied and important phenomenon. Neo-orientalists have sounded the alarm at the new threat to global peace and harmony that is the 'Green Peril'. As Turner points out, this version of Islam is 'defined by a limited, but highly persistent, bundle of interpretative themes which have the effect of bringing into question the authenticity of Islam as religion and culture' (1994, p. 67).

Arab Spring and Islamist Autumn

Political Islam is but one of a multiplicity of factors that have emerged to challenge the hitherto stability and prevailing resilience of a variety of authoritarian regimes in the region. Furthermore, there is no single variety of Islamism that can be used to account for the Arab Spring. Assigning politi-cal Islam its place in the Arab Spring is difficult and complex and not at all as simple as some commentators or pundits would have European audi-ences believe. This is because of the complicated and dynamic role played by a variety of actors, usually – though not exclusively – residing within the Islamist spectrum.

Firstly, political Islam was relatively absent from the Arab Spring. This proved somewhat of a surprise for those pundits and academics who have long described the Arab world as in the grip of Islamists. The banner of Islam was but one of many under which protestors rallied. For example, in Yemen in its capital Sana'a, where thousands set up tents in 'Change Square' to mobilize for the removal of President Saleh, we witnessed the representation of a truly diverse spectrum of Yemeni society, and not just Islamists. Certainly, the members of the Deaf and Dumb Youth Revolution Alliance, the 'Actors' tent and 'Diplomats' tent were not calling for an Islamist theocracy to replace the regime. Here, Islamism in its many varieties was compelled to reside among a plurality of interests and groupings that today represent Yemeni society.

Islamists, of course, played their part in the unfolding events, but it was not centre stage. Indeed, the call for democracy, constitutional rule and multi-party elections heard in the demands of Arab protestors was and remains markedly dissimilar from violence-based radical jihadist agendas commonly associated by the West in the post 9/11 era with the politics of the Arab world and Islamism. Nevertheless, such demands have not meant the wholesale rejection of Islamist discourses in favour of a region-wide embrace of secularism or western democracy templates. For this approach, too, had failed to bring freedom to the majority Muslim populations of the Middle East, and indeed had been hijacked by some incumbent tyrants to try to legitimate authoritarian rule.

Hence, political Islam has become one part of a multi-dimensional constituency that emerged to demand and agitate for change. Arab protestors have expressed a new discourse based around more equalizing notions of power, democracy and citizenship. Islamists who desire power have had to be responsive to such demands.

The Arab Spring and Islamist input have also demonstrated an iteration of the plurality within Islamism. No single Islamist group can claim a monopoly. This is a plurality within a plurality compelled to recognize the challenge of other discourses within Islamism, as well as the possibility of alliance-formation with political and social elements outside it. Post-revolution Tunisia, for example, illustrates this point. Since the fall of President Zine El Abidine Ben Ali, Islamists in the Ennahda movement and fundamentalist Salafi elements vied with each other to establish and register new political parties. The Tunisian transition has led to electoral success for Ennahda but power has been achieved through coalition with centre-left secularists. This is a reminder that the Arab Spring is no triumph for the utopian political vision that Islam is the solution. The boundaries of the nation-state remain intact and mainstream Islamists have largely remained content to work within them. This has also been a form of Islamism tied to a demand for democracy, and even the Islamist demand for *shari'a* states is disappearing as a result (Roy, 2012).

The issue that preoccupied the West remained violent Islamism. Indeed, among some western opinion, there was scepticism that, even if Islamists had not led the Arab Spring, they would take control and bring with them their jihadi violence. Yet, in part, the initial multi-faceted manifestation of Islamism confounded expectation, not least of all because the jihadi threat represented by al-Qaeda, and its networks in the region, appeared to be largely marginal. When revolt and revolution came, they were not led by al-Qaeda. Their leaders did not mobilize the popular Muslim masses who have challenged authoritarian regimes across the region.

While the objective of reform or regime change may have been one that was widely shared by the people of many states in the region, the jihadists with their violent means for change were largely rejected. In its mainstream representative form, political Islam has played a non-violent, rather than terrorist, part in the Arab Spring. To a certain extent, this demonstrated that al-Qaeda had failed to accommodate itself to the new realities created as much by its fellow Islamists as by any other incumbent regime or emergent social and political forces in the Middle East.

It is as if al-Qaeda, ideologically tied to the greater jihad against the USA and Israel, had simply overlooked the pressures, misery and constraints that millions of Arabs had lived under in the wake of 9/11. Yet, in so many ways, it was the protesting populace of the Middle East that had paid the price for al-Qaeda's fanatic rendering of Islam. It should be noted that an important, yet often overlooked, dimension of the Arab Spring is that most of the region's jihadi groups had actually created a disconnection from the very constituency they claimed to represent and broke the domestic link with the local political and economic struggles of the peoples of the Middle East. The Arab Spring demonstrated this.

The impact of jihadi violence and terrorism in the region only added to the domestic tyranny and militarization that most citizens of the region were forced to endure. This was particularly true of the post-9/11 era in which the state in the Middle East employed counter-terrorism and security measures as a means of suppression and denial of the rights and freedom which subsequently motivated the millions to mobilize in the rebellions that have characterized the Arab Spring. Of course, there are other factors which account for this seismic change in the region, but the point here is that jihadi violence against the citizens of the Middle East created the excuse for the employment of hegemonic power utilized by the state to target such citizens again and deny them their rights.

In terms of being effectively responsive to the Arab Spring, it is apparent that jihadi elements like al-Qaeda and its offshoots in AQIM, and AQAP, and the nascent Iraqi and Syrian offshoots in Jabhat al-Nusra and ISIS, could only bank on the failure of the transition across the region. Where states failed, became fragile and the transition was neglected or lost momentum, such elements violently exploited the situation.

Furthermore, as rebellion and protest ensued as part of the Arab Spring, there was initial silence from the normally vociferous jihadi ideologues. The Arab Spring appeared to take these ideologues by surprise. Contrary to expectation, the vanguard of the revolution in the Arab world has not been the radical bearded 'mujahids' who for decades promised to bring down apostate or *jahili* regimes, but largely urban-based young people who have no common cause with such ideologies.

Though the same 'enemy' was being challenged, the jihadis could not claim the events of the Arab Spring as their own. Even in Syria where, as noted above, by 2013 al-Qaeda affiliate Jabhat al-Nusra had become an increasingly entrenched part of the rebellion against the regime, it was but one of the potential challengers – alongside the Syrian Kurds, the Free Syrian Army, Palestinian elements and others – to any post al-Assad dispensation and newly emergent regional security order. So, even though violent extremists in groups like al-Qaeda and ISIS eventually had something to say about the Arab Spring and have become a dimension of the regional fallout in states like Syria, their attempts to claim such revolts have largely run aground.

So, what can we discern from the politics of transition and the place of Islamism? The orientalist trope of a region defined by bearded fanatics and their jihadi cultures of anti-Westernism were absent in the images projected of the popular mobilizations that unfolded in Tunisia, Egypt, Libya, Bahrain, Yemen, Syria, Jordan and elsewhere. The images on television and computer screens were in fact very ordinary, prosaic and all too easy to relate to – of people like 'us' who wanted freedom and democracy. There were no mobs filmed in Arab capitals burning American flags. The Arab Spring was taking place in the name of freedom and democracy, not jihad.

Nevertheless, Islamists are playing an important part in the politics of transition. They have proved to be the electoral victors in places like Egypt and Tunisia, and such outcomes have caused disquiet. Yet their success was explicable for reasons which have little to do with radical jihadi agendas and more to do with the politics of opposition and the resonance of their long-standing social conservatism. What is further apparent is that, since December 2010, the different trajectories of the Arab Spring have also impacted political Islam.

Transition and revolution are apparent in North Africa – yet there are only some superficial similarities between the outcomes, in Islamist terms, in Tunisia, Egypt and Libya. Elsewhere in the region, in the Levant states such as Syria, the role of Islamists has been manifest in a civil insurrection that metastasized into a sectarian revolt, proxy war and a new jihadist theatre that encompasses a broad array of Islamist actors on all sides of the conflict (Lister, 2015). In the Gulf states, the portent of popular mobilization was not lost on the region's rulers. The role of Islamists in the majority of Gulf states has been severely curtailed. Additionally, Gulf states – including Saudi

Arabia, the UAE and Qatar – have played key roles regionally in variously supporting the suppression of Islamist actors or in encouraging them in wider sectarian battles involving hostile competition with Iran.

Thus, the people's revolt across the Middle East presented challenges to political Islam. For decades, Islamists promised that 'Islam is the solution' and that their agendas could tackle the major socio-economic and political grievances of the people of the region. They promised also that their struggle had a transcendent quality that could unite the Muslim *umma* in jihad to obtain their objectives whether it was for an Islamic state in Egypt or the end of Israel's occupation in Palestine. Such promises have been received as a major threat sparking a counter-revolutionary and reactionary swing in states across the region, but most noticeably in Egypt under General, and then President, el-Sisi.

The transition heralded by the Arab Spring, however, is already proving by necessity to be a long and complicated affair and the effects not only have

Figure 5.2 *Young and at prayer, a future for Islam.* © Stephen Farrell

been domestic but clearly have had strategic region-wide and international implications as well. We can see that Islamists have been presented with as many challenges as opportunities as a result of the Arab Spring. Hence political Islam has its place in the transformations wrought by the Arab Spring, and it is to its most violent and extreme manifestation that most western attention has been paid.

Case study
The Islamic Republic of Iran

The mass-based revolution in Iran in 1978–9, which culminated in the exile of its monarchical ruler the Shah in January 1979, is commonly described as an Islamic revolution. In addition, the new political order which followed the departure of the Shah, led by the Shi'a leader Ayatollah Khomeini, has been characterized by theocracy rather than democracy or other types of rule. The establishment of the Islamic Republic of Iran in 1979 also heralded a new era in Islamic politics across the Muslim world. Whether Iran served as a model for Islamic revolution is debatable, because, as Ehteshami (1995) reminds us, 'the emulative potential of the Iranian "Islamic" revolution model was stunted. This does not mean, however, that at some future date and under the right circumstances it could not offer, at the very least, inspiration to other "Islamic" revolutions in Africa or Asia' (p. 199). These factors – revolution, theocracy and the Iranian model – have been perceived as important in understanding the nature of political Islam, the politics of the Middle East and the political character of the region in the twenty-first century.

The Iranian revolution was the culmination of decades of misrule, abuse of power, modernization for profit not welfare, and increasing foreign – particularly American – interference in the politics, culture and economy of the country. Spiralling economic and social problems were compounded by the Shah's increasing propensity to coercion as a means of rule. Iranians, irrespective of class, ethnic or religious background, or political differences, were increasingly aware of the immense wealth the country was generating and the growing indebtedness of ordinary people who failed to benefit from the Shah's programme of economic expansion and westernization. In addition, as Esposito (1984) highlights, 'Military and economic dependence were matched by progressive westernization of Iranian education and society. Religious and lay people shared a common concern about cultural alienation' (p. 188). From this body of concerned citizens, a number of thinkers would emerge, including Mehdi Bazargan, Ali Shariati and Ayatollah Khomeini – the 'symbol and architect' of the revolution. The contribution by figures such as Shariati in giving a voice to the discontented of Iran should not be underestimated. His thinking and ideas straddled the secular and sectarian worlds of Iran, combining reformist thinking with pure Muslim ideals, and he has been

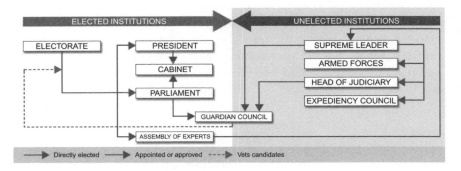

Source: BBC, http://news.bbc.co.uk/1/shared/spl/hi/middle_east/03/
iran_power/html.

Figure 5.3 *The power structure in post-revolutionary Iran*

described as 'an innovative Islamic thinker who stood in sharp contrast to the traditional religious interpretation of the *ulama* and the westernized secular outlook of many university professors' (Esposito, 1984, p. 193). Following Shariati's death in 1977, however, it was Ayatollah Khomeini who would harness Iranian opposition and determine its Islamic character in revolution. The religious character of the revolution makes it unique and distinguishes it from other revolutions in the contemporary era. In addition, other features, such as its 'reactionary, non-materialistic and anti-history' character, mark it out from the so-called ordinary business of overthrowing one existing political order and replacing it with another (Halliday, 1996, p. 44).

Post-revolution, with the establishment of a new state structure, Khomeini offered a vision for politics, advocating the abolition of the monarchy and political rule, and government by the Muslim clergy. This conception of leadership set Khomeini apart from other Islamists. He believed that the political rule best suited to an Islamic state included the clergy in key positions, a rule 'of Divine Law as interpreted and applied by the Just Faqih' (Zubaida, 1993, p. 17). Not only did this conception of rule empower the Shi'a clergy, but it also involved the Muslim people in the matter of rule and government and required their total obedience. Khomeini and his supporters succeeded in promoting this vision, and although the revolution involved all sectors of Iranian society in ousting the Shah, it was Khomeini who won the battle to direct the political future of the country.

The state system which emerged from the revolution was Islamic in character and theocratic in style (see figure 5.3 above). In addition, it was anti-western, anti-Soviet, anti-Israeli, opposed the claim to Islamic rule by leaders in Gulf states such as Saudi Arabia and Kuwait, and embarked on the entire reform of Iranian society. Whether Iran itself qualifies as an Islamic state is considered by some to be questionable. As Zubaida (1997) asserts:

Box 5.6 Imposed symbols and empty rhetoric

We shall see that the basic processes of modernity in socio-economic and cultural fields, as well as in government, subvert and subordinate Islamization. The Islamic authorities are often forced to adapt their policies and discourses to practical considerations. 'Secularization' has not been reversed, but disguised behind imposed symbols and empty rhetoric.

(p. 105)

Nevertheless, an Islamic state ruled by Islamic leaders was the goal for which Khomeini (until his death in 1989) and his supporters strove. The first decade of the republic was characterized by the zealous rhetoric and Islamic agenda-setting that would set Iran apart within the region. It is worth remembering, however, as Abrahamian (1989) highlights, that in many respects the real revolutionaries of 1979, the mujahideen, were all but eliminated by Khomeini's 'populist version of Islam' (p. 1). His agenda met with varying degrees of success.

Indeed, the era following Khomeini's death has been termed by writers such as Ehteshami as Iran's 'Second Republic', one characterized this time by the following features: accelerated economic and political reform, improved international and regional relations, and better cultural and social conditions. Evidence of such changes can be discerned in 'the leadership style of Khomeini's heirs, the content of the policies of the post-Khomeini leadership and the ways in which their policies differ from those of the Khomeini era' (Ehteshami, 1995, p. xiv). This change in affairs, however, should not be mistaken for a 'second revolution' or a change in the outwardly Islamic character and image which the Iranian Republic seeks to promote, both at home and abroad. Iran's leaders still struggle internally to balance the call for theological purity with improvements in real economic terms among the country's population. Increasingly, Iranians have demanded greater democratic practice and economic benefits, but the ability of the political authorities to deliver is highly questionable.

Difficulties at home can only mean difficulties abroad. The fears of the international community in the 1980s that Iran would inspire a tidal wave of Muslim revolution sweeping the entire Middle East proved fallacious. The model proved far too unique and sectarian in character to inspire the majority Sunni Muslim population of the region. The Islamic Republic of Iran, however, has emerged as a significant actor in the Middle East and has vied, in particular, with Arab Gulf states, for influence and impact. Moreover, successive US administrations grappled to contain Iran. In 2005, George Bush described Iran as the 'world's primary state sponsor of terror'. International sanctions had long been imposed on Iran, especially in relation to fears over its developing nuclear capacity. Inevitably, given the history of post-revolu-tionary US–Iranian relations, the issue has drawn in and mired other actors and regional dimensions have been added (Chubin, 2010).

It would be a decade before any diplomatic progress ameliorated such a view. In April 2015, Iran and world powers concluded the P5+1 Iran Nuclear Deal. Iran was committed by the deal to reducing its nuclear ambi-tions, and in return related sanctions would be lifted, which would release tens of billions of dollars in frozen oil revenues and other assets (Kaussler 2015). The certainties of the deal were shaken to some extent in the wake of the 2016 election victory of Donald Trump. President Trump made no secret of his hostility to Iran, and this chimed with the perspective held by the Israeli government headed by Prime Minister Netanyahu. Iran has also become significantly embroiled in the Syrian conflict by siding with President al-Assad along with the Russians. In Yemen, the Houthi rebels that took power have been supported by Iran. These instances of action in the region have played their part in the escalation of major sectarian tensions between Iran and its Arab Gulf state neighbours (Bahgat, Ehteshami and Quilliam, 2017)

Back on the domestic front, the Islamic Republic has entrenched, but is not immune to protest and opposition. Significant political controversy erupted over the results of the 2009 presidential elections, with popular protest erupting onto the streets of Iranian towns and cities. The pro-tests were violently suppressed by Iranian state forces but nevertheless found support among elite leaders such as former President Rafsanjani. Opposition tensions have continued to simmer, casting the stability of Iran into some considerable doubt. Iran remains a significant example not only of theocratic statehood in the Middle East, but of the broader manifestation of political Islam in state form, domestically and in terms of foreign policy.

Case study

ISIS – the case of the 'so-called Islamic state'

It started in the summer of 2014. Do we remember the ice-bucket challenge and viral contagion associated with it? Do we remember that Ed Sheeran's 'Sing' (with Pharrell Williams) was battling it out with Sam Smith's 'Stay with me' for the number one spot in the singles charts? The gossip magazines covered a feud, but it wasn't Islamist – this was one between Beyoncé and Kim Kardashian. At the same time that all that summer fun was taking place, a hitherto virtually unknown group called Islamic State of Iraq and Levant – *ad-Dawlah al-Islāmiyah fī 'l-'Irāq wa-sh-Shām* – a.k.a. ISIL, ISIS or Daesh, was conquering a third of Syria, a quarter of Iraqi territory and threatening the latter's capital city Baghdad. All of a sudden, TV screens and social media feeds jumped alive with talk and images of tens of thousands of fleeing Iraqi soldiers and terrified persecuted citizens – many of them from religious (including Christian) minorities. Then came the killing.

There are many perspectives from which to study the phenomenon of ISIS and, in the scholarship to emerge since the organization took control of territory in Iraq and Syria and declared a caliphate, it has been examined in relation to: social media, Islamism, gender, home-grown terrorism, foreign fighter flows, regional foreign policies of the Middle East, international relations and power balances, migration and refugee crises, culture and politics, state-formation, and the resilience of the nation-state in the Middle East. There is more. It has been examined within debates about proxy wars and conflicts, anti-terror legislation, drone strikes, air strikes and the legacies of the wars and occupations by the West in Iraq and Afghanistan, the Arab Spring, human rights and international norms, and the war on terror.

In this respect, we can contend that the ISIS phenomenon and responses to it are deeply symbolic of a number of features as they relate to the politics of the contemporary Middle East. For the purposes of this case study, we will examine three factors as they relate more specifically to discourses about political Islam and the Middle East region. Evident, then, is a phenomenon that is: terrorist, insurgent, governing power, home-grown and foreign, has enjoyed territorial control, generates sectarian conflict, and is resource-rich (human and economic). It is, also, Islamist. We need, however, to understand the genesis of this phenomenon in terms of its status within the spectrum of political Islam and how representative it may be with respect to discourses and debates about Islamist threats in the post-9/11 era.

Source: Wikimedia.

Figure 5.4 *The 'flag of ISIL' with the 'seal of Mohammed' design*

ISIS begins and is found among those motivated by a very specific set of hybrid extremist *salafi*-jihadist beliefs (Kepel, 2006). Its origin also lies within al-Qaeda in Iraq (AQI), led by Abu Musab al-Zarqawi, which in turn was one part of the violent insurgent – and then sectarian – Sunni and Shi'a response to US-led western occupation from 2003 onwards. The rise of ISIS in Iraq is accounted for in relation to the vacuum created in the wake of the US withdrawal in 2011. ISIS was able to achieve territorial control due to weaknesses within the Iraqi army, structural and other, the political outworking of sectarianism under Prime Minister al-Maliki, hostility from Baghdad towards Sunni majority regions such as Anbar, and lack of coordination between the Iraqi army and other armed forces, including Kurdish Peshmerga. In the Syrian civil war, ISIS first emerged as one among other Sunni *salafi*-jihadist and other rebel forces (Lister, 2015). It engaged in fierce rivalry and then domination over such forces, including Jabhat al-Nusra. By 2014, up to 50 per cent of Syria was under ISIS control, with regions and cities such as Raqqa considered formidable strongholds.

ISIS is inspired by specific ideologues of extremist salafist-jihadist thinking and antipathies to others, including other Sunni Muslim believers. It has declared open sectarian war on Shi'a Muslims and other religious minorities and groups. It has declared Arab regimes and their leaders apostate. ISIS calls for jihad and declares it an obligation (*fard ayn*) for Muslims. In this they have appealed to Muslims to enjoin them in their cause from many parts of the globe (Byman and Shapiro, 2014). They want to be dominant over other competing jihadist groups. ISIS is headed by Abu Bakr al-Baghdadi who emerged as a leader of al-Qaeda in Iraq around 2010. On 29 June 2014, ISIS declared a caliphate and al-Baghdadi as Caliph. It seeks to eradicate the pre-existing nation-state system in the Middle East. Furthermore, its goals are dynamic and evolving and include local, regional and increasingly global dimensions. These goals are often acted upon concurrently; they may be both proactively and reactively pursued and re-assessed in light of developments.

ISIS violence is manifest in a variety of ways. ISIS leaders legitimate violence as part of a political goal. It is simultaneous over more than one sovereign jurisdiction, including Iraq (weak state), Syria (weak state), and beyond where sovereignty is weak, failing or failed in the Middle East and West Asia. Its violence is also multi-faceted, public and performative. It employs violence as a force to subdue populations and exert a monopoly of control – militarily in contest against other armies and national militaries, as an insurgent in violent outbidding and rivalry, as a sectarian against Muslim co-religionists and others. It engages in gender-based violence as part of its violent discourse and modus operandi.

ISIS also employs forms of political violence that define it as a terrorist group: they deliberately target civilians – local populations as well as, more recently, in transnationally organized and executed attacks on civilian targets. ISIS terrorism instils fears among a number of 'audiences'. Its terrorist acts have included mass rape; massacre of minorities; suicide bombings; using civilians as human shields; the beheading of western and other – including Arab – hostages in graphic, public, propagandist fashion designed to establish fear, their power (communicative dimension), and to recruit and warn. ISIS breaks international, national and Islamic norms in its use of violence.

The security response to ISIS is complex. There is a consensus that ISIS has made an array of enemies locally, regionally and globally, both Muslim and non-Muslim, Islamist and secularist, theocratic and democratic, western and eastern. On the ground, for example, ISIS have contended with counter-offensives from local and regional state and non-state actors, including the Iraqi state and its armed forces, Popular Mobilization Units, Syrian state forces, Iran, Kurds, Yazidis and Alawites and Shi'a. Additionally, other jihadist rebel elements and insurgent groups in Syria have fought against them.

This means it faces an array of forces against it and fighting it on a variety of fronts: on the ground, economically, diplomatically, through military action, surveillance, etc. By 2017, the counter-offensive against ISIS had begun to pay off. Large swathes of Iraq were liberated and ISIS-controlled territories in Syria were also vulnerable. Iraqi Prime Minister Haider al-Abadi – supported by Iran and the US-led Operation Inherent Resolve – has risen to the challenge of defeating ISIS. What is less certain is the future of such countries after ISIS is defeated. ISIS is unlikely to fade away and will continue to threaten security in the Middle East and other regions of the globe, including Europe.

Case study
Palestinian Islamists – Hamas

In 1987, following the outbreak of the Palestinian uprising against the Israeli occupation, a new Islamist movement was established. The organization was called the Islamic Resistance Movement, its Arabic acronym was Hamas (Milton-Edwards and Farrell, 2010). Since its birth, Hamas has proved a formidable Islamist actor and has played an important role in shaping the Palestinian–Israeli conflict and the way in which it can be resolved. Some authors define Hamas purely as a terrorist movement (Schanzer, 2008). Its suicide bombers have claimed hundreds of Israeli lives and undermined prospects for peace between Israel and the Palestinians. Others highlight that Hamas symbolizes political Islam in other ways (Gunning, 2007)

The agenda of Hamas – initially encouraged by the government of Israel, as a foil to the popular support engendered by the PLO – is Islamist and nationalist at the same time. Hamas is also as much a movement against the social forces of Palestinian secularism as against Israeli occupation.

When Hamas was first formed, it wanted to compete on an equal basis for popular support under the framework of the uprising. The movement organized strikes, special committees for education, welfare, and policing and first aid. Hamas was able to mirror the activities of the nationalist movement while making a bid against the PLO's claim to be the 'sole legitimate representative' of the Palestinian people. It effectively challenged the last bastion of effective nationalism in the Middle East, in its Palestinian guise.

Since the late 1980s, Hamas has established a large organizational structure. The political, military, welfare, educational, religious and fund-raising activities of the organization have spread throughout the Palestinian territories. Hamas supporters are in most schools, universities, hospitals, professional associations and businesses. Hamas also builds and runs its own mosques, which also serve as libraries, sports centres, classrooms and kindergartens. As many observers are fond of stating, Hamas provides something for everyone, from the cradle to the grave. Political support for the organization has fluctuated, largely shaped by external changes, such as the Gulf crisis of 1990–1 and the Declaration of Principles signed by Israel and the PLO in 1993. Nevertheless, the organization has become a part of the political fabric of Palestinian society, and won elections to government in 2006 (Milton-Edwards and Farrell, 2010).

Over time, Hamas has changed. Initially, Hamas was the product of the Islamic revival that took place in the Gaza Strip and West Bank in the early 1980s. From that period to 1987, the Islamic movement preached a reformist agenda and concentrated on social, education and welfare issues. Its political wing concentrated on discrediting the secular nationalist ambitions of the PLO. The Islamists were more likely to wage a campaign for the re-Islamization of society than to organize demonstrations against the appropriation of Palestinian land or the building of illegal settlements by Israel.

After 1993, when the PLO signed up for peace settlement negotiations with Israel, the strategy of armed violence by Hamas against Israel was criticized. Indeed, the issue turned on whether Hamas was innately violent. The violence that Hamas has engaged in has included armed attacks against Israeli soldiers and civilians, suicide bombing campaigns and rocket fire from the Gaza Strip on Israeli targets.

Hamas leaders claim they are waging a legitimate war against a foreign occupation and that a Hamas attack on Israeli civilians is no worse than Israeli soldiers who kill Palestinian civilians in far higher numbers (Milton-Edwards and Farrell, 2010).

In terms of popular support, Hamas has maintained a large constituency of followers among Palestinians. They have supported Hamas for a variety of reasons. In part, Hamas wins support because of the negative effects of the PLO's reputation for corruption and its failure to progress peace negotiations with Israel. Supporters also admire the commitment of the Hamas leadership to continuing armed resistance against Israel's illegal occupation of Palestinian land. Others subscribe to Hamas because they believe in its Islamist character.

This support was evident when Hamas won the Palestinian elections of 2006. That support did not translate into cooperation from their rivals in the PLO. The international community responded by demanding that Hamas comply with three principles: recognize Israel, denounce violence and respect previous agreements. Hamas – as a resistance organization – said it could not give up on the Palestinian right to resist. The international community withdrew aid support from the Palestinians. In 2007, inter-Palestinian relations had deteriorated to an all-time low and Fatah was routed from the Gaza Strip leaving Hamas in charge. Aid assistance resumed to the Palestinians in the West Bank but not to the 1.9 million Palestinians living under Hamas rule in Gaza.

From 2008 to 2014, the citizens of the Gaza Strip endured three major military assaults by Israel in its attempt to contain or destroy Hamas. Thirty years after it was founded, the Palestinian movement for political Islam has tenaciously endured, but it has had to do so through some considerable compromise. In 2017, for example, it agreed to a pact with its old enemy Mohammed Dahlan, in order to ensure its survival as a governing force in the Gaza Strip. Yet, it can still count on the popular support of Palestinians who subscribe to its ideology.

Questions for discussion

- Explain the resurgence of Islam.
- What can we learn from states governed according to Islam?
- Is the era of populist Islamic radicalism over?

Recommended reading

- Currently, there is a vast amount of literature on the phenomenon of Islam and politics in the Middle East. The most comprehensive introductory accounts can be found in Milton-Edwards (2004) and Esposito (1984). The handbook edited by Shahin and Esposito has an impressive array of chapters authored by leading scholars in the topic, such as Margot Badran on gender and political Islam (2016). A text edited by Euben and Zaman (2009) offers readers a chance to access the writings of the most prominent Islamic leaders and thinkers of the modern age. Accounts of Muslim politics by Eickelman and Piscatori (1996) and Zubaida (1993) are particularly useful, as they analyse popular forms of politics as well as government and institutions.
- The state and politics dimension of Islamism has occupied many writers, including Piscatori (1986), and Jaadane writing in Luciani (1990). Beinin and Stork's (1997) reader on political Islam covers a diverse range of subjects from economy to Rai and Rap music, civil society to Shi'ism in Lebanon, and parallels Guazzone (1995).

- Roy (1994) on political Islam questions its saliency in the contemporary Middle East. A. S. Ahmed (1992), Ahmed and Donnan (1994) and Sayyid (1997) debate extensively the impact of Islam on postmodern thinking, including cultural and post-colonial theories. Aspects of this subject are also covered in Choueiri (1990), al-Azmeh (1993) and Salvatore (1997).
- On the Muslim Brotherhood, Hassan al-Banna and the Qutbists, interesting insights can be garnered from Mitchell's classic study of the Muslim Brotherhood (1969). Milton-Edwards (2016) examines the Muslim Brotherhood in the wake of the Arab Spring across the Middle East. Tadros (2012) and al-Arian (2014) provide very helpful historical analysis of the Muslim Brotherhood, especially in the Egyptian context.
- Contemporary thinking on Islamic fundamentalism and the debate on Islamism, and the threat it either does or does not pose, may be found by reading Ramadan (2012), Hamid and Ruekert (2014), Osman (2016) and Roy (2017).
- On the Iranian example, a number of excellent texts can be found, including Afshar (1985), Arjomand (1988), Abrahamian (1989), Zubaida (1993) and Ehteshami (1995). Aspects of Shi'a politics are also examined in Saikal (2015), as well as Ansari (2017), Tabaar (2017).
- Scholarship on ISIS is relatively incipient but it is well worth reading Cockburn (2015) and Lister (2015). Gerges (2017) gives a strong account of the rise and growth of ISIS. McCants (2015) offers an overview of ISIS in terms of its strategy and apocalyptic visioning.
- On Hamas, read Milton-Edwards and Farrell (2010), along with the work of Gunning (2007), Hroub (2006) and Tammimi (2007). Texts by Roy (2013), Dunning (2017) and Mukhimer (2016) offer specific analysis and insight on Hamas, particularly in the context of its governance of the Gaza Strip, or in terms of social service.

CHAPTER SIX

The Ephemerals of Democracy in the Middle East

Introduction

Democratization, political liberalization and the promotion of liberal democracy in the Middle East became the catchwords of the 1990s, and were subsequently resurrected in the wake of the US-led invasion of Iraq as a post-bellum justification for deposing the regime of Saddam Hussein, and in the wake of the Arab Spring in 2011. In many respects, the Arab uprisings were termed the 'pro-democracy moment' of the region in the twenty-first century, heralding what many believed might be a new era of politics.

Democracy promotion has been a way in which the West has once again used its economic and political influence in the region: 'in virtually every case', as is argued in *MERIP* (*Middle East Report*), reforms (liberalization or democratization) 'have been abetted by the intervention of institutions representing international capital' (*Middle East Report*, 1992, p. 4). The drive towards democracy and associated freedoms and rights has presupposed the absence of democratic trends in the region that is borne out in surveys such as those of Freedom House, which in 2016 described the Middle East and North Africa region as having the worst freedom ratings in the world. (See table 6.1.)

There is also a belief in the incompatibility of Arab and Muslim ideologies with accompanying notions of freedom, pluralism, participation, equality of opportunity and justice. As Bromley (1997) notes, the conventional view is that 'democracies are strangers to the Middle East … The limited post-independence experiments with democratic politics did not survive the rise of nationalist forces seeking modernization and independence, or were thwarted by monarchical rule and oil wealth' (p. 329). In the 1990s, the path of democratization was seen as a positive phenomenon with accompanying social and economic preconditions which should be encouraged in the region, albeit in a piecemeal rather than wholesale fashion. Such thinking lay at the heart of European Union democracy promotion efforts (Börzel et al., 2015).

In reality, however, many have ruled out any prospect for democracy, arguing that the combined forces of Arab and Muslim political cultures promote the region as an exception to the global movement. These

TABLE 6.1 The democracy deficit in the Middle East and North Africa 2017

Country	Status
Algeria	Not Free
Bahrain	Not Free
Egypt	Not Free
Iran	Not Free
Iraq	Not Free
Libya	Not Free
Oman	Not Free
Qatar	Not Free
Saudi Arabia	Not Free
Syria	Not Free
UAE	Not Free
Yemen	Not Free
Jordan	Partly Free
Kuwait	Partly Free
Lebanon	Partly Free
Morocco	Partly Free
Turkey	Partly Free
Israel	Free
Tunisia	Free

Source: Freedom House, *Freedom in the World 2017*

culturalist arguments then lead to a concept of exceptionalism: 'the idea of an Arab or Islamic exceptionalism has thus re-emerged among both western proponents of universal democracy and established orientalists, and this in turn has encouraged a great many local apologists of "cultural authenticity" in their rejection of western models of government' (Salame, 1994, p. 1).

An example of a proponent of the traditional orientalist perspective is Bernard Lewis (1993a) who has argued that the gap between western and Arab notions of 'freedom' highlights the antipathy of Arab culture to democracy. Indeed, it has been judged by a variety of authors (Huntington, 1984, 1993; Kedourie, 1994) that the political, economic and cultural conditions prevalent in individual states of the region (bar Israel) did not go any way towards encouraging the development of liberal democratic models of government and politics. The countries and political cultures of the region were largely viewed as weak, unstable, lacking in unity, authoritarian and lacking political legitimacy. Such authors contended that processes of modernization recognized as conducive to democracy had broken down, encouraging only limited opportunities for political participation in the Middle East.

Indeed, even within the modernization approach, there was still room to air doubts over the Arab or Muslim temperament with regard to notions of pluralism and democracy. An example is the following claim by Lerner that a 'complication of modernization' in the Middle East is 'its own ethnocentrism – expressed politically in extreme nationalism, psychologically in passionate xenophobia … wanted are modern institutions', he continues, 'but not modern ideologies, modern power, but not modern purposes' (Lerner, 1958, p. ix).

In the decades, therefore, that followed the collapse of early democratic projects in the region, and the era of authoritarianism and dictatorship, orientalist scholars found all the evidence they needed to doubt the chances of democracy. Even the process of economic liberalization from the 1970s onwards was not considered to be as significant in promoting political change and democracy as it had been in other parts of the developing world, and in Latin America in particular. Yet there has been a critique of this approach, argued by authors such as Bromley, claiming that, 'seen in comparative perspective, the Middle East may only be exceptional in the timing and fragility of its democratization rather than constituting a wholesale departure from patterns found elsewhere' (1997, p. 329).

Since the 1990s, this view has altered both within and outside the region. Democracy has been seen as a western 'peculiarity' and it has been rejected in the Middle East because of its more recent associations with promotion down the barrel of a gun (Carothers, 2006). Nevertheless, many states were seen to engage in some form of political liberalizing process, such as the more open elections in Jordan, Yemen, Egypt, Algeria, Israel and Iran, to name a few (Tessler and Gao, 2009). The early rush to declare democratization as a process in the Middle East, however, has to be tempered with the important distinction between liberalization and democratization. As Brynen, Korany and Noble pointed out, liberalization 'involves the expansion of public space through the recognition and protection of civil and political liberties', while democratization 'entails an expansion of political participation … to provide citizens with a degree of real and meaningful collective control over public policy' (1995, p. 3). The two terms, however, are not one and the same thing, nor are they reflective of the same structural changes in government, politics, economy or society. Moreover, for authors like Parekh, it is not the promotion of democracy that should be abandoned but the means which should be reconsidered for more successful outcomes in Middle Eastern states (Parekh, 2010). This, however, contrasts strongly with the enduring view that the Middle East is resistant to democracy (Brownlee, Masoud and Reynolds, 2013).

A number of important themes, therefore, have emerged from the debate about democracy and liberalization in the Middle East. The first theme, as I have noted above, has rested on the critique and counter-critique of Arab and Muslim cultures being uniquely exceptional in their undemocratic tendencies, which means that the Middle East can never truly achieve democracy according to the liberal values and principles associated with it. Indeed, authors like Hamid highlight the innate illiberal character of Islamism to drive this point home (Hamid and Ruekert, 2014). This debate has raged for a number of years, resting largely on Huntington's 'clash of civilizations' thesis, as well as work on Arab political culture by authors such as Stepan and Robertson who have contended 'Arab political culture ... helps to sustain political exceptionalism' (2003, p. 42). A number of other authors, however, refute this approach and contend that there is room within Arab and Islamic political culture for a meaningful discourse on democracy and to not take it too seriously as a challenge (El-Affendi, 2010).

The second discernible strand is the emergence of a democratization thesis that is distinct from the discussion about political liberalization in the region. This discussion focuses not just on the theoretical dimensions of the concept of democracy but on the manifestations of democratization that can be identified within the region. The third strand of this debate looks at the impact of so-called economic liberalization on the democratization and political liberalization theses, exploring whether or not a particular approach to the development of the economy in the region is a prerequisite feature of any experiment in democratization. The fourth motif focuses on the relationship between democratization and civil society, and questions whether it is correct to assert that, in light of the democratization and liberalization debate, it would be better to refer to civil society. For example, Richards and Waterbury argued that civil society has not reached the appropriate level of development in the region to support a process of 'redemocratization' (1990, p. 329). The fifth motif looks at the relationship between democracy and Islam and analyses the continuing dispute within the discipline over this issue (Paya, 2010). The final theme of this debate will focus on the Arab Spring and the apparently ill-fated fortunes of democracy promotion in its wake.

Clash of civilizations

The promotion of democracy has been a significant agenda item for the Middle East for the last quarter of a century. The collapse of the former Soviet Union, the fall of the Berlin Wall, the rise of democracy in Eastern Europe and the Gulf crisis of 1990–1 all contributed to the apparent rise of a new world order, in which the USA would dominate the world stage and political change was inevitable. The end of the Cold War and America's triumph gave the victory to liberal democratic values and market capitalism, without which, it was argued, the world was doomed to dictatorship and tyranny. Within the Third World in general, the mantra of democratization was preached by western governments, international corporations, aid agencies and development experts. In the Middle East, in particular, the message was broadcast loud and clear: democratization was the only way forward, a path out of the legitimacy crisis, a vehicle by which failed economic policies, the demands from the masses and external pressures could be harnessed by a variety of regimes of differing political hues to promote democracy by diktat. As Norton explained, 'No doubt, the defining concept of the 1990s is democracy. Like Coca-Cola, democracy needs no translation to be understood virtually everywhere. Democracy, however, is easier to say than to create' (1993, p. 206).

A difficulty was apparent in this mantra of democratization in relation to the Middle East. In particular, Huntington highlighted it in his thesis of the clash of civilizations. In brief, the thesis argued that 'the fundamental source of conflict' in the present day and future will rest on a 'clash of civilizations that will dominate global politics' (1993, p. 22). Huntington, believing that identity from civilization was more important than other types of identity, argued that religion is the most important feature

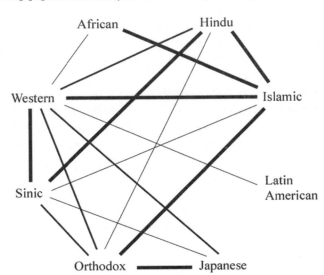

"Emerging alignments" of civilizations, per Samuel Huntinton's theory in *The Clash of Civilizations* (1996).

Greater line thickness represents more conflict in the civilizational relationship.

Figure 6.1 *Clash of civilizations*

contributing to this new identity: 'even more than ethnicity, religion discriminates sharply and exclusively among people' (1993, p. 27). The basis for conflict, he argued, lies in the 'fault line' between civilizations and, in particular, the one between Islam and the West. For Huntington, the relationship between the West and Islamic civilization has always been, and will always be, based on military conflict. Muslims and, by association, Arabs are an aggressive civilization, Islam has 'bloody borders', violence is repetitively cited almost as an innate trait of Muslim people. This theme had been developed from Huntington's earlier reflections in an article written in 1984, in which he declared:

> ## Box 6.1 Inhospitable climate
>
> Islam has not been hospitable to democracy ... the prospects for democratic development seem low. The Islamic revival, and particularly the rise of Shi'ite fundamentalism, would seem to reduce even further the likelihood of democratic development,
>
> (1984, pp. 208, 216)

The combination of violence, Islam and anti-democratic tendencies highlighted by Huntington painted a picture of the Middle East (with Israel as the notable exception) in which Arab and Islamic civilization was portrayed as backward, static, barbaric and vicious. The shift to democracy, in whatever form, could, therefore, be immediately ruled out in Huntington's opinion. In echo of this approach, Waterbury added that, 'whether Islam and Middle Eastern culture are separable phenomena the two work in ways that do not augur well for democracy. I believe that basic tendencies in regional culture and in religious practice must be overcome rather than utilized in any efforts to promote pluralism and democracy' (1994, p. 33).

Other authors have gone a considerable way in supporting Huntington's thesis. The relationship between Arab and Muslim identity is cast in stone, they are perceived as one and the same thing, and as such democracy is declared 'alien' to this mind-set. Whether Arab or Islamic, Kedourie declared that democracy in the region will always fail. Representative government and other features associated with democracy are, he wrote, 'profoundly alien to the Muslim political tradition' (1994, p. 6). Political tradition, such authors argue, is based on a form of 'oriental despotism' which has dominated the region for centuries. This tradition of rule, which survives to the present day, is best articulated as authoritarianism. Thus, even those Arab states that claim a populist, nationalist base were regarded as highly dubious by writers such as Kedourie, who stressed the region's proclivity for anti-democratic political practices. In addition, the appalling human rights record of many Arab regimes cast further doubt on the professed claims to pluralism and freedom for all in their societies.

The future for promotion of democracy within the region, according to such writers, then, was far from rosy. The despotic Orientalism school also drew little distinction between types of state and government. All Arab or Muslim regimes, irrespective of whether one was talking about Wahabi Saudi Arabia, consociational Lebanon, populist Yemen or monarchical Jordan, were the same in this respect. From this perspective, the 'problem of Arab authoritarianism' persists and continues to vex sponsors of democracy in the region (Masoud, 2015, p. 85). The predominantly Muslim basis from which most, if not all, Arab governments within the region worked therefore also inhibited the development of liberal democratic approaches. This view, however, has its resistors, with authors arguing that both Arab and Islamic political cultures are open to expressions of democracy (Khatami, 2010).

Democratization or liberalization?

Democracy and liberalism, democratization and liberalization are related terms, but in the context of our particular analysis should be scrutinized very carefully. While it is the case that democratization cannot truly take place without liberalization of political systems, government and institutions, the same cannot be said of liberalization. Indeed, in the Middle East it is true to say that the processes of reform that have taken place in countries as politically diverse as Egypt, Kuwait, Tunisia and Oman are more akin to a trend towards liberalization than towards democratization. Indicators that in the early 1990s were seized upon as signs of democracy sweeping the Middle East were, in reality, a series of minor and major acts of liberalization. They were prompted by factors as diverse as the Gulf crisis, the rise of ethno-national discontent, religious persecution, changes in the global economy, and the deepening crisis of identity within the Arab world as it faced pressure from the outside to change and emulate 'other' western cultures.

The trend towards liberalization in the Arab world and the Middle East in general even predates the momentous political changes that swept the former Soviet Union and the communist states of Eastern Europe in the late 1980s. Glasnost Arab-style was manifest in the *infitah* (open door) policies of Egypt and Tunisia in the late 1970s and early 1980s. As the state opted for reform through liberalization, Syria and Egypt's citizens saw the 'open door' as an opportunity also to press for greater political changes and liberalization. Thus the leaders of the Arab world hoped that policies of economic liberalization would strengthen the role of the market and capital in the economy but not extend to the incorporation of democracy. As Heydemann argued, 'Arab regimes have become proficient at containing and disarming democracy promotion – if not exploiting it for their own purposes.' Specifically, Arab states employed such approaches to 'upgrade' the authoritarian state and build resilience (2007, p. 9).

Conceptually, the debate about democratization and liberalization must focus on the differences inherent in the two terms. Liberalization, for example, may be taken to mean any activity that generates greater individual freedom in societies. Individual and collective freedoms are separate constructs and the process of liberalization enhances one, the individual, over the other, the collective. In turn, such perspectives are related to the tradition of liberalism that has dominated western political thought. At the heart of this approach is an emphasis on and protection of the individual, economically, socially and politically, and on a weakened state. Liberalism and liberalization, then, are essentially western constructs that have been promoted in the Middle East for a variety of reasons. In theory, this approach relegates the state to the periphery; state interference in economic activity, social issues and other areas is to be avoided at all costs. In reality, however, the picture is a little more complicated. The Arab state in countries like Egypt has actively engaged in promoting liberal economic orders to perpetuate crony capitalism (Hinnebusch, 2015b). Such examples highlight the paradox and limits of liberalization from above (Chekir and Diwan, 2012). In the Arab world, much of the political and economic change since the late 1970s in countries like Egypt, Tunisia and Syria, did not promote freedom, liberalism or democracy.

Democracy, meanwhile, as I have discussed above, enjoys a relationship to liberalism and processes of liberalization but remains a different creature. Democratic socialism, for example, promotes an agenda that is often largely at odds with liberal democracy as it is currently understood. Nevertheless, the generic term, particularly in relation to the Middle East, is currently understood or interpreted in a number of ways. As we shall see in subsequent sections, democrats in Algeria are very different from democrats in Israel. In the contemporary era, then, democracy has largely reflected on the process of electoral politics or press freedoms and human rights. Yet larger structural impediments relating to the process of state formation, allocation of resources, state bureaucracies and citizenship have been ignored. As Bromley remarked, 'the relative absence of democracy in the Middle East has little to do with the region's Islamic culture and much to do with its particular pattern of state formation' (1994, p. 169). The failure or weakness of the state in the region is thus an important constraint on the emergence of truly democratic processes.

Processes of liberalization have been under way in the region. As such, they allow for – relatively – greater degrees of political participation in existing political systems without necessarily embracing widespread democratic reforms. Political changes in some Gulf states illustrate this point. For example, Kuwait's experiment in parliamentary politics has been fraught with both opportunities and setbacks. It is not yet a harbinger for liberal democracy or constitutional monarchical democracy. Instead, the opportunity for Kuwaitis to elect parliamentarians has resided alongside what can be referred to as elements of royal autocracy residual in the ruling al-Sabah family (Herb, 2014). In another example, Iran, rates of electoral participation have been significant in the second Islamic Republic. Opportunities for participation in the political system are provided for according to the rules of *shari'a* law, and since 1979 there have been more than twenty-eight elections in the country for the head of state and government (the president), legislature (the *majlis*), the Assembly of Experts – which in turn elects the 'Supreme Leader' – as well as municipal elections. With such a significant number of opportunities to vote and universal suffrage, Iran exhibits elements of what Ehteshami declared a 'fledgling democracy' but historically they have been restrained by authoritarian theocratic tendencies exhibited throughout the post-revolutionary period.

Liberalization developed into an important trend in the region. How this factor is balanced by demands for democracy and the continued socio-economic changes that have characterized the area are explored below.

Socio-economic indicators

The relationship between economic, social and political factors in a discussion of liberalization is complex and multivalent in relation to the Middle East. Nevertheless, there does seem to be a meaningful relationship between economic changes – or, more specifically, economic liberalization – and the social and political factors that precipitate and accompany it. As discussed above, for more than forty years, forms of political liberalization have occurred within certain states in the region, primarily because of some kind of domestic economic crisis. An unfortunate coincidence of spiralling inflation, and high levels of unemployment have often heralded the path to liberalization and the promise of democratization. In other words, the decision to undertake new economic programmes, moving from a centrally state-planned economy to the privatization of state assets and removal of state controls, is normally a result of crisis rather than a change in government through election. Economic crisis heightens demands for political reform to fix problems too. Once again, the reasons for political opening have more to do with preservation of the status quo – usually in the form of the authoritarian state – than with real change.

Box 6.2 System maintenance

The main purpose of liberalization from above is system maintenance in a situation of acute socio-economic crisis, by co-opting wider circles of the political public, distributing responsibility for future austerity policies more broadly, directing political and religious organizations into controllable channels and excluding all those outside the 'national consensus' defined by the regime.

(Kramer, 1992, p. 24)

Initially rapid but uneven patterns of socio-economic development have characterized the Middle East, playing their part in the economic and widespread societal crisis that has affected many of the region's countries. The difficulty, politically, with the path of economic liberalization has been that the state's role has not diminished. Vested interests associated with political leadership, power and business remain strong. Hence, the reluctance by political leaderships in the Arab world to opt for even limited economic liberalization and a limited path of political reform. As we have already discussed, in some cases liberalization has little – or nothing – to do with economic reform, and in others, despite huge economic problems, the path to political reform or democratization is strongly resisted and even reversed. Indeed, some authors argue that change and reform have to be de-coupled from western agendas. As far back as the early 1990s, Vitalis contended that:

Box 6.3 Terribly fashionable

Beneath the last fashionable rhetoric, 'democracy' in the hands of the AID (US Agency for International Development) serves as an instrument for the pursuit of other ends – specifically, more market-friendly economies ... [development practitioners] should show why contemporary political engineering projects by US agencies are any less likely ... to retard indigenous democratic currents and institutions.

(1994, p. 46)

In addition, this perspective might help explain why liberalization has been limited and why it has not been a resounding success vis-à-vis the economic problems it was supposed to address. Finally, this model of economic activity takes little account of the prevailing social conditions of the region. The process of state-formation, independence and state-consolidation that has occurred within the Middle East over the last sixty years has wrought significant social changes, such as decline of rural for urban life, widespread immigration and migrant labour patterns, changes in levels of education, a drop in infant mortality rates, and so on. The issue here is whether these social changes and patterns of life, with the creation of new economic interests which often abut family, tribal, religious and other pressures, can withstand the liberalization process in terms of both economic and political change.

One might add that such limited economic liberalization only widens the inequalities within society, keeping the underclass down and removing it even further from whatever state assistance is available. This has been apparent in Egypt, where the liberalization of the economy has resulted in a huge bureaucracy but declining state provision in terms of welfare assistance and health care. By 2016, state social security nets had been proved inadequate in terms of a disconnect from the most vulnerable elements of society whom they are supposed to help. The crippling poverty and economic inequalities that have been created as a result of the partial liberalization of the economy through the Mubarak era had not been resolved through the limited process of political appeasement. For example, the introduction of a multi-party system in Egypt had a minimal impact on the continued authoritarian nature of the state and did not make it any more accountable to its citizens. Instead, the sense of frustration grew and the tendency to authoritarian rather than democratic rule became strengthened. After all, the process of economic liberalization is a double-edged sword that can both weaken and strengthen the state. In the case of the Middle East, state control has been exerted and the autonomy of society significantly weakened.

Democracy and civil society

Civil society, the amalgamation of non-governmental and autonomous social organizations such as trade unions, women's groups, professional associations, trade guilds, religious groups, chambers of commerce, and voluntary associations concerned with issues such as children, disability or welfare rights, are perceived as a prerequisite of democracy and democratic life in any society, and its relations to the state. As Turner noted, 'the theory of civil society was part of the master dichotomy of nature/civilization, since it was within civil society that the individual was eventually clothed in judicial rights of property, possessions and security' (1994, p. 25). The existence of civil society protects the individual from a monopoly of state control. The individual lies at the heart of this concept, as do individual rights, notions and concepts that scholars such as Kedourie and Huntington regard as anathema to the collectivism ever-present in Arab and Muslim societies.

The promotion of democracy in the Middle East has been strongly associated with the study of whether civil society exists in the region, together with its strengths and weaknesses and future prospects. One of its most passionate proponents writes: 'a vibrant and relatively autonomous civil society is integral to democracy ... no discussion of political change in the contemporary Middle East will be complete unless it takes into account the status of civil society' (Norton, 1993, p. 203). The issue of autonomy from the state has been debated extensively, with little resolution of the issue. States in the Middle East strong-arm – through licensing and registration processes – civil society actors. A case in point are the Islamic welfare and charitable societies of Egypt that include *zakat* committees. Interestingly, Atia argues that the neoliberal authoritarian state in Egypt 'created the prime context in which' Islamic charity and other pious activity were not only regulated but oriented to 'particular political economic arrangements between the state, the private sector, and individuals (2013, p. 158).

It should be noted from the outset that certain battle lines are drawn around the issue of whether civil society exists in the Middle East, or is likely ever to exist in the region. In the past a number of writers, identified by Sadowski (1997), including Patricia Crone, Daniel Pipes, Samuel Huntington and Bernard Lewis, have rejected the possibility of any form of civil society existing in the Arab countries of the region. According to these authors, civil society cannot exist because Arab and Muslim societies are despotic in nature, and despotic rule presupposes the absence of any social institutions between the individual and the despot. Others, including Augustus Richard Norton, Muhammad Muslih, Michael Hudson and Bryan Turner, believe that evidence of civil society can be found in the region and that, as states weaken, these groups have grown in strength, acting as an important check on a number of regimes.

In addition, this flourishing sector supports the case for localized routes to democratization and greater pluralism in Arab and Muslim societies. Muslih, writing about the Palestinian context of civil society and its relation to the PLO as 'state surrogate', outlines evidence of a flourishing civil society existing 'in the absence of a democratic state' where 'it is precisely because the state surrogate has sustained political pluralism that it may be inclined to sustain a pluralistic civil society if independence is achieved' (1993, p. 272). While evidence of civil society is clear, Muslih is perhaps slightly over-optimistic about the maintenance of autonomy. Since the establishment of the Palestinian Authority (PA) in the wake of the 1993 Oslo Peace Accords, there has been a squeeze on the relatively autonomous activities of Palestinian non-governmental organizations, trade unions and other sectors of civil society. Nevertheless, many of the gatekeepers of democratic traditions among the Palestinians remain at large, continuing their work in the large civil-society sectors of welfare, human rights, education and professional associations. Under the Fayyad government of 2007 onwards, however, many civil society associations were forced into closure as part of a PA-orchestrated campaign.

For the neo-orientalists or cultural theorists, however, civil society in the Middle East is the harbinger of authoritarianism, not democracy. They 'assert that the proliferation of social movements will discourage any trend toward power sharing and greater tolerance in the region, if it does not breed civil war and anarchy' (Sadowski, 1997, p. 42). Either way, as far as the neo-orientalist and cultural perspective is concerned, democracy cannot be linked positively with either the absence in the past or the contemporary growth of civil society in countries such as Syria, Egypt or Lebanon and among such communities as the Palestinians of the West Bank and Gaza Strip.

In contrast, however, there is a growing body of writers, some of whom are mentioned above, who believe that there is empirical evidence from cases in the region that supports the argument for an important link between the birth of civil society and the promotion of democratization. In Egypt, for example, since the early 1970s, liberalization of the economy by the state through the process of infitah has resulted in the unintended by-product of a growth in civil society that in turn made some governmental concessions to forms of democratization impossible to resist. Under President Mubarak, the regime sought a balancing act between pressure for reform of the political system, the creation of pluralism and a space between the state and the individual for civil society to flourish. This highlights the resilient nature of the authoritarian state in the region and the power of coercive apparatus (Bellin, 1994). Hence, there is an enduring and deep-seated fear within the regime concerning any relinquishment of political power to the people or their representative associations. What the regime failed to see was the reluctance of the people to recognize the legitimacy of state power as it was constituted. In part, this explains the societal mobilization evidenced by the Arab Spring.

In the example of Lebanon, the relative autonomy of large sectarian elements of civil society undermined the capacity of the state for a considerable period. The strength of civil (or civic) society in Lebanon (sustained by vertical lines of kinship, confessional allegiance and other affinities) weakened the state in a dramatic manner. To the present time, the state in Lebanon remains a fragile edifice.

In Lebanon, the prospects for political liberalism and democracy are surely promoted by the respect for economic liberal practices for which so many of its people are infamous; as the economy of Lebanon is reconstructed according to capital and free-market principles, the inevitable pressures for political reform became increasingly difficult for Lebanese leaders to suppress. The turning point came following the 2005 assassination of former Prime Minister and businessman Rafik Hariri and the protests that led to the Syrian withdrawal. In this context, civil society, as it is currently constituted, could play a contradictory, ambiguous and confused role in political reconstruction, particularly as civil society has had the power in the past to play a part in the collapse of the Lebanese state.

Clark and Salloukh refer to a 'recursive' relationship in Lebanon between the state, elites and civil society actors. 'On one side of this relation', they explain, 'sectarian elites pursue their political and socioeconomic interests at the expense of civil society organizations (CSOs); on the other side, civil society actors instrumentalize the sectarian political system and its resources to advance their own organizational or personal advantage. These mutually reinforcing dynamics enable sectarian elites to penetrate, besiege, or co-opt CSOs as well as to extend their clientelist networks to CSOs ...' (2013, p.731).

It remains clear – the objections of the neo-orientalists notwithstanding – that the existence and promotion of civil society have been considered an important component of democratization in the Middle East. Certainly, the state and its elites remain deeply hostile to civil society actors and the forms of democracy they are seen to symbolize. Ironically, as the examples of Lebanon and Egypt above illustrate, there is no longer an easy equation between democracy and civil society in the Middle East. Co-optation can lead such actors to serve, as they have done in Syria under the regime of Bashar al-Assad, as handmaidens to an authoritarian state.

This is a dynamic landscape. Nowhere is this more apparent than in analyses of the role of online civil society in the Arab world in understandings of the Arab Spring (Howard and Hussain, 2013). It is no surprise that civil society, hand in hand with democracy, seems remote in authoritarian regimes. Finally, much of the debate about civil society, democratization and political liberalism has spun on the axis of Islam. As the next section highlights, the addition of this particular ingredient to the debate has provoked fierce passions.

Islamism and democracy – an oxymoron?

In most monotheistic religions, a tradition of monolithic interpretation is not present. Whether one reflects on Christianity, Judaism or Islam, the diverse expression and interpretation of one faith is always apparent. The history of these religions is one of schism, denomination and other differences. Islam, therefore, like Christianity and Judaism, is capable of having multiple and major interpretations or orientations. Political Islam has been used both to oppose and to legitimate a variety of political models and state types. There are Islamist supporters of democracy. Ayubi, while challenging Huntington's approach, reiterates this point by asserting, 'I would argue myself that Islamic culture contains elements that may be both congenial and uncongenial to democracy, depending on the particular society and on the historical conjuncture' (1995, p. 399). Democracy, or *shura* (consultation) as some Muslims prefer to think of it, is part of a contemporary practice of politics that is appropriated by both opposition and ruling groups to state their political case. Yusuf al-Qaradawi, a well-known Islamic theologian, states the following about democracy:

Box 6.4 Essence of democracy and Islam

The essence of democracy ... is that people choose who rules over them and manages their affairs; that no ruler or regime they dislike is forced upon them; that they have the right to call the ruler to account if he errs and to remove him from office in case of misconduct ... This is the essence of real democracy, for which humanity has found such forms and practical approaches as elections and referenda, majority rule, multi- party systems ... In fact, whoever contemplates the essence of democracy finds that it accords with the essence of Islam.

(al-Qaradawi, 2009, p. 233)

Nevertheless, it is important to recognize that, within the diverse body politic that is Islam in the Middle East, there resides a discourse that democracy is deeply incompatible with Islam. In states ruled in the name of Islam, democracy is absented. In groups such as ISIS or al-Qaeda, democracy is rejected as a foreign and inauthentic imposition.

Using evidence of such absence and rejection, some scholars also argue that Muslims in the Middle East only embrace democracy in an instrumentalist and short-term fashion as a strategy for Islamic statehood, which is both authoritarian and anti-democratic. 'Democracy', writes Kramer, 'diversity, accommodation – the fundamentalists have repudiated them all. In appealing to the masses who fill their mosques, they promise, instead, to institute a regime of Islamic law, make common cause with like-minded "brethren" everywhere, and struggle against the hegemony of the West and the existence of Israel' (1993, p. 41).

Ayubi believed the picture to be more complicated than this, particularly at a time in the Arab world when Islamists formed the main base of opposition. He admitted that there was some currency in the argument that, 'in the immediate instance, most "fundamentalist" groupings act as a counter-democratic force'. But he concluded that,

Box 6.5 Delaying the inevitable?

whereas some of the factors that explain the delay of democratization in the Middle East are purely economic or technological, rather than religious or cultural, there is little doubt that the refusal by ruling elites to allow an element of participation for Islamic movements is an added cause for the slow pace of democratization in many Muslim societies.

(1997, p. 364)

Nevertheless, orientalists and cultural theorists, as explained above, contend that the attempt to impute democratic qualities to Islamic culture is the dangerous and naive preoccupation of apologists who fail to recognize the threat implicit in all Islamist movements in the region. Some in the administration of President Trump, including his 2017 chief strategist Steve Bannon, attach this threat to the religion of Islam itself. According to this school of thought, therefore, there is no place or hope for democracy in the region.

Others argue for a different approach to the Islam–democracy paradigm in the Middle East (Esposito, 2010b). On whichever side of the spectrum opinion falls, there is no denying, as Esposito and Piscatori point out, that 'whether the word democracy is used or not, almost all Muslims today react to it as one of the universal conditions of the modern world. To this extent it has become part of Muslim political thought and discourse' (1991, p. 440).

The school of thought within Islam – rather than those outside it – that rejects the idea that Islam and democracy could be compatible fears for the future of the faith in the same way that European clergy feared the impact of the Enlightenment and the rise of secularism in Europe. There is a genuine spiritual desire to protect the faith, rather than a predilection for conflict with the traditions of western political thought that champion democracy as part of the great secular experience. The hostility to this type of secular democracy that is found in Islam is not unique.

In theory, then, the Islamic intellectuals who voice their opposition to democracy do so because of its secular associations. They question how a believer can embrace a secular notion of equality that is associated with democracy when Islam already encourages believers to accept equality as part of their faith. This debate has been examined by Ismail who pointed out that the 'confrontation' between Arab secularists and Islamists 'is not without its links to the protagonists' hopes and fears regarding democracy', yet it takes place, she adds, at a time when 'the interpretation of divine sovereignty … is not agreed on among the various thinkers of the Islamist movement' (1995, p. 102). Issues of sovereignty are rejected for the same reason; the efficacy of Westminster-type legislative bodies is questioned because Islam is supposed to legislate for all aspects of life, and ultimate sovereignty rests not with the people, as is common in secularized democratic practice, but with God (Esposito, 1983, p. 79). And yet contemporary Islamist movements, such as the Muslim Brotherhood, regularly compete in elections to Westminister-type legislative bodies.

Most Muslims have, however, accepted some notion of democracy, but, as I have already stated, they do have differences over its precise meaning. Muslim

Source: Wikimedia.

Figure 6.2 *Free to vote, Shi'a leader Abdel Aziz Hakim, Iraqi elections 2005*

interpretations of democracy place varying degrees of emphasis on the degree to which the people are charged with power, and which actors protect democracy and are able to exercise their duties (Masoud, 2015). This can only be done in the context of acknowledging the higher authority of God, who remains the supreme ruler of the people. Nevertheless, the people do have some authority over their earthly rulers, leaders or caliphs, who guide the community according to Islam.

A corrupt, unjust or un-Islamic ruler does not have to be tolerated by the people, and the assent of the community should be regularly sought by the ruler, whoever he may be. All members of a community should be treated equally and bias must not be shown because of race, class or creed. This approach recognizes the importance of consensus within the community of believers without which Islam cannot flourish. It is not democracy per se, then, that is problematic within Islam, as Halliday reminds us: 'If there are in a range of Islamic countries evident barriers to democracy, this has to do with certain other social and political features that their societies share' (1996, p. 116).

While many focus on the rejection of western liberal democracy, others have discovered the important debates taking place within Islam that encompass not just the problems of democracy but the role of Islam in a world of nation-states, capital-led economies and the technological boom. These new modernists and reformers, Islamic democrats and advocates of human rights are embarking on the formulation of an authentic Islamic response to contemporary conditions and challenges in the Middle East. They do not engage with soundbite populist quick fixes that unravel as quickly as they are formulated, the kind of fix-it-all response which many wish the Middle East would undertake; rather, they form the backbone of the truly intellectual response which must evolve through important discourse and problem-solving. As Abou el Fadl contends, 'democracy is an appropriate system for Islam because it both expresses the special worth of human beings … and at the same time deprives the state of any pretence of divinity by locating ultimate authority in the hands of the people rather than the ulema' (2004, p. 36). In practice, the formation of political Islamist parties such as al-Ennahda in Tunisia is evidence of a liberalization of Islamic thinking on issues of plurality, democracy, partisan politics and elections. Masoud argues that 'if Tunisia manages to hang onto its hard-won democracy, it will constitute a living rejoinder to the argument that Muslims or Arabs lack the capacity or desire for democratic government' (2015, p. 83).

The Arab Spring and democracy

The Arab Spring in 2010 appeared to set the stage for an era in which new political dispensations would address the democracy deficit of the Middle East. There were hopes that, as calls for reform of government echoed around the region and autocratic regimes fell, the political class would establish new democratic polity in the Arab states of the Middle East.

In the transition states of Tunisia, Egypt, Yemen and Libya, democratic indicators – such as the formation of new political parties, and elections – gave cause for optimism. Moreover, even in states which did not topple, such as Jordan, the political elite appeared to engage with democratic reform debates as a means of responding to the rise of popular protest and demonstration. Protestors had highlighted the absence of democracy among their grievances. Moreover, opinion polls (see figure 6.3) have highlighted consistent support for varieties of democracy in the region (Doha Institute, 2015).

By 2013, the political transitions were unfolding in Tunisia, Egypt, Yemen and Libya, and the impact of the Arab uprisings remained palpable in Syria, as well as other countries across the region. Millions of Arabs had participated in presidential and legislative elections, indicating burgeoning democracy. In Egypt, for example, twenty-eight political parties registered for the country's first ever free and fair election in 2011. Egyptians used their ballot box opportunities to choose a new head of state and members of the legislature. The constitution was about to be rewritten and there were hopes that the institutional checks and balances associated with democracy – such as popular referenda, an independent judiciary and civil government – would be incorporated into the transition.

In Tunisia, there was encouraging evidence of democratic practices taking root in this previously authoritarian state. Yemen, as Alley argues, evidenced even greater possibility as the route through transition epitomized inclusive and negotiated frameworks for democracy building (2013). In Libya, even at the outset of the transition of power, hopefulness for democracy was tempered with an astute understanding of the task ahead. For, after all, under President Gaddafi, Libyans had endured forty-two years of autocratic rule in which any semblance of democratic governance was almost impossible to

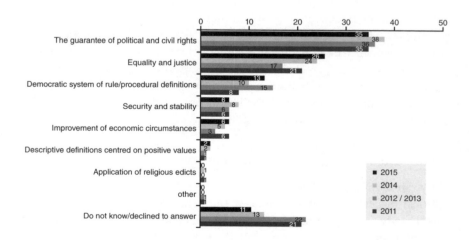

Figure 6.3 *Arab respondents' definitions of democracy (Doha Institute 2015)*

discern. In the wake of Gaddafi's fall, a National Transitional Council (NTC) established a transition framework which included elections for a General National Congress (GNC) held in July 2012.

Yet for all these demonstrations of democracy, powerful elites would act to halt, and even derail, progressive-change approaches. Re-emerging from behind the scenes, the Arab military and security actors in countries like Egypt and Syria have pushed democracy efforts back. Military and security courts have become the destination of choice to try local civilians, and effectively suppress the spirit of reform and democratic change.

By 2014, in Egypt, the popularly elected Muslim Brotherhood had been replaced by former army General Abdul Fattah al-Sisi. He used ballot box opportunities to become the winner of the 2014 presidential election. In Syria, the regime of President Bashar al-Assad was employing the tool of democracy – elections – to remain in power in a country torn apart by a vicious civil war. In Libya, the so-called governing elements have been unable to withstand the assaults of armed actors – including militia elements – to establish strong enough institutions of governance to underpin democracy-building. The societal and institutional base in Libyan society and politics is not strong enough for this country to engage in rapid democracy as it recovers from decades of authoritarianism. Furthermore, in Libya, as with the other examples above, external security interests have driven democratization efforts. Governments of the region, including in Libya, have been vulnerable to external pressures from competing western actors and other regional rivals. Even the formation, with international recognition, of a United Nations-backed unity government headed by Prime Minister Fayez Sarraj, and installed in Tripoli in March 2016, has thus far failed to kick-start democracy.

Tunisia, as we discuss in the case study below, is increasingly cited as the 'single success' story when it comes to addressing the democracy deficit in the wake of the Arab Spring. Here, civil–military relations have tipped back in favour of the civil. Civil society actors and a variety of political actors and groupings have negotiated, compromised and worked out democratic power-sharing arrangements. Elsewhere in the region, the uncertainties wrought by the Arab Spring have encouraged state actors to deepen autocratic control. Increasingly, state actors and elite have labelled civil actors, particularly Muslims or Islamists, as enemies of democracy. Moreover, elite manipulation of differentiated identity politics, particularly of a sectarian variety in countries like Lebanon and Iraq, inhibits plural values considered inherent to democracy. Elections become confessional or sectarian 'events' reifying difference rather than building democratic nations. In the monarchical states of Morocco and Jordan, the response to locally inspired Arab Spring protests is mixed. In Morocco, constitutional reforms, Benchemsi argues, 'at first glance look like major concessions', yet he notes, 'the king may not have abandoned all his powers … further inspection reveals that the monarchy may have succeeded in outfoxing its opponents by producing an elaborate constitutional smokescreen' (2012, p. 57). Leaders and rulers in the majority of Arab Gulf states still argue that the consultative function of the customary *majlis* system is a democracy substitute.

Such limited efforts have led Masoud to conclude,

Box 6.6 Nasty, brutish and short

[O]ne thing that the Arab Spring and its aftermath have made clear is that we should not expect democracy to come as a result of an intifada that sweeps dictators from power and enables the masses to erect liberal institutions ... The Arab world today gives us more cause to think it is inching toward the Hobbesian state of nature than decent government.

(2015, p. 79)

Case study
Jordan – a façade democracy

At the beginning of the 1990s, academic literatures often cited Jordan as the most encouraging example of democratization in the region. By the middle of the decade, however, analysis that is more circumspect emerged, calling for a proper assessment of the conditions of change that were prevailing in the country. Jordan has not democratized successfully. There is also strong evidence to suggest that democratization was never truly the aim of the ruling regime. Rather, appropriate conditions were created to maintain a 'façade democracy', satisfying both local demands for greater participation and international – and particularly so-called western – conditions of democracy for aid-giving and other financial assistance (Milton-Edwards, 1993). In addition, as the kingdom faced further internal crises due to factors such as peace with Israel, the continuing political fallout of the Gulf crisis, and the succession debate prompted by King Hussein's episodes of cancer throughout the late 1990s, and his death in 1999, the process of political liberalization stalled.

According to its constitution, the Hashemite Kingdom of Jordan is a constitutional monarchy with a bicameral system of parliament, including an elected legislature known as the House of Representatives. The Senate makes up the other institution of parliament and its members are appointed by the monarch. The Prime Minister and government are also appointed and dismissed by the monarch, who has the right to exercise this power as frequently as he deems fit (Milton-Edwards, 2017).

In practice, until 1989, the government and politics of Jordan were severely circumscribed by the power of its monarchy through King Abdullah and then his grandson King Hussein. Although there has always been a formal provision of plural and democratic institutions of government and legislation, Jordan, particularly since the period of intense political instability of the late 1950s when the monarchy looked precarious, has not been famous for its unfettered practice of democracy. Indeed, the make-up of the state – a majority Palestinian population ruled by a Hashemite monarchy – and a history of intense conflict, including the civil war of 1970 (Sayigh, 1997), have been used to legitimate coercion to create stability at any price. In return, Jordan earnt the enduring moniker that it was an 'island of stability' in the region.

For more than twenty years (from the late 1950s onwards), full elections were suspended, political parties were banned, the press was censored and the internal security service (*mukhabarat*) imprisoned hundreds – if not thousands – on political charges. Allegations of human rights abuses and tortures were widespread and consistent. These conditions highlighted a tradition of autocratic rule which was described by Finer as a 'façade democracy', one where 'historic oligarchies govern from behind a façade of liberal-democratic forms which serve as a screen for their rule' (1970, p. 124). The palace, rather than the people, ruled the political roost in Jordan for many decades. King Hussein's Hashemite lineage to the Prophet Mohammed bolstered the monarchy's claims to legitimacy in this troubled state. Oligarchy rather than democracy prevailed, and the opposition remained largely circumscribed, forced underground by the security network that hounded it. In this shackled political arena, only one other political actor stood apart from the palace and those tribal leaders whose fealty lay with the king, and that was the Islamic movement (Milton-Edwards, 2016a). The Islamic movement, primarily the Muslim Brotherhood, as discussed in chapter 5, acted largely as a body of loyal opposition, actually doing little if anything to press for democratic reform.

In early 1989, following a series of riots throughout the country against IMF-imposed price increases on basic foods, the status quo was threatened. King Hussein, aware of the increased pressure from below for political concession of some sort, announced that full elections would be held. In addition, it was widely believed that the monarch had decided to embark on a process of democratization that would encourage greater plurality of opinion, increased opportunities for participation, freedom of speech and assembly, and an end to the high levels of corruption that had almost paralysed the business of government. Economic crisis had severely weakened the king's coercive powers, as Jordanian citizens demanded greater freedoms at a time when the IMF was making it clear that any assistance would be dependent on a certain liberalizing of political control.

Clearly, Jordan's path to democratization has not been smooth. In 2016, the *Economist* Democracy Index ranked Jordan as 'authoritarian' (*The Economist*, 2016). In many ways, this kind of democracy promotion reflects Ayubi's (1997) manifestation of cosmetic democratization 'for the Yankees to see' and must be viewed as a continuing process in which the destination – full democracy – is still a long way off.

The election that was held in November 1989, however, was an unheralded spectacle and a roaring success. The campaign and polling day were the freest ever experienced in the country, although it should be noted that political parties were still prohibited, the press was still censored and human rights abuses were still reported by organizations such as Amnesty International (Milton-Edwards, 1996b). The elections to the eighty-seat House of Representatives, the lower house of parliament, resulted in a victory for the Muslim Brotherhood, delivering thirty-four seats and a high participation rate of some 60 per cent of the eligible electorate. The Cabinet and Senate, the upper house of parliament, however, still remained subject to appointment by the king himself, who has also retained the power to dissolve parliament and call elections.

Since 1989, aspects of political liberalization have been episodic in nature, and characterized by a 'one step forward two steps back' approach. Jordan's rulers have continued with plans to push for forms of economic liberalization at a pace dictated by the palace not the people. The government signalled some advance in the announcement in 1992 of the National Charter, which called for greater freedom for the individual and equality in society, including the establishment of a multi-party system and greater freedom for the press. Notably, particularly in relation to the debate about the compatibility of Islam and democracy, the Jordanian charter also enshrined the principle of Islamic law by declaring that *shari'a* (Islamic law) would be the source of all law in the kingdom. Yet opponents complained that such steps would serve to inhibit democratic mechanisms rather than encourage them. In the same year, the king permitted the legal formation and registration of political parties and announced that further elections to the House of Representatives would be held. Those elections resulted in the undermining of the Islamist vote and a further consolidation of the traditional tribal allegiances to the king.

By the end of the 1990s, the new monarch constrained further the forces of political liberalization and democracy. Additionally, he grappled with the severe economic conditions in his country and had to plead for debt forgiveness from the big-power players in the international community (Yom, 2009). Subsequent elections have seen participation rates drop and boycotts by certain political elements such as the Muslim Brotherhood. Of greatest significance is the fact that Jordan's Islamist elements found themselves increasingly on the margins of parliamentary and governmental power (Schwedler, 2006). The parliamentary elections of June 2003 illustrated this change in the balance of power: independents known for their loyalty to King Abdullah II won the majority of the 110 seats to the parliament. The November 2007 elections witnessed the further narrowing of plural politics and the consolidation of increasingly authoritarian rule (Lust-Okar, 2006, 2009). In 2016, the kingdom held general elections. New electoral legislation permitting multiple votes for open proportional lists replaced the decades-old single-vote system but did nothing to encourage political participation rates from the electorate.

Since the late 1990s, the pace of political reform for promotion of democracy in the country has slowed. The government has reintroduced curbs on fundamental freedoms – such as on free speech. Democracy Jordanian-style is taking a long time in terms of reflecting a plurality of political voices in the country. Prospects for further democracy promotion in the kingdom are, according to Yom, 'exceedingly low' (2009, p. 151).

Case study

Moroccan parse

Morocco's journey to democracy is one that many western states would like to see repeated elsewhere in the region. They see this modern monarchy as one of the most liberal Arab states of the Middle East. To all intents and purposes, it was an ideal breeding ground for democracy promotion. Morocco has some of the most progressive social legislation in the Arab world, particularly as it pertains to family law and the rights of women.

The state has a multi-party system and elected parliament. Yet, like other monarchical states in the region, there is a degree of façade to the political system. The king, as indicated earlier in this chapter, enjoys extensive executive powers. The legislature does not actually enjoy autonomy. The palace controls political parties, ensuring their compliance with monarchical rule. Historically, parliament has served mostly as a glorified debating forum. Elected representatives know this better than anyone else, and most have chosen not even to show up when parliament is in session. In many respects, the parliament has been nothing more than a 'rubber stamp' body for the decisions of the monarch. There has been little public confidence in the government, and public bureaucracy is also plagued by corruption and nepotism. The king's power has extended to other realms as well. He has appointed the Prime Minister and also influenced whom the Prime Minister picks for government.

Elections are relatively free and fair. Yet participation rates – with the noticeable exception of the 2011 constitutional referendum – are low. This has been disappointing for purveyors of democratization who hoped that such elections could demonstrate the extent to which this form of popular participation in governance had become rooted in the country.

Morocco has developed close relations with western states, and the USA in particular. In return, it has enjoyed healthy inputs of development assistance, and ties with respect to security issues. In 2007, the call for legislative elections was perceived in the West as an opportunity to demonstrate that democracy was working in the Middle East and that it could also be used to contain Islamists rather than give them an alternative route to power. Participation rates and the actual outcome of the election in terms of other indicators of democratic governance, however, turned out to be unimpressive and led to further questions with respect to the US policy of democracy promotion in the region (Storm, 2007).

Democracy was a key aspect of protests when they broke out in Morocco during the Arab Spring. A broad pro-democracy coalition emerged – 'the February 20th Movement' – calling for political reform. King Mohammed VI responded with a commitment to increase constitutional improvement and reduce his powers. Indeed, Morocco's monarch, King Mohammed VI, has been key to the democracy experiment. Succeeding his father in 1999, this pro-western leader has encouraged the West, and the USA in particular, to buy into his vision for democracy, in the belief that it meets twin demands for security first and degrees of liberalization second. Once again, economic and political liberalization are intimately tied together. The USA has backed the king's vision of democracy rather than investing in bottom-up civil society and non-governmental initiatives, or even a mixture of the two.

In reality, as with other pro-western monarchical states in the region, such as Jordan, Moroccan democracy promotion and reform have been limited in substantive impact. Initial reform efforts that the king undertook in the 2000–5 period then stagnated in the following five years. In 2008, the Democracy Index continued to describe the country as an authoritarian regime, scoring only 3.88 out of 10 in terms of democracy indicators such as freedom of association, women's rights and press rights. Egypt, Iraq, Turkey and the Palestinian territories all have higher indicators. Even in the wake of constitutional reform efforts in 2011, the King is criticized for not going far enough with relinquishing power and permitting true democracy (Ghafar and Jacobs, 2017). The 2016 elections had returned a number of parties to power but the palace has interfered to stymie power-sharing and authentic coalition-building.

Morocco appears to have become nothing more than a western-backed Arab pseudo-democracy. The king is critiqued for 'maintaining control over major policy issues', as well as succeeding in 'co-opting the two main opposition parties of long-standing without being forced to give up any power or change policies' (Ottaway and Riley, 2006, p. 6). Indeed, the opposition, including reformist Islamist elements of the Party of Justice and Development (PJD), has been effectively constrained by curbs on electoral laws, press laws, freedom of association, power-sharing and securitization policies (Dalmasso and Cavatorta, 2013). Hence, true participative democracy and governance, with the usual checks and balances on power expected in a liberal democracy, are absent from the Moroccan experience.

While it is true that the USA and the EU have attempted and funded democracy promotion in Morocco and that their starting point was a regime that was one of the most liberal in the Middle East, such efforts have not been fully rewarded. Reform has been initiated by the king but, thus far, it has not resulted in full-scale transition to liberal democracy. As such, this has now made it difficult to promote Morocco as a success story or model for the rest of the region to follow – if true liberal democracy is the desired end. If, however, as many suspect, the USA and EU demand nothing more than stability, co-option of the opposition including Islamist elements, security, manageable economic liberalization and a passive Arab citizenry, then Morocco could prove to be a case in point (Ottoway and Riley, 2006). Indeed this kind of 'top-down' approach to democracy promotion has become the primary outcome of such external inputs over the last decade in the region. Morocco's neighbour, Tunisia, is now increasingly scrutinized for such potential.

Case study

All hopes in Tunisia

Tunisia provides the student of the politics of the Middle East with cause for optimism when it comes to the topic of democracy. This was not always the case. For decades, under the rule of President Ben Ali, scholars regarded the state as lacking democratic features. The framework of exclusion that defined the state limited elements of reform that were introduced by the governing regime in the 'name of democracy 'or 'plural governance'. Hegemonic control essentially characterized the state and inhibited demands for democracy and principles of power-sharing.

Democratic politics under Ben Ali was state-managed to preserve control and establish sufficient distance from society so as to disempower it. In the early 1990s, along with some of its other neighbours, the state embarked on processes of liberalization while managing to avoid relinquishing any meaningful power. For example, electoral reform occurred but it succeeded in co-opting the 'official' opposition, regulating it and controlling it. Such measures scarcely opened the way for meaningful opportunities for political participation. The new election laws placed the approval of opposition-party candidates in the hands of the ruling regime, and other freedoms and rights were still squeezed by the state. Furthermore, the state and its ruling party – the DRC – ensured its control of patronage networks throughout the country, making it even harder for opposition elements to feel as if they were competing on an even playing field. Open public discourse was discouraged unless it reinforced the hegemony of the President and his ruling party. Under such stifling conditions, Islamist opponents were also subject to fierce control, repression, imprisonment and exile (Lust-Okar and Zerhouni, 2008).

Thus, in Tunisia, as in other regimes across the region, forms of electoral 'democracy' were utilized by the state to consolidate control and policies of pacification of its citizens. From the 1990s the regime of Ben Ali embarked on so-called political reform. Such reforms did not, however, bring an end to processes of political exclusion for major social and political groupings, including the Islamist movement (Milton-Edwards, 2016a). Electoral opportunities were not signs of a burgeoning democracy but stage-managed to defeat the nascent Islamist opposition: 'Tunisia has been trying to enter the democratic era in a way that does not challenge the dominant party but still retains voter participation' (Zartman, 2015, p. 208). Islamists did not find succour among other opposition elements in their attempts to become incorporated into democratization processes. As Willis notes,

Box 6.7 The danger within

the opposition parties tried to maintain a common front to protest the clear restrictions on the political system, but were weakened by divisions between and within them about the extent to which they should confront or cooperate with the regime. Many opposition figures saw Tunisia's large Islamist movement as a greater danger and threat than the regime, and when Ben Ali moved against the Islamist Ennahda party in the early 1990s they felt they should side with the president.

(2012, pp. 131–2)

This is all the more ironic when one of the more positive features of the post-revolution democracy transition has been alliance and coalition-building between such elements.

Civil society in Tunisia has always had a strong organized character, but represented a form of challenge to Ben Ali's regime that he actively sought to repress. In many respects, Ben Ali was successful until the events of December 2010 when the Jasmine Revolution erupted, heralding the rapid change of power and end to authoritarian rule.

After the revolution, there were concerns that Tunisia's Islamists – principally but not exclusively Ennahda – would harness the transition and steer the country away from democracy. In some respects, the fears were both founded and unfounded. Unfounded because, as Gelvin noted, the Islamists were not the catalysts or drivers of the Jasmine Revolution when it broke out in December 2010. Founded because, even though 'it did not guide or even participate [in the revolution] … The speed with which Ennahda regrouped after Ben Ali left, however, demonstrates it had not lost its appeal' (2012, p. 58).

Those fears heightened when the October 2011 polls put Ennahda and its leaders into power. This was conditional on having to share power and enter into coalition with Tunisia's secular parties (Alexander 2012).

To be sure, the transition to democracy in Tunisia is constantly being negotiated between new state leaders and society. Powerful labour and trade union forces existing alongside resurgent Islamist and secular social elements shape civil society in Tunisia. Negotiating democracy has been apparent around a range of issues. Some are fundamental to democratic frameworks such as the constitution. Others are about how to build democracy while facing major economic challenges, alongside other national security threats. The two Ennahda-led governments (2011–13) struggled to meet such challenges and proved increasingly unpopular and reactive programmatically, especially in relation to the economy. There were evident reasons for some of this, which Guazzone outlines as including 'the difficulties of the overall context and the ideologically and politically fragmented nature of the government ... the opposition of the still unreformed state institutions, ... the lack of experienced personnel among the ruling parties and the related tendency to make new appointments on the basis of political loyalty and family ties, rather than competence' (2013, p. 36). In the 2014 election contest, voters opted for the secular alternative, electing Nida Tounes into power over Ennahda.

The transition to democracy in Tunisia has not been seamless. There has been a significant challenge in recreating democratic values beyond the amorphous imaginings of Tunisians and an array of external actors. References to the 'model' of democracy that Tunisia offers to the wider Middle East and North Africa region are only partially helpful as they overlook the incompleteness of the transition process currently underway. Nevertheless, the democratic transition in Tunisia is focusing attention away from the monopoly of the state onto the establishment of new relationships and forms of union with society. This has necessitated the negotiation of a new social contract. The challenges remain but the efforts of Tunisians to build democracy were recognized in 2015 when the Tunisian Dialogue Quartet (consisting of workers, employers, lawyers and activists) were awarded the Nobel Prize for Peace (Nakhle, 2017). The outlook is not assured but Tunisia does demonstrate that democracy in the region can arise from deeply authoritarian states, and that Islamists – alongside other actors – can play an important role in constructing new political frameworks that are increasingly plural, rights-based and open, and focus on establishing security and stability for prosperity.

Questions for discussion

- Is there an argument for the exceptionalism of the Middle East when it comes to democracy?
- Is Islam and democracy an oxymoron?
- What does Tunisia, post-Arab Spring, tell us about democracy promotion?

Recommended reading

- Esposito, Sonn and Voll (2016), along with Saikal and Acharya (2014), provide introductory overviews to some of the themes associated with the debate in the Middle East. Owen (2004) gives a historical account of the emergence of political parties, aspects of electoral politics and the emergence of one-party political regimes in the earlier half of the twentieth century.
- On the theme of Islam and democracy in the Middle East, there is insight offered in the account of authors such as Hamid (2014), Akyol (2013) and Mirsepassi and Fernee (2016).
- On Jordan, the debate about democracy can be found in Milton-Edwards and Hinchcliffe (2009), while politics in general in the country are discussed in Jonasson (2016) and Braizat (2010). Jones (2007) has a chapter on both Morocco and Jordan in his volume on new politics in the Middle East.
- On Morocco, the following are recommended: Bergh (2017) and Boukhars (2010), which take account of democratic reform in the wake of the Arab Spring. Ottaway and Riley (2006), Boukhars (2010), Storm (2007) and Sater (2007) debate democracy dynamics in Morocco.
- The case study of Tunisia throws up fresh debate about the country as a future model for transition in the Middle East, and this is apparent in the works of Fergany (2016), M'rad (2015) and Winiarek (2015).

CHAPTER SEVEN

Women: the Invisible Population

Introduction

Women in the Middle East have traditionally been relegated to a minor role in the dominant patriarchal systems of religious, social, economic and political relations. Women remain a largely marginal force who are often absent from the public and political domain – literally, as figure 7.1 graphically illustrates, obscured from view.

However, women have been and remain an important influence in society; their apparent marginal role has much to do with Eurocentric orientalist and feminist views on the subject, among other factors (L. Ahmed, 1992). In the contemporary era, their battle for rights has been linked with the early twentieth-century anti-colonial Arab nationalist movements that achieved independence in the 1950s and 1960s. Arab independence, state-encouraged or state-directed feminism, state socialism and social reform have, however, impacted in unexpected ways on women's rights.

One aspect of this impact is reflected in the important debate about the rights and status of women in the laws of various states, including their rights to education, work, and relations to men, inheritance and property. In addition, many would argue that the root of women's oppression in much of society in the region lies in the Islamic religion and its attitude to women. Yet, as Kelly noted, 'a substantial deficit in women's rights persists in every country in the MENA region … [and] women throughout the Middle East continue to face systematic discrimination in both laws and social customs. Deeply entrenched societal norms, combined with conservative interpretations of Shari'a (Islamic law), continue to relegate women to subordinate status' (Kelly, 2010, pp. 1–2).

Both western and Arab feminist authors have been critical of Islam in respect of women's rights. Arab feminist authors such as Fatima Mernissi, for example, have developed a thesis which questions not only the way in which Islam (or Muslim men) has created a particular place for women in the social order, but the way in which certain orthodox interpretations of the religion perceive women as actively threatening sexual beings undermining Muslim male order and authority (Mernissi, 1985). But as Judith Tucker reminds us, 'there is actually little agreement on what the central texts of

Figure 7.1 *Women: not seen and not heard.* © *Stephen Farrell*

the religion have to say about gender. The Quran … is rather vague or so all-encompassing on most gender questions as to offer only very general guidance on the subject' (Tucker, 1993, p. ix).

Debate then, has focused on Islam in relation to gender issues and is used as a guide. Issues of marriage rights, polygamy, inheritance and dress are not as fixed as many associated with one perspective or another might have us think, and are open to the same methods of interpretation as other issues. As Leila Ahmed (1992) has outlined, there is no single blueprint of behaviour for Muslim women – rather, an accretion of roles determined as much by faith as by history, class, culture and economic context. Indeed, the Islam–women debate has created two distinct approaches. The first promotes the argument outlined above: that dimensions of Islamic culture(s) have created significant problems for women in the Middle East. The second approach, discussed further in this chapter, claims that Islam and the current revival of the religion is actually responsible for the liberation of women, protecting and respecting their status and role rather than objectifying and denigrating them as has occurred in the secularized West. The ideological impulse behind both positions is very dynamic and not difficult to discern. It reflects the ways in which women's issues have become a significant site of contest between opposing forces, within the region as well as globally.

Islam, however, is just one factor contributing to the current status endured by women in the Middle East today. It is important, therefore, to address indicators of socio-economic status – work, the domain of the home and associated issues – to gain a deeper insight into women's lives as they are currently experienced across the region. In societies that have prospered and remained largely static politically, like the Arab states of the Gulf, women have by and large remained powerless, marginal and excluded. Inroads in terms of formal participation in the political systems of such states – enfranchisement for women, women being able to stand as candidates in elections, women elected to parliaments for the first time – have been incremental and limited.

Issues of citizenship, suffrage, economic independence, violence and education for women are only given limited address in national government agendas. While some states have made a few advances more than others, the political patriarchy of these states has ensured the continued control of women and debates about their status, rights and political roles in society. The creation of wealth in these societies, therefore, has not always empowered women. Feminist debate and discourse has played an important part in the way in which not only women in the Middle East, but the region as a whole, are viewed. An increasing number of writers are reflecting on the import of Eurocentric feminist debates, the dominance of liberal feminism or state feminisms, and have contributed further to the debate about the 'other' initiated by Said in the late 1970s. As such, the gendering of the Middle East remains in a state of constant evolution, constructing the 'other' not just in the post-orientalist sense but in terms of gender and the rights of women in the region more generally.

The role of women in nationalist movements

The rise of Arab nationalism, anti-colonialism and the independence movement in the Arab world has a strong link with women's rights. The earliest stirrings of the women's movement coincided with, and involved women who were also engaged in, national struggles against colonial powers in the region.

The history of the women's struggle during this period, then, may be reflected through the lens of nationalism, be it Egyptian, Iraqi, Syrian or Palestinian. As such, the independence, development, progress, setbacks, concrete gains and perceived losses of the movement for women's rights can only be understood by appreciating the political climate of the time, which dictated the role that such individuals and movements would have.

This climate also ensured that, although the issues of women's rights, suffrage, political participation and so on were given attention, the agenda for action was male-dominated – very few women, if any at all, were able to achieve real positions of power, and the political activities which women began to engage in were often associated with traditional female occupations such as education, or through the burgeoning networks of women's charity associations which were established during this period. Arab nationalism was largely an expression of patriarchy, and although the leaders of such movements appealed to women to support their cause, it was as mothers, daughters and wives, not as women with independent rights.

As Botman (1987) noted, using the example of Egyptian nationalism, 'With few exceptions, political work was performed by Egyptian men who, through family prominence, wealth, political connections or the patronage system, rose up the legislative ladder. Women participated in public affairs only sporadically, essentially because Egyptian society was socially traditional and highly conservative' (p. 14). These national movements for independence presented women with an opportunity to play a role on the margins of their own history and society, and a double-edged dilemma in the quest for their rights in the legal, social and religious spheres. As such, they were constantly reminded that, while their struggle must take second place to the larger fight for national independence and freedom from colonial rule, their liberation would come only when the people were freed from the yoke of colonialism and imperialism.

It might have been assumed that the national independence movements of the Arab world would achieve the social, political, economic and legal reforms that some women dreamed of when independence was gained. In reality, however, the outcome was somewhat different. First, it has to be remembered that, although some women did play an important role in independence movements in countries like Algeria in the 1960s, their involvement was never a primary objective or the result of a widespread social revolution that had taken place as nations struggled against colonial powers. Indeed, in Algeria, despite the fact that as many as 10,000 women played a role in the revolution, the leaders of the FLN and the Armée de Libération Nationale (ALN) absorbed many of the reactionary ideological positions on the subject of women that were prevalent in Algerian society at the time. As Knauss (1987) highlighted, patriarchy and control of women after French attempts to define their role were ways of resisting the colonial onslaught. Fanon, as quoted by Gerner (1984), sums up the French colonial position: 'If we want to destroy the structure of Algerian society, its capacity for resistance, we must first conquer the women; we must go and find them behind the veil where they hide themselves in their houses where men keep them out of sight' (p. 76).

The women heroes of revolutions were a minority, predominantly drawn from the Arab bourgeoisie and leftist forces. The primary goal of the Arab nationalist movement was independence from foreign rule, not necessarily the transformation of society. While it was inevitable that the transition from one order to another would incorporate some changes, traditional patterns of social and power relations within society between men and women would remain largely unchanged. During the Algerian war of independence (1957–62), women did play a role in the ranks of the FLN, mainly in a gendered service function such as that of a cook or cleaner, yet the legends of women fighters, such as Djamila Bouhired, Djamila Bouazza, Zahia Khalifah and Djennet Hamidoh, and the nature of the role they played, have been reassessed, as Minces (1978) argued:

Box 7.1 Hardly a word of their own

In the milieu of Algerian society and traditions, women, as such, hardly had a word of their own to say … [when] the men had to go underground or flee the country, then they turned over to women tasks that they themselves could no longer carry out. That is to say … women were utilized … it appears that very few women entered the battle on their own initiative.

(p. 162)

Whether these experiences in themselves were liberating for women should also be questioned. Unfounded hopes and false dawns might be a more appropriate description of what was offered to women by national movements throughout the region during the era of independence. The making of myths, the women fedayeen, resistance fighters and bombers, and heroines of the struggle could be manipulated by the leadership of progressive national movements to portray their struggles as social revolutions in traditional societies where women were a silent force. Yet the great national consciousness-raising of women in these societies never occurred, either during or after such revolutions. Indeed, the leaders of Arab independence hoped to satisfy women with incremental rather than full-scale reform of legislation relating to their status post-independence. As Knauss (1987) highlights in the case of Algeria, post-independence rhetoric was firmly rooted in patriarchal attitudes; as such, 'the imperative needs of the male revolutionaries to restore Arabic as the primary language, Islam as the religion of the state, Algeria as free and fully independent and themselves as sovereigns of the family' communicated a clear position on the role of women in all this (p. xii).

Bourgeois feminism emerged among the small elite of women in cities such as Cairo, Damascus, Beirut, Algiers and Baghdad. As a result, associated with the nationalist movement for independence in the Arab world, it did achieve some important changes. As Hatem highlights, 'they created a new social climate and a political economic system that accepted women's rights to public space, where they were expected to pursue public activities like

education, work, and some forms of political participation, especially suffrage' (Hatem, 1993, pp. 39–40).

The achievement of public space for women was a remarkable step forward
in itself, as Badran highlights in the example of Egypt in the 1990s: 'Feminist
movements ... in the first half of the century and public policy under
Nasser's programme of Arab socialism assisted women in making vast inroads
into all aspects of society. Today they are found in virtually every sector of
the economy and all levels, although generally not heavily clustered at the
top' (1994, p. 209). As we shall see in the following sections, the battle to
maintain women's rights to public space throughout the Middle East has
been hard fought, with as many defeats as victories. In addition, although
the street may have belonged to women, other improvements regarding their
rights would either be slow in coming or would never materialize at all.

As I have already pointed out, the nationalist agenda did not incorporate
a clear position on women's rights and steered clear of controversy by declaring that discussion would be postponed until after independence. Bourgeois
feminism was too much in its infancy to challenge the whole edifice maintaining the traditional balance of power in Arab patriarchal society. The
freedom that these women enjoyed had not been taken by them but had
been granted by men within the framework of a modern movement for
national liberation and independence. As such, the granting of the right to
public space was about anti-colonialism and the portrayal of women through
the lens of Orientalism as much as – if not more than – it was about truly
recognizing the rights of all women irrespective of their class, religion, education or position in society. The issue of women's rights during this era of
nationalism, then, can be described as a battle between the colonial and the
Arab male for the possession of women and control over their lives, and as
a rearticulated patriarchal agenda in Arab society with a façade of modern
themes regarding the rights of women.

Identity and independence

The end of colonialism and the birth of national independence for the states
of the Middle East should have heralded an era of democracy and freedom.
Issues of Arab, Zionist and Iranian identity post-independence, however,
would often be forged through a prevailing patriarchal lens and tendency to
authoritarianism. From the Maghreb to the Gulf, the new Arab order would
change in many ways – agrarian, economic and educational – but the traditional patterns of patriarchy would be maintained. One interesting exception to this position is found in the example of post-independence Tunisia,
where the liberal position of President Habib Bourguiba in 1956 was reflected
in the new Personal Status Code (1957). This removed religious authority
from issues directly affecting women such as marriage, divorce and custody,
while at the same time it outlawed polygamy (as previously permitted by

shari'a) (Salem, 1984). The patriarchal attitudes which prevailed in society, however, were rarely challenged, and the state – socialist, progressive or conservative – played an enormous part in presenting an idealized vision of women which consolidated chauvinistic values. In Iraq, for example, the Ba'th Party slogan of 'unity, socialism and independence' was interpreted for Iraqi women by the male-dominated military dictatorship led from 1979 to 2003 by Saddam Hussein. Women's visions of independence and freedom were largely ignored and subordinated to the national agenda, post-independence, of state-building and then state-consolidation.

The fate of women in the radical, progressive regimes of the Middle East did improve in some respects, but in others women have found their notions of identity and freedom challenged by the very state apparatus which they played their part in establishing. On the issue of women's rights, the progressive state has often turned its back and maintained the traditional relationship based on patriarchal dominance. In addition, state feminisms have promoted a particular vision of women which has more to do with national economic and political agendas than meaningful rights. Instead, such issues have been harnessed by the state and certain women have been promoted as symbols of particular state policies and visions, which have been sold as reflecting a deep-seated concern with what women want. This useful coalescence of approaches has been particularly pertinent as secular state and Islamist forces entered into battle to win public opinion and support throughout the 1980s and 1990s.

One area of progress has been literacy. There has been a step increase in Arab female education. By 2015, the UN's Economic and Social Commission for West Asia (ESCWA) reported that female literacy levels in the region were as high as 80 per cent (UN ESCWA, 2015). Unfortunately, such progress has not translated into a compelling outcome in terms of female employment rates in the region.

Very often, women are being held back by the fate of motherhood, which remains idealized by the state and often lacks meaningful state assistance in any form. The rapid expansion of population in most Middle East countries, coupled with poor support from the state through education, welfare, health, employment or childcare programmes, policy or planning, means that women in the region are continually burdened and compelled to conform to ideal types which the state constructs as part of its efforts at nation-building and consolidation. In Syria, for example, Ba'th Party posters presented an image of women which emphasized the multiple roles they have had to play.

Women, even post-independence, often remain defined by their status as wife, mother or daughter, rather than as individuals with a variety of roles to play in society. In reality, women are regularly denied meaningful political equality and are barely represented in formal spheres of power associated with the state. Their economic rights are also constrained by the marginal role they are compelled to play in the labour force (Momani, 2016). Employ-ment opportunities outside the home remain limited to say the least, and are governed by a variety of family- and society-imposed restrictions. In Iraq, under the regime of Saddam Hussein, for example, employment outside the home often only occurred as a result of war and associated labour shortages. Emancipation for women through the Ba'th Party, however, was designed to strengthen the Ba'th within the powerful arena of the home and the family. The women were compelled to serve as vehicles for ideology.

In Libya, under the rule of President Gaddafi (1969–2011), an all-woman personal bodyguard was supposed to symbolize the notion of equality pro-moted by the Jamahiriya. In reality they were no more independent from men than the women of Saudi Arabia confined to their homes and prohibited from freedom of movement. In Egypt, the coup d'état led by Gamal Abdel Nasser and the Free Officers in 1952 proved a setback for the nascent feminist movement. The leftist relations enjoyed by these small feminist groups and leaders proved fatal following Nasser's policy of suppression against the left as he consolidated his power in the late 1950s and early 1960s. Nevertheless, Nasser and his government did incorporate some changes into the socialist state which was established following the coup. Like other progressive regimes, there was some attempt to improve women's opportunities in areas of education, rights to suffrage and health. The similarity, however, did not end here, as Badran noted: 'Women, other than tokens, did not make it to the top echelons of the government bureaucracy or professions, and they were virtually segregated in areas of work deemed more fitting for females … Finally, the old personal status laws remained in force, symbolically and practically oppressive to women' (1993, p. 139). In Egypt, as in other post-independence states, the demise of one male leader and the rise of another did little or nothing to improve the position and rights of women within the state. To date, there is little evidence of Arab women playing a decisive role in any government in the region. This is not to say that women have not achieved government positions. In 2016, the business magazine *Forbes* pub-lished a list of the 'The 10 Most Powerful Arab Women in Government', citing the names of Ministers of State from Qatar, Egypt, Jordan, UAE, Oman, Morocco, Algeria, Bahrain and Kuwait. The list illustrated that, despite being highly successful, women oversaw portfolios associated with so-called tradi-tional female concerns, such as social development, welfare, health and education (Forbes Middle East, 2016). Even within Israel, where there has been a female Prime Minister, where women serve in the army, and certain rights are legally protected, the battle for equality between the sexes is far from over.

In the 1980s and 1990s, as Arab regimes grappled with internal conflicts, dissension and power struggles, the Arab feminist struggle continued. These feminist movements were secular, religious and activist in nature, though they were largely elite-based (Afshar, 1998). Increasingly, the Arab world was becoming caught between two conflicting creeds. The first was the pressure for modernization, westernization, a liberal economy and more democratic governance. But there was an emerging argument that this had brought disruption to Arab society and to the second creed, the traditional way of life.

Modernization has been coupled to debates about empowering women. In 2004 (and subsequent reporting), the UNDP Arab Human Development (AHD) Report highlighted the debilitating effects on the region's development arising from the exclusion of women in terms of education, employment, politics and society. The report also highlighted the lack of political opportunities available for women evident in voting rights (or rather the lack of them) and participation in the region's legislatures. Women have begun to make incremental progress in terms of representation in legislatures across the region. In 2015, the Inter-Parliamentary Union (IPU) reported that Arab women only accounted for 17 per cent of legislative representation, as opposed to 27 per cent in Europe (IPU, 2015). Much of this progress is linked to the growing impact of gender quotas in legislative contexts in states such as Egypt and Jordan (Shalaby, 2016). Such data are further contrasted negatively by the limited progress on political rights for women in Gulf states. Thus, even where political participation advances for women across the region, it is a hard-won and tortuously slow process and remains woefully inadequate when compared to the political rights of women elsewhere across the globe.

There is considerable gender-based violence against women and girls in the region, and this is manifest in violence in domestic and intimate settings. It is also evident in female genital mutilation or cutting as well as so-called honour violence. Violence associated with conflict in the Middle East has grown exponentially in the wake of the Arab Spring as states become increasingly fragile or broken and a number of armed state and non-state elements target women and perpetrate violence (including rape) against them (Human Rights Watch, 2016). This has led to what is described as a significant denial of women's fundamental human rights in the region. In all of these situations, women are targeted and subjected to forms of tyranny and abuse. As Tetreault and al-Mughni asserted, 'The conceptualization of women as the "intimate enemy" makes their control by men a primary focus of concern, especially for men whose status and power are threatened' (1995, p. 415).

Women and Islam

The debate about women and Islam reflects, to a great extent, the issues which have been discussed in the sections above. Crudely stated, the debate has a dichotomous character and is centred on the question of whether or not Islam contributes further to the enslavement or liberation of Muslim women living in the Middle East. In reality, this question has no clear-cut answer, but it can be said that the resurgence of Islam across the region has had an important impact – positively and negatively – on women's lives.

Islam does embrace certain attitudes towards women, and in the contemporary era these attitudes have been utilized to portray images which have been dominated by conservative Islamists. Islam has a lot to say about women; the Koran and the *hadith* both address the rights, roles, behaviours and ideals of women inside and outside the faith. Women are frequently perceived as the most visible sign of the current resurgence of Islam, and questions concerning their dress, behaviour and rights have been hotly contested across the region (Jawad, 1998). From the West, the continuing fascination with the oriental 'Arab' or 'Muslim' woman persists through cultural stereotypes of two extremes – the belly-dancing siren of the harems or the black chadour-clad and niqab-wearing female fundamentalists of revolutionary Islamic Iran. Both stereotypes fetishize Muslim women and reflect forms of cultural appropriation. In 2015, for example, 'reality celebrity' Khloe Kardashian instagrammed pictures of herself (see figure 7.2 below) on a visit to the Gulf country of the United Arab Emirates, fully veiled and captioned 'habibi love'. The post was criticized for cultural appropriation and absenting of respect for Islam and women either choosing or compelled to wear the niqab, and the symbolism associated with it.

Islam is perceived as significant in the lives of women and the question of women's issues, which is in itself important in understanding the changes

Figure 7.2 *Habibi love (@khloekardashian, 2015)*

wrought in Middle Eastern societies. The contest has centred on who has the right or legitimate interpretation of women's role according to Islam, rather than the attention paid to women in the Koran and the Sunna (Karam, 1998). Should this interpretation be literal or should it reflect the modern era in which we live? The contest is undertaken by both men and women, secularists and Islamists, fundamentalists and liberals, activists and reactionaries, feminists and non- feminists. Indeed, whether one believes the term 'Muslim/Islamist feminist' to be an oxymoron or not, the debate which women themselves have engaged in provides the most beneficial insights (Karam, 1998).

A large number of verses (*sura*) in the Koran deal with women and the issues affecting them. These verses proclaim on marriage, including polygamous relations for men; divorce; inheritance; child-rearing; menstruation; discipline against disobedient women; adultery; and relations with men. It is also contended that the Koran empowers women – giving them rights in divorce and inheritance, as mothers of children and widows: 'Divorce must be pronounced twice and then [a woman] must be retained in honour or released in kindness. And it is not lawful for you that ye take from women aught of that which ye have given them' (Sura of the Cow, verse 229). On inheritance, the Koran declares: 'Unto the men [of the family] belongeth a share of that which parents and near kindred leave, and unto the women a share of that which parents and near kindred leave, whether it be little or much – a legal share' (Sura of Women, verse 7). Thus, for many Muslim women, their religion has acted as an important shelter and protector of their rights. Islam provides honour, dignity and strength within the faith, society and the family. In the era of Islamic resurgence, many nominally Muslim women have returned to active expression and adherence to their faith as a new means of independence. This return has been facilitated by the Islamic movement itself, particularly the conservative and radical elements which have campaigned to bring women back to the Muslim faith – conservative regimes in the Gulf have provided the money for Islamic dress for thousands of women, facilitated segregated education from primary to tertiary levels and funded the thousands of books, leaflets, magazines and articles written by Islamists for women. For these women, wearing the veil is an act of empowerment which means they can remain in the workplace with respect and move freely in public male-dominated space.

The conservative Islamist view of women is, however, contested, by those within the religion and outside it. From within the faith, authors such as Mahmoud have identified a 'mixed [or] hybrid discourse' which Islamist thinkers such as Tunisian Rashid al-Ghannushi have promoted to contest the issue of gender. This discourse, while going 'beyond the traditional Islamic position … does not go far enough to satisfy the legitimate aspirations of women in Muslim societies to see inequality and gender discrimination redressed' (Mahmoud, 1996, p. 262). As Eickelman and Piscatori remind us,

'The regime, established religious authorities, and counter-regime Islamists all claim to be the defender of family integrity and of the role and rights of women in an Islamic society. In so doing, each makes the ideas of family and women pivotal to contemporary Muslim politics' (Eickelman and Piscatori, 1996, p. 99). Thus, the authenticity of the conservatives is challenged. This challenge, however, has been marginal historically, and in the present day represents a minority view within the region. At the turn of the twentieth century, Islamic modernists emphasized the need for reform within Islam and a new interpretation of women's rights and roles. The modernists have seen 'reform on women's issues as centrally important to the reform of society as a whole, and ... [it] includes women's participation in the public sector (politics and work)' (Stowasser, 1993, p. 14). For modernists, the education, welfare and health of women remain central to a positive regeneration of Islam that empowers them in the contemporary era and withstands the scrutiny of the West.

Outside the religion, secular Arab critics of Islam have bemoaned its treatment of women. Writers such as Moroccan sociologist Fatima Mernissi (1985) have argued against the image of Islam which the religion promotes. They point to the important role women have played in society and politics and criticize the Islamists' objectification of women as a sexual threat. Such critics argue that Islam is holding women back and that if fundamentalists had their way women would be further enslaved by Islamists and their literal interpretations of seventh-century scriptures. Secular critics also identify the state as a chief culprit in aiding and abetting the Islamists in their task. By failing to take the initiative on family and civil law, the state allows the Islamists to win the argument and the state-paid clergy play their part in reinforcing the enslavement of women. Few examples exist in the region where the state has taken the initiative and used the law to change women's status for the better. The former People's Democratic Republic of Yemen (PDRY) is a rare exception, where, as Molyneux (1991) claims, 'the transformations in the structures and practices of law which were brought about ... had far-reaching implications for women ... the changes that were introduced can be recognized as important without exaggerating their overall impact or their contribution to "women's emancipation"' (p. 266). For the main part, the debate about women and Islam remains unresolved, with neither side able, to date, to claim victory. What will remain important is the path that women themselves choose in relation to Islam, rather than the route that men are currently claiming for them. One example of the new paths which women themselves are choosing is cited by Badran as 'gender activism': in Egypt in the 1990s, feminist, pro-feminist and Islamist women, while remaining grounded 'in divergent ideologies which in turn reflect their different configurations of identity and overlapping and yet distinct visions of the good society', found common ground and issues around which a common activism has been developed

(1994, p. 222). During the Arab Spring in Egypt in 2011, women were initially described as uniting together in such common call and indeed played a key role in the mobilization to protest against President Hosni Mubarak and call for change and reform. Political authorities soon assaulted that dynamic.

Box 7.2 Protest virginity tests

During the early months of the revolution, the military subjected female protesters to so-called 'virginity tests', acts of sexualized violence committed against women, ostensibly to prove that no other forms of sexualized violence had occurred. An unnamed general eventually admitted that the military had authorized these tests: 'We didn't want them to say we had sexually assaulted or raped them, so we wanted to prove that they weren't virgins in the first place', he said. 'The girls who were detained were not like your daughter or mine. These were girls who had camped out in tents with male protesters in Tahrir Square, and we found in the tents Molotov cocktails and [drugs].'

(Zaltsman, 2012)

In 2013, Islamist women were targeted by counter-revolutionary forces during the bloody episodes of violence that witnessed the end of the democratically elected government of President Mohammed Morsi and the installation of General el-Sisi. As McRobie argued, 'We must conceptualise the epidemic levels of sexual violence in post-revolutionary Egypt at least partly as "state violence", and resist the state's attempt to selectively appropriate women's rights. Every post-revolutionary Egyptian regime has the blood of women on its hands' (McRobie, 2014).

Subjugation

The ideal type represented to women in the Middle East through their state, family, society and religion depicts the relationship between women, wealth and work as purely domestic in location (Roded, 2008). For many decades, this idealized notion was generally accepted by researchers and writers. It was assumed that the harem, seclusion and the marginal space which women occupied in Middle Eastern society prohibited their role in the creation of wealth, in employment or work outside the home. In other words, women were perceived as invisible in the world of work and income generation, as they were in the realm of formal and state politics. It was understood that predominant religious and cultural values played their part in excluding women and regulating their absence at a formal level. This assumption stemmed from the absence of women's research in the subject, the domination of social science and other disciplines by men and their failure, as a result either of unwillingness or of inability, to come into contact with women in the Middle East and experience the impact of work on their lives. Ultimately, it is surprising that for so long the fundamental changes in the socio-economic environment of the region – modernization, rapid economic growth, industrialization, urbanization, decline of agriculture, population growth, migrant labour patterns, the growth of modern capital-led econo- mies and state-led economic liberalization – were deemed insignificant to women and their lives.

While earlier observations of women and work (or lack of it) in countries like Saudi Arabia or Kuwait may be valid, they assume that women's work patterns in the region are both uniform and the same as, or similar to, male work patterns. But they do not take into account the ways in which women in the Middle East generate income and own property, or the role of wealth creation that they play both inside and outside the home. Many studies pro- duced in the 1970s and 1980s only reinforced existing stereotypes of Arab women as marginal or absent in relation to productive economy. Indeed, it was argued that a woman's productive capacity was located in the family through her 'reproductive' abilities, as well as her duties to rear offspring. In conditions where rates of unemployment have been high, this role has been further emphasized, as Mernissi (1985) argued: 'a society having diffi- culty creating jobs for men tends to fall back on traditional customs that deny women's economic dimension and define them purely as sexual objects – and to write those customs into law' (p. 148).

Women in the Middle East are workers, both in the home and, increas- ingly, outside it. Levels of participation in the workforce have increasingly risen but are not 'commensurate' with the strides taken by women in educa- tion rates (Momani, 2016, p. 3). According to World Bank data, female par- ticipation rates in the workplace outside the home have only risen by a meagre 0.17 per cent annually since the late 1980s (World Bank et al., 2011).

Work trends within the region have changed, and with them the role of women. Where previously women's work was underestimated, present-day studies are starting to focus on the role women play as key economic figures in family units (extended and nuclear) and the impact this has on the relative wealth of society as a whole. Yet the argument which is repeated time and again is that, without the increased integration of women into the Arab workforce, the economies of the region will continue to fail to achieve their potential. While such analysis reflects the class-based divisions within society, regional and generational differences, marital status, as well as the predomi- nant Muslim cultural norms, it also recognizes that, while the prospects for women's financial independence may be highly restricted, they do enjoy increased levels of financial decision-making and freedom within the family unit. At official levels, particularly where the state draws up legislation bestowing a concept of national identity and duty, the role of women as independent economic actors is prohibited, as the Personal Status Code of

Morocco outlines: 'Every human being is responsible for providing for his needs (*nafaqa*) through his own means, with the exception of wives, whose husbands provide for their needs' (in Mernissi, 1985, p. 148). Within the family, however, wives, daughters and sisters do have an important economic role to play.

In many countries throughout the region, women are entering the workforce (see figure 7.3) and rates of income generation within the home are also increasing.

But, with the exception of Qatar, they are far below other regions of the globe, such as Europe or even other Muslim states. As the costs of living rise, the size of families continues to burgeon and one income becomes insufficient, women from the urban and rural lower classes begin to enter the workforce.

The informal sector encourages the majority of women entering paid employment for the first time, for a variety of reasons: it is seasonal, requires low if any capital outlay, is flexible and often located either within neighbourhoods or in other locations where women in particular may feel free to bring their children with them. The impact of this sector on the economy in general is difficult to estimate, but it has been concluded that the urban informal sector plays a significant role in a number of countries in the region.

While women's patterns of work have changed, particularly through entrance into the informal economic sector, it is still apparent that, across the region as a whole, there is little evidence to suggest that women are economically independent. In addition, 'their access to such resources [financial] is overwhelmingly tied to the mechanism of marriage ... What this means is that women's standard of living seems largely to be determined by

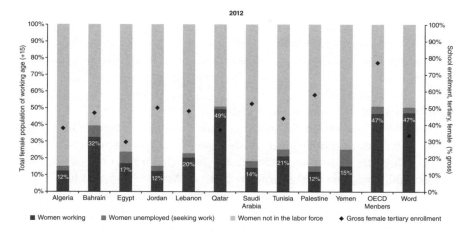

Figure 7.3 *Women in the labour force*

either the spouse or the family – they are, in other words, overwhelmingly dependent' (Hammami, 1997, p. 309). The state, through personal status legislation, often reinforces this dependency and inequality. Cultural pressures, meanwhile, are evident against women seeking to carve out an independent role.

Yet without women in the workplace, as drivers of the economy, international organizations such as the UNDP and IMF argue that the region will find it impossible to achieve economic recovery in the wake of a two-decade slump (IMF, 2015). Yet work has not necessarily resulted in the political empowerment of women; rather, it has tended to circumscribe further their role within the family structure and prevent their emancipation on an individual level, 'where women first enter the paid workforce, the decision to do so should not automatically be celebrated as a sign of emancipation. It is as likely to be a sign of distress – prompted by approaching landlessness in a peasant economy for example, or increasing impoverishment as a consequence of crisis in an urban economy' (Cammack et al., 1993, p. 242).

Feminism and gender discourses

It remains an unfortunate fact that many introductory textbooks on the subject of the Middle East consistently fail to address the issue of women in the region. A glance through the index and chapters of these books throws up little or no reference to the subject. When women are cited, they are always associated with, or cross-referenced within, a narrow vocabulary: women – and wearing hijab; clothing of; equality; or rights. The impression given from these books is that when it comes to telling the story of politics in the Middle East, the state, Islam, democracy and the military are all vital ingredients, while women and the issues affecting them are not even worthy of a single citation in an index. For example, a 2010 text specifically addressing globalization and the politics of development of the Middle East omitted the topic of women. What the major textbooks lack, new scholarship, mostly by women, seeks to redress in books dealing with this subject that have emerged with increasing frequency. Scholarship on the subject, however, has not emerged in any universal form, as Kandiyoti reminds us: 'advances in feminist scholarship have been incorporated into studies about the Middle East in a partial and selective manner' (1996, p. 18).

Feminist scholarship on the Middle East has traditionally been Eurocentric. Even Arab feminist scholars from within the region have viewed their experiences through a European social science lens. One impact of colonialism, for example, has been a small educated elite of Arab women who have been schooled by Europeans or according to European traditions of teaching and scholarship. A subsequent outcome of this has been a tendency in the past for Arab feminist scholars to base their work on western political science, sociological or anthropological approaches. Kandiyoti believes that, since the

1960s, contemporary feminist scholarship in Middle East studies has passed through four 'waves' – from writing which has concentrated on the colonial experience and independence movements of the earlier part of the twentieth century ('feminism and nationalism'), through 'the rise of social science paradigms and developments' and 'dialogues within feminism,' to the current wave in which feminist theorists debate which path women should take as one millennium has ended and another begins (Kandiyoti, 1996, pp. 1–18).

Feminist scholarship in the Middle East also encompasses a variety of disciplines, from anthropologists engaged in traditional studies of women's dress, embroidery and jewellery to social scientists studying the lives of urban Egyptian women in Cairo. In sociology, economics, politics, literature, art, agricultural and development studies, international relations and politics, feminist researchers and authors from inside and outside the region are attempting to rewrite women into the landscape of the Middle East. This in turn moves women from segregated spaces into wider forms of scholarship.

In 1986, feminist theorist Beverly Thiele argued that 'it is common knowledge among feminists that social and political theory was, and for the most part still is, written by men, for men and about men' (1986, p. 30). It takes no great leap of imagination to apply this statement to current writing on the Middle East. The literature on contemporary politics in the region, like so many other aspects of life, has reflected a predominantly male-centric agenda and thus its 'subject matter reflects male concerns, deals with male activity and male ambitions and is directed away from issues involving or of concern to women' (1986, p. 30). The arrival of feminist authors who seek to gender the politics of the region stands as a glimmer of hope in this barren landscape. They are putting women back into the study of politics, particularly in the realm of informal politics where they have greater influence and power. These authors are also challenging the current conceptualization of the region, making it clear that 'ostensibly neutral political processes and concepts such as nationalism, citizenship and the state' are not only Eurocentric but 'fundamentally gendered' and therefore biased as well (Waylen, 1996, p. 5). Given the contested nature of these concepts in the Middle East, the additional gender bias must also go some way in reshaping the ideas and lenses through which the region can successfully be viewed and understood, particularly in terms of Islamism.

To what extent the above-stated goals will ever be achieved, particularly in the short term, is highly questionable. What remains important, however, is the process by which feminist approaches have, in one form or another, encouraged women to rethink their place – politically, culturally, religiously and economically. Through a gradualist approach, women are starting to look at themselves anew. This is not to say that political emancipation or opportunities for greater personal freedoms and rights have an assured future; the gatekeepers to such processes enabling the transformation of women's lives in the region remain male. Iran, for example, prohibited women in 2016 from taking selfies with footballers, women in Saudi Arabia are still banned from driving, and women in Iraq have faced the prospect of legislation that would ban them from holy cities such as Karbala unless veiled. In a clearly retrograde step, military officials in eastern Libya, in the spring of 2017, banned women under the age of 60 from travelling on their own.

In addition, the traditional barriers to women's progress need to be removed in a campaign to win support, not create enemies. Islam, at least in theory, can, for many Muslim and Islamist women, provide a degree of freedom and independence which hitherto remained largely unchallenged. Indeed, there is an increasing trend within the region, from Morocco to Iran, of women challenging the so-called authenticity of male-imposed prohibitions. The challenges mounted by Saudi women in terms of the public spaces they inhabit and occupy are just one such example (Le Renard, 2014). Also, outside as well as within the Muslim realm, aspects of womanhood in the region are celebrated. There is hope. Kurdish women and the role they have played in the nationalist movement in regions such as Rojava are explained as part of a 'double revolution' in which feminist and nationalist agendas 'prove to be complementary' (Bengio, 2012; 2016, p. 30). Amongst their own company women enjoy a freedom that celebrates multi-layered identities that are liberated from the male gaze. The gendering of the Middle East provides the opportunity for new frontiers to be established.

Case study

Palestinian women in the West Bank, East Jerusalem and the Gaza Strip

Traditionally, the call for women's rights and equality in Palestinian society was muted by the broader and stronger appeal for national unity in the struggle against Zionism and later Israeli occupation. From the 1920s, Palestinian women were either involved in charity work or served as adjuncts to the male-dominated national movement. In the late 1970s and early 1980s a change in the women's movement occurred: women organized politically affiliated committees to address the issues of work, economy and childcare. Women's participation in decision-making at a national level or in the leadership of the PLO was almost non-existent. However, the committees, although a step forward, were always subordinated to the PLO, and the issues they addressed were subordinated under the call for national unity until independence (Kuttab, 2008).

The outbreak of the Palestinian Intifada against Israel's occupation in December 1987 went some way to altering the traditional patriarchal hold over political activism and women's issues that Palestinian men had previously enjoyed (Said, 1989). The Intifada also presented women with new problems, and serious attempts were made by conservative nationalists and

Islamists to undermine the position of women in society and the limited freedoms that many were enjoying for the first time. For better or for worse, then, the Intifada changed the lives of many Palestinian women.

For the better, women from all backgrounds and classes, particularly in the first two years of the uprising, enjoyed unprecedented freedom to organize politically, in terms of both formal and informal activities. Thus, as well as literally taking to the streets to protest against the Israeli occupation, they were also key figures in the network of popular committees which sprang up throughout the West Bank and Gaza Strip (Jad, 1991). The public space which they occupied was shared, temporarily, with men, but the political structure of the Intifada, the United National Leadership of the Uprising (UNLU), which was the local arm of the PLO, remained male-dominated, and women were largely excluded from decision-making about strike days, demonstrations, strategy and tactics designed to maintain national unity and achieve the goal of ending the occupation.

The uprising also presented women with other dilemmas and difficulties, excluding them in a number of ways. The closure of schools and universities prevented them from gaining or finishing their education, and many young women were pressured into marrying early in the absence of opportunities for education and employment. At home, women were left to carry the burden of responsibility while many thousands of men were imprisoned by the Israeli authorities. The rise of traditional Islamic values fostered by the mainstream Hamas movement also led to increasing authority exercised by men over women's lives (Milton-Edwards and Farrell, 2010). The return to traditional values led to campaigns, organized by Hamas and tacitly supported by the mainstream nationalist movement, to compel women to stay at home, look after the family, raise and educate children, and dress in a modest and Islamic fashion. As Hammami noted, the impact of the hijab (headscarf) campaign waged by Hamas in the early 1990s was manifold, yet initially resulted in women feeling frightened and marginalized from the public space. One unforeseen outcome, however, was the resistance to this issue mounted by Palestinian women, feminists and activists: 'If Hamas succeeded to some extent in Islamicizing Palestinian national culture, it simultaneously succeeded in bringing parts of the Palestinian women's movement to a new feminist awareness ... that ignoring social issues had been extremely short-sighted' (Hammami, 1997, p. 205).

These campaigns communicated a powerful message to Palestinian women: they must subordinate their claims to equality, their calls for freedom and choice, and these desires must be sacrificed for the greater goals of an end to the Israeli occupation of the West Bank and Gaza Strip and national independence for the Palestinian people. While the majority of Palestinian women bowed down in the face of political demands from the patriarchal leadership of the nationalist movement, a small minority refused to put their demands to one side. As Glavanis-Grantham noted, 'Palestinian women activists warn of the dangers of subordinating the social struggle to the national struggle to the extent that women may have the gains of the Intifada subverted and return to and be forced to return to the domesticity of former years, as were women activists in post-liberation Algeria' (1996, p. 176). In reality, however, this is what happened. First, feminist agendas were, and are still, regarded with suspicion, even by progressive and leftist elements of the nationalist political patriarchy. Second, over the decades since the signing of the Oslo Accords between Israel and the PLO in September 1993, the Palestinian national leadership has only scored a few modest successes in terms of women's issues.

Palestinian self-rule in the West Bank and Gaza Strip has been beset with a variety of problems since the establishment of the Palestinian National Authority (PNA) in 1993. One major issue associated with the interim period of limited autonomy was the question of how democracy could survive the authoritarian tendencies of the PNA and the cadres of the PLO who returned from Tunis, and then, after 2006, Hamas rule and entrenchment of control in the Gaza Strip after the latter took complete power in June 2007. The promotion and maintenance of democracy are inextricably linked to the debate about equality and women's rights, as well as to the feminist agenda that Palestinians embrace. To date, the outlook is not encouraging; the institutions of the PLO, PNA, the Palestinian Legislative Council and the nationalist and Islamist hierarchy remain male-dominated.

Women candidates to the Palestinian legislature and municipal councils, however, have been encouraged through quotas applied to women candidates in electoral lists. Nevertheless, women's issues are not being given the long-promised attention they deserve. Indeed, like most nationalist and nationalist-religious movements which have attained some form of power within the Middle East, the position of the PNA on women's rights is depressingly familiar. As Hammami noted, the PNA's stance on the role of women in nation-building is tokenistic: 'wives of the elite as representatives of national womanhood; and a preference for modernist appearances ... avoidance of changing the real underpinnings of women's oppression by addressing legislation or unequal power relations' (1997, p. 206).

Hamas too has been critiqued for its agenda on women and the restricting of their freedoms and rights in the Gaza Strip (Milton-Edwards and Farrell, 2010). Even at community level, the battle for equality has fared little better. As Giacaman and Johnson noted in the 1990s: 'the increase in feminist consciousness, often remarked on, has so far found little resonance in institutional struggles over women's issues, whether at schools and universities, factories or hospitals – three sites where women's presence and gender inequalities might reasonably engender women's demands' (1994, p. 25). More than twenty years on, little has changed in relation to gender inequalities.

Palestinian women have also long borne the burden of the Israeli occupation and its consequences, both as individuals and as a dimension of society.

> **Box 7.3 No normal life**
>
> There is no such thing as a normal life. All there is are closed spaces, enclosed feelings, pressures which are social and political. And the fight for women's rights is related to the occupation because we are now an ugly mutilated society that cannot naturally unfold or deal with its own issues.
>
> ('Laleh', women's activist, author interview, Hebron, West Bank, May 2013)

The political, social and economic conditions on the ground remain challenging for Palestinian women in particular. Conditions of occupation – whether in respect of obstacles and barriers to freedom, right to freedom of assembly, food insecurity, health or unemployment – affect women and girls differently from Palestinian men because of gender-based discrimination and inequalities from both Israel and fellow Palestinians (United Nations Economic and Social Council, 2012). Available data show that women's unemployment rates during the second quarter of 2012 remained high, at 47.2 per cent in the Gaza Strip and 21.4 per cent in the West Bank. Women's participation rates in the labour force stood at only 14.9 per cent (compared with 65.9 per cent for males) in Gaza, and at 18.6 per cent (compared with 71.5 per cent for males) in the West Bank (www.peacewomen.org/assets/file/situation_of_and_assistance_to_palestinian_women.pdf).

The Palestinian women's movement is today, however, diverse in terms of its voices and its discourse, but it faces an uphill struggle in bringing the rights and equality debate to the forefront of local political discourse. It is argued that Palestinian women still struggle to break down patriarchy which views them as passive and detaches them from the struggles taking place around them and which affect them deeply.

Case study

From beyond the veil – Iran since the revolution

While the issues of nationalism, feminism and revolution have been addressed in previous sections, the example of the Iranian revolution of 1979 allows us an opportunity to ask the same questions of Islamic nationalism and the theocracy that was established in its name. The women's movement in Iran since 1979 has experienced mixed fortunes and the rise and fall of two distinct approaches to women's rights – the secularized approach which has been all but forced into exile, and the emergence of an Islamic feminism which has struggled to maintain its autonomy from the state. Antagonisms remain, yet there is a consensus that the issue of women and their rights was and remains an important platform in legitimating the populist appeal of the Islamic republic, as well as resistance to it.

Under the regime of Mohammed Reza Shah Pahlavi, progress in women's rights and the women's movement was a state-sponsored exercise. Women enjoyed little if no autonomy from the regime to organize themselves. Social progress under the Shah was dictated by the state not in response to popular will or sentiment, but in an attempt to continue the modernization and westernization of Iran. The remit of modernization and westernization, slavishly replicating the values of the West and rejecting indigenous and authentic tradition, was a public exercise where women were concerned. While the Shah's father had outlawed the veiling of women and his son maintained the public façade of progress, in private – in the home – little progress was made. There the rights of men – the husband, brother, father or nephew – prevailed. Women were still left unprotected, legislation did not emerge, and women lived a dual existence. In the workplace and in public, they wore mini-skirts, make-up and worked in a mixed environment, because the state dictated it. At home, they obeyed the laws of the family, laws determined by religion and their men. As Paidar (1996) astutely remarked, 'The Pahlavi regime opposed women's independence in the family and their independent presence in the public sphere, and this influenced the logic behind state-sponsored women's organizations which made sure that women's lives inside and outside the home remained under the control of male guardians' (p. 56).

It was this controlling environment that encouraged a generation of Iranian women to turn to Islam as a source for the construction of their identity as women and opposition to the state and its image of the modern Iranian woman. The revolution of 1979 was notable for the wide-scale participation and support of women. Khomeini and the Shi'a clergy promoted a vision of an Islamic utopia where Iranian women believed their rights would finally be recognized. The theocracy went some way, at least initially, in encouraging women in this belief. The new political leadership was as quick to utilize the issue of women as their predecessors had been. In this version of the story, however, women were idealized in a different way. They were the guardians of Islam; their veiling, their segregation, education and role as mothers and daughters would symbolize the strength of the theocracy. If, under Reza Shah, women were the epitome of modern Iranian society, then under Khomeini they would be depicted as the symbols of the revolution. This view, however, was almost immediately challenged by women themselves, who in March 1979 organized marches to protest against enforced veiling. The impact of this political challenge to Khomeini, however, went unsupported, as a variety of political and social organizations struggled to adjust to the new realities. State repression of this form of activism automatically followed, and this first battle by women was lost (Moghissi, 1994). Once again women were deemed unacceptable in the public space.

Box 7.4 Purifying space

The 1979 Islamic Revolution ... wanted to 'purify' public space in the name of Islam by clearing out women. Thousands of women were coerced into early retirement; many lost their jobs; many were forced into exile. Women were segregated in mosques, schools, universities, beaches and buses. They disappeared as entertainers and singers. They faded away from the silver screen. Women's place, it was argued, was not public but private, not out in the streets but inside the house.

(Milani, 2011, p. 1)

The state image of women, following this early defeat, was further embedded in the Iranian consciousness during the eight-year war with Iraq (1980–8), when millions of Iranian men were at the battlefront while women maintained the economy and their families at home.

Islamicization of Iran following the revolution of 1979, therefore, impacted on women's lives in a variety of ways. First, however, there was the unexpected privilege of increased political rights for women, including the franchise and the constitutional right to stand for public positions, except as President. Contrary to western and other expectations, the theocracy in Iran did not ape the conservative regime of Saudi Arabia or other parts of the Gulf in prohibiting women from voting or denying them other rights to political participation. As citizens in their own right – another progressive step away from traditional Islamic fundamentalist approaches – Iranian women were afforded the right to vote in the many elections that would take place for the President, constitution and national assembly. While women who stood for election in Jordan were condemned by Islamists, who issued fatwas declaring them heretics, in Iran the Shi'a clergy actually empowered women in this sphere.

The state set the agenda and women's independence and autonomy were severely undermined (Zubaida, 1997). Thus, while it is true that some considerable difficulties were encountered by women in the early stages of the revolution, aspects of their political, employment, legal and other rights were eventually improved and institutionalized by the state. These early setbacks may have had much to do with the overwhelming desire by Khomeini and his followers to impose an idealized Islamic vision of state and society, which was subsequently followed by the much remarked-upon progression to pragmatism. Pragmatism, combined with the idealism of the conservative wing of the ruling *ulama*, has, however, resulted in an often contradictory policy emanating from government on issues such as population control, employment rights and education, which affect Iranian women on a daily basis (Hoodfar, 1997).

Once again, many of the changes have been cosmetic, and patriarchy has been strengthened through religious sanction from Iran's hard-line clergy. Initial hopes of the realization of a utopia have been reassessed by Iran's feminists, whether they be secular or Islamic. Women once again sit on the margins of society; real political power is consistently denied to them. The parameters of their power lie in the strict confines of the home, but even here the state has managed to reinforce male dominance and legal rights. Yet, as Paidar (1996) reminds us, there have been some notable changes: 'the trans-formation of Islamist feminism from post-revolutionary idealism to realism and pragmatism of the late 1980s has been remarkable. This being the case it is no longer inconceivable to envisage strategic alliances between Iranian strands of secular and Islamist feminisms on women's rights issues' (p. 63).

The battle for women's rights in Iran is far from over, but it would be wrong to assume that the establishment of the theocracy in 1979 really did so much to change the nature of the issues affecting women's lives. Nor would it be right to assume that the status of women in Iran is any worse by nature of the Islamic republic in which they live. Indeed, the issue is far more complex and problematic than this. Does the woman of Tehran enjoy more or fewer rights than her sister in Riyadh, Cairo or Algiers? Increasingly, the question can only be answered by talking of degrees of change, not substan-tive social revolutions that have changed forever the way the women of the Middle East live their lives. In the wake of protests in 2009 at the result of Iran's presidential elections, it certainly appeared as if 'Iran's body politic was invaded by feminine power', but their repression was all too apparent in the state response as well (Tahmasebi-Birgani, 2010, p. 78).

Case study
Turkey, the state of women

As is often the case with any debate about women's rights, the 'success' of the Turkish women's movement is a relative one in terms of state, society and other comparator countries in the rest of the Middle East. Successes in terms of winning rights from the state and addressing patriarchal societal norms are also ones that have come in historical ebbs and flows for Turkish women, who have mobilized around such issues. As with other cases, the genesis of the women's movement in Turkey can be found in the late Ottoman period of the 1870s–1890s when women began to mobilize around issues of rights and emancipation through the formation of the first women's associa-tions, publishing and public meetings. The central focus of such activities were initially aspects of constraint with respect to the Islamic law which the state was ruled by at the time. By the first and second decades of the twen-tieth century, women were more forcefully mobilizing around rights to the franchise.

Such issues would receive significant propulsion with the establishment of the Republic by Mustafa Kemal Ataturk in 1922–3. The new state, in breaking completely with Ottoman tradition, was founded on distinct principles of secularism, and was perceived as providing women with new opportunities in terms of their formal rights in relation to the state. Ataturk also condemned the wearing of traditional Ottoman dress as backward-looking and at odds with the symbols of a modernizing secular state. As such, the headscarf (hijab) was banned; this prohibition extended to public sector employees too. Turkish women would be granted legal, political and social rights that were unprecedented in terms of a modern Muslim-majority Middle Eastern state. In 1926, the Turkish legislative assembly passed the Civil Law giving women the right to vote. It also dealt with aspects of Ottoman laws on social status, including polygamy and other religious strictures that the women's movement had long campaigned against. Hence, the early decades of the Republic were an era in which women emerged as participants in the formal political life of the state.

By the mid-1930s they were competing in elections. But women were never able to attain a significant representation in the Turkish parliament, and discrimination in these formal realms of politics was as strong as in other realms. Women have usually accounted for no more than between 2 and 4 per cent of the seats. It was only in the election of 2015 that women achieved a historically unparalleled 18 per cent of seats, raising the number of women parliamentarians to 98 out of 550. In a snap election later that year, however, the number fell back to 82 sitting in the legislature.

Moreover, Turkish women have experienced the usual obstacles in the corridors of political power, encountering sexism in their own party ranks and in the legislature. Women's groups have attempted to overcome this by calling for the state to introduce electoral quotas that might encourage greater representation and participation of women. Some political parties have responded by introducing gender quotas, and this may in part explain the relative success in terms of parliamentary representation in recent elections.

The military coup in 1980 appeared to extinguish the hopes and aspirations of Turkish women mobilized around issues of their rights. The military regime was critiqued for its patriarchal backward-looking agenda with respect to women. Its presence, however, galvanized a new generation of Turkish women to marshal debates and activities around an emerging feminist agenda (Arat, 1994). This agenda was influenced by western feminist discourses, and in particular critiqued state laws that pertained to the status and rights of women and their definition in both the private and public realms. In 1985, Turkish feminist elements began to call for reform of the 1926 Civil Law, and in 1987 Turkish women took to the street in protest at the illiberal position of Turkish state courts in dealing with women victims of domestic violence and divorce rights. Such campaigns and protests gained momentum so that, by the early 1990s, the state was compelled to review particular laws that perniciously discriminated against women. Hence the constitutional court repealed old laws and the state introduced new laws, such as the 1998 Protection of the Family Act, which went some way to enhancing women's rights.

With Islamic revivalism in Turkey taking place from the late 1970s onwards, issues pertaining to the rights of Muslim women took centre stage in a drawn-out battle between secularists and Islamists (Saktanber, 2002). Inevitably, the headscarf issue came to the forefront in such contests of ideas and power. Controversy arose over the ban when, in 1999, an Islamist parliamentarian was prevented from taking her pledge of office in the Turkish parliament because she insisted on wearing her headscarf. State and political parties and even the European Court of Human Rights (ECHR) were soon mired in the issue. The state and ECHR upheld the ban and rejected legal contest in terms of human rights. But Islamist parties and, in particular, prominent leaders such as JDP head Racip Erdogan campaigned to lift the ban, promising that it would be repealed if they got into power. And indeed, as Prime Minister, he has attempted to overturn the law, only to be thwarted by Turkey's constitutional court, which ruled in 2008 that such legislation was a betrayal of the principles of the Turkish constitution. Since 2013, however, Erdogan and his supporters have progressively reversed such bans for women in various parts of public life. For example, in 2016, it was reported that Turkish policewomen would be allowed to wear the headscarf as part of their uniform.

Today, the political movement of Turkish women continues to campaign for their rights, freedom and equality. The rights that have been won have succeeded in letting them play a role, albeit minor, in the public and political life of the country. The state, however, still remains the ultimate gatekeeper in this particular political game.

Questions for discussion

- How can the role of women in politics in the region be improved?
- Islam or patriarchy stops the advance of women in the Middle East – discuss.
- What socio-economic factors impact the status of women in the Middle East?

Recommended reading

- A number of general texts on women and the Middle East have been published, including Shalaby and Moghadam (2016) and Touaf, Boutkhil and Chourouq (2017), which address the issue of women in North Africa and elsewhere across the region in the wake of the Arab Spring.

- In addition, Sadiqi and Ennaji (2010), as well as Haghighet-Sordellini (2010), look at women in the region – including important developments in North African Arab states, involving social as well as political and economic issues.
- Themes of Islam, gender and sexuality are explored in Eltahawy (2016) and Mernissi (1985, 1991).
- Relations between contemporary Islamic movements and gender rights are covered in a variety of texts, including Ahmed (2011), Lovat (2012) and al-Rasheed (2013), the latter of which employs the case of Saudi Arabia. Krause (2012) looks at the Islamic/secular dichotomy in terms of the roles women play in civil society in the region.
- On dynamics as they relate to the experiences of Palestinian women, some recent works by Dahan-Kalev et al. (2012), Muhanna (2016) and Hamdan (2013) add to an important corpus of works.
- There are some excellent works on Turkey including Saktanber (2002), Keddie (2007) and Tuncer (2017).

CHAPTER EIGHT
Endangered Species: Ethnicity and Minorities

Introduction

Ethnic issues, concepts of ethnicity and ethnic rights are familiar in one way or another to all of us. The twenty-first century has seen an explosion of ethnic conflict which hitherto had been suppressed under forms of authoritarian rule in many parts of the world. As ideological conflict of the type witnessed during the Cold War appeared to go into decline, new forms of contestation arose. As Moynihan has argued: 'Nation-states no longer seem inclined to go to war with one another, but ethnic groups fight all the time. Inevitably, many of these ethnic clashes make their way into the realm of international politics' (1993, p. 5). The horror of ethnic cleansing has entered our vocabulary, whether referring to the destruction of Aleppo and the flight of its population in December 2016, the Kurds in the 1990s, or ISIS' sexual violence against Yazidi women, designed to eradicate their population (Human Rights Watch, 2016).

The rise of transnational corporations, the telecommunications revolution and the global village also means we experience the ethnic without venturing from our own shores. Through social media, ethnic music, food, art, literature and clothing, the ethnic 'other' is streamed, posted, fed, tweeted and represented. The boundaries of ethnic identity are constructed.

Ethnic identity is a variable in politics (domestic, regional or international); it is also malleable, and whether one agrees or not that it has either certain primordial or ascribed characteristics, it is also shaped by subjectively interpreted historical experiences, combining, as Barth explains, to give both objective characteristics – such as language, religion, territory, social organization, culture, race and common origin – and subjective characteristics, which are a mix of any of the above or of any other 'markers' used by a group to assert its identity (Barth, 1969). Terms of reference that may formerly have incorporated class or other factors are increasingly substituted by the ethnic label, which thus, it is presumed, becomes an explanation in itself. Ethnicity, ethnic rights and ethnic claims are symptoms of the continuing inability, whatever way things are presented, to solve, at a global level, the myriad of conflicts involving competing ethnic or minority claims (Horowitz, 1985).

Box 8.1 Fighting, bleeding, burning a path

Our present-day concerns are recent in origin, 'connections among Biafra, Bangladesh, and Burundi, Beirut, Brussels, and Belfast were at first hesitantly made – isn't one "tribal", one "linguistic", another "religious"? – But that is true no longer. Ethnicity has fought and bled and burned its way into public and scholarly consciousness'.

(Horowitz, 1985, p. xi)

It is the inability to resolve what are now referred to as ethnic conflicts that concerns policy-makers and opinion-setters when they look to the Middle East. It is the rise of ethnic-based demands from the Kurds in Iraq, for example, that have made the state-building project there difficult for international actors. The continuing tension and internal conflict between Turkey and its native minorities have also significantly hindered its attempts at consideration for candidature in the EU.

Across the region, minority Christians are now identified by the most powerful leader of the free world, President Trump of America, as worthy of his attention and focus. 'Christians in the Middle-East have been executed in large numbers', he tweeted in January 2017, 'we cannot allow this horror to continue!' (Trump, 2017). ISIS ruthlessly and violently persecuted minorities, seeking to extinguish them. By and large, it is not ethnic communities or minorities themselves that present a problem – rather, their conflicts, lack of rights and claims to self-determination and independence, which lie at the heart of the issue and are seen as threatening stability within the region.

Ethnic and minority politics have assumed a new importance. In addition, this overview of the ethnic dimension once again highlights the important linkages between themes such as the colonial legacy, political economy, nationalism and political Islam, which were discussed in earlier chapters. In the Middle East, then, ethnicity and minority status have developed a special meaning. The concept is perceived as a relative newcomer to the region, linked to conflicts within nation-states. Some might argue that the ethnic tensions of the twenty-first century are the inevitable result of the failure of the colonial powers decades ago to take account of such factors when they carved up the region into new nation-states and forced distinct and diverse groups to live alongside each other under 'one flag and one nation'.

The issues of ethnicity and minority rights are inextricably linked with the nation-state, nationalism, popular sovereignty and citizenship. The rights of many ethnic groups and minorities in the region have been ruthlessly suppressed, irrespective of the governing ideologies of states as diverse as Iraq and Saudi Arabia. As such, the debate about ethnic and minority rights in the region has as much to say about the nature of the nation-state and its legitimacy as it does about demands for self-determination or independence.

Defining ethnicity

The debate about ethnicity, ethnic rights and ethnic politics in the Middle East reflects a number of changes in the scholarship of the region. While ethnic group ties and solidarity have always existed there, politics has been regarded as significantly unaffected by such issues. Analysis of politics was tribal, class-based or centred on the classical orientalist and post-orientalist positions. Ethnic groups were largely confined to the realm of anthropological study and to debates about tribe and clan, and removed from the political study of nation and state (Tibi, 1996). Indeed, it was only when politics broke down – such as in the confessional state of Lebanon during its civil war between 1975 and 1990 – that such elements were considered. It is useful, therefore, at this point to raise some key theoretical perspectives on the importance, definition and concept of ethnicity within the region.

The first debate is defined as one between primordialism and instrumentalism. In brief, primordialists believe that rooted 'given' identities are a major feature of ethnicity and politics in the region. Islam, for example, is commonly cited as one of these rooted 'givens' and presented as unchanging, rigid and monolithic in shaping politics and political outcomes in society. Instrumentalists, however, appreciate a more subjective construction of ethnicity among the peoples of the region, and its relationship to the construction of nation and nationalism. In addition, 'to the more extreme instrumentalists', argue Esman and Rabinovich, 'ethnic and confessional solidarities survive only as long as they pay – as long as they provide more security, status and material rewards than do available alternatives' (1988, p. 13).

The extent to which one accepts either argument or definition will also influence any subsequent analysis of ethnic politics or interaction in the many ethnically plural societies of the region. Brown, for example, perceives ethnic 'givens' – primordial loyalties – as an important factor in characterizing the political culture of the region, exhibited by jealous loyalty to a small-group particularism (religious, ethnic, linguistic, tribal) (Brown, 1984, p. 143). Brown refers to and talks about the persistence of traditional Middle Eastern political culture in the modern age. This political culture is based on a mosaic of ethnic, tribal and religious groups which, when faced with the modernizing forces of nation, nationalism and institutions of government based on universal rather than specific characteristics, retreats to primordial loyalties and associated behaviour. This 'given' pattern of political culture, for Brown, explains communal resistance to change and the appeal of so-called traditional religious political forces.

This notion of resistance to a particular type of political change is apparent when scholars address the issue of ethnic communities challenging the state. A riposte to this perception of ethnic politics and primordial identity can be detected in Zubaida (1993), who argues for a more dynamic reading of ethnicity. In turn, Anderson's (1983) concepts of constructed and imagined identities also contribute to the debate. In this respect, Zubaida also embraces the instrumentalist approach to explaining the 'political field', pointing out that 'in many countries the ultimate triumph of a particular group or current culminated in the monopolization and the suppression of the whole political field' (1993, p. 146). Ethnic identities and ethnic politics in relation to new political units such as the nation-state, therefore, can be conceived, argues Zubaida, in new ways. He argues that, while 'communalist sentiments enter into the political field … the form they take is shaped and sometimes transformed by the forces and conjunctures of that field' (1993, p. 149). In illustrating his argument, Zubaida reflected on the example of Iraq's Shi'a majority while under the rule of Saddam Hussein, pointing out that 'the Iraqi Shi'a, for instance, never constituted a unitary political force, but that Shi'a interests and outlooks contributed significant inputs into various political movements and forces at different points in time' (p. 149). Post-2003, however, we see a subsequent inversion of this process whereby Iraq's Shi'a have asserted themselves, with Iranian support, as the major unitary political force of the state, leading to the progressive exclusion of Sunni Iraqis (Haddad, 2016).

The same might also be argued in the example of the Armenian community of the West Bank and its role in the Palestinian articulation of national identity and struggle for self-determination and independence from Israel as an occupying state. In addition, this debate engenders a need for both a historical and a comparative perspective that recognize new scholarship on this subject.

In the past, much of the debate about ethnicity in the Middle East was posited on a comparative historical and often orientalist perspective. The region was always defined as the exception, in relation to, first, comparative experiences in the West and, second, historical observations of politics in the region since the collapse of the Ottoman Empire. In this respect, as I have previously argued, analysis and understanding of ethnicity were tied to debates about the meanings of nationalism and political Islam. If one returns to the first point, however, it is not difficult to discern the myopic Eurocentric tendencies inherent in the approach of, say, Kedourie and his notion of ethnicity and nationalism, which he argues is a modern western doctrine which, when translated within the region, led to an abuse and destruction of this particular vocabulary of European politics (Kedourie, 1988, p. 31). Yet Kedourie's complaints about abuse of vocabulary and outcomes should be reflected back on the European standard-bearer. Connor (1994) has done this, pointing out that, in the case of nation, 'there is no formula', which presumably leads one to question what will be exported (p. 99). Indeed, in place of a formula, there are myths, lies and notions of ethnic and racial superiority, which will always alter the way in which writers like Kedourie and Lewis view ethnic bases, identity and loyalties in the region.

In the past, then, ethnicity was viewed from a broad base; the region chiefly consisted of Arabs and Persians and was largely constructed as Arab. The Arab world, however, hides a multiplicity of ethnic, sectarian and minority difference, which is evident in a variety of Arab states, as well as Israel and Persian Iran. Anthony Smith writes that, by 'ethnic groups' we mean 'a type of cultural collectivity, one that emphasizes the role of myths of descent and historical memories, and is recognized by one or more cultural differences like religion, customs, language or institutions' (1991, p. 20). From this definition, a variety of groups throughout the Middle East may be described as ethnic – Jews, Arabs, Amazighs, Persians, Alawites, Tuareg, Armenians, Maronites and Marsh Arabs, and so on. In addition, a variety of countries in the region have in the past experienced, or are currently experiencing, degrees of ethnic conflict or tensions within and across their borders.

Ethnicity is perceived as an important element of the politics of identity in the region. While some identities and associated ideologies have waxed and waned, others have risen to fill the vacuum of ideological retreat and crisis. In an earlier chapter, I identified Islam as currently playing this role, co-existing with, and attempting to replace, other identities and loyalties, yet, according to Smith's definition, Islam is but one element of ethnic solidarity, and alongside this religious marker, co-existing or competing, are other identities, which people also believe in. From this emerges stratified identity, which includes a variety of elements, from the religious to nation and family. This point is discussed at length by Khalidi (1997) in his historical treatment of the emergence of Palestinian identity at the beginning of the twentieth century, and still animates debates in the present time.

Ethnic identity, as I have already mentioned, also created, through belief and perception, something Anderson (1983) aptly described as 'imagined communities'. The example of Israel is a case in point. Until the establishment of the Zionist movement in the late 1890s, the Jews were regarded as a religious minority in the region. Herzl's vision of a revived Jewish nation transformed this dispersed community into an ethnic group from which the establishment of a nation-state would emerge. Israel is a self-declared Jewish state. For example, in 2014, Israel's Prime Minister Bibi Netanyahu tried to persuade his government and the Israeli legislature to amend Basic Law to define Israel as a Jewish state. Netanyahu said, 'I will promote a Basic Law that will define Israel as the nation-state of the Jewish people' (Heller, 2014). Israel is predicated on the survival of the Jewish people, not as a religious collective but as a national and ethnic collective. The Jews, according to Anderson's approach, achieved this task through the imagined community, creating, maintaining and sustaining Zionism and the establishment of Israel. Thus, in so far as there is an Israeli nation, it is because its members believe in their difference, sustain difference, celebrate it and have consolidated it through the foundation of a nation-state (Milton-Edwards, 2008). The construction of a gulf of ethnic division between the Palestinians and Israelis has, thus, appeared so wide it is almost impossible to breach. Constructed ethnic identities, therefore, are proving highly durable and a lasting issue for the entire region.

Ethnic conflict in the region is not rare; it is an all-too-frequent fact of political life. Although the majority of state systems in the region have vigorously pursued policies designed to repress and hide from the rest of the world their ethnic problems, one way or another their secrets emerge. Obviously, there is a danger in ascribing to conflict an ethnic dimension which is artificially construed. Disputes which were previously described as nationalist, class-based or otherwise have been reassessed and pronounced as ethnic.

While ethnicity may be just one of the identities the people call on, the conclusion in terms of the Middle East is that it currently assumes greater importance than other factors. Protracted ethnic/minority conflicts in the Middle East have been described as having 'caused more misery and loss of human life than has any other type of local, regional, or international conflict ... and [as] the source of most of the world's refugees' (Gurr and Harff, 1994, p. 7). For example, since 2011, the outbreak of civil conflict in Syria alone has triggered the world's largest humanitarian crisis since the Second World War. Refugees from Syria are now the biggest refugee population from a single conflict in a generation. There are over 4.8 million Syrian refugees, many of whom are from the country's diverse ethnic and minority population groups, in neighbouring countries and the wider region. A further 6.3 million have been internally displaced in Syria. It is estimated by the UN that more than 400,000 Syrians have been killed (Hudson, 2016). Syria's own economy has also been shattered (Gobat and Kostial, 2016)

As such, any hope that, if the various regimes could change and reform their political systems to accommodate the demands of their minority, ethnic and religious communities, that conflict would subside, has been increasingly hard to maintain. In post-war Iraq, the result of such an attempt is abject failure. Since the toppling of Saddam Hussein's regime in 2003, the extent to which Iraq's main ethnic and sectarian elements have been able to reconcile their demands with the emergence of a federal state dominated by sectarian and ethnically hostile interests is exceedingly poor. Even democratic power-sharing through arrangements for some autonomy in Iraq has thus far sold short its ethnic and minority interests. I say democratic because, as we know from the chapter on democratization, it has been argued that without a democratic injection the politics of ethnicity in the Middle East can never be accommodated in a way which actually reflects the plural nature of society and those individuals living in the region. As Cammett et al. assert:

> **Box 8.2 By one's own definition**
>
> It is the case that no sectarian or ethnic groups can be analysed or understood within their own terms of reference. In every instance there will be at stake elements of the distribution of scarce resources, of making concessions that might jeopardize national unity, of reacting to minority demands in such a way as to call the regime's legitimacy into question.
>
> (2016, p. 406)

The prospects for the translation of ethnic and religious pluralism into patterns of politics of power-sharing or accommodation, however, are not good. There is a belief that pluralism will naturally be associated with instability and the breakdown of lasting political order – though, of course, the inverse was being witnessed in states such as Syria and Iraq. The promotion of politics that recognizes the rights of minorities to parity of esteem within the region is absent from the largely unitary and coercive state. The desire, for example, by the Wahabi majority in Saudi Arabia to maintain stability of the state structure and perpetuate the rule of the al-Saud family has effectively stifled any hope for pluralism for other religious or ethnic groups living in that state. The situation is exacerbated by the argument that the al-Saud family forwards in defence of this state of affairs. They use their particular Wahabi interpretation of Islam to argue for stratified notions of citizenship and discrimination on sectarian grounds against other sects within Islam, as well as other faiths.

> **Box 8.3 Islam and tolerance**
>
> Islam has been known to be tolerant, pluralistic and integrative ... In some of these cases, Islam is the ultimate community ... But this does not necessarily undermine the possibility of other communities existing on other levels ... Therefore, Islamic resurgence and ethnic reassertion are not at odds.
>
> (Ben Dor, 1988, p. 88)

Minority status

Many minorities populate the Middle East and thus it is important to highlight that this chapter is reflecting principally on religious, ethnic or linguistic minority groups, such as the Assyrians of Syria, Sabaean Christians in Iraq, and Armenians in Lebanon, or the Jews who used to live in Yemen. There is also an argument to be made for distinguishing the debate about minorities from ethnicity for two very important reasons. First, while the issue of ethnicity and ethnic politics in the Middle East does have some bearing on the minority status of groups within certain states – such as the Kurds in Iran – not all ethnic politics or ethnic conflict is necessarily about minority–majority relations. In addition, not all minority–majority conflict can be ascribed with a strictly ethnic characteristic. It would be unhelpful, for example, to describe the civil war which started in Syria in 2011 between the Alawite minority of the Assad government and Sunni-majority rebel elements as ethnic, when both groups are Arab in ethnic origin but differ in terms of internally driven religious identities and power-holding. In addition, conflicts between Iraq's majority Arab Shi'a and minority Arab Sunni population is not ethnic in nature but has more to do with the emergence of distinct sectarian frames of politics that also speak to the state-to-state proxy ambitions of Iran and its foes. The role of minorities in the Middle East has been and remains an important factor in understanding the nature of the state and politics.

Historically, the Middle East has acted as a magnet for minorities, in particular for the religious of the monotheistic faiths of Judaism, Christianity and Islam. Within each faith, the region has hosted the numerous sects and schisms which have emerged over the centuries. Minority status in religious terms has had both its advantages and disadvantages, as the course of history has shaped the majority composition of the area. For 700 years, before the collapse of the Ottoman Empire, the religious status of the majority community had been Muslim. As a result, minority religious and linguistic communities in the region were largely tolerated. By the time of the Ottoman reform period (*tanzimat*), Jews and Christians were also afforded forms of equal status in law (see box 8.4, 'Supreme Edict of the Rosehouse'). Islam was still regarded as a superior and final revelation, but the Prophet Mohammed had passed on God's word and ruled on the special respect and treatment

Figure 8.1 *Threatened minority, Sabaean Mandean follower of John the Baptist.* © *Stephen Farrell*

that co-existing religious groups could expect to enjoy. The Ottoman caliphs in Istanbul continued this tradition until the defeat of the Empire and the fall of the Middle East into largely colonial hands.

Box 8.4 Supreme Edict of the Rosehouse

Excerpt from the Supreme Edict of the Rosehouse. The edict was proclaimed on behalf of Sultan Abdulmecid I. In 1839, it proposed a variety of reforms, including rights for all, irrespective of ethnic or religious group:

> In short, without the several laws, the necessity for which has just been described, there can be neither strength, nor riches, nor happiness, nor tranquility for the empire; it must, on the contrary, look for them in the existence of these new laws.

> ... From henceforth, therefore, the cause of every accused person shall be publicly judged, as the divine law requires, after inquiry and examination, and so long as a regular judgment shall not have been pronounced, no one can secretly or publicly put another to death by poison or in any other manner.

> No one shall be allowed to attack the honor of any other person whatever.

> Each one shall possess his property of every kind, and shall dispose of it in all freedom, without let or hindrance from any person whatever; thus, for example, the innocent heirs of a criminal shall not be deprived of their legal rights, and the property of the criminal shall not be confiscated.

> These imperial concessions shall extend to all our subjects, of whatever religion or sect they may be; they shall enjoy them without exception. We therefore grant perfect security to the inhabitants of our empire in their lives, their honor, and their fortunes, as they are secured to them by the sacred text of the law.

(Edict of Gulhane, 1839)

Of course, the picture outlined above is a general one and cannot account for specific ethnic/religious tensions, such as those in Lebanon in the nineteenth century between Christian and Druze. Yet it does remain relevant to the issue of communal relations, say, between Jew and Arab in Palestine at the turn of the century, before the country fell into British hands.

The colonizers, the imperial powers of France and Britain, treated the existence of a multiplicity of religious groups in the region quite differently. They had used the claim of defence of their co-religionists to gain a foothold in the region in the latter half of the nineteenth century – this was particularly true in the Levant. Once in the region, they not only further used the 'religious card' as a means of pursuing a policy of divide and rule to weaken Arab claims to national unity, independence and self-determination but also actively promoted pliant minority elements into power over and above majority communities. In Syria and Lebanon, the French pursued a policy of divide and rule among the Druze and Maronite Christian community, which exacerbated pre-existing tensions that had already erupted in the Mount Lebanon civil war of 1860 (Fawaz, 1994).

In Palestine, from 1920 to 1948, the British policy of divide and rule among Jew, Muslim and Christian tore the country apart and plunged the region into a conflict from which it has yet to recover. While it would be untrue to argue that religious tension was absent during the centuries of Ottoman rule, one can assert with certainty that the advent of colonial power over parts of the region corresponded strongly with an upsurge in tension of this nature. In a world where the boundaries of the region were literally redrawn, where new states were created and new leaders appointed to positions of power, there is an argument that religious loyalty, along with tribal and family affiliations, was resurgent. Under these new political conditions, there were perceived advantages among minority groups in seeking alliances and, therefore, benefiting from the colonial rulers, even at the expense of fellow citizens.

Box 8.5 Divide and Rule

As Firro reminds us in the example of the Druze in Syria and Lebanon, the French pursued a policy of divide and rule among and between religious communities, encouraging them to 'establish Alawi, Druze and Lebanese states and grant each of them domestic autonomy … the French hoped to co-opt the … Druze and thereby gain a weapon to do battle against the Syrian nationalist movement' (1988, p. 188).

Some minority communities gained much from this game of politics, but colonial patronage had its price when the region's states gained independence from the colonial masters.

Religious minorities fared less well in the 1950s and 1960s when universal ideologies such as Arab nationalism and pan-Arabism attempted to render divisive pre-existing primordial loyalties that had encouraged people into religious or linguistic minorities and particularism. With a few notable exceptions, one of which – the Alawites – is discussed below, religious and other minority groups in the region have experienced decades in which their status has been regularly undermined by autocratic politically monolithic and anti-plural states.

The irony of the situation is that, until states are threatened by minority groups, little is done to encourage them to identify with the state. Yet the rise of minority consciousness has been a global phenomenon; religious minorities in a variety of states are demanding, at the least, fair and equal status. In the Middle East, there is barely a country that does not experience serious tensions and conflicts between majority and minority populations. The question this poses is to what extent this tension is the product of authoritarian governance approaches in a variety of states across the region.

No doubt the answer does lie, to a great extent, in anti-democratic forms of rule which exist in the plural societies of the region, and also reflects the marginal role many minority groups play in these political systems and governments.

The state and ethnicity

The nature of the state in the Middle East has greatly affected the debate about ethnicity and ethnic politics. Predominant state types, be they monarchical, one-party, imam-chief or post-colonial, have all sought to overcome the problems of creating identity in territorial units which have been considered inauthentic. State-building, under these conditions, whether in post-colonial Algeria or Hashemite Jordan, has always incorporated a strong desire by the ruling elite to create a new identity, including new symbols, which in one way or another seek to transcend pre-existing ethnic, religious, linguistic or tribal loyalties. The process of transcending past loyalties has occurred through a variety of methods, mostly associated with strategies of aggressive statist assimilation or, at the other extreme, marginalization and even ethnic cleansing / genocide. Whatever the strategies, the ruling elite of a variety of states in the region have all faced the same problem – creating new identities in territorial units in which a variety of distinct ethnic or other groupings co-exist.

The nation-state, the dominant political unit of the region, demands much and has created a variety of problems in relation to the region's ethnic, religious and linguistic plurality. This should not be surprising given the debates about national identity within the nation-state that are currently under way across Europe and the United States of America, where populist politics seeks to reduce plurality, especially when it is seen as threatening to identities and values claimed as primordially national. In other words, the states of the Middle East are not alone in establishing these factors as issues and threats.

Primarily, however, the nation-state, by its very definition, demands the loyalty of a nation; a sense of national consciousness must exist and the state should derive its legitimacy from its citizens. The nation-states of the region have encountered a variety of difficulties in achieving this consensus among its citizens. Many ruling elites have had to set about creating new identities where other loyalties previously existed. Iraq, for example, is a nation-state, a territorial unit created by the British. During the mandate, the British established monarchical rule through the Hashemite Prince Faisal, and the new nation-state of Iraq over which he (nominally) ruled incorporated a diverse ethnic and sectarian population. The British and their monarch failed to unite the country's diverse population, and communal conflict became a regular feature on the political landscape.

Following Iraq's independence in 1932, a constitutional monarchy was established but the new independent ruling elite still struggled to create national identity that could transcend pre-existing loyalties, particularly ethnic and sectarian ones. Monarchs, nationalists, a Ba'thist regime and post-war political dispensation in Iraq have all failed to establish a system of governance which is both plural enough and strong enough to manage successfully the ethnic and sectarian communities which exist within its borders. In the present time, this is evident in the ungoverned spaces of Iraq and the rise and subsequent territorial control (albeit relatively brief) of ISIS over large swathes of the country from 2014 to 2017.

Not all states within the region have suffered the same type of difficulties as Iraq in harmonizing the task of state-building and consolidation with strategies for managing the competing claims of diverse ethnic groups. But the majority of countries in the region 'do suffer from the malintegration of state and society, and consequently from limited legitimacy among ethnic groups that are excluded from political power or consider themselves the victims of discriminatory treatment' (Esman and Rabinovich, 1988, p. 277).

This malintegration exacerbates ethnic tension and highlights the lack of formal political mechanisms for plurality, and the continuing problem that many states in the region have in generating legitimacy among all of their citizens. This in turn encourages the dominant regime to employ draconian coercive powers to manage demands from those groups that remain marginal and outside the political system. In countries such as Lebanon malintegration has occurred, in large part, because the state is weak, but also because the state has failed to balance the demands of its intensely plural society through consociational power-sharing arrangements that reflect demographic parity. The system collapsed, resulting in civil war (1975–90), because formal mechanisms for plurality were still providing advantages to one group (the Maronites) over others, such as the Druze, Shi'ites and Sunni Muslims. In addition, in common with other states in the region, in Lebanon communal problems, ethnic tensions and sectarian differences have been and remain exacerbated by the interference of external actors – in this case, the French, Israelis, Syrians, Americans, Iranians and Saudi Arabians.

Thus, very few, if any, state types in the region have successfully managed the pluralism of the societies existing within their borders. Obviously, in some states, the contrivance of 'nation' is more meaningful than in others. In Egypt, up to 2012, successive post-colonial rulers did manage to establish the semblance of a nation to which many citizens felt an allegiance without denying other loyalties. Since 2012, however, that semblance of unity is but one casualty of a disastrous transition from uprising to revolution, election and counter-revolution.

Modernity in the post-modern age

There is some debate about the impact of modernity and post-modern discourses of identity on the issue of ethnic politics. It is clear, however, that, whichever way one looks at it, the politics, government and institutions of the region have been affected by the processes of so-called modernization. Modernization in the Middle East, it has been believed, is meant to imply a process of economic and political development leading to a decline of traditional agricultural and rural-based societies in favour of modern industrialized, urban societies. These urban societies are symbolized by technological support, increased rates of literacy, decline of the infant mortality rate, improved health care and democratic pluralism. As such, the process of modernization should have comfortably incorporated ethnic and minority demands, which concurrently would become less important, the more democratic and responsive government became. In addition, it was presumed that the process of modernization would go some way in weakening traditional 'primordial' loyalties to faith system, clan, tribe, ethnic group, etc.

This approach, however, is problematic to say the least. First, there is a huge credibility gap between the idealized and utopian vision of modernization and modernity, as represented above, and the reality as represented in the contemporary Middle East. Second, unlike the plural societies of the West, the plural societies of the Middle East have not benefited in the same ways, if at all, from the process of modernization. Finally, it has been argued that modernization in the region has strengthened not weakened pre-existing loyalties and ties that people feel to their ethnic group, religious community, tribe, clan and family, and as such the national unity project in the nation-states of the region has been extremely difficult to achieve without regular resort by the state to extreme coercive measures.

For ethnic and minority groups, the process of modernization in their societies has resulted in two types of situation, both of which only serve to heighten their ethnic and communal claims. In the first situation, incorporating a perspective that was prevalent in scholarship of the subject in the 1950s and 1960s, it was argued that failure of the modernization development approach in the Middle East was evident in the continuing importance that people attached to their ethnic, religious or linguistic origins. This situation was evident in Iraq where, despite the coup d'état led by Abdel Karim al-Qasim in 1958 and the early promise of modernization and democracy, the Kurdish community and nationalists soon clashed. The revolt of 1961–3 reflected the rapid disillusionment that spread throughout the Kurdish community. While the national government of al-Qasim promoted modernization and economic development, the Kurds witnessed a rise in unemployment in their communities, peasant indebtedness, evictions by landlords, and uncertainties within the community over the issue of land reform (McDowall, 2007, p. 310). Modernization in Iraq was promoting a sense of isolation within the Kurdish community as it became more marginal, both politically and geographically, from the centre of power in Baghdad.

It would not be true, however, to claim that all ethnic minorities emerged from processes of modernization in the same way. In Algeria, following the war of independence in 1962, the ethnic minority Amazighs from the areas of Kabiliya and Aures maintained their role in the nationalist movement and benefited equally from the modernization process, in particular the modernization of Algeria's natural gas industry. The Amazigh political elite, whose leaders had played such an important role in the war of independence, continued to perpetuate and assimilate itself into the new structures of the state form, the bureaucracy and technocratic positions.

It is notable that, during the Boumedienne period, positive policies of development were instituted for Amazigh areas, all resulting in the gradual drawing-in of Amazigh groups. Problems arose as a result of the government policy of the 1970s to 'Arabize' Algeria, eliminate French as the official language and promote a new sense of national identity. Amazigh dissent, based on the argument that the evolution of national culture should be determined by a free policy of social forces mediated by the state, not directed by it, resulted in a number of disturbances throughout the 1970s and 1980s. Amazighs have resisted the assimilationist tendencies associated with modernization and promoted by the regime (Hoffman, 2010).

By the late 1990s, following the alleged government assassination of Amazigh cultural personalities and leaders, the imposition of Arabic-only legislation and the continuing civil chaos, Amazigh communal sentiments led to the formation of an armed movement, forcing the government of Lamine Zeroual into a grudging climb-down on certain Amazigh issues (Silverstein, 1998, p. 3). Yet, by 2015, Amazighs in Algeria were still awaiting formal incorporation of their language rights (Tamazight) into the constitution. In 2016, however, the Algerian government finally granted Tamazight official status. The decision was not without its critics and Amazigh supporters were still cognisant of the fact that Arabic remained the official language of the state.

Many scholars continue to believe that modernization exacerbates ethnic conflict and contributes to it. From this perspective, communal conflict rises out of the increased sense of competition generated by the political and economic developments associated with modernization. This places an emphasis on communal and ethnic solidarity and the power attributed to group rather than individual dynamics, leading ethnic or sectarian groups into competition and then conflict, as the case of Lebanon well illustrates. The Lebanese example highlights the strength garnered from strong communal links in the face of a weak state. Without close communal links in Lebanon, individuals would not derive any benefit from the state. The weakness of the state in Lebanon can be linked to the nature of modernization in the country. It is concluded, therefore, that civil war in Lebanon was a result of the nature of modernization in the country and the need for communal solidarity in opposition to a weak and ineffective government that failed to disburse basic services to its citizens. Modernization, including its failures, has altered forever the nature of a citizen's links to the state and the ties and support to be derived from ethnic, religious or linguistic communities.

Ethno-national and religious battles

The demands of the Middle East's ethnic, linguistic and religious minorities and groups range from modest requests for rights of worship – such as the calls of many Christians living in some Gulf states – to the demand for self-determination and independence made by the Polisario in Morocco's Western Sahara, representing the Sahrawi people. The means by which such groups pursue their claims are dependent on a number of factors, including whether a minority group is compact or scattered, the political character of the state they reside in, the leadership of such communities and the ability or willingness of the dominant regime to concede to a particular group's demands. The strategies employed by minority groups to pursue their various claims range from non-violent petitions and sit-ins to campaigns of civil disobedience and outright wars of secession.

The nature of such strategies is again often determined by the nature of the state in which the groups live. For example, Israel's Palestinian Arab minority are granted citizenship, and allowed to participate and compete in the country's democratic elections, run their own municipalities and become members of the Knesset. As such, their grievances are not expressed in terms of secessionist claims or calls for self-determination, but instead focus on issues of equality of rights, opportunities and privilege. While Israel, despite being democratic, continues to privilege the rights of one community, the Jews, over the rights of another, the Palestinian Arabs, the latter will remain marginal. Consciousness-raising might occur for a number of reasons, including calls for greater rights for a subordinate community, autonomy or independence.

Political mobilization around these issues may take place in a variety of ways – for example, a vanguard approach might be taken, with the political elite (intellectuals, professionals, etc.) claiming to act on behalf of the community. On other occasions, the same group or minority will mobilize the whole community into mass-based political acts. In addition, it is worth remembering that internal mobilization around demands for greater autonomy, political or cultural rights, or even self-determination will result in factionalization – a variety of groups and leaders claiming the support of the minority community. Evidence of such behaviour can be found in the Kurdish example, in which a plethora of Kurdish nationalist groups, from the Turkish-based PKK (Kurdish Workers' Party), PUK (Patriotic Union of Kurdistan) to the Iraqi-based KDP (Kurdish Democratic Party), have, on occasion, ended up in conflict with each other rather than with the dominant states in which they are located. Mobilization around minority and ethnic rights has also resulted in tactics which, in turn, have resulted in episodes of political violence. It is argued that, when other avenues of mobilization and expression are closed or have been exhausted, then ethno-nationalist movements will resort to violence in an attempt to achieve their goals.

The fortunes of such movements are dependent on a variety of elements, chiefly the nature of both the demands and the state to which those demands are made. One might look at the Copts in Egypt to illustrate this point. Christian Copts are Egypt's largest minority group, accounting for some 10 per cent of the population. In the past, they held important political positions in government, but since the 1950s the community has been subject to episodes of discrimination and persecution. The Coptic community mobilized to resist such changes, and by the 1980s the state was supporting their calls. Coptic claims were not radical, the state could support them as part of its ongoing anti-Islamist crackdown, and tolerance could be promoted as part of Egypt's policy of political and economic liberalization.

The majority of ethnic and religious groups, however, have not been so successful, and even the Copts have some way to go before they feel secure in Egyptian society. Following the ouster of President Mubarak in Egypt, Copts subsequently became the target of violent attack. When General Abdel Fatah El-Sisi overthrew the Muslim Brotherhood and President Morsi, Coptic Christians celebrated. Three years later, El-Sisi had not sufficiently addressed Coptic grievances, and protests against the government grew. Indeed, the prevalence of authoritarian and anti-democratic states in the region, as we shall see below, inhibits even the most modest demands for justice, pluralism and equality. Without pluralism and equality, the demands of ethnic and minority groups will result in those unwanted episodes of violence and terror which seem to grip the region and further slow the pace of reform and change. The rigid nature of most state systems in the region promotes a vicious circle that seems impossible to break. Political violence and acts of terror become instruments of control and counter-control in which both sides engage. The state is accused of seeking the ethnic cleansing of minority populations, and acts of terror are, in turn, perpetrated by the politically powerless and voiceless ethnic and religious minorities of the region.

Conflict management and regulation

In multi-ethnic or multiple-minority states, concessions by the government to one group might result in the same demands from others, thereby undermining national unity and possibly fragmenting the state for ever. As already noted, many states in the region find themselves engaged in ethnic or sectarian conflict with their populations. The state has at its disposal a variety of means for 'regulating' such conflicts. By this, I mean that the state can employ a variety of strategies to deal with, react to or end the conflicts in which they are engaged. It is useful for us to employ McGarry and O'Leary's (1993) taxonomy of 'macro-methods of ethnic conflict regulation' in this particular overview of the region. While the approach is not entirely comprehensive, it does allow us to examine the variety of strategies that state elites in the region have employed. As such, McGarry and O'Leary outline their taxonomy in the following way: first, they refer to 'methods for eliminating differences', which can include the act of genocide, thereby physically eliminating the subordinate group. Forced mass population transfers, partition and/or secession, and creating displaced populations are also discussed. The final method or approach for eliminating difference is cited as integration and/or assimilation. The second major category revolves around 'methods for managing differences' and embraces themes such as hegemonic control, arbitration (third-party intervention), cantonization and/or federalization, and consociationalism or power-sharing (McGarry and O'Leary, 1993, p. 4).

In the contemporary Middle East, all of these strategies for conflict regulation have been found at one time or another. Sometimes, a variety of strategies is pursued at the same time; at other times, just one. Nevertheless, the depressing evidence exists for all cases. Acts of genocide, the elimination of a race or ethnic group, have been perpetrated, for example, against Iraq's Kurds by the Ba'thist regime led by Saddam Hussein. As the case study below illustrates, the express intention of the Iraqi regime against not only the Kurds, but also the majority Shi'a population and Marsh Arabs who inhabit the southern regions of Iraq, had been to engage in acts of ethnic cleansing and elimination through large-scale murder. Other regional actors accused of playing a role in forced or mass population transfers include Israel, which in both 1948 and 1967 played its part in creating a Palestinian refugee population now numbering in the millions (Morris, 1988). Turkey too stands accused of a brutal campaign of killing against Armenians in 1915 and also against its Kurdish population throughout the 1980s and 1990s (Jongerden, 2007). ISIS clearly deployed forced transfer against Iraq's Yazidi minority. The threat of mass population transfer has not declined and remains a real threat to a number of ethnic groups and minority populations.

The empirical evidence of successful partition and/or secession (self-determination) in the Middle East is extremely limited. The 1948 partition of Palestine into two states, one for the Jews and another for the Arabs, did nothing to resolve ethnic and communal conflicts between the two peoples, and has only served to heighten the tensions between them. While a variety of secessionist movements have arisen in the region, including the Kurds, Palestinians and the Polisario of the Western Sahara, the state system in the region has strongly resisted any attempt to resolve ethnic conflicts by pursuing this strategy. Interestingly, when the option of secession/partition was at its strongest, i.e. in Iraq in February 1991 after the US and allied forces encouraged Kurdish and Shi'a uprisings, the coercive arm of the state still resisted fragmentation and kept a firm grip on the institutions of government. Further fragmentation through partition or secession, as a means of regulating or resolving conflict, is unlikely, given the lack of internal and international support for such proposals.

Evidence of hegemonic control as a system of managing difference in the multi-ethnic states of the region is widely available, from Algeria's management of the Amazighs to Israel's management of its Palestinian Arab minority. Hegemonic control, as defined by McGarry and O'Leary, is 'coercive and/ or co-optive rule which successfully manages to make unworkable an ethnic challenge to the state order' (1993, p. 23). The Arab nationalist regimes of Syria, Iraq, Libya, Algeria, Yemen, Egypt and the Islamic Republic of Iran have all pursued ideological agendas designed to transcend ethnic or sectarian loyalties, and all, for the most part, have failed in their task. Arbitration in the region has largely failed to resolve ethnic- or sectarian-based clashes. A difficulty there has been associated with the identification of arbiters – particularly on the external level, where even the United Nations is regarded with suspicion. The prospects for cantonization within the region as a mechanism for conflict-resolution are poor, especially given the associated fear of instability which the further breakdown of states such as Iraq, Syria or Iran might provoke as a result of such a policy. The canton option has proved to be an emergency measure, as in the creation of 'safe havens' for the Kurds in northern Iraq in the 1990s. The Kurds proclaimed autonomy in their federated state (KRG) in northern Iraq in the early 1990s and subsequent elections in 1992, 2005, 2009 and 2013. KRG has a population of 5.2 million people and enjoys autonomous rule over territory that is four times larger than Lebanon. Kurdish ambition is kept in check through a fractious relationship with Baghdad.

Consociationalism – power-sharing, grand coalition in government, proportional representation, community autonomy and constitutional vetoes for minorities (Lijphart, 1977) – stands a very limited chance of success in the region. The consociational experiment in Lebanon did not prevent the outbreak of civil war in 1975, though it was resurrected as part of the Taif peace accord. Six years after the outbreak of the Arab Spring and the descent of the region into unrelenting instability, calls for consociational arrangements for power-sharing within the borders of states like Iraq, Syria, Libya and Yemen appear unrealistic 'pie-in-the-sky'. Civil conflicts act as a significant obstacle to such ambitions.

Through these conflicts, sectarian, ethnic and extremist religious non-state actors, including the Islamic State (ISIS) and others, emphasize that power can be accrued without the state. Primordial identity issues – sectarian, religious or ethnic – increasingly dominate the regional conversation. These threaten to create conflicts and exacerbate existing ones, and in weak or failing states they have led to wars. Yet the state remains resilient. The partition of Iraq, Syria, Yemen or Libya may seem a forgone conclusion and the vision of Kurdish independence may seem alive, but still the Arab state stands.

There is a fear that ethnic partition or divorce in the region may not necessarily lead to peace and prosperity. Nevertheless, territorial break-up is still

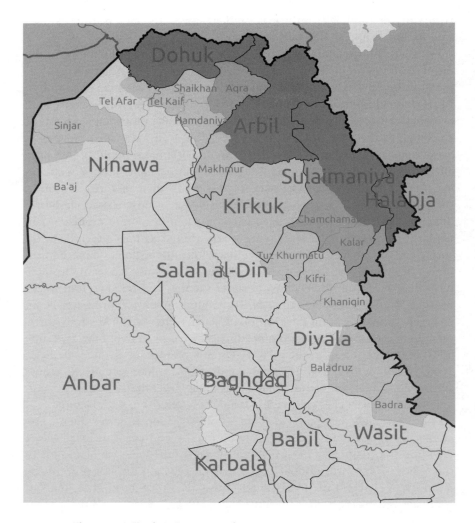

Figure 8.2 *Kurds in Iraq, an evolving map*

considered by distinct and mobilized ethnic or minority elements as the only way to redress their historic grievances. While the nation-state may remain a permanent feature of the region, the demographic realities of mosaic communities in large numbers require a more plural approach to politics, rights and privileges than is currently evident.

Case study

Lost within the Jewish state – Israel's Arabs

'Are Israeli Arabs the new African Americans?' asked a prominent Israeli historian and columnist in 2010 (Segev, 2010). Locating his article on the

Martin Luther King 'I have a dream' speech and the debate about the advance of African American rights, the author pointed to Israel's own vision of a democratic state with principles of equality for all its citizens and found it wanting.

In the twenty-first century, Israel's Arabs – Palestinians who remained on their lands after 1948 when Israel achieved independence – constitute an important 20 per cent of the population. Nevertheless, as a non-Jewish minority, they have endured what many contend to be systematic discrimination and denial of minority rights because of their ethnic Arab and Palestinian origin. This Arab minority includes a variety of sub-groupings such as Muslim and Christian Arabs, Druze and Bedouins. Their communities are increasingly segregated and isolated from other parts of Israel. The north and Galilee area has the greatest density of Arab Christians, Muslims and Druze. Bedouins have traditionally resided in southern areas of the Israeli Jewish state around Beer Sheba. The emphasis on the 'Jewish' state is an important feature of political discourse in the present era.

Back in the late 1940s the Palestinians of the new Israeli state were actually granted citizenship. This meant that they could vote in elections to the Israeli legislature (Knesset) and form political parties. But, in distinction to their Jewish neighbours, they were compelled to live under martial law, and then other restrictive commands such as curfews, detention without trial and deportations. Furthermore, the Israeli state used legal means to take control of Arab-owned lands (the Absentee Property Law of 1950) and put them into Jewish hands. It is argued that the Israeli state has subsequently failed to ensure equitable land distribution between its Jewish and Arab citizens. State laws and policies have curtailed Arab land rights, with consequences in terms of fundamental rights to human security and development. In 1966, martial law was lifted, but it is alleged that discrimination continues unabated.

It is contended that many of Israel's Arabs perceive the state and wider society as actively hostile to their presence. They are regularly described as 'second-class citizens', treated more as enemies than equals. In 2006, a group of notable Israeli Arabs issued a document entitled 'The Future Vision of Palestinian Arabs in Israel'. It argued that the Israeli state, in defining itself as Jewish first and foremost, is discriminatory. 'Exploiting democracy in service of its Jewishness excludes us', argued the authors of the document, 'and creates tension between us and the nature and essence of the state.' It was argued that, through mechanisms of ethnic preference for Jews protected in law, Arabs would never enjoy full equality (Ghanem, 1998).

It is alleged that discrimination takes place in terms of state provision of services across the board, as reflected in traditionally lower budgetary allowances. In terms of education, this has meant that Arab students have not enjoyed the same opportunities as their Jewish counterparts. In turn, this has limited employment opportunities. At other levels of local government and service provision, Arabs again have been found to be discriminated against. Political activism, however, has continued to characterize Israel's Arab minority. Arab MPs have served in every Knesset since the founding of the state in 1948. Arab Druze are drafted into the Israeli Defence Forces, but other Arab citizens of the state do not serve. In the history of Israel, only a handful of Arabs have served in the Supreme Court. Others would highlight that Arab Israelis are apparent in all aspects of business, and public service as well.

There are three main political parties traditionally considered representative of the community: Hadash (Arab–Jewish), Balad and the United Arab List (which has included members of the Islamic Movement in Israel). In the past, Arab voters would also have voted for leftist Jewish parties as well. The Knesset, however, has also passed legislation curbing party activism, which has had the greatest implications for Arabs.

Inter-communal relations have also been poor. Jew and Arab in Israel have each traditionally come to distrust the other. Israel's Arabs are perceived, by some, as a potential fifth column. Inter-marriage, a common feature of integrated societies, is almost non-existent between Jew and Arab in Israel. Indeed, in 2014, right-wing Israeli Jews protested at the wedding of one such couple and shouted 'Death to Arabs'. Instead, 'demographic' fears are propagated regarding a growing Arab population and increased segregationist tendencies. In an Israeli state commission of inquiry following violent clashes between Israeli Arabs and the state's armed forces in 2000, a former high court justice admitted that:

Box 8.6 Discriminating

The Arab citizens of Israel live in a reality in which they experience discrimination as Arabs. This inequality has been documented in a large number of professional surveys and studies, has been confirmed in court judgments and government resolutions ... Although the Jewish majority's awareness of this discrimination is often quite low, it plays a central role in the sensibilities and attitudes of Arab citizens.

(Orr Commission, 2001, p. 33)

Successive Israeli governments, even in the wake of serious inter-communal protests, clashes or violence, have been slow to address such disparities. Human rights organizations and foreign governments such as that of the USA have critiqued Israeli Jewish policies that deny Arabs rights in terms of accessing land for development, natural growth and purchase, and government house-demolition policies that are unfairly executed against them.

Towns with Arab population majorities have continued to be omitted from government social and economic expansion, development and growth plans, leading to further inequity in favour of the majority Jewish population. In closing his article, Segev compared the issues of rights enjoyed by African Americans and by Israeli Arabs. He quoted one of three Arab MPs to the First Knesset in 1949: 'Denying democracy and freedom to a national minority leads to the denial of democracy and freedom to all the country's inhabitants. It is impossible to portion out democracy and freedom' (Segev, 2010). Majority Israeli opinion would disagree with such contentions. For them, Israel remains the only democratic state in the region and one that offers equal rights to all its citizens, whether an Arab minority or other. Much contemporary scholarship on the topic, however, warns of entrenched tensions and conflicts within Israel if the state and successive governments continue to restrict the rights of non-Jewish citizens in Israel (Yiftachel, 2006).

Case study
'All the President's men' – the Alawites of Syria

Syria is not an ethnic or sectarian homogeneous state. In fact, since the creation of a new nation-state of Syria in 1920, initially under the French mandate, a mosaic of minorities have made up its population. The minorities include Alawites, Kurds, Druze, Christians, Turks, Circassian, Armenians, Assyrians, Jews and Maronites. While some 90 per cent of the population is Arab, minority status in terms of religious confession and sect is also important. The largest religious group consists of Sunni Muslims who live in the urban areas of Damascus, Aleppo and Homs and Hama. The Alawite Muslims, a Shi'a sect from the coastal areas of Syria, constitute 15 per cent of the population and form a distinct religious minority group that dominated the Ba'thist state. Druze and Christian Arabs form the other major religious groups of the country. The Christian Arabs make up some 10 per cent of the population and include among their number Greek Orthodox, Syrian Orthodox, Greek Catholics, Maronites and others. Jewish emigration from Syria throughout the twentieth century significantly diminished their presence.

The Alawites were concentrated in the coastal area of the Mediterranean near Latakia. Despite the rise of nationalism, and more specifically Ba'thism, Alawites and other minorities in Syria have preserved religious, linguistic and ethnic identities. Minorities remain an important factor in Syrian politics. While some minorities, such as the Kurds (as discussed above), have failed or refused to assimilate into the state, others, such as the Alawites, have been assimilationist. The Alawites had had a taste of autonomy under French rule in Syria, and integrated themselves into the Syrian armed forces at a rate disproportionate to their number (Nisan, 2002). The Alawites avoided challenging state policies, and in many respects have become identified with the state itself.

In considering the formation and structure of the modern Ba'thist state and the role of the Alawites within this, the crucial point is the rise of

Alawites in the Syrian armed forces and the Ba'th Party. While the French had pursued a policy of divide and rule among Syria's minorities, the founders of the Ba'th Party encouraged all Arabs in the country to join their struggle. The Ba'thist agenda had a particular appeal to the rural poor of areas like Alawite-dominated Latakia, and this openness facilitated their entrance into and rise within the party. The army, however, remained Sunni Muslim-dominated until the military coup of Ba'thists, Nasserists and independent officers in 1963. From this period onwards, a power struggle within the officer corps of the Syrian army took place between the Sunni and minority-background officers. This period of internal struggle had serious consequences, undermining military and national morale, and was only resolved in the late 1960s following the purge first of Sunni officers, then Druze officers, and finally an internal Alawite power struggle in which Hafiz al-Assad defeated his co-religionist and fellow officer Salah Jadid.

President Hafiz al-Assad, and his successor son Bashar, promoted fellow Alawites in the army, the Ba'th party and state institutions. They surrounded themselves with a cadre of loyal co-religionists. As Tibi noted as far back as the late 1990s, the Alawites 'constitute major segments of the ruling military and civilian elites in the current Syrian regime' (1996, p. 176). Al-Assad also faced the delicate task of promoting Alawites, while at the same time avoiding antagonizing the Sunni majority. Alawite leaders did not always achieve this balance. Sectarian tension, particularly between the Alawites and Sunnis, has always been in evidence.

Over decades of rule, the al-Assads presided over the repression of the majority Sunni population. For their part, the Alawite minority in Syria served to highlight the degree to which such groups can dominate politics in the inherently non-plural and authoritarian political systems. The failure to provide a plural and democratic basis for politics and representation in minority states like Syria, however, led to internal crisis and communal conflict. It explains in large part the growth of Sunni opposition in the country.

Since 2011, one defining feature of the civil war in Syria has been sectarianism (Potter, 2014). One dimension of the war is that it has become an Alawite versus Sunni contest. Brutal crackdown against the opponents of the regime of Alawite President Bashar al-Assad has been supported by Shi'a Iran and the Shi'a Lebanese militia Hizb Allah. Iran has trained and equipped Shi'a militia against Sunni Muslim rebel and opposition elements. In turn, these groups have drawn support from Sunni state actors in the region, such as Turkey and the Arab Gulf states. This has opened the floodgates of sectarian tension across the region. Thousands of Syrian Sunnis and foreign Sunni fighters have joined or been recruited to rebel groups such as Ahrar al-Sham, the Islamic Front and al-Qaeda's Jabhat al-Nusra (re-branded in 2016 Jabhat Fateh al-Sham) or ISIS. Such groups have promoted vehement anti-Shi'a messages. Similarly, thousands of Syrian Shi'a and foreign Shi'a fighters from Lebanon, Iran and Afghanistan have fought in the Syrian war against Sunni rebel militias. Sectarianism has become rife and led to violent purges and displacement of entire communities across the country.

Syria's Alawites, along with other minorities such as Christians, Druze, Ismailis, Kurds, Turkmen, Twelver Shi'a and Yazidis, have been affected by the conflict. Due to their minority status and demographically small size, the future of the Alawites in a post-conflict Syria where President al-Assad is removed from power could prove an existential threat. For the time being, President al-Assad views his co-religionists as highly important strategic allies. This has also made the prospects for peace and reconciliation through negotiated agreement all the harder to achieve. Left to their own sectarian devices, it would have been a significant challenge for Syrians to reach a political settlement that reflected plural democratic options. But, with the drawing-in of external actors – each with their own sectarian agendas – the task that lies ahead of anyone seeking a peaceful settlement to the Syrian civil conflict is almost unachievable.

Case study

Fear on a mountain – the Yazidis

In August 2014, a hitherto unknown minority group – the Yazidis of Iraq – burst into global consciousness. Following the capture of large swathes of Iraqi territory, ISIS had targeted and corralled thousands of Yazidis on the barren mountains of Sinjar. On social media and TV, pictures of the men, women and children huddling against each other for shelter highlighted their frightening plight. Tens of thousands more fled to the relative safety of Iraqi Kurdistan.

Yazidis are one of the oldest ethno-religious minorities in Iraq. There are an estimated 700,000 of them, the majority of whom live in the Sinjar area of Iraq. They derive their beliefs from a mixture of Islam, Christianity and Zoroastrianism. They centrally worship a fallen angel – Melek Tawwus. They are accused by other sects and religions of being devil-worshippers. This is a group on the religious periphery in a region of the globe where primary identities are either Sunni or Shi'a Muslim.

Yazidis have always been a persecuted minority. The Ottomans perpetrated massacres against them. The predecessors of ISIS, al-Qaeda in Iraq, were responsible for car bomb attacks targeting the Yazidis. In 2014, however, it became clear that ISIS were intent on a genocide against this syncretic minority community. The reason why ISIS targets such minorities lies in their conception of a homogeneous Sunni Muslim space as a fundamental component of their caliphate project. ISIS, in its attempt to establish a unitary Sunni Islamic caliphate, has engaged in religious cleansing of persons and physical structures that sit outside this parameter of their singular-manifestation faith. As al-Marashi highlights, 'eliminating these religious sites severs the opportunity for religious pilgrimage for these minority diaspora and destroys the only spiritual link these exiled, refugee communities possess to their ancestral lands' (al-Marashi, 2017, p. 144).

ISIS attempts to legitimize its brutality by reference to religious edict and injunction. It has subjected Iraq's Yazidi population to massacres, abductions, forced conscription and conversion. ISIS has assaulted and brutally raped Yazidi women and girls and forced them into sexual and other forms of slavery. It has institutionalized the sex trade in Yazidi women and girls; thousands are enslaved and a network has grown up to incarcerate, supply and sell them. According to a Human Rights Watch report, 'Islamic State has developed a detailed bureaucracy of sex slavery, including sales contracts notarized by the ISIS-run Islamic courts. And the practice has become an established recruiting tool to lure men from deeply conservative Muslim societies, where casual sex is taboo and dating is forbidden' (Human Rights Watch, 2016).

Propaganda in service of their cause – in *Dabiq* magazine – was employed to publish articles on the validity of their enslavement of Yazidi women. In an article entitled 'Slave-girls or prostitutes?', ISIS offered justification based on religious interpretation to suggest that it was 'permissible' to make slaves of Yazidi women and girls:

Box 8.7 Possession: excerpt from Dabiq

... The right hand's possession (*mulk al-yamīn*) are the female captives who were separated from their husbands by enslavement. They became lawful for the one who ends up possessing them even without pronouncement of divorce by their *harbī* husbands.

... Saby (taking slaves through war) is a great prophetic Sunnah containing many divine wisdoms and religious benefits, regardless of whether or not the people are aware of this ...

... So I say in astonishment: Are our people awake or asleep? But what really alarmed me was that some of the Islamic State supporters (may Allah forgive them) rushed to defend the Islamic State – may its honor persist and may Allah expand its territory – after the kāfir media touched upon the State's capture of the Yazīdī women. So the supporters started denying the matter as if the soldiers of the Khilāfah had committed a mistake or evil.

... I write this while the letters drip of pride.

Yes, O religions of kufr altogether, we have indeed raided and captured the kāfirah women, and drove them like sheep by the edge of the sword. And glory belongs to Allah, to His Messenger, and the believers, but the hypocrites do not know!

... Therefore, I further increase the spiteful ones in anger by saying that I and those with me at home prostrated to Allah in gratitude on the day the first slave-girl entered our home. Yes, we thanked our Lord for having let us live to the day we saw kufr humiliated and its banner destroyed. Here we are today, and after centuries, reviving a prophetic Sunnah, which both the Arab and non-Arab enemies of Allah had buried.

(Al-Muhajirah, 2015)

In June 2016, a UN report asserted that ISIS had perpetrated genocidal acts against the Yazidi minority in Iraq and Syria (United Nations Human Rights Council, 2016). Support for Yazidi victims of ISIS violence in their own countries is woefully inadequate. It is estimated that, since 2014, 120,000 Yazidis have had to seek asylum in Europe, amounting to a significant forced displacement of this vulnerable minority population (Brown, 2016). Areas, such as Sinjar, that were liberated from ISIS occupation have not seen a Yazidi return due to a climate of fear that is perceived as palpable by governing authorities in Baghdad and the KRG.

The political future for the Yazidi population in Iraq – even post-ISIS – has seemed uncertain. One solution offered was to establish a 'safe zone' in Northern Iraq where guarantees of security and autonomous governance could help minority groups like the Yazidis. Yazidi and other minority leaders have proposed the establishment of three autonomous provinces (Ninevah plains, Sinjar and Tal Afar) as safe zones with government in Baghdad making direct financial provision.

Box 8.8 Future protections

Such arrangements, while appearing attractive in the abstract, could make matters worse. While power-sharing in Mosul before ISIL took over in 2014 was far from perfect, it did represent forms of power-sharing which accommodated and balanced minority interests. The 2013 governorate elections returned a coalition of parties from the Kurdish KDP and PUK, Atheel al-Nujaifi's tribal, Sunni-dominated al-Hadba coalition, and other tribal, Shabak, Yazidi, Chaldean, and nationalist parties, reflecting the possibilities of representation without territorial carve-ups.

(Milton-Edwards, 2016b)

Proposals to develop such religious cantons are normally about carve-ups between self-interested local warlords and their external backers. Unless they are the product of constructive approaches to managing long-standing sectarian and ethnic problems, that are inclusive and representative of minorities like the Yazidis, they will fail. Such proposals are motivated by largely undisguised sectarian, patriarchal, tribal or ethnic interests at the expense of the rights and protections of other parties. They do not secure the future of Yazidis in the Middle East.

Questions for discussion

- Is the nation-state inhospitable to minorities in the region?
- How could Palestinian Arabs of Israel be assimilated into a Jewish nation-state?
- Do religious minorities have a future in the Middle East?

Recommended reading

- For scholarship on the Middle East and its ethnic and religious minorities, Robson (2016), Roald and Longva (2016) and Castellino and Cavanagh (2013) provide valuable insights and accounts. Zabad (2017) looks at the enhanced dimension of minority status in the region in the wake of the Arab Spring.
- Accounts of Israel's Palestinian Arab citizens can be found in seminal works by Smooha (1990), Yiftachel (2006) and Ghanem (2001, 2009). For other accounts, see Louer (2006) and Kanaaneh (2008), which reflect the personal accounts and narratives of Israel's largest minority population. Nassar (2017) employs the work of poets such as Mahmoud Darwish to explore Israel's Palestinian Arabs and their disconnected existence from their fellow Palestinians.
- On Syria and Alawite influence and power over the political system, the accounts in Seale (1989), Hopwood (1988), Van Dam (1996), the edited text by Kienle (1996) and Lawson (2009) all provide an insight. Historical overview of the Alawite political and military ascension can be found in Nisan (2002) and Hourani (1991). Further insights into the dynamics of Alawite, military, Ba'thist and state power are touched on in Kienle (1990), Hinnebusch (1990, 1993) and Perthes (1991, 1992). Goldsmith (2015) tackles Alawite precariousness and their future in the wake of the civil conflict.
- On the Yazidis, there are academic studies that have emerged to examine their status and persecution and these include Maisel (2016), Acikyildiz (2014), and Russell (2015) – who also looks at other minorities in the Middle East, such as the Copts and Zoroastrians.

CHAPTER NINE

Them and Us: the United States, EU and Russia in the Middle East

Introduction

In September 2002, one year after the al-Qaeda bombings in the USA, the Bush administration issued a national security strategy document that outlined its mission in terms of its bid for global leadership in the twenty-first century. US global leadership would deliver a form of pax Americana 'in the service of a balance of power that favors freedom'. This strategy would be manifest in three priorities: first, the USA would 'lead the world in defending the peace against global terror and against aggressive regimes seeking weapons of mass destruction'. Second was a commitment to peace through diplomacy; and, third, America would 'extend the peace by working to extend the benefits of liberty and prosperity as broadly as possible' through free trade mechanisms (US State Department, 2012). Without a doubt, such policy aspirations had a major impact on the Middle East region and would endure beyond Bush through to the two terms of President Barack Obama.

Nearly fifteen years later, in January 2017, the inauguration of President Donald Trump took place at the White House. Within days of assuming office, the Trump administration had issued Executive Orders and statements immediately signalling a change of course in US – Middle East and North Africa relations. President Trump indicated his immediate intention to issue an Executive Order halting and banning the entry into the USA of residents of seven Muslim-majority countries, five of which were in the Middle East and North Africa: Iraq, Iran, Syria, Libya and Yemen. Amidst claims that it religiously discriminated against Muslims, especially from the Middle East, US courts subsequently blocked the Executive Order. President Trump issued a similar order in an attempt to counter the judicial intervention. The tussle over the so-called Muslim ban would continue. Additionally, Iranian–US relations began to unravel with threats and counter-threats; both sides resorted to Twitter-bashing and diplomatic attempts at censure, ban and counter-ban. The auguries did not look positive. The incoming President had also issued a claim that within thirty days he would reveal a new plan to defeat ISIS.

Since 1945, the USA's relationship with the Middle East has in one way or another focused on the three themes of: (i) fighting terrorism; (ii) peace through diplomacy; and (iii) prosperity through free trade. Until 1989, this national security strategy was also shaped by the Cold War superpower rivalry with the former Soviet Union. Thus, there are elements of immutability in terms of the Middle East and American policies towards it.

In January 2009 when Barack Obama assumed the presidency, he ignited widespread hope across the Middle East. There was hope that he would reverse some of the more unpopular dimensions of the Bush administration's policies in the region. Such hopes were soon tempered by the realities that faced the new administration: Iran and its nuclear development programme; stasis in the Palestinian–Israeli conflict; Iraq; the ongoing threat of al-Qaeda and radical Islamism. President Obama would end his two terms of Presidency amid accusations that, notwithstanding the Iran Nuclear Deal of 2015, US policies had contributed to a worsening of instability, violence, conflict, abuses of human rights, poor economic performance, and terrorism in and from the Middle East. At best, his legacy was considered to be mixed; and at worst, pundits opined that he had undermined American credibility and power in the region and proved ineffective at tackling the scourge of terrorism (Gardner, 2017). President Obama was also criticized in some quarters for conducting a US retreat from the Middle East. This was a retreat that other states – such as Russia – have appeared to exploit.

Throughout the period of American engagement in the Middle East, commentators and critics have argued either for or against greater American intervention in the region. On the one side, many critics decry American intervention in the Middle East for being severely biased and dangerous in terms of longevity of local regimes, and exploitative in terms of the region's oil and other resources. Others, however, maintain that, despite a disdain for intervention, various US administrations have been compelled to intervene in the region in the name of the protection of values of freedom and independence, in the promotion of democracy, and to stop terrorism threatening the security of the global order. In early 2017, all the indications from the Trump administration were that he would avoid intervention. During his campaign for election, President Trump had indicated that he would not involve the USA in costly (human and otherwise) embroilments in the Middle East. Previous Republican administrations have pursued policies of state-building in the Middle East. President Trump's instinct is to aver.

National interest

When America was first involved in the Middle East, a number of issues – particularly in relation to the furtherance of national interest – emerged as key to establishing a set of policy objectives that remain largely unchanged some eighty years later. Elements of what defines American national interest vis-à-vis the Middle East are, of course, historically dynamic – some interests

Figure 9.1 *Anti-American sentiment: Tehran mural*

wax and wane according to circumstance – but there are some essential elements that have remained relatively unchanged.

Historically, one element that has remained so is the extent to which energy resources (principally oil) in the region led the USA to establish important relations. The US government has long considered energy to be at the nexus of its economy and national security.

The question here is: why is it that oil from the Middle East was so important to the USA? The main answer lay in the development of America's advanced industrial economy, and growing dependence of the economy on oil. While America was able to produce some of its own oil, it had become increasingly dependent on oil produced in the Middle East. In the early 2000s, experts had predicted that US energy consumption would increase while domestic production was likely to decline, leaving the country increasingly reliant on the free flow of oil from the Middle East (Bahgat, 2001). The US, for example, was dependent on Saudi Arabia alone for some 20 per cent of its crude oil imports. By 2017, America still relied on Saudi Arabia for oil but, as figure 9.2 illustrates, imports had gone into decline since the highs of the early 1990s and 2000s.

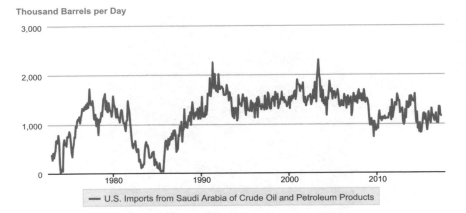

Source: US Energy Information Administration (2016).

Figure 9.2 *US imports from Saudi Arabia of crude oil and petroleum products*

Unimpeded access to energy resources from the region has thus been vital to US national interest. While there have been significant changes in energy markets and America has expressed its ambitions to be an 'energy superpower', it remains aware that maintaining positive diplomatic relations with some key energy producers in the region remains in the national interest. President Trump's positioning around Iraqi oil resources, however, was considered less than helpful, and contributed to the emergence of a bullish relationship between Baghdad and Washington. In 2017, for example, Iraq's Minister of Oil emphasized that the prosperity and stability of his country (including its ability to fight ISIS and act as a bulwark against it) were dependent on the development of its energy sector.

Secondly, trade with the Middle East has long served as a cornerstone of US national interest, and the region is particularly significant in terms of US arms exports and military assistance. The states there are seen as major consumers and markets for America. For example, in 2017, during his visit to Saudi Arabia, President Trump announced an arms deal worth more than $100 billion to the American economy. Furthermore, as the USA is the most important arms exporter in the globe, it is significant to note that, between 2011 and 2015, Gulf states such as Saudi Arabia and the UAE were the top receivers of American-made arms (Stockholm International Peace Research Institute (SIPRI)). The Middle East accounts for as much as 40 per cent of American global arms sales.

Additionally, the USA has given considerable support to certain states in the Middle East, through grants and loan assistance, to engage in major military spending programmes with US manufacturers. The US State Department's 2017 budget request included approximately $5.7 billion as Foreign

Military Financing. Of the top five recipients of US foreign military financing, four are from the Middle East: Israel ($3.1 billion), Egypt ($1.3 billion), Jordan ($350 million), Pakistan ($265 million) and Iraq ($150 million).

The example of Israel is illustrative.

Box 9.1 The golden ticket: aid and assistance for Israel

According to the US government, it 'has provided Israel $124.3 billion (current, or non-inflation-adjusted, dollars) in bilateral assistance. Almost all US bilateral aid to Israel is in the form of military assistance.'

Furthermore, 'Strong congressional support for Israel has resulted in Israel receiving benefits not available to any other countries. For example, most US military assistance is required to be used to purchase equipment from US manufacturers, but Israel can use some US military assistance both for research and development in the United States and for military purchases from Israeli manufacturers.

... In addition to receiving US State Department-administered foreign assistance, Israel receives funds from annual defense appropriations bills for rocket and missile defense programs.'

(Sharp, 2017, p. 2)

The export of arms produced in the USA to the Middle East, in terms of national interest, is thus clearly a means of supporting friendly regimes against threats that emanate against them from elsewhere in the region. American arms sales to Iran in the 1970s, for example, were essential to national interests in that a well-armed Iran was a bulwark in the northern tier states against the Soviet Union during the Cold War. Of course, the fact that American-supplied arms were also deployed internally against Iran's citizens was simply overlooked at a time when an authoritarian regime sought to control the masses.

The third feature of American national interest in the Middle East is the survival of Israel. For a variety of reasons, successive American governments have adhered to and maintained a commitment to preserve not just the security but also the prosperity of Israel. The nature of the 'special relationship' means that the USA perceives Israel as *the* strategic ally of choice in the Middle East. As illustrated above, the factors behind this relationship are significant in terms of diplomacy, aid, arms sales, and the increasing importance of religion in American politics as well as strategic considerations.

Finally, US national interest in the Middle East has always been concerned to stop forms of expansionism. During the Cold War, American policy was focused on halting Soviet expansion in the region. After 1990, American policy-makers increasingly worried about the growing expansion of the Islamist threat in the region and the consequences therein for their allies and their ability to access and secure oil, sell arms and promote American values. This has led to important dimensions of containment policy, as well as approaches to counter the threat.

The Middle East, however, has been a region that has presented American policy-makers with formidable challenges. By 2015, the impact of those challenges in Iraq, Libya, the resolution of the Palestinian–Israeli conflict, fighting al-Qaeda and then ISIS had dented America's image abroad and its pride at home. The election of Donald Trump, in 2016, was a telling reminder of the change in America's attitude to the Middle East.

Relations and rivalries

The policy relationship between the USA and the Middle East was established shortly after the First World War when American President Woodrow Wilson enunciated American support for the right to self-determination and independence for the inhabitants of the region. Such aspirations were, however, thwarted by the continuing imperial ambitions of the British and the French. The true rise of American policy within and towards the region emerged in the years of the Second World War and shortly thereafter. It would result in the establishment of a series of 'special relationships' that would benefit American interests in the region.

In many respects, the USA was regarded as an heir to the British colonial presence that went into such rapid decline during the years 1945–56. The US was motivated to become involved because of its own national interest in securing access to the oil reserves of the region as well as in keeping Soviet influence at a minimum. Containment of the Soviet threat would become a major preoccupation.

The USA, as I have previously mentioned, developed an early dependency on oil that compelled it to secure a place for itself in the region. By the 1930s and 1940s American oil companies rivalled British interests in oil-rich states such as Saudi Arabia, Kuwait, Bahrain and Iran. In states such as Saudi Arabia, American oil companies became, in tandem with the ruling family, the engine for the economic growth and development of the kingdom. US technical expertise and know-how played an important part in redefining the infrastructure and political allegiances of states in the Middle East. The USA quickly became the major western power there. Policy would be developed to protect this position and it meant that the USA was prepared to forge a variety of relationships with client states in the region. Thus, from the late 1940s, US diplomats would forge important footholds in countries such as Iran, Saudi Arabia and Israel. These client states would serve to maintain US interests in the region. The aim here was to build an axis of pro-western regimes that would act as a foil against Soviet ambition in the region and ensure access to oil.

America was aware that it would need to contain the Soviet threat to the region as well as keep an eye on the burgeoning and restive movements for nationalism and independence. The Soviet threat meant that the Middle East was largely regarded by both superpower rivals as an alternate theatre of the Cold War. The Eisenhower Doctrine of 1957 was part of the American policy of containing Soviet influence in the Middle East and securing American interest there. The doctrine was a response to growing Soviet influence in Egypt and Syria in the late 1950s and betrayed a desire, particularly in the wake of the Suez Crisis of 1956 and the diminishing esteem of western states as a result, to steer the maintenance of stability in the region according to American national interest. The strategic and economic implications of the Middle East going 'red' under the communist grip of the Soviet Union also compelled the Eisenhower administration to extend its involvement in the region. But Polk contends that the doctrine was ultimately unsuccessful, and 'largely redundant since all that it gained was public endorsement by those states [in the Middle East] that had already indicated their friendly attitude toward the same policy in a former guise' (Polk, 1991, p. 399). Moreover, it did not seem to play a part in deterring a number of events in the region – in Syria, Lebanon and Iraq – in the late 1950s, all of which were construed as harmful to America. The prospect of Arab or Iranian nationalists seizing control of natural assets such as oil and gas was inimical to American interests. Thus, throughout the late 1940s and 1950s, American policy-makers were compelled to rise to the challenge inherent in Arab and Iranian movements for nationalism and greater independence.

By the 1950s, both the Soviet Union and the West competed to offer aid to Egypt as its post-revolutionary leader Gamal Abdel Nasser set about building the Aswan Dam on the Nile River. The West stepped back after it was clear that Egypt would look to the communist East for its arms. Tensions rose as Nasser unilaterally announced the nationalization of the Suez Canal, prompting a crisis that led to a British, French and Israeli invasion in 1956. Much to the surprise of the old western powers, the USA and the Soviet Union supported a United Nations resolution demanding an immediate ceasefire. Nevertheless, it was the Soviet Union that was able to capitalize quickly on the Suez Crisis, winning new friends for itself in the Arab world. Indeed, an alliance of the 'radical' Arab states, such as Egypt, Iraq, Syria and Yemen, supported by the Soviet Union, soon emerged in opposition to the pro-western conservative states of Saudi Arabia, Jordan and Morocco.

This environment of superpower rivalry not only led to the establishment of contention over client states in the region but meant that both states were vulnerable to getting caught up in regional skirmishes. This was demonstrated during the 1970s when the superpower détente was seriously threatened by the war-like actions of their client states. In such a context, it was increasingly difficult to discern whether the dog was wagging the tail or the tail was wagging the dog! If client states were locked in enmity, the superpowers were often pulled in.

The policy of containment soon emerged alongside increased support for America's pro-western friends in the region. One result of this was an ever-escalating arms race within the Middle East that was conveniently supported and aided by the USA and the USSR. Throughout the Cold War, both the USA and its opponent sought to use arms sales and military aid as a way to gain and maintain a foothold in the region. The USA was keen to establish military bases there. By the mid-1970s, America had offered more than $65 billion in terms of military assistance to friendly states. By the early 1980s, 50 per cent of total global arms exports went to the Middle East (Gresh and Vidal, 1990, p. 14).

Furthermore, by the mid-1970s American arms sales to Iran and Saudi Arabia were playing a large part in determining their regional importance vis-à-vis other states. Oil revenues were now being used to fuel the arms race and allow the USA and other suppliers to preserve their place in the region. Oil for arms and arms for oil established a deep relationship of dependency that in turn created new perceptions and illusions of power and control within the Middle East. In the case of Iran, American backing encouraged the regional ambitions for power that the Shah had harboured. Halliday asserts that, 'throughout this period [1960s–1980s], Iran's growth as a regional power has gone hand in hand with the growth of its co-operation with the USA ... The USA has therefore been the key external factor in Iranian foreign policy since the Second World War' (Halliday, 1979, p. 252). Power-seeking at a regional level was translated into the barrel of the guns, missiles, warplanes, military technology and communications that successive US administrations offered to their Iranian ally. Iranian expenditure on US-supplied arms ran into the billions. By the late 1970s, however, when the Shah was deposed, and with the revolution harnessed by the Ayatollah, control of the Iranian arsenal fell into the hands of a theocratic regime that would declare the USA its number one enemy. Shi'a Iran was now a threat in the region – particularly to Iraq and Saudi Arabia, where there were concerns about their own restive Shi'a populations – but also to America where diplomats and policy-makers feared the fundamentalist tide would sweep the region and end unhindered access to oil. This fear was largely born out of their own experiences in the region in the early 1980s when those they believed to be linked to Iranian fervour kidnapped, held hostage and killed Americans in cities like Beirut and Tehran.

This fear played a significant part in a major policy reorientation towards the Gulf region in the early 1980s. This coincides with the end of the Carter administration and the controversy of the Iranian siege of the American Embassy in Tehran and the ascension of Republican Ronald Reagan to the White House. For Reagan it appeared as if the omens were good. As he swore his oath of office in January 1980, the Iranians released the 52 American hostages that they had held for 444 days. He talked tough on the Middle East and looked across the region for new alliances and with a determination to end the Israeli–Arab conflict. It would not be long before the Reagan administration began to pay a high price for its new policy orientation. In Lebanon in 1983,

241 American service people were killed in a bomb attack that eventually led the administration to withdraw its troops. America had intervened in Lebanon at the height of the civil war there. Their presence was seen by many there as evidence of American complicity in the Israeli invasion and occupation of the country in 1982 and as an attempt to influence the Christian militia elements. The Americans were shocked by the attacks on them. They blamed a Lebanese Islamist Shi'a organization called Hizb Allah (party of God) for the 1983 Marine barracks bombing. This new actor on the scene of Lebanon's scarred landscape of civil war also enjoyed close ties with the revolutionary regime led by Shi'a Ayatollahs in Iran, who were keen to export their revolutionary model elsewhere in the Middle East. By 1983, President Reagan ordered a retreat from Lebanon that demonstrated that American policy had been altered by the wrath of militant and violent Islamists. Moreover, by the mid-1980s, the Reagan administration was exposed for its double-dealing as news of the Iran–Contra arms deals filtered across the globe.

In 1980, the Iranian regime and neighbouring Iraq became embroiled in a war that would engulf both countries for the better part of a decade. Midway through this war, Iran's leaders embarked on a secret quest for US arms. Elements within the Reagan administration encouraged the President to accept the request, arguing that it would enhance their position in the region. Despite a US-imposed embargo on arms sales, President Reagan approved the deal with Iran. The revenues would allow him to fund, covertly, Contras in Nicaragua. A Lebanese newspaper exposed the deal in 1986 but by that point Iran had already received over 1,000 American missiles. The US investigation into the deal revealed that millions of dollars of Iranian funds had been received by America and then diverted to fund the Contras. While Reagan eventually emerged from the scandal largely untarnished (enjoying high popularity ratings as he left office), the significance of the affair was not lost on the many capitals of the Middle East region.

Successive American administrations, from Eisenhower to Carter, pursued policies of direct interference and subterfuge in the political and economic arenas of the Middle East. When in 1953 Iranian Prime Minister Mohammed Mossadegh, for example, announced the nationalization of the country's oil industry and an end to foreign assistance, alarm bells rang in Washington. American officials moved to intervene. By the summer of 1953, the USA (in cahoots with the British) had engaged the CIA in 'Operation Ajax' in a move to oust Mossadegh from power and restore the authority of Reza Shah Pahlavi. The mission was a great success as the CIA and MI6 stoked unrest which led to the flight of Mossadegh and the restoration of the Iranian throne to a Pahlavi Shah eternally indebted to the USA for his position. The USA considered the Shah a key client in the Middle East and sustained his authoritarian and crooked regime with billions of dollars in aid and arms.

During the 1960s and early 1970s, US policy in the region was restructured. As Soviet influence and Arab enmity grew, Washington's traditional reluctance to supply advanced weapons to conservative Arab states and Israel abated. The war of 1967 had transformed the military and political balance of power in the region. As a consequence, Israel's relationship with the USA became strengthened. This special relationship was pursued throughout the Nixon era and the furtherance of this relationship was seen as being on an economic–military basis.

These acts of intervention established local and regional distrust of American policy. In the case of Iran, this was to prove fatal both to the regime of the Shah and the American position there. During the revolution of 1979, the Pahlavi regime collapsed and with it American influence over this state. The regime of the Islamic Republic led by Ayatollah Khomeini declared the USA a major enemy of the Iranian people and the wider region. Thus, from 1979, Iran was lost to America and its policy within the Gulf region severely strained. After 1973 and the oil boycott, however, US policy had shifted again towards the conservative Arab regimes of the Gulf. By 1979, arms sales had become a political fix-it for obstacles in the way of US policy. The Iranian revolution of 1979, however, upset the US applecart, leaving the Gulf bereft of a US agent. Israel became the only agent in the region and American policy-makers were compelled to secure a resolution to the Arab–Israeli conflict while promoting Egypt as a new client of American aid and support. This was achieved through American sponsorship of the Israel–Egypt peace treaty and the significant promise of aid to be given to Egypt by the USA. The Camp David Peace Accords signed between Israel and Egypt formally ended the enmity between the two states, but the import of American intervention in this case was the way in which Egypt was neutralized as a threat to American interests in the region more widely. The decision by Sadat to enter into the American-brokered peace treaty with Israel effectively severed the claim to leadership of the Arab world and radical Arab nationalism that was previously so strongly identifiable with President Nasser.

As the USA was to discover, as a result of other encounters in the region, the desired outcomes of their foreign policy agendas were not always understood by those states or elements that they were interacting with. This led successive American administrations to increase their interactions with the region. As a result, dependencies have been established that have often made it difficult for the USA to change course or tack. This was true of the US–Iranian relationship, and is true of the US–Egyptian relationship, and the US–Israel relationship. Moreover, as a result of these special or particular relationships, the USA conversely chose to disestablish other actors in the region who were then accused of acting like Soviet sympathizers, enemies of America and rogue states. This meant that, in many states in the region, the USA was simply no longer welcome.

The policy of the Republican Reagan (1980–8) and Bush (1988–92) administrations was dominated by the realization that the attainment of Israeli objectives had, perhaps for the first time, been inimical to American interests, objectives or priorities. In light of this perception, the USA appeared to try and balance its objectives by pursuing a policy more favourable to some Arab states. However, on closer examination it became clear that the policy change only favoured the objectives of the Gulf states and further enhanced the hold of the USA in the Middle East. The 1980s and early 1990s were also characterized by the American attempt to stem the tide of Islamic fundamentalism in the Middle East – which it believed had been triggered by the revolution in Iran. This led them to forge many deals in the region, and amongst the region's near neighbours in states such as Afghanistan, that would later come back to haunt them.

Under the Clinton administration, there did appear to be movement with respect to the greatest political bugbear of the region: the Israeli–Palestinian conflict. There was certainly a ripple effect within the Clinton administration with respect to peace and intervention efforts in Europe (Northern Ireland, where his peace envoy George Mitchell achieved success, and the Balkans) and the Middle East. However, the Clinton administration did not effectively contain other actors and threats within the region. Moreover, his government left office without having brokered a final resolution to the Israeli–Palestinian conflict.

George W. Bush entered the White House in January 2001 with very little intention of engaging the efforts of his Republican administration in the politics of the Middle East. The attacks orchestrated by al-Qaeda against American targets on 11 September 2001 changed all that and they have had a significant impact on American foreign policy orientations in the Middle East.

In the wake of the attack, President Bush declared a war on terrorism. In the Middle East, not only were Iraq and Iran in his target sights, but pressure grew to look afresh at a variety of foreign policy issues. These included the Israeli–Palestinian conflict, Libya, Saudi Arabia, Yemen, Lebanon, Syria, regional security and arms defence issues, Egypt, the absence of democracy in pro-western regimes such as Jordan, as well as economic factors such as oil and global capital development. The re-engagement was bullish and confrontational in tone.

This tone was a reflection of how deeply the need to recover the myth of US hegemony and invincibility was felt. The attacks had revealed a sense of vulnerability on the home front that the Bush administration was keen to compensate for abroad. The events of 9/11 were a 'wake-up call' for the USA (Kupchan, 2002, p. 31). In the aftermath of these events, every aspect of US governance came under scrutiny. Some commentators argued that American 'imperial over-reach' had bred radical, hostile, anti-American forces in the region that were rooted in the fundamentalist Islamic tradition (Chomsky, 2003). Other thinkers and commentators, especially on the American right, argued for a different interpretation and policy with respect to the Middle East. They argued that the very fabric of American society – democracy and freedom – was under attack from fanatical Muslim terrorists. In this sense, their commentary lent credence to the 'clash of civilizations' thesis. They argued for strong intervention in the politics of the region to prevent further threats arising against America.

Intervention took the form of military action against Afghanistan – with its effects felt in neighbouring Middle Eastern states such as Iraq. As one such commentator remarked:

Box 9.2 America responds

[The] most realistic response to terrorism is for America to embrace its imperial role ... Occupying Iraq and Afghanistan will hardly end the 'war on terrorism', but it beats the alternatives. Killing bin Laden is important and necessary; but it is not enough. New bin Ladens could rise up to take his place. We must not only wipe out the vipers but also destroy their nest and do our best to prevent new nests from being built there again.

(Boot, 2001)

This thinking accounts for the changes in US policy in the Middle East in the wake of 9/11, the occupation of Iraq and involvement in Libya in 2011. It has also created a legacy of new and more direct US intervention that successive administrations have had to deal with. The new thinking was reflected in a growing antipathy towards the Middle East that was reflected more widely in American public opinion and popular culture (Sardar and Wyn Davies, 2003).

President Obama's administration highlighted the importance of the realist approach to America's role in the region and a growing disinclination for intervention. While President Bush took the USA into Iraq in 2003, President Obama charted the route out. He was also disinclined to intervene in Syria. There was little evidence from either President of significant traction in resolving the Israeli–Palestinian conflict or in reassessing support for authoritarian regimes. While the advent of the Arab Spring did initially disrupt strategic visioning in the USA, the ultimate corrective was evident in ongoing support for resilient authoritarian powers. Yet this was, as Gerges highlights, the key moment that has signalled

Box 9.3 America's moment

the beginning of the end of [America's] hegemonic moment in the Middle East. The end of American hegemony ... stems from internal and external causes, including an awakened public opinion in the Middle East, the emergence of geostrategic and geo-economic regional powers with assertive foreign policies, America's relative economic decline and the high costs of war, and the shift in US foreign policy priorities to the Asia–Pacific region.

(2013, p. 299)

Europe, the EU and the Middle East

At the close of the twentieth century, driving Europe's relationships in the Middle East were factors such as politics, economics and strategic rivalry. European colonial powers such as Britain and France had established elements of territorial control through colonization in the region, and political administrative control, in the wake of the First World War. Such powers had competed with each other to exert political influence, extend trade ties and exploit newly discovered oil resources. The historic backbeat of such relations, as detailed in chapter 1, was broken and loosened during this period. Indeed, in the twenty-first century these factors still drive relations but they are institutionally structured to take account of a post-colonial age, and a global age in which trade, migration and refugee flows have strained ties between the two regions, and the supranational influence of the EU has wavered under the strains wrought in the wake of the Arab Spring (Börzel, Dandashly and Risse, 2015).

The reassertion of the EU's role in the Middle East came in the wake of the ending of the Cold War. Taken in its totality, the MENA region is the EU's third-largest trading partner. The rising threats within and from the region impact more deeply on the EU than on other international actors. European states compete with each other for Middle Eastern markets but also grapple in differing ways with immigration issues.

From 2015, the migration crisis in Europe has focused on those fleeing countries in the MENA region where conflicts have forced the displacement of major population groups. The majority of migrants have fled war in countries like Syria and Iraq, making hazardous journeys to reach the relative safety of Europe. Transit through states of the region such as Turkey and Libya to the southern countries of the Mediterranean has also added to the EU's concerns with wider security and political implications. European consciences were pricked by the human tragedy symbolized in September 2015 when the photo of the body of a 3-year-old Syrian refugee child, Aylan Kurdi, spread around the globe. Aylan had drowned in the Mediterranean Sea as his family sought refuge in Europe.

The EU has clearly struggled to act in concert on these issues. It has discovered that its advantage on the ground in the Middle East and North Africa is limited in an era of security uncertainty and with the influence of other international actors such as Russia and China. The EU wants to encourage regional stability and security but cannot ensure this alone. Security concerns, including maritime security, migrant flows, terrorism and border security, have only seemed to expand in proportion to the EU's engagements and concerns with the region. The EU has become apprehensive that the 'neighbourhood' within which it has formed relationships has soured and turned 'bad'. Nevertheless, there is evidence of EU balancing in terms of relations with Gulf states, where, as well as strengthening cooperation with the GCC, the EU was key in establishing the 2015 nuclear deal with Iran.

In the wake of the Arab Spring, much-vaunted democracy efforts have quietly gone into abeyance in states such as Egypt, where a counter-revolution against democratically elected representatives has re-established authoritarian resilience. It is clear that the idealism of democracy promotion has run up against the realities of pragmatism and security for a number of EU actors in the Middle East.

The EU has tried to act as a major force in the quest for a resolution to the Arab–Israeli conflict (Yacobi and Newman, 2008). Understanding that the conflict is the nexus of relations both in the region and between the region and the EU, particular attention was paid to it and its resolution (Musa, 2010). The EU's support has been manifold but one can point to two primary inputs: political and economic. The EU is also a member of the international quartet, founded in Madrid in 2002, to promote Arab–Israeli peace. In respect of its actions, the EU supports UN resolutions on resolving the conflict that call for Palestinian self-determination and a two-state solution.

The EU has been involved in the development of the Euro-Mediterranean Partnership (EMP), launched in 1995 (also referred to as the Barcelona Process). The EMP has met with mixed success. There are major asymmetries between the EU member states and Middle East states in the partnership. These have only eroded incrementally through mostly bilateral rather than multilateral agreements and arrangements on such issues as trade, industry and immigration (Orhan, 2010).

The Syrian conflict has also drawn in the EU and member states such as France and the UK (Pawlak, 2016). By 2017, however, as the conflict appeared entrenched, it was also apparent that the EU's influence over events was limited. Russia dominates the diplomatic landscape in alliance with the regime of al-Assad, Iran and Turkey. Despite the EU's limited influence, it has had to deal with major humanitarian fallout from the crisis. The EU's role in the conflict and in terms of dealing with its consequences is thus mostly evident in the major humanitarian burden it has had to shoulder. The EU has emerged as a leading humanitarian donor to Syria. Since 2011, the EU has disbursed more than €5 billion to Syrians in the country and to refugees and their host communities in neighbouring Lebanon, Jordan, Iraq, Turkey and Egypt. In addition, the EU pledged €3 billion at the 'Supporting Syria' conference held in London in February 2016. In terms of security, the EU must contend with the largest refugee/migrant crisis in its history.

In terms of other regional efforts at containment and conflict resolution, the EU has also played an important role – this was the case particularly with Iraq, where strains were apparent and consensus broke down among EU member states over US ambitions and strategies for control. These strains have impacted negatively on common security and foreign policy in the region. This lack of consensus has become apparent again with respect to policy and positions over the Syrian conflict. The appetite of the states of the Middle East to look to the EU and EU states to temper or balance US policy outcomes has increasingly diminished. Hence, the importance of the EU as external actor with respect to the whole of the region, from the Maghreb in the west to Iran and the Arab Gulf to the east, has weakened in the transition period since the Arab Spring.

The bear awakens: Russia and the Middle East

President Putin's strategic approach to the Middle East and North Africa is evident from the Valdai International Discussion Club meeting, held annually in Russia. During the 2014 meeting, Russia conveyed key messages about its role. It also offered itself as an alternative to western states in the Middle East and North Africa. Nevertheless, the 2014 meeting also offered an instructive note. Russian officials stated that they had to rebuild alliances and establish strategic depth after an absence from the MENA region for more than two decades.

The officials were recognizing the historic and deep role played by the former Soviet Union, which partially terminated during the 1990s. The Soviet Union, as a rival to the USA during the Cold War, had built important alliances in the Middle East. These alliances included Arab socialist states, such as Syria, along with patronage of local Arab communist movements. There has been some evidence that, along with re-building Arab alliances, Russia has used the last decade to augment its position in the Middle East with non-Arab state actors such as Israel, Iran and Turkey.

In the wake of the Arab Spring, Russia's interests in the region have grown considerably. Russia recognizes the strategic importance of relations within the region especially as growing turbulence has threatened the wider global order. This has seen the military and diplomatic footprint of the Russians increase. Nevertheless, economic ties with the Arab states have not yet been sufficient, especially when compared to trade relations with other regional actors such as Iran and Turkey. Russia has sought to maintain a strategic status quo with allies such as Iran and Syria. It has been prepared to support both countries in regional as well as global contexts. In the case of the Arab Spring, Russia exhibited cautious support for populist mobilization, preferring the certainties of relations with leaders of stable regimes – even if such regimes are decidedly authoritarian. On Libya, however, there was evidence that Russia had a strategic interest. Russia refrained from voting on UN Resolution 1973, which authorized the establishment of a no-fly zone in Libya. It then claimed over-reach when NATO militarily intervened to oust the regime. In the succeeding break-up of the Libyan state, there is evidence that Russia has aligned with key Libyan military figures such as General al-Haftar, to keep its strategic interest.

Russia has been motivated to maintain an important strategic military foothold in the Middle East, including a naval foothold in Tartous in Syria and, therefore, the eastern Mediterranean. It is wary of full-scale presence. From Moscow, the motivation to involve it in Syria is as a consequence of lessons learned from the Libyan intervention (or rather lack of it) in 2011. Russia initially claimed it was seeking to avoid a Somalization of the conflict – working to ensure that Syria remained unified territory under President al-Assad's control. Russia has thus simply averred from international strategies or approaches that involved the 'toppling of regimes' – as was the case with NATO intervention in Libya in 2011. Nevertheless, as Russian fighters joined the jihadi flows to the Syrian theatre, there were concerns regarding national interest back home as well.

In the wake of populist revolutions and the transitions across the Middle East, but particularly in Egypt and Tunisia, Russia struggled with the ballot box victories and ascendance of the Muslim Brotherhood. Due to allegations of links with the Chechen cause, the Muslim Brotherhood had been prohibited by Russia. Along with other state actors, Russia was worried that a rise of region-wide support for the Muslim Brotherhood and its ascension to power would inspire Russia's own Muslim citizens. President Putin did establish relations – albeit limited – with the government of Mohamed Morsi, but these strengthened following the coup of July 2013 led by General el-Sisi. This has opened up a new era in Russian–Egyptian relations, especially in terms of trade, economy and the energy sector.

Critics of Russia highlight that it has not acted as a positive force within the region, nor as a useful counter-balance to the USA. Furthermore, they highlight its role in Syria and in particular in supporting the regime of Bashar al-Assad. Russia's relations with Iran also bemuse and annoy regional strategists. Russia will have to devise an exit strategy from Syria if it is to avoid helping President al-Assad win a contentious peace. Even if Russia's approach to the region appears to be piecemeal and idiosyncratic, it still reflects an ambition, under President Putin, to secure its interest for the near future.

Case study

America and Israel – the really special relationship

The relationship between the governments of Israel and the USA stems – at the level of inter-governmental bilateral relationships – from the historic fall-out of the Holocaust, and American repositioning in the wake of the end of the Second World War. These events have gone some considerable way in shaping a bilateral diplomatic relationship that in turn has had many layers added to it. This relationship is, in many respects, unlike any other diplomatic relationship that the USA has conducted with a foreign ally. Both sides term this relationship as 'special'.

In 1977, as Israel stood on the brink of peace with its Arab neighbour, Egypt, American President Jimmy Carter affirmed his commitment to Israel declaring, 'We have a special relationship with Israel. It's absolutely crucial that no one in our country or around the world ever doubt that our number one commitment in the Middle East is to protect the right of Israel to exist, to exist permanently, and to exist in peace' (Carter, 1977). Forty years later, President Trump re-affirmed the relationship between America and Israel, addressing ways to 'advance and strengthen' it (White House Office of the Press Secretary, 2017).

Successive administrations of the US government have, since 1945, acted as staunch allies of Israel when other actors in the international community have criticized the state for its illegal actions with respect to its occupation of the Palestinian territories and its treatment of the Palestinian people. At international forums such as the United Nations, when UN resolutions to remind Israel of its obligations to the Palestinians according to international law are passed, the USA has consistently applied its veto power. UN resolutions condemning Israel for its 'policies and practices in the occupied territories', 'expropriation of land in East Jerusalem', 'settlement activity in East Jerusalem' and 'killing by Israeli forces of … U.N. employees' have all been vetoed by the US representative at the United Nations. One way of interpreting this support is to reflect on the extent to which Israel's interests are a part of, or a reflection of, American foreign policy interests in the Middle East. In December 2016, in the dying days of the Obama administration, the USA permitted the UN to censure Israel. This was the first time in thirty-six years that the USA did not block the way for such a resolution against Israel.

The US–Israel relationship has been subject to a process of institutionalization and close links that are reflected in more than one area of the American system of governance and more broadly in American society, where pro-Israel sympathies and support for the Zionist cause remain widespread. Pew Center data, for example, show pro-Israel support to be consistently higher than that for Palestinians (Pew Research Center, 2016).

Institutionally, the extent to which Israel and issues associated with it form a crucial element of American foreign policy in the Middle East is reflected in the office of the President, the State Department, Congress and Senate.

This is due in no small measure to the presence and influence of an important pro-Israel lobby in the USA, the mobilization in the past of the Jewish vote in national elections, sympathies in the highly influential Christian Zionist movement and the current impact of all of these on Republican and conservative discourse in the USA. Israeli peace activist Uri Avinery argues, in respect of the influence of the pro-Israel lobby, that, 'if the pro-Israel lobby were to sponsor a resolution on Capitol Hill calling for the abolition of the Ten Commandments, both Houses of Congress would adopt it

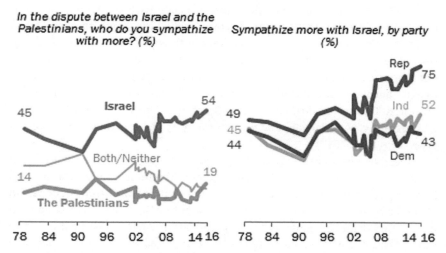

In the dispute between Israel and the Palestinians, who do you sympathize with more? (%)

Sympathize more with Israel, by party (%)

Note: 1978-1990 data from the Chicago Council on Foreign Relations. Don't know responses not shown.

Source: Pew Research Center, survey conducted 12–19 April 2016, Q52

Figure 9.3 *Middle East sympathies, 1978–2016*

overwhelmingly' (2005). The main lobby group is the American Israel Public Affairs Committee (AIPAC) and it focuses on Congress and other parts of the American political system directly in an attempt to influence legislation and policy in support of Israel. In other words, it seeks to ensure that American foreign policy is supportive of Israel – particularly as a 'lone democracy' in the Middle East.

Israel has benefited greatly from US support. Israel receives more of America's foreign aid budget than any other country (US State Department, 2012). As noted above, 'Israel is the largest cumulative recipient of US foreign assistance since World War II' (Sharp, 2016).

Given the depth of the relationship between Israel and the USA, many have examined and questioned it in terms of American interests and their policy agenda vis-à-vis the wider Middle East. The natural sympathies that the USA shares with Israel are understandable, but dependence rather than mutuality is an issue that has featured in critiques of this relationship. America is understood as an actor in the region in relation to Israel first and other states second. This in turn has shaped Arab attitudes towards the USA and its policies in the region. Such commentators complain that 'every issue in the region has to go firstly through the door of Israel before it can be discussed with the US and we simply don't feel this way about everything' (Moussawi, 2005).

In sum, a combination of factors, including the ethical debt America feels that it owes Israel, the impact of the pro-Israel lobby, as well as material interests in terms of relations between these two states, continues to account for American foreign policy with regard to this tiny state. Under the Obama administration, relations between the USA and Israel were characterized by unprecedented strains with respect to inter-personal relations between the US President and the Israeli Prime Minister Netanyahu, along with dispute in respect of Israeli defiance of a US call to halt illegal settlement construction and expansion in Palestinian territories. A Trump presidency was a fundamental reversal of this positioning.

Case study
America and Saudi Arabia – oil on troubled waters

The foreign relations that the policy-makers of the USA have sought with the Kingdom of Saudi Arabia are rooted in a relationship that was largely motivated by securing access to or control over Saudi Arabia's energy reserves. Successive US governments have had to remain cognizant of a diplomatic, political, economic and security relationship with an Arab state that also claims significant Islamic, and in particular Wahabi, credentials. The cities of Mecca and Medina in Saudi Arabia are the most holy to millions of Muslims from across the globe. Saudi Arabia is a monarchical Islamic state that does not reflect the democratic political profile that the USA claims for itself.

Over the years, the association between the United States and Saudi Arabia has been cultivated more by necessity than by natural political affinity. Since 1932, Saudi Arabia has been a monarchy ruled by the al-Saud family. The al-Sauds are adherents of the fundamentalist Islamic doctrine of Wahabism, which they have incorporated into the structures of the state they control. The Saudi possession of energy reserves such as oil and the country's strategic location in the Gulf region have made it important in terms of defined American national interest. Shortly after independence in 1932, diplomatic relations with the kingdom were established and cemented in a historic meeting in 1945 between President Roosevelt and King Abdul Aziz al-Saud. This relationship extended to the facilitation, by the USA, of the participation of a growing number of US-owned oil corporations in the economic development of the country. The oil industry would contribute to the rapid development of Saudi Arabia as a modern state governed by the conservative pro-western monarchy.

The pivot in this relationship was the extent to which successive US governments could secure American national interest (oil and strategic influence) with a government guided by principles so radically different from their own. The USA achieved this largely by treating the relationship with Saudi

Arabia as primarily economically driven. Oil from Saudi Arabia was increasingly key to US industry and the economy. By the 1970s, the USA derived 20 per cent of crude oil imports from Saudi Arabia. The USA, in turn, became Saudi Arabia's most important trading partner. A key element in US enjoyment of access to Saudi oil exports was, of course, security – particularly in a region traditionally viewed as one of the most volatile on the globe.

US administrators understood this issue as early as the 1950s and persuaded the Saudi monarchy to accept a US base in the Saudi town of Dahran as early as 1953. Increased spending on US-supplied weaponry plus the role of American oil companies in promoting the modernization of infrastructure in Saudi Arabia contributed to the establishment of a meaningful relationship between the two sides. The depth of meaning to this relationship, however, extended to certain areas of policy such as economic and military issues. By the early 1980s, for example, there were complaints within the Reagan administration of preferential treatment for the Saudis after the President agreed to sell the advanced AWACS system, as well as Sidewinder missiles, to the kingdom. There were fears – particularly in pro-Israel circles – that American support for the supply of advanced weaponry to Saudi Arabia could upset the advantage that Israel traditionally enjoyed in the regional arms race.

The importance of the military and security relationship between the USA and Saudi Arabia was underscored following the invasion by President Saddam Hussein of Saudi's neighbour Kuwait in August 1990. Iraq's occupation of Kuwait brought a threat direct to Saudi borders and imperilled the American principle of unhindered access to Arab oil. Nearly 500,000 Iraqi troops were in occupation of Saudi Arabia's neighbour. There was an immediate fear in both Saudi Arabia and the USA that an emboldened Saddam Hussein would order his troops into Saudi Arabia. Hence, in early August, at the invitation of the Saudi monarchy, President George Bush ordered the deployment of over 200,000 troops. By early January 1991, these numbers were boosted with the arrival of a further 200,000.

In 2003, more than a decade later, this deployment of US troops was terminated. The presence of American troops in Saudi Arabia was a potent indication of the extent to which the kingdom (one of the wealthiest in the world) was reliant on another power for national security. Moreover, extremist jihadists such as Usama bin Laden exploited the presence of US troops in territory considered by Muslims to be the most holy in Islam. The decision, moreover, to leave Saddam Hussein in Iraq, until he was deposed in April 2003, also left the region, including Saudi Arabia, with a strategic 'threat' that would have to be contained. This ultimately tied Saudi Arabia to the USA – security for the kingdom remaining a linchpin of their relationship.

The events on 11 September 2001 tested the limits of the US–Saudi relationship. It became apparent that many of the bombers from al-Qaeda had originated from Saudi Arabia and that Usama bin Laden was behind the plot. There was an inevitable growth in American pressure on the kingdom to take action against what many believed to be the problem of Islamic terrorism that was rooted in Saudi Arabia. Bin Laden had singled out America as an enemy and accused it of occupying Islam's most holy places (Mecca and Medina in Saudi Arabia). He had demanded an immediate withdrawal of American troops from the country. A growing critique of Saudi Arabia in America galvanized rulers in Riyadh to join the American-led war on terrorism.

In the post-9/11 era, US–Saudi relations have strained further. Increasingly, US politicians had criticized Saudi Arabia's support for Islamic extremism, manifest, they argued, in growing terrorist attacks. In 2015, the conclusion of the Iran nuclear deal dismayed policy-makers in Riyadh. 'Washington's relationship with Riyadh will never find many enthusiastic defenders in the United States', argues Gause, '[but] the United States should not distance itself from one of the few Arab countries still able to govern itself and influence the region' (2016, p. 124).

The USA, as discussed in chapter 3, has tried to break itself from its energy dependence on Saudi Arabia, in part to release itself from this relationship. For the foreseeable future, however, geostrategic considerations as they pertain to the Gulf are likely to direct President Trump's sway towards Saudi Arabia rather than Iran. This was evident in the spring of 2017 on President Trump's first visit to the Middle East, where he was lauded by his Saudi host and he, in return, heaped rich praise on this regime.

Case study

Russia and Syria – the embrace

The embrace between Russia and Syria has been strong and enduring. The former Soviet Union supported Syrian independence from France in 1946. In the 1970s, as President Hafez al-Assad established his authority through the Syrian state, he permitted the Soviet Union to open a naval base in the Syrian port of Tartus (Ginat, 2000). Underpinning relations between the two states are near-continuous treaties, deep economic ties and patterns of military assistance from the former Soviet Union and, latterly, Russia. For the Soviet Union, an alliance with Arab socialist Syria allowed it leverage in the Middle East against its American foe and its regional proxies, such as Iran (until 1979) and Israel. Additionally, Ba'thism and Soviet ideology elided strongly, making it easy to develop ties between the two states. The Soviet Union developed economic ties to Syria that also created a form of dependence for the Arab state on this global power. Such manoeuvrings did not go amiss. British diplomats noted:

> ## Box 9.4 Russian long game
>
> They [the Soviets] are clearly taking a long-term view and have apparently decided that the advantage of securing for themselves a central place in the Syrian economy, possibly for the next generation, is a political and economical prize well worth having, and that all future Syrian regimes, whatever their complexion, will be bound, if only on account of the strength of Syrian–Soviet trade and aid ties, to give due weight and consideration to the policies and wishes of the USSR as regards Syria and the Middle East area as a whole.
>
> (Ginat, 2000, pp. 156–7)

The collapse of the Soviet Union in 1989–90 inevitably led to some re-ordering of regional relationships. In essence, however, while the ideological impulse to pursue relations with Syria declined, economic and strategic levers were ascendant. Strategic considerations go a long way in explaining the re-admission of Syria into the Russian orbit and the regional calculus at work under President Putin. This was evident in 2005 when Putin invited Bashar al-Assad to Moscow. The invitation was accompanied with the announcement that Russia would forgive nearly three-quarters of a $13.4 billion debt owed by Syria and supply arms and military training to al-Assad's regime (Bourtman, 2006, p. 5). The move also signalled a growing alliance between the two states at a time of relative diplomatic isolation for Syria. Since 9/11, Washington had emphasized that Syria was a security threat. In American parlance, Syria was ascribed status as a 'rogue state', close to – if not part of – the 'Axis of Evil', and political leaders raised concerns about Syrian support for terrorism and weapons of mass destruction (WMD).

In 2011, the Arab Spring protests broke out in Syria, and the regime of Bashar al-Assad faced a growing mutiny, rebel forces and populist protest. Syria looked to its alliance with Moscow and President Putin for support. This support was evident in two principal ways. Firstly, as a major international power, Russia could employ its advantage and UN veto to stymie diplomatic consensus against al-Assad. For example, Russia has consistently employed its veto power at the UN Security Council against moves by western or Arab states to sanction Syria or consider intervention. Secondly, Russia's direct intervention on behalf of al-Assad in the growing Syrian quagmire helped effect decisive battleground victories that he would otherwise not have gained. Russia has not only continued to support the supply of arms to Syria but, on 30 September 2015, it commenced a military engagement there. The intervention constituted:

Box 9.5 Big guns

Russia's biggest intervention in the Middle East in decades. Its unanticipated military foray into Syria has transformed the civil war there into a proxy US–Russian conflict and has raised the stakes in the ongoing standoff between Moscow and Washington. It has also succeeded in diverting attention away from Russia's destabilization of Ukraine, making it impossible for the West to continue to isolate the Kremlin. Russia is now a player in the Syrian crisis, and the United States will have to find a way to deal with it.

(Stent, 2016, p. 106)

In total, these Russian efforts have contributed to the endurance of the al-Assad regime and played into the strategic calculus of President Putin regarding his adversaries and allies in the Middle East region.

Nowhere is this more evident than in Russia's support over Aleppo. Aleppo, the second-largest city in Syria, became a major battleground between Syrian government forces, an array of rebel groups and a benighted civilian population. Rebels had taken control of large swathes of the city and effectively pushed al-Assad's regime forces out. The loss of this strategic site significantly

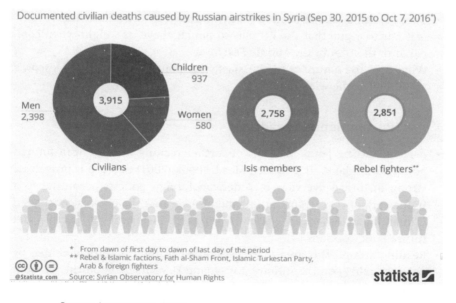

Documented civilian deaths caused by Russian airstrikes in Syria (Sep 30, 2015 to Oct 7, 2016*)

Children 937

Men 2,398

3,915

Women 580

Civilians

2,758

Isis members

2,851

Rebel fighters**

* From dawn of first day to dawn of last day of the period
** Rebel & Islamic factions, Fath al-Sham Front, Islamic Turkestan Party, Arab & foreign fighters

@Statista_com   Source: Syrian Observatory for Human Rights

statista

Source: Armstrong, 2016

Figure 9.4 *People killed by Russian airstrikes in Syria*

undermined the chances that President al-Assad might have of holding on to power. It is widely agreed, therefore, that Russian airstrikes – which began ostensibly against terrorist forces in the autumn of 2015 – and other support to Syrian government forces helped achieve a decisive rout against the rebels by the end of 2016. By early 2017, the Russians were scaling down their military presence in Syria and on the verge of announcing 'mission accomplished'. Russian intervention proved to be a game-changer in the contest for power over Aleppo, boosting the regime of President al-Assad over rebel groups that, in turn, a variety of regional and international backers supported. The Aleppo 'victory' also allowed momentum to Russian rather than US-supported 'peace efforts', favouring an outcome that would permit al-Assad to remain in power. This was evident in the swing away from the American-mediated Geneva peace track to the Russian-supported Astana talks of 2017.

The victory for Russia underscores its effective presence in the Middle East and ability to maintain important strategic alliances with states such as Syria and Iran. It has induced other regional actors to consider Moscow as an increasingly important destination in terms of power and advantage in the region. It was also a timely reminder of the eclipse of US influence and the extent to which powers like Russia or China will move to exploit this. For the near future, the embrace between Russia and Syria remains enduring.

Questions for discussion

- Does oil and oil alone explain US involvement in the Middle East?
- Is it fair to argue that the EU fails to punch above its weight when compared to the USA in the Middle East?
- What does the nature of the Russia–Syria alliance tell us about Moscow's ambitions in the wide region?

Recommended reading

- A good starting point in terms of further reading on American foreign policy would be Walter Russell Mead's book (2001) because it provides a strong historical overview of American foreign policies according to a framework of US categorization, and also because the book is considered influential in American circles in terms of historical perspective and future policy options.
- Reading around this area more generally can then be supplemented by Bacevich (2017) on US military policy, and Hassan (2014) on the freedom agenda in the Middle East.
- There are many critiques of American foreign policy as it relates to the Middle East. It is worth considering Chomsky's contributions (2003) for a perspective on American 'imperial' ambition and its consequences for the

rest of the international community and the resolution of conflicts in the Middle East in particular. Additionally there is work by Khalidi (2009) and Tyler (2009).

- The theme of American withdrawal is also explored in Gerges (2013) in relation to the two-term Obama administration and the consequences of the Arab Spring. Pollack and Byman (2011) also addressed themselves to America and the Arab Spring. Bin Hethlain (2010) takes both a historical and contemporary overview of the Saudi–US relationship. Riedel offers a compelling perspective on US–Saudi relations from 1945 to the present day (2017).
- There are many good works on the relationship between Europe, the EU and the Middle East, and these include Orhan (2010), Musa (2010) and Dosenrode and Stubkjaer (2002). Popular intellectual Slavoj Žižek (2016) has written about Europe and refugees. Betts and Collier (2017) offer significant insight on the refugee issue from the Middle East.
- In terms of Russian foreign policy in the Middle East and Russian intervention, Kozhanov (2016) and Phillips (2016) provide timely assessments, particularly as it pertains to Syria. Moore (2017) and Andreeva (2010) discuss different dimensions to the Russian–Iranian relationship, and its wider impact or consequences for the balance of power in the Middle East.

CHAPTER TEN

The Arab Spring and the New Era of Uncertainty

Introduction

The protest-driven downfall and removal of authoritarian leaders in Tunisia (President Zine El Abidine Ben Ali), Egypt (President Hosni Mubarak), Libya (President Muammar Gaddafi) and Yemen (President Ali Saleh) marked the Arab Spring. Major demonstrations, worker strikes, e-protests and uprisings occurred throughout the Middle East, challenging autocratic regimes in Bahrain, Jordan and Syria. Stirrings of popular unrest actually first occurred in non-Arab Iran in 2009 following gerrymandered elections but did not result in any form of regime change – in this case, Iran proved resilient. Within the Arab Spring phenomenon that emerged, many of the key themes discussed in this book – such as gender, political Islam, political economy and the Arab state – were tellingly apparent.

In many respects, such protests, as we outline in this chapter, were unprecedented – or at least the response to them and their region-wide impact were considered so. Yet there were other dimensions of the Arab Spring, such as popular discontent, economic woes, frustration at authoritarian rule, cronyism, corruption and the mobilizing power of organized political Islam, that were not unprecedented in the least. Instead, they reflected long-standing concerns among the citizens of the region at the ways in which the state and its rulers had ill served, marginalized, and even abandoned them, and yet still claimed legitimacy.

The outcomes of the Arab Spring have been highly fragmented. Some commentators rushed to declare the events that unfolded a victory for democracy, freedom and universal rights. Others hurried to pronounce that the Arab Spring had turned into an 'Islamist Autumn' in which gains would be reversed. There has been evident impatience at the transition. What is uncontested is the extent to which the Arab Spring has affected politics across the entire Middle East and disrupted security and political arrangements with its allies in the West as well as elsewhere in the globe.

While it is the case that in the seven countries mentioned above the significant impact on politics, state–society relations and the economy is apparent, other states were made vulnerable, and still remain so, to the same motivating dynamics. Indeed, many diverse voices within and outside the region were still warning in 2017 that the events of 2010–12 were the 'first wave' of a liberation movement that has struck the politics of the region and established an era of uncertainty.

The Arab Spring was epitomized by a powerful coalescence of factors that marked the politics of repression long endured in the region. Yet what was unprecedented was that the change of power in Arab regimes was effected as a result of actual non-violent popular mobilization of a type previously not witnessed in the regime-change movements of the past. Authoritarian incumbents were forced from power by popular dissent.

Underlying factors

In the wake of the Arab Spring, the flurry of op eds, news reports and analyses making sense of the rash of events breaking out across the Middle East blamed academic scholars for their lack of foresight. In truth, scholars of the Middle East had spent decades looking at, accounting for and objectively presenting analyses that stressed the underlying factors that led to the outbreak of the Arab Spring. The only thing such scholars were guilty of was not naming the day when the region would tilt.

The underlying factors that gave rise to the outbreak of protest and the calls for change, reform and even revolution had been steadily rising in most states of the Middle East and North Africa for at least a decade before 2011. They represented the discontent of a variety of groups and non-state strata in Arab society. Frustration grew at a variety of factors that included suffocating state repression, economic downturn and corruption (Haddad and Atassi, 2013). For example, the global economic crisis of 2008 had serious repercussions, such as growing youth unemployment rates, in the states of the Middle East where the uprisings took place. Furthermore, industries – such as tourism – that played a major part in driving revenues in countries like Egypt and Tunisia were hit. Once again it was the young that were hit hardest. In Tunisia, for example, where the uprisings first broke out, youth unemployment was, according to the World Bank, at nearly 30 per cent (World Bank, 2009). In rural regions and periphery towns and villages, the state was virtually invisible in terms of providing services to its citizens. Neo-liberalization, as discussed in chapter 3, had not delivered benefits to all in society but had instead exacerbated existing inequalities. In countries like Egypt, this depressed wage costs and did nothing to stop spiralling price rises or cuts in government subsidies on basic foods such as flour or bread. While structural adjustment policies in Egypt and Tunisia may have satisfied the IMF, which had forced them to undertake such moves in the first place, and contributed to economic growth rates, they were not actually benefiting the majority of the population. The state was averse to large-scale public investment in the regions or social strata of their countries that needed it most. Grassroots initiatives were sidelined so as to distance the state from its obligations to society.

Corruption, nepotism and a propensity to kleptomania by regime leaders and their families was also an underlying factor that played a key part in popular revolution. It was no surprise then that this dissatisfaction was reflected in the Corruption Perception Index of 2011, in which most of the states of the Arab uprising achieved a score of less than 4 on a scale of 0 to 10. A score of 0 implied that a respondent believes a country is highly corrupt (Transparency International, 2011). It should be noted that corruption in the Arab states came in many guises, but all were a product of a culture of impunity, and lack of transparency and accountability, in such states. High-profile instances of corruption, especially among 'ruling families', were played out 'soap-opera' style. For example, the excesses of wealth amassed by President Ben Ali and his family, including his wife Leila Trabelsi, were exposed on social media and on websites like WikiLeaks, which provided details of high-end luxury car concessions and the family's private business interests in banking, shipping, drugs and transport, to name but a few (Embassy Tunis, 2008). The sons of Egyptian President Hosni Mubarak were investigated for amassing an estimated $340 million wealth fund (AlMasry al-Youm, 2011). The barely disguised hold of such ruling families and their business interests over national economies actually discouraged direct foreign investment because this would require dealing with the 'gatekeepers' through their networks of bribery and corruption. These were practices that could not easily be carried through the books of legitimate businesses.

Box 10.1 Key factors of corruption

First, the lack of institutional reforms accompanying economic liberalisation programmes has created new opportunities for rent seeking ... Second, the prevalence of authoritarian rule in the region constitutes a major hindrance to transparency and accountability at both state and private sector levels. ... Libya's oil revenues, for example, constituting 95 per cent of the nation's exports, are held in secret funds controlled exclusively by Colonel Muammar al-Qaddafi and his associates. ... Furthermore, most MENA governments compensate for low popular support or poor legitimacy by granting opportunities for bribery to leading families or cliques to ensure political survival.

(Leenders and Sfakianakis, 2002)

Corruption, and the perception that interfacing on a daily basis requires bribery to ensure access across the states of the region, established the politics of antagonism and frustration. A simple bureaucratic procedure, such as changing car ownership, which in open societies can be completed quickly and at relatively small cost, is not simple in some countries of the Middle East. Corruption also means that nepotism works strongly to stifle professionalism and meritocracy in public service. This is a problem when such states are also characterized by overblown bureaucracies.

Another major underlying factor, which scholars and analysts had long warned was problematic, centred on the politics of the authoritarian state. States such as Egypt, Syria, Jordan, Tunisia, Yemen and Libya had long featured in reports – from Human Rights Watch or Amnesty International, for example – as repressive and lacking in freedoms for their citizens. The citizens of such states, and others in the region, were prevented from voicing dissent, calling for reform or any form of criticism against state power-holders. In Jordan, for example, where widespread protests broke out in 2011, criticism of the monarchy was considered a punishable offence with a three-year prison term (Zacharia, 2010).

Moreover, in such states, security oversight was so pervasive that they were routinely referred to as 'police states'. Citizens could be arrested and held in indefinite detention, 'disappeared', tortured and killed. In countries such as Syria, secret prisons, state emergency law and the all-pervasive secret police (*mukhabarat*) ensured that politics was a state-run affair carefully stage-managed to keep dictators like President al-Assad in power. The citizens of these states were prevented from airing any form of dissent. Journalists, activists, comedians, artists and human rights workers were all considered fair game.

The state employed an array of legislative measures – under the 'national security threat' mantra – to harass its opponents and limit freedoms. Political opposition was effectively de-fanged by state policies. State rulers could arbitrarily appoint and dismiss their governments, send their citizens to notorious state security courts, shackle the independence of their legislatures, co-opt political parties and repress meaningful organized opposition. Opponents were spied on, harassed, sacked, regularly detained, prosecuted, kidnapped, disappeared into secret prisons and detention facilities, exiled or killed. Free media, freedom of association and free speech were aspirations, not real rights.

The Arab Spring – the public and mass mobilization of discontent – was, then, an event just waiting to happen. The citizens of so many countries in the region lived in a constant state of fear and insecurity. Fear of their rulers and state-agents, insecurity at the limited opportunity to participate in economies and societies building for national prosperity, and lack of freedom were catalysts for change.

Winds of change

As should be abundantly clear by now, there is a challenge to expound the upheavals of the Arab Spring and to find ways to explain objectively the unfolding events in the Middle East and their portents. We need to avoid over-simplistic descriptions like 'the Facebook Revolution' or 'Arab Spring Islamist Autumn' because the changes that are taking place are extremely complex. They involve a variety of local and external forces. This is in fact a long and uncertain transition. There are a number of ways of looking at factors that commonly characterize the uprisings that took place across the region.

Teenage kicks: youth and the Arab Spring

At the vanguard of the Arab Spring were the youth. This may be explicable by the simple fact that young people (aged 18–25) in the Middle East make up the majority of the population in most states. Indeed, this is frequently referred to as the 'youth bulge', affecting diverse societies across the region and transcending national, ethnic, sectarian and other boundaries. This means that the region has one of the youngest populations on the planet. As such, youth are a fundamental factor in the socio-economic picture of society. Politically, however, young people tend to feel excluded and marginalized from even those limited forms of political participation that were formally offered by the state before the Arab Spring. They were also largely presided over by political leaders who represented their grandparents' generation.

In the mid-2000s, the issue of youth was central to research and policy debate across the MENA region. In 2007, the World Bank report on *Development and the Next Generation* contended that regional prosperity hinged on utilizing the potential of young people. Since that time, however, progress in youth inclusion has been distinctly unimpressive (see figure 10.1). It is not simply that youth endure high rates of unemployment, but that they are increasingly marginalized politically.

Young people are considered to be developmental assets for the struggling economies of the Middle East and North Africa. Yet their potentialities have still to be truly realized. Youth unemployment, for example, in Jordan was estimated by the World Bank in 2014 as being at 28.8 per cent. Not only was this figure more than double the national unemployment level, but it also meant that more than one in every four young people was out of work (World Bank, 2016b). Jordan is not a special case. Across the region, youth unemployment is at an average of 25 per cent, including well-educated university and high school graduates among its growing numbers.

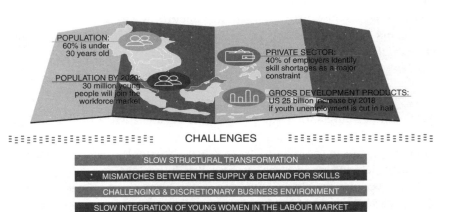

Figure 10.1 *Youth unemployment landscape in the MENA region*

Young people clearly acted as agents of change in the unfolding events of the Arab Spring. There were pronounced gendered differences in such actions. Young men were often portrayed by the media in defining images of the organization of protest, demonstration and forms of resistance against incumbent regimes. Young women were incorporated at a secondary level. They tended to be framed by their veils and hijabs in public spaces, but, as we discussed in chapter 7, were at least or at last visible. Young people were the chief articulators of grievance against the state, and against authoritarian governance for denying them opportunity. Yet what also confounded many scholars of young mobilization in the region is that the Arab uprisings did not witness droves of young people – and young men in particular – rushing into the arms of violent extremist movements. Quite the opposite. Young people employed strategies of non-violent protest, social media, popular culture and mainstream youth activities, such as music and clothing, to promote a strategy for change. But the 'Youth movement' that appeared to typify the Arab Spring was a convenient label applied to a highly disparate phenomenon. In truth, there was no such thing as an organized youth movement marshalling events or strategizing for change. Young people in Tunisia, for example, represented a complex dynamic of interests and identities alongside goals which they believed should be achieved once power changed.

When the ruling powers were overthrown, however, the youth faced significant obstacles from the incumbent generations, in both state and non-state organizational form, in the consolidation of their triumphs. The youth remain excluded from power-holding in both the formal and informal realms of society, economy and politics in the Arab world. In tribal contexts, in countries as diverse as Jordan and Yemen, young men have tried to lobby for a share of influence among 'elders' but they have failed. In Jordan, for example, tribal youths had lobbied to be included as candidates on tribal voting lists. Elders excluded them. Young women remain completely excluded from such structures. They remain firmly outside the tent. In non-state opposition movements, such as the Muslim Brotherhood, the energy and political agenda of young people, both during the Arab Spring and in its aftermath, were resisted by those much older leaders presiding over the organization (Milton-Edwards, 2016a). Middle East states, even in the wake of the Arab Spring, still offer too few prospects for youth participation in decision-making, and generally inhibit youth access to governance. The media will highlight some exceptions, such as the Gulf princes in their thirties heading ambitious economic reform agendas, but in general young people remain marginalized. This is illustrated by the example of a young Jordanian graduate. In 2016, Mohammed, who had graduated with top honours in Civil Engineering from university, had been unemployed for over a year. He was driving an Uber car several hours a day just to escape the pressure, frustration, boredom and expectation that home and family represented to him. He had not voted in the general election that had been held in September 2016. He had abstained, his friends had abstained and no one he knew had voted. It was contended that such a vote was a waste of time. For young people like Mohammed, the vote would not make any difference to how parliament worked or how it was controlled, as he believed it was all in the hands of his monarch. This is not to say that there had not been some progress, but rather that the majority of states in the region do not encourage young people to be invested in governance and politics. It is for this reason as well that, in the past, so many young people were drawn to opposition movements such as the Muslim Brotherhood. There they found plenty of opportunities to be involved in political debates and discourses that incorporated a variety of issues. Such exclusion of youth, who are naturally agents of change, makes the rebellions that took place from 2010 onwards entirely explicable.

Rebellion and extremism

General rebellion against authoritarianism was also identified as a common feature of the Arab uprisings. This was perceived as an indicator that the 'third wave' of democratization was finally washing up in the Middle East. As discussed in chapter 6, there was some initial evidence that this was the case. The movements for change in Tunisia, Egypt, Libya, Yemen, Bahrain and Syria were all characterized as centred on demands for democratic reforms and greater freedoms and rights. In Bahrain, for example, an array of opposition elements joined together on 14 February 2011 to call for democratic reforms from their leadership. Notably, as many as one in five citizens in this small Gulf state congregated at the Pearl Roundabout in Manama, to call on their ruler to establish an elected legislature and a new constitution. The state responded swiftly and brutally to put down the calls for democracy and protests. The ruling al-Khalifa family also relied on the deployment of thousands of troops from neighbouring Saudi Arabia (as part of the Gulf Cooperation Council (GCC) Peninsula Shield Force) to conquer the protest movement definitively. Jones argues that, six years after the uprising in Bahrain, authoritarianism has deepened:

Box 10.2 Bahrain's non-revolution

While the pro-democracy movement may have prompted minor concessions on the part of the government, the extent of the popular mobilization triggered the Al-Khalifa regime's authoritarian reflex, and they have reacted to throttle the Uprising by putting in place legislative, ideological, and political barriers to reform, which points not only to a current de-democratization, but also a lack of future democratization.

(Jones, 2016, p. 251)

Authoritarian regimes fought back. By 2017, the Pearl Roundabout was a bulldozed remnant of the past, only distinguished by the ever-present armoured vehicles of the Bahraini state The third wave of democracy has, for the time being, been ruthlessly suppressed.

The fear that the Arab Spring would be hijacked by the forces of Islamism proved partially founded. Yet it was extreme Islamism that has gained the most from the instability and uncertainty of the transition era. Powerful states within the region have employed tropes that have demonized groups like the Muslim Brotherhood to force them from power while at the same time they have pursued sectarian agendas that have led them to support and arm Sunni extremist rebellions in Syria. Yet, despite the tensions between the Muslim Brotherhood in power and the military in Egypt, and the electoral and power-sharing successes of Ennahda in Tunisia, this was not where the threat lay. These elements of reformist and moderate Islam have partially demonstrated their ability to transition from the authoritarian milieu to different forms of governance. In the case of the Muslim Brotherhood in Egypt, there is speculation that the movement was not given enough time or autonomy to promote transition to democracy. Others vehemently disagree with this argument, reasoning that this lack of progress towards democracy was why a counter-revolution was launched and that, once again, the Egyptian military stepped into the breach. Egypt today contends with a violent Islamist threat in North Sinai and other relatively ungoverned spaces across the country.

In Yemen and Libya, Islamist elements now account for newly dispersed and extreme varieties of Islamism. Similarly, in Syria, the democratic opposition, which mutated dangerously into armed rebellion against the government of al-Assad, has spawned a plethora of rival Islamist cells, brigades and groups (Lister, 2016). As in the past, extreme Islamist elements have capitalized on the ungoverned spaces to embark on violent jihad and contest for control of the state, or to declare new caliphate states themselves.

This also brings us to the issue of the Arab state itself in the wake of the uprisings. The notion of statehood, its roles, its foundations and claims to legitimacy have been challenged and questioned. As such, basic conceptions – for example citizenship, nation, nation-state, sovereignty and nationalism, as discussed in chapter 2 – have been tested and found wanting by millions of people in the region. This has led academics and policy-makers to ask whether, in the wake of the Arab Spring, the state has reformulated and changed, particularly in respect of the social contract with its domestic constituencies.

There is little evidence that state rulers have been capable of such change or an ability to negotiate new ways of governing. If anything, as we discuss below, the authoritarian state has remained resilient and has been 'allowed' to defend the interests of entrenched governing elites with little interference from the liberal-democratic states of the West. The so-called statist threat posed by ISIS and its caliphate claims have proved to be a disruption – albeit temporary – to norms of sovereignty and nationalism in the Middle East. If anything, the threat evident in the ferocious self-rule norms of the caliphate state of Raqqa in Syria and Sunni lands in Iraq has established a foundation for the reactionary rhetoric of power-holding elites in Arab states across the region. Furthermore, in the wake of the Arab Spring, the Arab state is increasingly epitomized by the array of coercive instruments it deploys against its own citizenry, as enemies within. As such, civilian–military relations are largely in abeyance as state military and security institutions preside over the political frameworks of governance. By 2017, the military, security and other state agencies of coercion were actively inserted in the broken polities of Syria, Libya, Egypt, Yemen and beyond. In Libya, for example, General Haftar was put in charge of the Libyan National Army and has remained a pivotal political actor in the pre- and post-Gaddafi era. In the wake of the Arab Spring, he has actively inserted himself into the evolving and fissuring domestic political drama, as well as cultivating important external alliances with states like Russia.

In essence, in the wake of the Arab Spring, the social actors that tried to re-define a new relationship have, with the notable exception of in Tunisia, largely failed. The empowerment of a broad array of social actors, including women, youth, labour activists, business people and the middle classes, that was so evident in the dynamic of the Arab Spring, has butted up against a reactive state that recovered and then went on an all-out offensive against them. The state has continued to treat its social actors with disdain. State rulers have, as we have demonstrated, employed a variety of means to portray such social actors and their grievances as a national security threat. State elites will portray these as 'agents of a hostile foreign state' or as a threat to public order. In Bahrain, for example, the state prosecuted and jailed doctors and nurses on charges equivalent to treason, for treating protestors injured in the Pearl Roundabout uprisings. In Syria, many civil society organizations established out of necessity in response to the state's lethal approach to thwarting the uprisings have been subsequently targeted as hostile actors. Medical organizations, for example, have been deliberately targeted by the Syrian state. It is questionable whether such civil society actors and organizations can survive in hostile environments like these. Yet the state, in such contexts, is frequently incapable of offering the kinds of public service that keep society functioning and the social contract intact.

Unfolding spectacle of political change

It is necessary to have a timeline in order to demonstrate the reach of the Arab Spring. The countries that have been included are the states in which widespread protest was most apparent, and also where some regimes actually toppled. This was an unfolding spectacle that spread like political wildfire from one country to another across North Africa and the Middle East. At first it appeared uncontainable and the ruling regimes of states across the region looked, for the first time in decades, to be uncertain of their much-vaunted authoritarian stability.

There were 'features' attributed to the Arab Spring. Such features included the fact that the initial demonstrations and protests were distinctly pacifist and non-violent. Protestors also deployed and enacted forms of creativity in their defiance of their political rulers and governing elite. There were claims that, in specific instances, social media formed a key determinant of mobilization and bringing people together in the public spaces of the largest cities and the smallest towns or villages. As the state sought to counteract protest by employing repressive and violent measures, the protestors organized themselves to care for the injured in makeshift clinics, triages and treatment centres. The people themselves challenged the all-pervasive fear that had, in the case of states like Syria, effectively controlled entire populations.

The uprisings were also shaped by the majority of the youth who streamed to the streets from their homes to occupy public spaces and act as captains of the revolution. Many major barriers enshrined in the patriarchal state and a paternalistic society were also fractured as women emerged as actors in their own right. This is evident from the role played by journalist and activist Tawakal Karmon in the Yemen uprising. Karmon was awarded a Nobel Peace prize in 2011.

Tunisia

- **17 December 2010** Tunisian Mohammed Bouazizi sets himself on fire outside the local municipal office in an act of protest after being humiliated by local police officers for not having a permit to run a vegetable stall. Popular protests break out across the country.
- **14 January 2011** Ben Ali announces his resignation and flees to Saudi Arabia, ending twenty-three years in power.
- **27 March 2011** Tunisia unveils a new cabinet of technocrats, none of whom has served in governments under Ben Ali.
- **23 October 2011** Tunisia votes in the first election of the Arab Spring, choosing from among eighty political parties to form an assembly charged with drafting a constitution within a year.
- **19 February 2013** Tunisia's Prime Minister resigns. Former Interior Minister Ali Laareyedh is appointed in his place.
- **28 September 2013** After talks with the opposition, Tunisia's Ennahda-led government agrees to resign.
- **2014** Presidential and parliamentary elections are successfully held.
- **2015** The Tunisian National Dialogue Quartet, an alliance of workers, employers, lawyers and activists, wins the Nobel Prize for Peace.

Egypt

- **25 January 2011** Mass protests in Egypt demand for Mubarak to resign.
- **28 November 2011** Egypt's first free elections. Islamist parties, including the Muslim Brotherhood, sweep the polls to win a parliamentary majority.
- **2012** Egyptians vote in the first round of the presidential elections.
- **2 June 2012** An Egyptian court sentences former President Hosni Mubarak to life in prison.
- **24 June 2012** Egypt's election commission announces that Muslim Brotherhood candidate Mohamed Morsi has won Egypt's presidential elections.
- **22 November 2012** Morsi issues a new constitutional decree, giving himself sweeping powers and banning any challenges to decisions he makes. The move later triggered mass protests in front of the presidential palace.
- **June 2013** Anti-government protests break out.
- **3 July – 17 August 2013** President Morsi deposed. General Abdel Fattah el-Sisi installs Supreme Court Chief Justice Adly Mansour as interim president. Muslim Brotherhood leaders arrested. Morsi supporters take to the streets in protest. Egyptian security forces raid al-Nahda Square and Rabaa al-Adawiya Square, leaving more than 500 dead.
- **23 September 2013** Egypt's Muslim Brotherhood banned.
- **May 2014** General el-Sisi wins 97 per cent of the vote in election.

Yemen

- **27 January 2011** Protests erupt in Yemen, as opposition groups call for President Saleh to stand down.
- **23 November 2011** President Saleh agrees to transfer power under an agreement brokered by the GCC.
- **27 February 2012** Abd Rabbuh Mansur al-Hadi becomes new President.

Bahrain

- **14–17 February 2011** More than 100,000 Bahrainis participate in demonstrations. State responds by forcibly and violently suppressing protest.
- **14 March 2011** Saudi troops enter Bahrain. The GCC agrees to send troops of the Peninsula Shield Force at the request of the Bahraini government. About 4,000 Saudi Arabian troops and 500 UAE police arrive.
- **18 March 2011** The Pearl Roundabout is demolished. An important symbol and focal point of the Bahraini uprising and opposition movement is destroyed.

Libya

- **15–17 February 2011** Protests erupt in Libya.
- **March 2011** UN Resolution 1973 authorizes 'all necessary measures' to protect civilians in Libya from pro-Gaddafi forces.
- **19 March 2011** NATO starts bombing Libya.
- **20 October 2011** Gaddafi is captured and killed by rebel fighters in the city of Sirte. A few days later, the National Transition Council officially declares an end to the 2011 Libyan Civil War.

Morocco

- **20 February 2011** Moroccans take to the streets to demand a change of government and constitutional reforms.
- **1 July 2011** Moroccans vote to approve constitutional changes that curb monarchical power, amid calls by activists to boycott the referendum because changes fall short of popular demands.

Syria

- **6 March 2011** Demonstrations in the southern town of Deraa calling on the regime of President Bashar al-Assad to reform. Protests soon spread to Damascus, Aleppo and other cities. The regime orders state forces to put down the protests.
- **March 2011** Rebel groups spring up across the country to represent a myriad of often competing ethnic, confessional and sectarian interests, alongside the Free Syrian Army, Syrian army defectors. Al-Qaeda off-shoot Jabhat al-Nusra established and recruits foreign fighters.
- **10 January 2012** President al-Assad makes his first public speech in months, mixing defiance with promises of reform and an insistence that 'victory' for his regime is imminent.
- **15 July 2012** The International Committee of the Red Cross officially declares that the Syrian uprising is a civil war.
- **12 February 2013** Syria's death toll since the start of the civil war exceeds 70,000.
- **21 August 2013** Syrian activists claim that government forces have carried out a poison-gas attack in Damascus.

Algeria

- **3 January 2011** In Algeria, violence erupts as protestors claim the government is responsible for corruption, limitations on freedom of speech, and poor living conditions.
- **8 January 2011** The Algerian government lowers food prices and cuts taxes on sugar and cooking oils.
- **12 January 2011** Algeria faces a state of emergency as protests quickly escalate.

- **February 2011** The government announces measures aimed at boosting employment and reducing the cost of food.
- **10 May 2012** Legislative elections are held, which retain power for the incumbent coalition of President Bouteflika's National Liberation Front and Prime Minister Ouyahia's National Rally for Democracy amidst accusations of electoral fraud.

Jordan

- **January 2011** Jordanians call for more jobs and an end to government corruption. They soon demand greater democracy and for the king's powers to be reduced.
- **March 2011** The National Dialogue Committee is established and tasked with matching government political reform with public opinion. Many decline offers of Committee positions due to lack of confidence in its effectiveness.
- **24 March 2011** Demonstrations include calls for action expressly to tackle over-reaching of the regime's security services.
- **November 2012** Clashes with security forces after thousands take to the streets to show their anger at the government's IMF-induced abolition of fuel subsidies.
- **January 2013** Parliamentary elections are held two years early, with the king promising to consult parliament over the choice of Prime Minister for the first time. However, opposition parties – led by the Muslim Brotherhood's Islamic Action Front – continue to boycott the polls in protest at electoral laws favouring royalist loyalists. (Al Jazeera, www.aljazeera.com/indepth/interactive/2013/12/timeline-arab-spring-20131217114018534352.html)

Authoritarian resilience

The momentum of change wrought by the Arab Spring across the region and the threat it posed to authoritarian regimes were resisted. The state struck back. In some states, like Bahrain, the regime was able successfully to manage and call upon aid from its near neighbour Saudi Arabia to effect a definitive repression of the protest movement. In other states, the counter-revolution or state response took longer to galvanize, but when it did it was fierce and deeply repressive. This demonstrated the resilience of authoritarian states in the region and their resistance to democracy-promotion approaches. This, in turn, reinforced the prevalent idea that the region was an exception when it came to plural politics and freedoms.

Authoritarian regimes had, in most cases, spent decades funding and building up their security apparatuses to use against their own citizens. The response by actors invested in the maintenance of such regimes was to 'adapt and protect' (Heydemann and Leenders, 2011). As the wave of protest broke out across the region, state incumbents devised approaches to put incipient demands from citizens in their own states down. A range of means were employed to mediate the ongoing tension between state and citizen. In some nations, like Egypt, state interest was evident in the role that the military played in the counter-revolution to end the presidency of the Muslim Brotherhood's Mohammed Morsi and to effectively install General-then-President el-Sisi in his place.

As discussed in chapter 4 of this book, the military in states like Egypt and Syria is a strong stakeholder in the state and economy. Keeping the military on board was key to regime maintenance. In other regimes, rulers resorted to stalling strategies, promising political reforms, delaying change and parsing promises to open up power structures and make them more transparent and accountable. This is evident in states like Jordan, where King Abdullah II responded to protests calling for an end to corruption and democratic transformation. To be sure, there was evidence of some adjustment – for example, to electoral laws – but more significantly the ruling Hashemite regime further consolidated executive power in the hands of the monarch. The regime has subsequently clamped down even further on reformist calls for freedom of association and the press.

Nevertheless, the Arab Spring has exposed the dynamic of power in incumbent authoritarian regimes and the lengths to which mutual dependencies have grown between rulers, the military and heads of powerful security and intelligence agencies. Military spending, as explained in chapter 4, has increased in the wake of the Arab Spring, at a time when the economies of the region can ill afford such expenditure (Small Arms survey, 2015). The state cannot incur the loss of the loyalty of its armed forces or security and intelligence agencies. They are the tool of power employed on an almost daily basis against the citizen. External backing is also apparent in the continuing and expedited support of arms sales and military assistance from countries like the USA, China and Russia to the regimes.

There is also evidence of a strategic calculus in a region-wide dynamic of support from one regime to another. This calculus of power has been complex and has simultaneously operated internally as well as in regional and international diplomatic relationships. Where possible, the status quo has been maintained, and international state actors have supported such states or provided the means of assistance to allow them to continue to repress their populations and inhibit rights and freedom. As such, there has been a region-wide consolidation of power and regime preservation to prevent Arab leaders – such as Bashar al-Assad in Syria – from being toppled from power.

It should be noted, however, that, in preserving power, the authoritarian state has also practised divide and rule tactics in their own nations as well as against others in the Middle East arena whom they consider inimical to their interests. This is most telling and apparent in the sectarian dynamic of the Arab Spring and conflicts that have subsequently ensued. In particular, Sunni state actors have employed sectarian tropes to demonize the Shi'a other. In Arab Gulf states, argues Matthieson, sectarianism during and in the wake of the Arab Spring has been 'encouraged by sectarian entrepreneurs, namely people who used sectarian politics to bolster their own positions' (2013, p. 7). The state has also succeeded in threatening their populations with fear of chaos and instability (*fitnah*). Here, the state has employed the threat of the uncertain in order to control and repress in perpetuation of the power of its existing and ruling elite. The state effectively struck back and, with few exceptions, the intervening period since 2011 has not led to meaningful opening of societies, improved economies or transition to plural democratic rule.

Uncertain future

The future of the region is almost impossible to predict. Many of the issues outlined in this book – such as political economy, political Islam, the state and its rulers – will probably continue to determine the political systems which will develop in the Middle East over the next decade – not least of which will be the unfolding legacy of the Arab Spring/Awakening. The resilience of authoritarian regimes – whether monarchical, presidential republican or theocratic – will continue to be tested and challenged by the region's citizens. The previous notion of enduring authoritarianism as key to the stability of the region has been partly debunked. New political systems and dispensations will be shaped by a number of factors including historic legacy and tradition, elite constellations, economic development, the role of the military in the state, regional and external interests, and – perhaps meaningful for the first time – the preferences of a truly enfranchised citizenry. The following case studies have been chosen because they are all examples of power being toppled, rather than regime resilience. Libya and Yemen have also been selected as they tend otherwise to be overlooked in many accounts of contemporary politics in the Middle East. Yet in these two states, the most fragile of political arrangements emerged. In both countries, the collapse of state authority and proliferation of violence, including that of al-Qaeda and ISIS, have major security implications for the wider region and the West.

Case study

Libya fracturing

After more than forty years in power, the resilience of the authoritarian regime of Muammar Gaddafi looked assured. It was not. Libya's Arab Spring, with America-led NATO support, toppled Gaddafi. The bloody collapse of the regime, however, would not herald the opportunities of stability, prosperity and equal governance for the country's 6 million citizens.

Instead, Libya's Arab Spring was typified by the proliferation of rival local militias that quickly overran the mostly peaceful civil protest that broke out in February 2011. Within a year of Gaddafi's death, the country was in the grip of a civil war. The opportunity for free and fair elections had led to the outbreak of violence as Islamist-aligned rebel militia took up arms against the elected government, forcing it in turn to flee from the Libyan capital Tripoli to the eastern city of Tobruk.

Since 2011, political change has been dislocated by the extent to which rebel militias have impacted transitional governance. The transitional ruling authorities have constantly struggled to address substantive governance issues such as the economy, law and order, security and post-conflict reconstruction.

The transition was initially heralded by elections to Libya's new legislative structures. Additionally, constitution drafting in the post-Gaddafi dispensation also got underway. By 2014, open dispute was occurring and the descent into civil collapse and crisis seemed inevitable.

Subsequent conflicts involving Libyans from all parts of the country immobilized the political transition. Since 2014, militia groups and locally organized political leaders (such as those from the Islamist Libya Dawn) remain the most powerful arbitrators of rule. Violent Islamist extremists such as ISIS have exploited these circumstances to gain a foothold in Libya – for example, in Sirte – to use it as a North African base from which to organize. Criminal elements, including human traffickers and smugglers, have also exploited Libya's ungoverned spaces to turn the country into one of the major embarkation points for migrants to Europe.

Despite the obviously ill-fated NATO intervention – which was perceived as an excuse for US-inspired regime change rather than protection of civilians – the international community remained engaged with Libya. In August 2014, the United Nations Security Council adopted Resolution 2174, authorizing financial and travel sanctions on individuals and entities found to be 'engaging in or providing support for other acts that threaten the peace, stability or security of Libya, or obstruct or undermine the successful completion of its political transition'. UN-supported governance-building has drawn in a variety of political groupings including: two competing parliaments, political parties and their activists, local municipalities (including mayors and representatives of local councils), tribes, militia and women. At meetings and sessions in Libya, Switzerland, Morocco, Algeria, Belgium and Tunisia, negotiating parties discussed ceasefires, frameworks for a political process, unity government formation, the phased withdrawal of armed groups, prison visits, the rights of the Tawergha, reopening airports, refugee return and enhancing the participation of women in politics.

By December 2015, some Libyan leaders had been encouraged to support a UN-negotiated agreement to create a Government of National Accord (GNA) to oversee the completion of the transition from dictatorship to a growing democracy.

The GNA Prime Minister would be Fayez al-Sarraj. In March 2016, the new Prime Minister and his government returned to Libya. Al-Sarraj has not enjoyed anything like unanimous support. Despite – or because of – UN backing, al-Sarraj cannot command authority or establish unitary legitimacy over the whole of Libya. In eastern Libya, for example, the governance of al-Sarraj is considered nothing more than a cover for foreign agendas. This has led to a spiral of competition to control oil installations, as well as in seeking to combat the threat from ISIS.

More than six years after the Arab Spring, Libya remains weak and vulnerable to exploitation. The US government considers Libya a terrorist safe-haven. The rise of ISIS, principally in Sirte, gave significant cause for concern both in and outside of Libya. By late 2016 though, a variety of Libyan forces (secretly supported by outside actors) had succeeded in mostly ousting ISIS from its strongholds. The US, the French and the Russians are among a number of stake-holding countries engaged in Libya's security situation.

Libya's oil plays a significant part in post-Arab Spring calculations and stability. Control of this resource has proven to be an instrument of war rather than peace. Nevertheless, the UN has given the GNA the right to export oil and use its vital revenues to combat the economic crisis that grips the country. Since 2014, the national oil company has resumed production and oil export routes have reopened. The fragile political structure and chaos of Libya, as armed elements engage in civil war-like practices, have, however, threatened the flow of oil.

The future for Libya in the wake of the Arab Spring is uncertain. The ruling bargain – mediated by the UN – struck between Libya's diverse representatives has failed to gain significant traction on the ground.

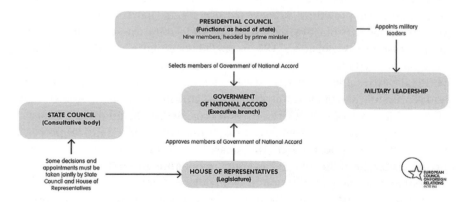

Figure 10.2 *Libya's institutions under the Libyan Political Agreement*

Case study

Egypt – children of the revolution

The Egyptian revolution began with the outbreak of protest on 25 January 2011. The revolution was mainly non-violent with protest consisting of demonstrations, marches, strikes and myriad acts of civil disobedience. Hundreds of thousands of Egyptians united in a common call to overthrow the thirty-year-old regime of ruling autocrat President Hosni Mubarak. Protests took place all over Egypt but spectacularly in the occupation of Cairo's Tahrir (Liberation) Square. The protestors waved placards declaring that it was 'game over' for Mubarak and his regime. His days looked numbered as, over the succeeding period, more and more people responded to social media exhortations to leave their homes and join the thousands of others in protest at Tahrir Square. In the Square, protestors significantly outnumbered state forces, such as riot police, who had been dispatched to break up the protest. Demonstrations that were incipient with calls for some reforms quickly transformed into a large-scale revolutionary uprising against the entire Mubarak regime.

For decades, President Mubarak concentrated power into his own hands. He appointed and sacked his Prime Minister and government, could dissolve the legislature, apply a veto to any legislation and ignore parliament by putting his proposals to the public directly through gerrymandered referenda. The ruling party – the National Democratic Party – anointed by Mubarak was permitted to enjoy a monopoly of power at his command. Like other rulers in the region, Mubarak also deployed security measures under the guise of emergency laws to give the state in effect a range of tools to repress and control its activist or opposition citizens. The state prevented free association, engaged in censorship of the media, banned most trade union organizations and used legislation to keep wages low.

President Mubarak had hoped to use these coercive tools of power to quash the uprisings. At first, his security forces, in particular the police and state-hired 'thugs', complied and attacked protestors. Yet when the Egyptian military appeared to side with protestors, the tide turned against Mubarak and he was forced from power. Interim arrangements in post-revolutionary Egypt kept the military at the centre of power. The Supreme Council of Armed Forces (SCAF) would govern through the post-revolutionary period. SCAF, in fact, became pivotal to the escalating tensions that unfolded between civil and military actors. While the military had long enjoyed autonomy and power, it clearly had an important political role (bolstered by popular support) in the transition. This inevitably led to clashes with civilian power-holders, especially when President Morsi attempted to rescind SCAF's political powers. Nevertheless, the military remained Egypt's most powerful institution and it was thus no surprise that General el-Sisi led the charge against the elected and ruling Muslim Brotherhood in 2013. A report posted by WikiLeaks highlighted 'the main priority of the military throughout the 2011 and 2012 elections was to ensure the election of a Parliament and executive who would uphold the military–industrial complex' (Bassiouni, 2016).

The Islamists also originally emerged to play a pivotal role in the transition. In effect, they had both the most to gain from the revolution and, ultimately, it would prove, the most to lose. As noted earlier, the Islamists did not initiate the revolution. Nor did they lead the broad coalition of social forces calling for Mubarak to go. The Muslim Brotherhood leadership was, instead, cautious. Yet, when the transition offered opportunities for elected power, not only were Islamists the best organized but they were ready to contend for power through opportunities offered at the ballot box.

There were always suspicions, however, that the Islamists would use power to institute their own form of authoritarian rule. The fact that President Morsi set about using power to shape Egypt's political landscape as it evolved post-revolution did not augur well. President Morsi gave himself far-reaching powers of governance while attempting to disarm the military politically at the same time. After the emergence of a popular backlash, he quickly rescinded his self-empowering decrees. Commentators wondered aloud whether post-Mubarak Egypt would simply be a reactive artifice of power dictated to by the power of popular opinion. Morsi had promised to lead the country in forms of democratic governance but he was constantly challenged by the power of the military and became increasingly embroiled in the 'unwinnable' fight with this deeply embedded state institution. Furthermore, the Brotherhood were ill equipped to govern a country – especially one where the institutions of state were tilted against them and had almost permanently excluded them. The impatience of the people with the Brotherhood grew as it clearly struggled to rise to the challenge of economic recovery. Again, these were challenges that did not play well to the skills of the Brotherhood. In their wake, the government of President el-Sisi, as was discussed in chapter 3, has also struggled to get the Egyptian economy back on its feet. In 2016 and 2017, sugar and bread riots broke out once again in Egypt and the President embroiled himself in domestic political controversy.

Morsi and the Muslim Brotherhood were pushed from power in the summer of 2013 and since that time they have been charged and tried in the Egyptian courts. President el-Sisi is considered to be a leader whom the administration of President Donald Trump can deal with. El-Sisi had joined in the regional reactionary steps of Gulf states such as Saudi Arabia and the UAE in demolishing the mobilizing power of political Islam in the guise of the Brotherhood. By 2017, the Arab Spring had clearly failed in the Egyptian context; even former President Mubarak had been released from jail. Yet the underlying causes of revolt remained, and were, in some cases, exacerbated. The authoritarian state was back in business – literally. The youth who had made the uprising possible couldn't organize themselves sufficiently to translate this into political power. The Egyptian military has evidently been contemptuous of democracy promotion, and state security forces have played their role alongside other actors in manufacturing insecurity and, in turn, creating a yearning for the stability inherent in repressive authoritarian rule. The Islamists were not truly prepared for power. It proved to be the case that they were ill equipped, beyond their slogans of 'Islam is the solution', to effect the sufficient internal organizational change necessary to engage in effective governance.

Case study

Yemen from hope to war

For the first-time student of the politics of the contemporary Middle East, Yemen can be a daunting topic. The politics of Yemen is defined by a complex convergence of highly competitive and fractious tribal elements, Islamist actors (including al-Qaeda), a history of secession and political reunification (North Yemen and South Yemen were reunified in 1990), as well as smaller religious factions, including the Houthi sect. The country has a strategic foothold on the tip of the Gulf peninsula.

Yemen has a political system vulnerable to the competing forces of tribal powers and violent extremism. Essentially, President Ali Abdullah Saleh had presided over a weak state for more than thirty years. Al-Qaeda in the Arab Peninsula (AQAP) has also exploited this weakness and lack of central government control to establish itself in Yemen. AQAP was a threat to regional security and of considerable concern to the USA. This explains why the USA was committed to supporting President Saleh's authoritarian regime. From its base in Yemen, AQAP had repeatedly attacked American, Saudi and British targets, and highlighted the extent to which absence of government control could be exploited in Yemen. Over the years, AQAP has, despite US drone strikes and counter-terrorist operations, continued to anchor itself in Yemen.

Hence, the Arab Spring revolt in Yemen was of great importance due to the country's vulnerability as the poorest state in the Middle East and as a base for AQAP. Popular protest broke out in early 2011 and persisted throughout the year. Yemenis, like their counterparts elsewhere in the region, were demanding freedom, democracy and better living conditions. President Saleh thought that, with minor concessions (and US backing), he could hang on to power, but this was proven not to be the case. In Yemen, tribal politics also played a role in hastening transition as powerful clan leaders swung behind the urban protests in Sana'a. Remarkably, Yemen is the only example of a negotiated Arab Spring transition. On 23 November 2011, President Saleh finally relinquished power to his Vice-President and, in early 2012, went into exile in neighbouring Saudi Arabia. In February 2012, Abd Rabbuh Mansour al-Hadi was inaugurated as President Saleh and his General People's Congress (GPC) had been overturned. Yet, as Durac contends, the popular protest 'was quickly overtaken and marginalized both by the established parties of opposition and by tribal actors. While Saleh's exit from office represents a major rupture in Yemeni political life', in the wake of the Arab Spring the deep state and forms of authoritarian power were reasserted (2012, p.161).

The transition phase did not lead to the establishment of national dialogue, unity and power-sharing. Instead, the country inched inexorably closer and closer to civil war. The transitional government of President al-Hadi failed to begin to reform the political institutions of the Yemeni state, to begin even the most incipient forms of effective economic reform needed to meet the challenges of rampant poverty, or to begin to tackle the endemic corruption that was the hallmark of President Saleh's rule. President Saleh remained an increasingly effective spoiler of the transition. Saleh has effectively sabotaged the transition, formed an alliance with the Houthi rebels and demonstrated the power of the deep state in the contemporary politics of the Middle East.

The international community failed to understand the fragility of the transition and to support the national government adequately. Moreover, for countries like the USA, the Yemeni imperative has been AQAP and the fight against it. The transitional government tried to join the anti-AQAP fray but, given other strains in Sana'a, were unable to strike against it effectively.

Houthis had long been on the margins of Yemeni society and had fallen foul of President Saleh's regime. Houthis are from the Zaidi Imamate of north Yemen that had enjoyed power until the revolution of 1962 (Boucek, 2010). Yet, as Baron noted, 'it is a testament to the faults of Yemen's transitional government that even many Yemenis with deep aversion to the Houthis initially welcomed their takeover of Sana'a in September 21st of last year' (Baron, 2015).

Since 2014, when Houthi rebels took control of the Yemeni capital Sana'a, the country has been embroiled in conflict. This in turn has drawn powerful regional actors into a proxy war (a pro-Hadi Saudi-led alliance against Iranian-supported Houthi rebels). By September 2014, the Houthi leaders had effectively forced President al-Hadi from power. He turned to Saudi Arabia to intervene. Since then, Saudi Arabia has led a regional military alliance that has targeted the Houthis with the aim of returning President al-Hadi to power. Houthi power was consolidated in early 2015 when they assumed full control over Yemen's governing institutions and moved against other political groups such as the Muslim Brotherhood (Milton-Edwards, 2016a). Regional and security actors condemned the moves. The UN, for example, affirmed support for President al-Hadi and called for a full reconciliation and dialogue effort mediated by their special envoy. The Houthi rebels averred and instead entered into dialogue and agreement with the government of Iran.

By March 2015, Saudi Arabia announced the formation of a coalition of GCC member states, as well as Jordan and Morocco, to launch Operation 'Decisive Storm', against Houthi forces and bases (Mazzetti and Kirkpatrick,

2015). Yemen's tribal groupings also joined the confrontation against the Houthis.

With the onset of civil conflict and military strikes by outside regional and international actors, Yemen's Arab Spring transition has come to a shuddering and irrevocable halt. In 2017, as the conflict in Yemen came to the end of its second year, official UN agencies reported on the mounting human toll. The situation was described as one of the worst humanitarian crises in the world. The acceleration of conflict had intensified an already existing long-drawn-out human catastrophe, characterized by endemic poverty, weak governance and almost non-existent rule of law. Tribal power was now holding more sway and influence in Yemen than both its elected representatives and the government of President al-Hadi.

Yemen has imploded further as the Saudi-led coalition has fought the Houthi rebels. This form of external influencing by outside Gulf actors has exacerbated conflict in a state that even before the Arab Spring had struggled to hold the national fabric together under decades of authoritarian rule. Its Arab Spring moment had promised change until authoritarian forces reasserted themselves and the power vacuums were exploited. The principal victims of the conflict in Yemen are not armed forces on either side but ordinary people. These people are also mostly unable to meet their basic needs and attain fundamental rights. Indeed, by 2017, as many as 3.5 million Yemenis were homeless, either internally displaced or refugees who had fled to other countries because of the conflict. Worse was to come when a cholera epidemic was declared by international health organizations.

International attempts to manage and negotiate an end to the conflict had largely failed. Yemenis have also contended with a humanitarian resource crisis. Moreover, international organizations and regional states were also subject to repeated criticism from organizations like Human Rights Watch for inaction and silence over the Yemen crisis, as well as coalition abuses. Houthi rebels drew censure for dragooning child soldiers into the conflict.

Regional interference has thus exacerbated the transition. In essence, since the Arab Spring Yemen has become a theatre of the Saudi–Iranian 'cold war'. As Salisbury notes,

Box 10.3 Unlikely allies

At first sight, Yemen appears likely to be another country where Saudi–Iranian tensions further complicate existing home-grown rivalries. At root, however, the latter are local disputes, far more than they are a proxy conflict between Saudi Arabia and Iran. The Houthis' recent expansion is partly a reflection of a newfound alliance with an unlikely bedfellow: former president Saleh is at heart a nationalist secularist – and historically an enemy of the group – but is for now an ally against their common rivals.

(2015, p. 12)

Saudi Arabia, along with some of its allies in the USA, is concerned at Iranian regional expansionism in the Gulf and other parts of the Middle East such as the Levant (Syria and Lebanon). Iran has supported the Houthis militarily and financially with respect to their ambitions to achieve functioning governance and the provision of basic services to the country's population.

Events since 2014, including the civil war, the continued presence of AQAP, tribal strengthening and the slide into humanitarian crisis, have reversed the gains of the Arab Spring. In Yemen, as in other countries in the region, the Arab Spring has highlighted that contemporary politics in the Middle East remains a contest for power between state rulers and their subject populations. The global importance of the politics of the region should never be underestimated.

Questions for discussion

- Popular movements overthrew dictators, but did they overthrow authoritarianism in the Middle East? Discuss with reference to Egypt, Tunisia, Yemen, Libya or Syria.
- What does the Arab Spring tell us about the future for Islamist groups in the region?
- If socio-economic indicators have not improved since 2011, does this mean that another Arab uprising is inevitable?

Recommended reading

- Books and publications that came out initially, in the immediate wake of the Arab Spring, were more likely to provide snapshot analyses and indications of events than measured analysis. For example, Filiu's (2012) and Gelvin's (2012) books fall into this category, but they are still good as scene-setters and indications of the energy and new horizons initially indicated by the events of 2010–12. Owen (2012) frames the debate about the Arab Spring through a strong analysis of the Arab state.
- In the years that followed, this changed. In the works of authors such as Gerges (2015), Dabashi (2012), Noueihad and Warren (2012), Sadiki (2015) and the edited work of Agathangelou and Nevzat (2013), we see the provision of good insight and framing of the Arab Spring to help make sense of the phenomenon and responses to it.

Haas and Lesch (2017), along with McMurray and Ufheil-Somers (2013), offer insights in edited collections that look at the challenges for democracy and popular resistance offered by the Arab Spring.

- The significant role played by Arab youth in igniting and leading the uprisings is accounted for in the work of authors like Floris (2012), the edited text by Schafer (2015), and Khalil (2016), who also adds an important gender perspective. The edited text by Sayre and Yousef (2016) demonstrates the extant factors that affected Arab youth and motivated them to action. The UN Human Rights video on youth bloggers and the Arab Spring (https://www.youtube.com/watch?v=ElpGfC5Vo_0) and the Al Jazeera programme which follows the 'April 6th' youth who were key in the Egyptian revolution (https://www.youtube.com/watch?v=BSZ7Ln5KzRU) are worth watching for the insights they bring.

- The Middle East in the wake of the Arab Spring and counter-response by authoritarian states is analysed in Kamvara (2016), Brownlee (2015) and Haseeb's (2014) edited collection. Lynch (2017) explores the dangerous and violent disintegration of the Arab Spring into the conflicts of the present day. In doing so he critically examines the role of external actors as well.
- Fraihat (2016) offers a strong account of the effects of the Arab uprisings in Yemen. Libya and Tunisia that contextualize civil mobilization and state resilience.
- On Libya, it is worth reading works that address the country under Gaddafi's rule, such as Pargeter (2012) and Wright (2012). The text from Engelbrekt and Mohlin (2015) focuses on regime change and international involvement in Libya since the Arab Spring, including the American-led NATO alliance. Erdag's book (2017) examines the post-Arab Spring disintegration of the Libyan state and the ensuing civil conflict. Sensini (2016) similarly addresses the nature of interventionism in Libya.
- On Egypt, there are all sorts of accounts of the Arab Spring, including one so-called comic account from Egypt's equivalent of John Stewart Bassem Youssef. If you like expletives, this is the recommended 'study' for you! Powerful academic analysis is offered by Ketchley (2017) and the edited text of Korany and El-Mahdi (2014) in terms of the revolution, social movement theory and contentious politics. Lacroix and Rougier (2016) also have an edited collection that incorporates these themes alongside chapters on religion and the revolution. By extension, Pargeter's 2016 contribution on the Muslim Brotherhood in Egypt (and Ennahda in Tunisia) is worthy of consideration.
- Yemen, as recognized earlier in this chapter, is a challenge for any student of the topic. To this end, a good route into the topic is Clark's excellent book from 2010. Although it was written and published before the outbreak of the Arab Spring, it still allows the reader to have an insight into the complex political structures of this often overlooked country. Fraihat (2016) and Lackner (2014) draw on dimensions of change in Yemen since 2011. Brandt (2017) and Hill (2017) reflect analysis that addresses important internal dimensions, such as tribal power and the Houthi rebellion, alongside the impact of Saudi (and other external) interventionism.

Bibliography

Names with the initial article 'al-' are alpabetized under the second element of the name.

Abboushi, W. F. 1985: *The Unmaking of Palestine*. Wisbech: Middle East and North African Studies Press.

Abdel Magid, F. 1994: *Nasser: The Final Years*. Reading, NY: Ithaca Press.

Abdo, G. 2016: *The New Sectarianism: The Arab Uprisings and the Rebirth of the Shi'a–Sunni Divide*. Oxford: Oxford University Press.

Abdul-Jabar, F. and Dawod, H. (eds.) 2003: *Tribes and Power: Nationalism and Ethnicity in the Middle East*. London: Saqi.

Abou el Fadl, 2004: *Islam and the Challenge of Democracy*. Princeton: Princeton University Press.

Abrahamian, E. 1989: *Radical Islam, the Iranian Mojahedin*. London: I. B. Tauris.

Abu Amr, Z. 1994: *Islamic Fundamentalism in the West Bank and Gaza Strip*. Bloomington: Indiana University Press.

AbuKhalil, A. 1992: A new Arab ideology? The rejuvenation of Arab nationalism. *Middle East Journal*, 46:1, pp. 22–36.

Aburish, S. K. 1994: *The House of Saud: The Rise, Corruption and Coming Fall of the House of Saud*. London: Bloomsbury.

Achcar, G. 2013: *The People Want: A Radical Exploration of the Arab Uprising*. London: Saqi Books.

Acikyildiz, B. 2014: *The Yezidis: The History of a Community, Culture and Religion*. London: I. B. Tauris.

Adib-Moghaddam, A. 2008: *Iran in World Politics, the Question of the Islamic Republic*. New York: Columbia University Press.

—— 2010: *A Metahistory of the Clash of Civilizations: Us and Them beyond Orientalism*. London: Charles Hurst and Co.

Afshar, H. (ed.) 1985: *Iran: A Revolution in Turmoil*. London: Macmillan.

—— 1998: *Islam and Feminisms: An Iranian Case Study*. Basingstoke: Macmillan.

Agathangelou, A. M. and Nevzat, S. (eds.) 2013: *Arab Revolutions and World Transformations*. London: Routledge.

Ageron, C. R. 1991: *Modern Algeria: A History from 1830 to the Present*. London: Hurst.

Ahmed, A. S. 1992: *Postmodernism and Islam: Predicament and Promise*. London: Routledge.

Ahmed, A. S. and Donnan, H. (eds.) 1994: *Islam, Globalization and Postmodernity*. London: Routledge.

Ahmed, L. 1992: *Women and Gender in Islam: Historical Roots of a Modern Debate*. New Haven: Yale University Press.

— 2011: *A Quiet Revolution: the Veil's Resurgence from the Middle East to America*. New Haven: Yale University Press.

Ajami, F. 1978: The end of pan-Arabism. *Foreign Affairs*, 57, Winter, pp. 355–73.

Akyol, M. 2013: *Islam Without Extremes: A Muslim Case for Liberty*. New York: W. W. Norton and Company.

Alaimo, K. 2015: How the Facebook Arabic page 'We Are All Khaled Said' helped promote the Egyptian Revolution. *Social Media + Society*, 1:2, pp. 1–10.

Alexander, C. 2012: Tunisia: the best bet. In R. Wright (ed.), *The Islamists Are Coming: Who They Really Are*. Washington DC: United States Institute of Peace, pp. 39–48.

Alley, A. L. 2013: Yemen changes everything … and nothing. *Journal of Democracy*, 24:4, pp. 74–85.

Allsopp, H. 2015: *The Kurds of Syria*. London: I. B. Tauris.

AlMasry al-Youm, 2011: News report, <http://www.almasryalyoum.com/en/node/505857>. Last accessed March 15, 2017.

Almulhim, M. 1991: *Middle East Oil: A Redistribution of Values Arising from the Oil Industry*. Lanham, MD: University Press of America.

Anderson, B. 1983: *Imagined Communities: Reflections on the Origin and Spread of Nationalism*. London: Verso.

Anderson, L. and Stansfield, G. 2005: *The Future of Iraq: Dictatorship, Democracy or Division?* New York: Palgrave Macmillan.

Andreeva, E. 2010: *Russia and Iran in the Great Game*. London: Routledge.

Ansari, A. 2017: *Iran, Islam and Democracy*. London: Gingko Library.

Antonius, G. 1969: *The Arab Awakening: The Story of the Arab National Movement*. New York: Putnams.

Arat, Y. 1994: Towards a democratic society: the women's movement in Turkey in the 1980s. *Women's Studies International Forum*, 17:2–3, pp. 241–8.

Arian, Asher. 1989: *Politics in Israel, The Second Generation*. New Jersey: Chatham House, the Royal Institute of International Affairs.

al-Arian, Abdullah. 2014: *Answering the Call: Popular Islamic Activism in Sadat's Egypt*. New York: Oxford University Press.

Arjomand, S. A. 1984: *From Nationalism to Revolutionary Islam*. London: Macmillan.

— 1988: *The Turban and the Crown: The Islamic Revolution in Iran*. New York: Oxford Uiversity Press.

Armstrong, M. 2016: *People Killed by Russian Airstrikes in Syria*. October. <https://www.statista.com/chart/6311/people-killed-by-russian-airstrikes-in-syria/>. Last accessed March 15, 2017.

Atia, M. 2013: *Building a House in Heaven: Pious Neoliberalism and Islamic Charity in Egypt*. Minneapolis: University of Minnesota Press.

Avinery, U. 2005: King George: the U.S.A sinking to new depths of ugliness and brutality. *Zope*, http://zope.gush-shalom.org/home/en/channels/avnery/archives_article340.

Ayubi, N. 1991: *Political Islam, Religion and Politics in the Arab World*. London: Routledge.

— 1995: *Overstating the Arab State: Politics and Society in the Middle East*. London: I. B. Tauris.

— 1997: Islam and democracy. In D. Potter et al. (1997).

Aziz, M. A. 2014: *The Kurds of Iraq*. London: I. B. Tauris.

al-Azmeh, A. 1993: *Islams and Modernities*. London: Verso.

—— 1995: Nationalism and the Arabs. *Arab Studies Quarterly*, 17:2, Winter, pp. 1–19.

Bacevich, A. J. 2017: *America's War for the Greater Middle East: a Military History*. Cambridge, MA: Harvard University Press.

Badran, M. 1993: Independent women: more than a century of feminism in Egypt. In Tucker (1993).

—— 1994: Gender activism: feminists and Islamists in Egypt. In V. Moghadam (ed.), *Gender and National Identity: Women and Politics in Muslim Societies*. Boulder, CO: Lynne Rienner.

Bagdonas, A. 2016: Russia's interests in the Syrian conflict: power, prestige, and profit. *European Journal of Economic and Political Studies*, 5:2, pp. 55–77.

Bagot-Glubb, J. 1948: *The Story of the Arab Legion*. London: Hodder and Stoughton.

Bahgat, G. 2001: Managing dependence: American–Saudi relations. *Arab Studies Quarterly*, 23:1, pp. 1–14.

Bahgat, G., Ehteshami, A. and Quilliam, N. (eds.) 2017: *Security and Bilateral Issues between Iran and its Arab Neighbours*. New York: Springer International Publishing.

Bank Audi. 2016: Between the Recovery of the Domestic Economy and the Burden of External Sector Challenges. *Egypt Economic Report*, www.bankaudi.com.eg/ Library/Assets/EgyptEconomicReport-2016-English-040615.pdf.

Bar, D. and Cohen-Hattab, K. 2003: A new kind of pilgrimage: the modern tourist pilgrim of the nineteenth and early twentieth century Palestine. *Middle East Studies*, 39:2, pp. 131–48.

Baram, A. 1991: *Culture, History and Ideology in the Formation of Ba'thist Iraq, 1968–1989*. Basingstoke: Macmillan.

Baron, Adam. 2015: What we get wrong about Yemen. *Politico*, 25 March, www. politico.com/magazine/story/2015/03/yemen-intervention-116396.html#. VXaxkc-qpBc.

Barr, J. 2012: *A Line in the Sand: The Anglo-French Struggle for the Middle East, 1914–1948*. New York: W. W. Norton & Company.

Barth, F. 1969: *Ethnic Groups and Boundaries: The Social Organisation of Culture Difference*. London: Allen and Unwin.

Bassiouni, M. C. 2016: *Chronicles of the Egyptian Revolution and its Aftermath: 2011–2016*. Cambridge: Cambridge University Press.

Batatu, H. 1979: *The Old Social Classes and Revolutionary Movements of Iraq*. Princeton: Princeton University Press.

Bazoobandi, S. 2013: *The Political Economy of the Gulf Sovereign Wealth Funds: A Case Study of Iran, Kuwait, Saudi Arabia and the United Arab Emirates*. London: Routledge.

Beblawi, H. 1990: The rentier state in the Arab world. In Luciani (1990).

Beinin, J. and Stork, J. (eds.) 1997: *Political Islam: Essays from Middle East Report*. London: I. B. Tauris.

Bellin, E. 1994: Civil society: effective tool of analysis for Middle East politics? *PS: Political Science & Politics*, 27:3, pp. 509–10.

—— 2012: Reconsidering the robustness of authoritarianism in the Middle East: Lessons from the Arab Spring. *Comparative Politics*, 44:2, pp. 127–49.

Benchemsi, A. 2012: Morocco: Outfoxing the opposition. *Journal of Democracy*, 23:1, pp. 57–69.

Ben-Dor, G. 1988: Ethnopolitics and the Middle Eastern state. In Esman and Rabinovich (1988).

Bengio, O. 2012: *Kurdistan in Iraq: Building a State within a State*. Boulder, CO: Lynne Rienner Publishers.

—— 2016: Game changers: Kurdish women in peace and war. *Middle East Journal*, 70:1, Winter, pp. 30–46.

Bennis, P. and Moushabeck, M. (eds.) 1995: *Beyond the Storm: A Gulf Crisis Reader*. Edinburgh: Canongate.

Bergen, P. L. 2001: *Holy War Inc.: Inside the Secret World of Osama Bin Laden*. London: Weidenfeld & Nicolson.

Berger, M. T. and Weber, H. 2014: *Rethinking the Third World: International Development and World Politics*. Houndmills: Palgrave Macmillan.

Bergh, S. 2017: *Democracy and Development in Morocco: Local Government and Political Participation in North Africa*. London: I. B. Tauris.

Betts, A. and Collier, P. 2017. *Refuge: transforming a broken refugee system*. London: Allen Lane.

Beydoun, K. 2016: *Donald Trump: The Islamophobia President*, 9 Nov., www.aljazeera.com/indepth/opinion/2016/11/donald-trump-islamophobia-president-16110906535945.html.

Bin Hethlain, S. 2010: *Saudi Arabia and the U.S. since 1962: Allies in Conflict*. London: Saqi Books.

Bina, C. 2013: *A Prelude to the Foundation of Political Economy: Oil, War and Global Polity*. Houndsmills: Palgrave Macmillan.

Blanford, N. 2008: *Killing Mr Lebanon: The Assasination of Rafik Hariri and Its Impact on the Middle East*. London: I. B. Tauris.

Boot, M. 2001: The case for American empire. *The Weekly Standard*, 7:5, 10 September.

Börzel, T. A., Dandashly, A. and Risse, T. 2015: Responses to the 'Arabellions': the EU in comparative perspective. *Journal of European Integration*, 37:1, pp. 1–17.

Botman, S. 1987: Women's participation in radical Egyptian politics 1939–52. In M. Salman, H. Kazi, N. Yuval-Davis, L. al-Hamdani, S. Botman and D. Lerman (eds.), *Women in the Middle East*. London: Zed Books.

Boucek, C. 2010. *War in Saada: From Local Insurrection to National Challenge*. Washington DC: Carnegie Endowment for International Peace.

Boukhars, A. 2010: *Politics in Morocco: Executive Monarchy and Enlightened Authoritarianism*. Abingdon: Routledge.

Bourdieu, P., Calhoun, C., Schultheis, F., and Frisinghelli, C. 2014: *Picturing Algeria*. New York: Columbia University Press.

Bourtman, I. 2006: Putin and Russia's Middle Eastern Policy. *Middle East Review of International Affairs*, 10:2, pp. 1–15.

BP 2016: *British Petroleum Statistical Review*, https://www.bp.com/content/dam/bp/pdf/energy-economics/statistical-review-2016/bp-statistical-review-of-world-energy-2016-full-report.pdf.

Braizat, F. 2010: *Islam, Muslims, and Liberal Democracy in the Middle East: Jordan in Comparative Perspective*. London: Lambert Academic Publishing.

Brandt, M. 2017: *Tribes and Politics in Yemen: a History of Houthi Conflict*. London: C. Hurst and Co.

Bresheeth, H. and Yuval-Davis, N. (eds.) 1991: *The Gulf War and the New World Order*. London: Zed Books.

Breuilly, J. 1993: *Nationalism and the State*. Manchester: Manchester University Press.

Brittain, V. (ed.) 1991: *The Gulf Between Us: The Gulf War and Beyond*. London: Virago.

Bromley, S. 1994: *Rethinking Middle East Politics*. Cambridge: Polity.

—— 1997: Middle East exceptionalism – myth or reality? In D. Potter et al. (eds.).

Brown, L. C. 1988: *International Politics and the Middle East: Old Rules, Dangerous Game*. London: I. B. Tauris.

Brown, J. 2016: Yazidis leave Europe and return to Iraq. *Al-Jazeera*, www.aljazeera.com/news/2016/04/yazidis-leave-europe-return-warring-iraq-160404074817769.html.

Brownlee, J. 1988: The June 1967 war: a turning point? In Y. Lukacs and A. Battah (eds.), *The Arab–Israeli Conflict: Two Decades of Change*. Boulder, CO: Westview.

—— 2015: *The Arab Spring: Pathways of Repressions and Reform*. Oxford: Oxford University Press.

Brownlee, J., Masoud, T. and Reynolds, A. 2013: Why the modest harvest? *Journal of Democracy*, 24:4, pp. 29–44.

Brynen, R., Korany, B. and Noble, P. (eds.) 1995: *Political Liberalization and Democratization in the Arab World*. Boulder, CO: Lynne Rienner.

B'tselem. 2017: *Statistics on Settlements and Settler Population*, www.btselem.org/settlements/statistics.

Burke, J. 2004: *Al-Qaeda: The True Story of Radical Islam*. London: Penguin Books.

Burton, D. (2016). Iraqi minorities advocate for the creation of new provinces, www.aina.org/news/20160512021117.htm.

Butterworth, C. E. 1980: Review of Orientalism. *American Political Science Review*, 74, March, pp. 174–6.

Byman, D. 2015: *Al Qaeda, the Islamic State and the Global Jihadist Movement, What Everyone Needs to Know*. New York: Oxford University Press.

Byman, D. and Shapiro, J. 2014: Be Afraid. Be A Little Afraid: The Threat of Terrorism from Western Foreign Fighters in Syria and Iraq. *Brookings Policy Paper*, 34. Washington DC: Brookings Institution.

Cammack, P., Pool, D. and Tordoff, W. 1993: *Third World Politics, A Comparative Introduction*. Basingstoke: Macmillan.

Cammett, M., Diwan, I., Richards, A. and Waterbury, J. 2016: *A Political Economy of the Middle East*. Boulder, CO: Westview Press.

Carothers, T. 2006: The backlash against democracy promotion. *Foreign Affairs*, 85:2, pp. 55–68.

Carter, J. 1977: Remarks at the White House. US White House, 12 May 1977.

Castellino, J. and Cavanagh, K. A. 2013: *Minority Rights in the Middle East*. Oxford: Oxford University Press

Chekir, H. and Diwan, I. 2012: *Crony Capitalism in Egypt*, CID Working Paper 250, November (updated August 2013), Center for International Development, Cambridge MA: Harvard University.

Chilcot. 2016: *Report by a Committee of Privy Counsellors*, Chairman Sir John Chilcot, www.iraqinquiry.org.uk.

Chomsky, N. 2003: *Middle East Illusions*. New York: Rowan and Littlefield.

—— 2005: *Imperial Ambitions*. Harmondsworth: Penguin.

Choueiri, Y. 1989: *Arab History and the Nation State: A Study in Modern Arab Historiography 1820–1980*. London: Routledge.

—— 1990: *Islamic Fundamentalism*. London: Pinter Publishers.

—— 2001: *Arab Nationalism: A History*. Oxford: Wiley-Blackwell.

—— 2003: *Modern Arab Historiography: Historical Discourse and the Nation State*. London: Routledge Curzon.

—— (ed.) 2005: *A Companion to the History of the Middle East*. Oxford: Blackwell.

Christie, K. and Masad, M. (eds.) 2013: *State Formation and Identity in the Middle East*. New York: Palgrave.

Chubin, S. 2010: The Iranian nuclear riddle after June 12. *The Washington Quarterly*, 33:1, pp. 163–72.

Clark, J. A. and Salloukh, B. F. 2013: Elite strategies, civil society, and sectarian identities in postwar Lebanon. *International Journal of Middle East Studies*, 45:04, pp. 731–49.

Clark, V. 2010: *Dancing on the Heads of Snakes*. New Haven: Yale University Press.

Cleveland, W. and Bunton, M. 2009: *A History of the Modern Middle East*. Boulder, CO: Westview Press.

Coates Ulrichsen, K. 2016: *The Politics of Economic Reform in Arab Gulf States*. Rice University: CME, www.bakerinstitute.org/media/files/files/717a5914/CME-GulfEconReform-060116.pdf.

Cockburn, Patrick. 2015: *The Rise of Islamic State: ISIS and the New Sunni Revolution*. London: Verso Books.

Collings, D. (ed.) 1994: *Peace for Lebanon? From War to Reconstruction*. Boulder, CO: Lynne Rienner.

Connor, W. 1994: *Ethnonationalism: The Quest for Understanding*. Princeton: Princeton University Press.

Cordesman, A. H. 1987: *The Iran–Iraq War and Western Security, 1984–1987*. London: Janes.

—— 1988: *The Gulf and the West: Strategic Relations and Military Realities*. Boulder, CO: Westview.

Coury, R. 1982: Who 'invented' Egyptian Arab nationalism? (parts 1 and 2). *International Journal of Middle Eastern Studies*, 14:2, pp. 249–81, 459–79.

Creighton, J. 1992: *Oil on Troubled Waters: Gulf Wars, 1980–91*. London: Echoes.

Crocker, C. A., Hampson, F. O., Aall, P. and Palamar, S. 2015: Why is mediation so hard? The case of Syria. In M. Galluccio (ed.), *Handbook of International Negotiation*. New York: Springer International, pp. 139–55.

Crystal, J. 2016: *Kuwait: the Transformation of an Oil State*. London: Routledge.

Culcasi, K. 2016: Warm nationalism: mapping and imagining the Jordanian nation. *Political Geography*, 54, pp. 7–20.

Dabashi, H. 2012: *The Arab Spring: the end of Postcolonialism*. London: Zed Books.

Dahan-Kalev, H. and LeFebvre, E., with El'Sana-Aih'jooj, A. 2012: *Palestinian Activism in Israel: A Bedouin Woman Leader in a Changing Middle East*. Houndsmills: Macmillan.

Dalmasso, E. and Cavatorta, F. 2013: Democracy, civil liberties and the role of religion after the Arab awakening: constitutional reforms in Tunisia and Morocco. *Mediterranean Politics*, 18:2, pp. 225–41.

Danilo, M. 2005: On globalization, Iraq and the Middle East, Noam Chomsky interviewed. *Z-Net*, www.zmag.org.

Darwin, J. 1981: *Britain, Egypt and the Middle East: Imperial Policy in the Aftermath of War*. London: Macmillan.

Davies, G. 2017: Saudi King visits Indonesia. *The Daily Mail Online*, 2 March, www.dailymail.co.uk/news/article-4270328/Saudi-king-visits-Indonesia-huge-entourage-tons-gear.html.

Dawisha, A. 2016: *Arab Nationalism in the Twentieth Century: From Triumph to Despair*. Princeton: Princeton University Press.

Dawn, E. C. 1988: The formation of pan-Arab ideology. *International Journal of Middle Eastern Studies*, 20:1, pp. 67–90.

De Bellaigue, C. 2017: Trump's dangerous delusions about Islam, 16 Feb., https://www.theguardian.com/news/2017/feb/16/trump-dangerous-delusions-islam-muslims-liberalism.

Dessouki, H. 1982: The new Arab political order: implications for the 1980s. In M. Kerr and S. Yassin (eds.), *Rich and Poor States in the Middle East: Egypt and the New Arab Order*. Boulder, CO: Westview.

—— 1991: *Foreign Policy of the Arab States*. Boulder, CO: Westview.

Devlin, J. 1976: *The Ba'th Party: A History of its Origins to 1966*. Stanford: Hoover Institution.

Dockrill, M. L. and Douglas Goold, J. 1981: *Peace Without Promise, Britain and the Peace conferences, 1919–23*. London: Batsford Academic and Educational.

Dodge, T. 2003: *Inventing Iraq: The Future of Nation Building and a History Denied*. New York: Columbia University Press.

Dodge, T. and Higgott, R. (eds.) 2002: *Globalization and the Middle East: Islam, Economy, Society and Politics*. London: RIIA.

Doha Institute, Center for Research & Policy Studies. 2015: *Arab Opinion Index 2015: In Brief*, http://english.dohainstitute.org/file/get/6ad332dc-b805-4941-8a30-4d28806377c4.pdf.

Dolatyar, M. and Gray, T. 2016: *Water Politics in the Middle East: A Context for Conflict Or Cooperation?* New York: Springer.

Doran, M. 2002: The pragmatic fanaticism of al-Qaeda: an anatomy of extremism in Middle Eastern politics. *Political Science Quarterly*, 117:2, pp. 177–90.

Dosenrode, S. and Stubkjaer, A. 2002: *The EU and the Middle East*. London: Sheffield Academic Press.

Drysdale, A. and Blake, G. 1985: *The Middle East and North Africa: A Political Geography*. London: Oxford University Press.

Dunne, M. and Revkin, M. 2011: Egypt: how a lack of political reform undermined economic reform. *Commentary for Carnegie Endowment for Peace 23.2.2011*, http://carnegieendowment.org/2011/02/23/egypt-how-lack-of-political-reform-undermined-economic-reform-pub-42710.

Dunning, T. 2017: *Hamas, Jihad and Popular Legitimacy: Reinterpreting Resistance in Palestine*. London: Routledge.

Durac, V. 2012. Yemen's Arab Spring – democratic opening or regime maintenance? *Mediterranean Politics*, 17:2, pp. 161–78.

The Economist. 2016: Oil and the Gulf states.: after the party, March, www.economist.com/news/middle-east-and-africa/21695539-low-oil-price-manageable-short-term-gulf-states-must-make.

Edict of Gulhane, also known as the Supreme Edict of the Rosehouse. 1839: www.anayasa.gen.tr/gulhane.htm.

Efrat, M. and Bercovitch, J. (eds.) 1991: *Superpowers and Client States in the Middle East: The Imbalance of Influence*. London: Routledge.

Ehteshami, A. 1995: *After Khomeini: The Iranian Second Republic*. London: Routledge.

Ehteshami, A. and Murphy, E. C. 1996: Transformation of the corporatist state in the Middle East. *Third World Quarterly*, 17:4, pp. 753–72.

Eickelman, D. and Piscatori, J. 1996: *Muslim Politics*. Princeton: Princeton University Press.

El-Affendi, A. 2010: Islam's future imperfect: fighting over camels at the end of history. In Paya and Esposito (2010).

Eligur, B. 2010: *The Mobilization of Political Islam in Turkey*. Cambridge: Cambridge University Press.

El-Katiri, L. 2016: *Saudi Arabia's Labor Market Challenge*, 6 July, https://hbr.org/2016/07/saudi-arabias-labor-market-challenge.

Eltahawy, M. 2016: *Headscarves and Hymen: Why the Middle East Needs a Sexual Revolution*. New York: Weidenfeld & Nicolson.

Embassy Tunis. 2008: Corruption in Tunisia: what's yours is mine. Wikileaks Cable 08TUNIS697_a. 23 June, https://wikileaks.org/plusd/cables/08TUNIS679_a.html.

Engelbrekt, K. and Mohlin, M. 2015: *The NATO Intervention in Libya*. London: Routledge.

Entessar, N. 1992: *Kurdish Ethnonationalism*. Boulder, CO: Lynne Rienner.

Erdag, R. 2017: *Libya in the Arab Spring: From Revolution to Insecurity*. Houndmills: Palgrave Macmillan.

Esman, M. J. and Rabinovich, I. (eds.) 1988: *Ethnicity, Pluralism and the State in the Middle East*. Ithaca, NY: Cornell University Press.

Esposito, J. (ed.) 1983: *Voices of Resurgent Islam*. New York: Oxford University Press.

—— 1984: *Islam and Politics*. New York: Syracuse University Press.

—— 1992: *The Islamic Threat: Myth or Reality?* Oxford: Oxford University Press.

—— 2002: *Unholy War: Terror in the Name of Islam*. Oxford: Oxford University Press.

—— 2010a: *The Future of Islam*. New York: Oxford University Press.

—— 2010b: The saga of Islam and democracy in the Middle East. In Paya and Esposito (2010).

Esposito, J. and Piscatori, J. 1991: Democratization and Islam. *Middle East Journal*, no. 45, Summer, pp. 427–40.

Esposito, J., Sonn, T. and Voll, J. O. 2016: *Islam and Democracy after the Arab Spring*. New York: Oxford University Press.

Euben, R. L. and Zaman, M. Q. (eds.) 2009: *Princeton Readings in Islamic Thought, Texts and Contexts from from al-Banna to Bin Laden*. Princeton: Princeton University Press.

Evans, Martin. 2012: *Algeria: France's Undeclared War*. New York: Oxford University Press.

Evans, Michael. 1988: *The Gulf Crisis*. London: Franklin Watts.

Fanon, F. 2001: *The Wretched of the Earth*. Harmondsworth: Penguin.

FAO. 2016: *Yemen Situation Report*, Sept., Food and Agriculture Association of the United Nations, www.fao.org/resilience/ressources/ressources-detail/fr/c/431610.

Farah, N. R. 2009: *Egypt's Political Economy: Power Relations in Development*. Cairo: Cairo University Press.

Faris, H. A. 2013: *The Failure of the Two-State Solution: The Prospects of One State in the Israel–Palestine Conflict*. London: I. B. Tauris

Farouk-Sluglett, M. and Sluglett, P. 1990: *Iraq Since 1958*. London: I. B. Tauris.

Fawaz, L. T. 1994: *An Occasion for War: Civil Conflict in Lebanon and Damascus in 1860*. Oakland, CA: University of California Press.

Fawcett, L. (ed.) 2016: *International Relations of the Middle East*, 2nd edn. Oxford: Oxford University Press.

Feldman, N. 2004: *What We Owe Iraq: War and the Ethics of Nation Building*. Princeton: Princeton University Press.

Fergany, N. 2016: *Arab Revolution in the 21st Century? Lessons from Egypt and Tunisia*. Houndmills: Palgrave Macmillan.

Fieldhouse, D. K. 2004: *Britain, France and the Fertile Crescent: The Mandates in Iraq, Palestine, Transjordan, Syria and Lebanon 1900–1958*. London: I. B. Tauris.

Filiu, J. P. 2012: *The Arab Revolution: Ten Lessons from the Democratic Uprising*. Oxford: Oxford University Press.

Findlay, A. M. 1994: *The Arab World*. London: Routledge.

Finer, S. 1970: *Comparative Government: An Introduction to the Study of Politics*. Harmondsworth: Penguin.

Firro, K. 1988: The Druze in and between Syria, Lebanon and Israel. In Esman and Rabinovich (1988).

—— 2003: *Inventing Lebanon: Nationalism and the State under the Mandate*. London: I. B. Tauris.

Fisk, R. 1992: *Pity the Nation: Lebanon at War*. Oxford: Oxford University Press.

Floris, S. 2012: Youth, those anti-heroes of the Arab Spring. *IEMed Mediterranean Yearbook 2*. Barcelona: IEMed Mediterranean Yearbook.

Forbes Middle East. 2016: *World's 10 Most Powerful Arab Women*, www.forbesmiddleeast.com/en/lists/read/2016/the-10-most-powerful-arab-women-in/listid/291.

Fraihat, I. 2016: *Unfinished Revolutions: Yemen, Libya and Tunisia after the Arab Spring*. New Haven: Yale University Press.

Fraser, T. 2015: *The Arab–Israeli Conflict*. Houndmills: Palgrave.

Freedman, R. O. 1991: *Moscow and the Middle East: Soviet Policy Since the Invasion of Afghanistan*. Cambridge: Cambridge University Press.

Freedom House. 2017: *Freedom in the World 2017*, https://freedomhouse.org/report/freedom-world/freedom-world-2017.

Fromkin, D. 1989: *A Peace to End all Peace: The Fall of the Ottoman Empire and the Creation of the Modern Middle East*. New York: Deutsch, Avon Book.

Galal, I. and Diwan, A. 2016: *The Middle East Economies in Times of Transition*. Houndmills: Palgrave Macmillan.

Galpern, S. G. 2013: *Money, Oil, and Empire in the Middle East: Sterling and Postwar Imperialism, 1944–1971*. Cambridge: Cambridge University Press

Gardner, D. Jan 2017: Barack Obama failed to fulfil promise of his Middle East policy, https://www.ft.com/content/eaa2622e-d74f-11e6-944b-e7eb37a6aa8e.

Gause, III, F.G. 2016: The future of U.S.–Saudi relations, https://www.foreignaffairs.com/articles/united-states/2016-06-13/future-us-saudi-.

Gellner, E. 1983: *Nations and Nationalism*. Oxford: Blackwell.

—— 1993: The mightier pen? *Times Literary Supplement*, 19 February.

—— 1994: Nationalism and modernisation. In Hutchinson and Smith (1994).

Gelvin, J. L. 2007: *The Modern Middle East: A History*, 2nd edn. New York: Oxford University Press.

—2012: *The Arab Uprisings: What Everyone Needs to Know*. New York: Oxford University Press.

Gerges, F. A. 2013: The Obama approach to the Middle East: the end of America's moment? *International Affairs*, 89:2, pp. 299–323.

— 2015: *Contentious Politics in the Middle East: Popular Resistance and Marginalised Activism beyond the Arab Spring Uprisings*. Houndmills: Palgrave Macmillan

— 2017: *ISIS: A History*. Princeton: Princeton University Press.

Gerner, D. 1984: Roles in transition: the evolving position of women in Arab–Islamic countries. In F. Hussain (ed.), *Muslim Women*. London: Croom Helm.

— 1994: *One Land, Two Peoples: The Conflict over Palestine*. Boulder, CO: Westview.

Ghafar, A. A. and Jacobs, A. L. 2017: *Morocco: The King's Dilemma*, 2 March, https://www.brookings.edu/blog/markaz/2017/03/02/morocco-the-kings-dilemma.

Ghanem, A. 1998: State and minority in Israel, the case of ethnic state and the predicament of its minority. *Ethnic and Racial Studies*, 21:3, pp. 428–48.

— 2001: *The Palestinian-Arab Minority in Israel, 1948–2000: A Political Study*. New York: State University of New York Press.

— 2009: *Ethnic Politics in Israel*. Abingdon: Routledge.

Giacaman, R. and Johnson, P. 1994: Searching for strategies: the Palestinian women's movement in a new era. *Middle East Report*, 186, January–February, pp. 22–5.

Gilbar, G. G. 2013: *The Middle East Oil Decade and Beyond*. London: Routledge.

Ginat, R. 2000: The Soviet Union and the Syrian Ba'th regime: from hesitation to rapprochement. *Middle Eastern Studies*, 36:2, pp. 150–71.

Glass, C. 2016: *Syria Burning: A Short History of a Catastrophe*. London: Verso Books.

Glavanis-Grantham, K. 1996: The women's movement, feminism and the national struggle in Palestine: unresolved contradictions. In Afshar (1996).

Global Agenda. 2005: *Egypt 2005: A Commitment to Growth*. London: World Link Publications Ltd.

Global Finance. 2017: Richest and poorest countries global data, https://www.gfmag.com/global-data/economic-data/worlds-richest-and-poorest-countries.

Gobat, J. and Kostial, K. 2016: *IMF Working Paper: Syria's Conflict Economy*, IMF WP/16/123, https://www.imf.org/external/pubs/ft/wp/2016/wp16123.pdf.

Goldsmith, L. T. 2015: *Cycle of Fear: Syria's Alawites in War and Peace*. London: C. Hurst and Co.

Gordon, J. 1992: *Nasser's Blessed Movement: Egypt's Free Officers and the July Revolution*. New York: Oxford University Press.

al-Gosaibi, G. A. 1993: *The Gulf Crisis: An Attempt to Understand*. New York: Kegan Paul International.

Gow, J. (ed.) 1993: *Iraq, the Gulf Conflict and the World Community*. London: Brassey's.

Gowan, P. 1991: The Gulf War, Iraq and Western liberalism. *New Left Review*, 187, pp. 39–71.

Gran, P. 1990: Studies of Anglo-American political economy: democracy, orientalism and the left. In Sharabi (1990).

Grawert, E. and Abul-Magd, Z. 2017: *Businessmen in Arms: How the Military and Other Armed Groups Profit in the MENA Region*. Maryland: Rowman & Littlefield.

Gray, J. 2004: *Al-Qaeda and What It Means to be Modern*. London: Faber and Faber.

Greenwood, S. 2008: Bad for business? Entrepreneurs and democracy in the Arab world. *Comparative Political Studies*, 41:8, pp. 837–60.

Gresh, A. and Vidal, D. 1990: *A–Z of the Middle East*. London: Zed Books.

Guazzone, L. (ed.) 1995: *The Islamist Dilemma: The Political Role of Islamist Movements in the Contemporary Arab World*. London: Ithaca Press.

—— 2013: Ennahda Islamists and the test of government in Tunisia. *The International Spectator*, 48:4, pp. 30–50.

Guazzone, L. and Pioppi, D. (eds.) 2009: *The Arab State and Neo-liberal Globalization: the Restructuring of State Power in the Middle East*. London: Ithaca Press.

Guibernau, M. and Rex, J. (eds.) 1997: *The Ethnicity Reader: Nationalism, Multiculturalism and Migration*. Cambridge: Polity.

Gulf Labour Markets and Migration (GLMM). 2016: *GCC: Total Population and Percentage of Nationals and Foreign Nationals in GCC Countries (International Statistics, 2010–2016)(with Numbers)*, http://gulfmigration.eu/gcc-total-population-percentage-nationals-foreign-nationals-gcc-countries-national-statistics-2010-2016-numbers.

Gunning, G. 2007: *Hamas in Politics, Democracy, Religion and Violence*. London: Hurst and Company.

Gunter, M. 2007: *The Kurds Ascending: The Evolving Solution to the Kurdish Problem in Iraq and Turkey*. Basingstoke: Macmillan.

—— 2013: The contemporary roots of Kurdish nationalism in Iraq. *Kufa Review*, 2:1, Winter, pp. 29–48.

Gunter, M. M. 2016: *The Kurds: A Modern History*. Princeton: Markus Wiener Publishers.

Gurr, T. R. and Harff, B. 1994: *Ethnic Conflict in World Politics*. Boulder, CO: Westview.

Haas, M. and Lesch, M. (eds.) 2017: *The Arab Spring: The Hope and Reality of Uprisings*. Boulder, CO: Westview.

Haddad, F. 2016: *Shia-centric State Building and Sunni Rejection in Post-2003 Iraq*. Washington, DC: Carnegie Endowment for International Peace.

Haddad, M. and Atassi, B. 2013: The youth of the Arab Spring. *Al-Jazeera*. Doha: Qatar, www.aljazeera.com/indepth/interactive/2013/07/201372992935843820.html.

Hafez, M. 2003: *Why Muslims Rebel: Repression and Resistance in the Islamic World*. London: Lynne Rienner.

Haghighat-Sordellini, E. 2010: *Women in the Middle East and North Africa*. New York: Palgrave Macmillan.

Halliday, F. 1974: *Arabia without Sultans*. Harmondsworth: Penguin.

—— 1979: *Iran: Dictatorship to Development*. Harmondsworth: Penguin.

—— 1996: *Islam and the Myth of Confrontation*. London: I. B. Tauris.

—— 2003: *Islam and the Myth of Confrontation*, 2nd edn. London: I. B. Tauris.

—— 2005: How to defeat terrorism. *Global Agenda*, www.globalagendamagazine.com.

Hamdan, S. 2013: *Palestinian Women: Rising above Limitations, Expectations and Conditions*. New York: Sharp Thinking Communications.

Hamid, S. 2015: What most people get wrong about political Islam. *Markaz*, 1 Oct., https://www.brookings.edu/blog/markaz/2015/10/01/what-most-people-get-wrong-about-political-islam.

Hamid, S. and Ruekert, L. 2014: *Temptations of Power: Islamists and illiberal democracy in the new Middle East*. New York: Oxford University Press.

Hammami, R. 1997: Women in Palestinian society. In Heiberg and Ovensen (1997).

Hanware, K. 2016: Vision 2030 may lead to Saudi ratings boost, 15 May, www.arabnews.com/news/vision-2030-may-lead-saudi-ratings-boost.

Harik, I. 1990: The origins of the Arab state system. In Luciani (1990).

Harrison, R. T. 1995: *Gladstone's Imperialism in Egypt: Techniques of Domination*. New York: Greenwood.

Haseeb, K. (ed.) 2014: *The Arab Spring: Critical Analysis*. London: Routledge.

Hassan, O. 2014: *Constructing America's Freedom Agenda for the Middle East*. London: Routledge.

Hatem, M. 1993: Toward the development of post-Islamist and post-nationalist feminist discourses in the Middle East. In Tucker (1993).

Hegghammer, T. and Nesser, P. 2015: Assessing the Islamic State's commitment to attacking the West. *Perspectives on Terrorism*, 9:4, pp. 14–30.

Held, C. C. 1994: *Middle East Patterns, Places, Peoples and Politics*. Boulder, CO: Westview.

Heller, J. 2014: Netanyahu wants to define Israel as Jewish state in law, Reuters, 1 May, www.reuters.com/article/us-israel-jewish-netanyahu-idU.S.BREA400EP20140501.

Henry, C. M. and Springborg, R. 2010: *Globalization and the Politics of Development in the Middle East*, 2nd edn. Cambridge: Cambridge University Press.

Herb, M., 2014: *The Wages of Oil: Parliaments and Economic Development in Kuwait and the UAE*. New York: Cornell University Press.

Hersh, S. 2005: The coming wars. *The New Yorker*, 24 January.

Hertog, S. 2016a: Challenges to the Saudi distributional state in the age of austerity. *LSE Research Online*, 12–13 December.

Hertog, S. 2016b: Late populism: State distributional regimes and economic conflict after the Arab uprisings. From mobilization to counter-revolution. *POMEPS Studies*, 20. https://pomeps.org/wp-content/uploads/2016/07/POMEPS_Studies_20_Mobilization_Web.pdf.

Heydemann, S. 2007: *Upgrading authoritarianism in the Arab world*. Washington, DC: Saban Center for Middle East Policy at the Brookings Institution.

Heydemann, S. and Leenders, R. 2011: Authoritarian learning and authoritarian resilience: regime responses to the 'Arab Awakening'. *Globalizations*, 8:5, pp. 647–53.

—— (eds.) 2014: *Middle East Authoritarianisms: Governance, Contestation, and Regime Resilience in Syria and Iran*. Redwood City, CA: Stanford University Press.

Hill, G. 2017: *Yemen Endures, Civil War, Saudi Adventurism and the Future of Arabia*. London: C. Hurst and Co.

Hinnebusch, R. 1990: *Authoritarian Power and State Formation in Ba'thist Syria: Army, Party and Peasant*. Boulder, CO: Westview.

—— 1993: State and civil society in Syria. *Middle East Journal*, 47, Spring, pp. 243–57.

—— 2015a: Syria's Alawis and the Ba'ath Party. In M. Kerr and C. Larkin (eds.) 2015: *The Alawis of Syria: War, Faith and Politics in the Levant*. Oxford: Oxford University Press.

—— 2015b: Globalization, democratization, and the Arab uprising: the international factor in MENA's failed democratization. *Democratization*, 22:2, pp. 335–57.

Hiro, D. 1993: *Lebanon: Fire and Embers: A History of the Lebanese Civil War*. London: Weidenfeld and Nicolson.

Hirst, D. 2010: *Beware Small States: Lebanon, Battleground of the Middle East*. London: Faber and Faber.

Hobsbawm, E. 1990: *Nations and Nationalisms Since 1780: Programme, Myth, Reality*. Cambridge: Cambridge University Press.

—— 1997: An anti-nationalist account of nationalism since 1989. In Guibernau and Rex (1997).

Hoffman, K. E. 2010: *Amazigh and Others, Beyond the Tribe and Nation in the Maghrib*. Bloomington: Indiana University Press.

Hoffman, S. and Bozo, F. 2004: *America's Imperial Temptation and the War in Iraq*. New York: Rowman and Littlefield.

Hogan, M., 2001: The 1948 massacre at Deir Yassin revisited. *Historian*, 63:2, pp. 309–34.

Höglund, J. 2008: Electronic empire: Orientalism revisited in the military shooter. *Game Studies* 8:1, http://gamestudies.org/0801/articles/hoeglund.

Hollis, R. and Shehadi, N. (eds.) 1996: *Lebanon on Hold: Implications for Middle East Peace*. London: Royal Institute of International Affairs.

Hom, A. R. 2016: Angst springs eternal: dangerous times and the dangers of timing the 'Arab Spring'. *Security Dialogue*, 47:2, pp. 165–83.

Hoodfar, H. 1997: Devices and desires: population policy and gender roles in the Islamic republic. In Beinin and Stork (1997).

Hopwood, D. 1985: *Egypt Politics and Society 1945–1984*. London: Unwin Hyman.

—— 1988: *Syria Politics and Society 1945–86*. London: Unwin Hyman.

Horowitz, D. 1985: *Ethnic Groups in Conflict*. Berkeley: University of California Press.

Hourani, A. 1991: *A History of the Arab Peoples*. London: Faber and Faber.

Hourani, A., Khoury, P. S. and Wilson, M. C. (eds.) 2009: *The Modern Middle East*, 2nd edn. London: I. B. Tauris.

Howard, P. N. and Hussain, M. M. 2013: *Democracy's Fourth Wave? Digital Media and the Arab Spring*. Oxford: Oxford University Press on Demand.

Hroub, K. 2006: *Hamas: A Beginner's Guide*. London: Pluto Press.

Hudson, J. 2016: U.N. Envoy revises Syrian death toll to 400,000. *Foreign Policy*, 22 April.

Hudson, M. 1977: *Arab Politics: The Search for Legitimacy*. New Haven: Yale University Press.

—— 2015: *The Crisis of the Arab State*. Harvard Kennedy School, Belfer Center, www.belfercenter.org/sites/default/files/legacy/files/CrisisArabState.pdf.

Human Rights Watch. 2015: *World Report*, https://www.hrw.org/world-report/2015, pp. 301–7.

—— 2016: Iraq: women suffer under ISIS, <https://www.hrw.org/news/2016/04/05/iraq-women-suffer-under-isis.

Huntington, S. 1984: Will more countries become democratic? *Political Science Quarterly*, Summer, pp. 193–218.

—— 1993: The clash of civilizations? *Foreign Affairs*, Summer, pp. 22–49.

Hussain, A., Olson, R. and Qureshi, J. (eds.) 1984: *Orientalism, Islam and Islamists*. Brattlebro, VT: Amana Books.

Hutchinson, J. and Smith, A. D. (eds.) 1994: *Nationalism*. Oxford: Oxford University Press.

ILO, International Labour Organization. 2017: Arab states: labour migration, www.ilo.org/beirut/areasofwork/labour-migration/lang–en/index.htm.

International Monetary Fund. 2009: *Regional Outlook: Middle East and Central Asia.* World Economic and Financial Surveys. Washington, DC: International Monetary Fund (IMF).

—— 2015: *Middle East and North Africa Report.* www.imf.org/external/pubs/ft/reo/2015/mcd/eng/pdf/menap1015.pdf.

Inter Parliamentary Union. 2015: *Women in National Parliaments,* www.ipu.org/wmn-e/classif.htm.

Ismail, S. 1995: Democracy in contemporary Arab intellectual discourse. In Brynen, Korany and Noble (1995).

Issawi, C. 1982: *An Economic History of the Middle East and North Africa.* New York: Columbia University Press.

Jaadane, F. 1990: Notions of the state in contemporary Arab-Islamic writings. In Luciani (1990).

Jabar, F. A. and Dawod, H. 2006: *The Kurds: Nationalism and Politics.* London: Saqi Books.

Jackson, R. 2016: *Suez: The Forgotten Invasion.* London: Endeavour Press Ltd.

Jad, I. 1991: From salons to popular committees: Palestinian women, 1919–1989. In Nassar and Heacock (1991).

Jawad, H. 1998: *The Rights of Women in Islam: An Authentic Approach.* Basingstoke: Macmillan.

Jenkins, B. M. 2012: *Al Qaeda in Its Third Decade: Irreversible Decline or Imminent Victory?* Santa Monica, CA: Rand Corporation.

Jonasson, A. 2016: *The EU's Democracy Promotion and the Mediterranean Neighbours: Orientation, Ownership and Dialogue in Jordan and Turkey.* London: Routledge.

Jones, J. 2007: *Negotiating Change, the New Politics of the Middle East.* London: I. B. Tauris.

Jones, M.O. 2016: Saudi intervention, sectarianism and de-democratization in Bahrain's uprising. In T. Davies, H. E. Ryan and A. M. Pena (eds.), *Protests, Social Movements and Global Democracy since 2011.* Bingley: Emerald Publishing, pp. 251–79.

Jongerden, J. 2007: *The Settlement Issue in Turkey and the Kurds: an Analysis of Spatial Policies, Modernity and War.* Leiden: Brill.

Juergensmeyer, M. 1993: *The New Cold War? Religious Nationalism Confronts the Secular State.* Berkeley: University of California Press.

Jwaideh, W. 2006: *The Kurdish National Movement: Its Origins and Development.* New York: Syracuse University Press.

Kamvara, M. (ed.) 2016: *Fragile Politics: Weak States in the Greater Middle East.* New York: Oxford University Press.

Kanaaneh, H. 2008: *A Doctor in the Galilee: The Story of a Palestinian in Israel.* London: Pluto Press.

Kandiyoti, D. (ed.) 1996: *Gendering the Middle East.* London: I. B. Tauris.

Karam, A. 1998: *Women, Islamisms and the State, Contemporary Feminisms in Egypt.* Basingstoke: Macmillan.

Karsh, E. 1997: *Fabricating Israeli History: The 'New Historians'.* London: Frank Cass.

—— 2014: *The Iran–Iraq War 1980–1988.* Oxford: Osprey.

Karsh, E. and Miller, R. 2008: Did Edward Said really speak truth to power? *Middle East Quarterly*, 25:1, pp. 13–21.

Kaussler, B. 2015: *Iran's Nuclear Diplomacy: Power Politics and Conflict Resolution*. New York: Routledge.

Keddie, N. R. 2007: *Women in the Middle East: Past and Present*. Princeton: Princeton University Press.

Kedourie, E. 1988: Ethnicity, majority and minority in the Middle East. In Esman and Rabinovich (1988).

—— 1992: *Politics in the Middle East*. Oxford: Oxford University Press.

—— 1994: *Democracy and Arab Political Culture*. London: Frank Cass.

Kellas, J. 1998: *The Politics of Nationalism and Ethnicity*, 2nd edn. Basingstoke: Macmillan.

Kelly, S. 2010: Hard-won progress and a long road ahead: woman's rights in the Middle East and North Africa. In S. Kelly and J. Breslin (eds.), *Women's Rights in the Middle East and North Africa*. New York: Freedom House.

Kepel, G. 1994: *The Revenge of God*. Cambridge: Polity.

—— 2006: *Jihad: The trail of political Islam*. London: I. B. Tauris.

Kerr, M. 1971: *The Arab Cold War: Gamal 'Abd al-Nasir and his Rivals, 1958–1970*. London: Oxford University Press.

—— 1980: Review of Orientalism. *International Journal of Middle Eastern Studies*, 12, pp. 544–7.

Ketchley, N. 2017: *Egypt in a Time of Revolution: Contentious Politics and the Arab Spring*. Cambridge: Cambridge University Press.

Khalidi, R. 1997: *Palestinian Identity: The Construction of Modern National Consciousness*. New York: Columbia University Press.

—— 2009: *Sowing Crisis: The Cold War and American Dominance in the Middle East*. Boston: Beacon Press.

Khalidi, R., Anderson, L., Muslih, M. and Simon, R. S. (eds.) 1991: *The Origins of Arab Nationalism*. New York: Columbia University Press.

Khalidi, W. 1991a: *The Middle East Post-war Environment*. Washington, DC: Institute of Palestine Studies.

—— 1991b: Why some Arabs support Saddam Hussein. In Sifry and Cerf (1991).

Khalil, A. 2016: *Gender, Women and the Arab Spring*. London: Routledge.

Khalil, S. 1989: *Republic of Fear: Saddam's Iraq*. London: Hutchinson Radius.

Khatami, S. M. 2010: Muslim world, theoretical perspectives and modern political discourses. In Paya and Esposito (2010).

Kheir-El-Din, H. (ed.) 2008: *The Egyptian Economy, Current Challenges and Future Prospects*. Cairo: American University of Cairo Press.

Khistainy, K. 2002: Author interview, London, December.

@khloekardashian. 2015: Instagram post, 26 May, https://www.instagram.com/p/3JXX89hRiS.

Khoury, P. S. 1983: *Urban Notables and Arab Nationalism: The Politics of Arab Nationalism 1880–1920*. Cambridge: Cambridge University Press.

—— 1987: *Syria and the French Mandate: The Politics of Arab Nationalism 1920–1945*. London: I. B. Tauris.

Kienle, E. 1990: *Ba'th versus Ba'th: Conflict between Syria and Iraq*. London: I. B. Tauris.

—— (ed.) 1996: *Contemporary Syria, Liberalisation Between Cold War and Peace*. London: I. B. Tauris.

Knauss, P. 1987: *The Persistence of Patriarchy: Class, Gender and Ideology in 20th-Century Algeria*. Boulder, CO: Westview.

Knudsen, A. and Kerr, M. 2012: *Lebanon: After the Cedar Revolution*. London: C. Hurst & Co.

Kohn, H. 1932: *Nationalism and Imperialism in the Hither East*. London: Routledge.

Korany, B. and El-Mahdi, R. (eds.) 2014: *Arab Spring in Egypt: Revolution and Beyond*. Cairo: American University of Cairo Press.

Kozhanov, N. 2016: *Russia and the Syrian Conflict: Moscow's Domestic, Regional and Strategic Interests*. Berlin: Gerlach Press.

Kramer, G. 1992: Liberalization and democracy in the Arab world. *Middle East Report*, 174:35, January–February, pp. 22–5.

Kramer, M. 1980: *Political Islam*. London: Sage.

— 1993: Islam vs. democracy. *Commentary*, January, pp. 35–42.

Krause, W. 2012: *Civil Society and Women Activists in the Middle East: Islamic and Secular Organizations in Egypt*. London: I. B. Tauris.

Kubba, L. 2010: Lessons from Iraq. In Paya and Esposito (2010).

Kupchan, C. A. 2002: *The End of the American Era: U.S. Foreign Policy and the Geopolitics of the Twenty-first Century*. New York: Alfred A. Knopf.

Kuran, T. 2004: *Islam and Mammon: The Economic Predicament of Islamism*. Princeton: Princeton University Press.

Kuttab, E. 2008: Palestinian women's organizations: global co-option and local contradiction. *Cultural Dynamics*, 20:2, pp. 99–117.

Kyle, K. 1991: *Suez*. London: Weidenfeld and Nicolson.

— 2002: *Suez: Britain's End of Empire in the Middle East*. London: I. B. Tauris.

Lackner, H. (ed.) 2014: *Why Yemen Matters: a Society in Transition*. London: Saqi Books.

Laclau, E. 1996: *Emancipation(s)*. London: Verso.

Lacroix, S. and Rougier, B. (eds.) 2016: *Egypt's Revolutions: Politics, Religion and Social Movements*. Houndmills: Palgrave Macmillan

Larson, A. P. 2003: Testimony before the Senate Foreign Relations Committee. *U.S. State Department*. Washington, DC: US State Department, 4 June.

Laub, Z., 2016: Yemen in crisis. Council on Foreign Relations 'Backgrounder', https://www.cfr.org/backgrounder/yemen-crisis.

Lawson, F. H. (ed.) 2009: *Demystifying Syria*. London: Saqi Books.

League of Nations. 1919: *Covenant of the League of Nations*, 28 June.

Leenders, R., 2012: *Spoils of Truce: Corruption and State-building in Postwar Lebanon*. New York: Cornell University Press.

Leenders, R. and Sfakianakis, J. 2002: *Middle East and North Africa, Global Corruption Report*, http://unpan1.un.org/intradoc/groups/public/documents/APCITY/UNPAN008450.pdf.

Le Renard, A. 2014: *A Society of Young Women: Opportunities of Place, Power, and Reform in Saudi Arabia*. Redwood City, CA: Stanford University Press.

Lerner, D. 1958: *The Passing of Traditional Society*. New York: Free Press.

Lewis, B. 1968: *The Middle East and the West*. London: Weidenfeld and Nicolson.

— 1976: The return of Islam. *Commentary*, January.

— 1982: The question of Orientalism. *New York Review of Books*, 24 June.

— 1990: The roots of Muslim rage. *Atlantic Monthly*, 266:3, September, pp. 47–60.

— 1993a: Islam and liberal democracy. *Atlantic Monthly*, 271:2, February, pp. 89–98.

— 1993b: *Islam and the West*. Oxford: Oxford University Press.

Lijphart, A. 1977: *Democracy in Plural Societies*. New Haven, CT: Yale University Press.

Lippman, T. W. 2004: *Inside the Mirage: America's Fragile Partnership with Saudi Arabia*. Boulder, CO: Westview Press.

Lister, C.R. 2015: *The Islamic State: A Brief Introduction*. Washington, DC: Brookings Institution Press.

— 2016: *The Syrian Jihad: Al-Qaeda, the Islamic State and the Evolution of an Insurgency*. Oxford: Oxford University Press.

Llewellyn, T. 2010: *Spirit of the Phoenix: Beirut and the Story of Lebanon*. London: I. B. Tauris.

Lockman, Z. 2004: *Contending Visions of the Middle East: The History and Politics of Orientalism*. Cambridge: Cambridge University Press.

Lockman, Z. and Beinin, J. (eds.) 1989: *Intifada: The Palestinian Uprising Against Israeli Occupation*. Boston, MA: South End Press.

Louer, L. 2006: *To Be an Arab in Israel*. London: Charles Hurst and Company.

Lovat, T. (ed.) 2012: *The 'Women's Movement' in Modern Islam: Reflections on the Revival of Islam's Oldest Issue*. New York: Springer.

Luciani, G. (ed.) 1990: *The Arab State*. London: Routledge.

— 1995: Resources, revenues and authoritarianism in the Arab world: beyond the rentier state. In Brynen, R. et al. (eds.).

— 2009: Oil and political economy in the international relations of the Middle East'. In Fawcett (2016).

— 2015: On the economic causes of the Arab Spring and its possible developments. In K. Selvik and B. O. Utvik (eds.) 2015: *Oil States in the New Middle East: Uprisings and Stability*. Abingdon: Routledge.

Lukas, A. 2000: WTO Report Card III, Globalization and Developing Countries' Trade Briefing Paper, 10, The Cato Institute, 20 June.

Lustick, I. 1993: *Unsettled States, Disputed Lands: Britain and Ireland, France and Algeria, Israel and the West Bank – Gaza*. Ithaca: Cornell University Press.

Lust-Okar, E. 2006: Elections under authoritarianism: preliminary lessons from Jordan. *Democratization*, 13:3, pp. 456–71.

— 2009: Reinforcing informal institutions through authoritarian elections: insights from Jordan. *Middle East Law and Governance*, 1:1, pp. 3–37.

Lust-Okar, E. and Zerhouni, S. (eds.) 2008: *Political Participation in the Middle East*. Boulder, CO: Lynne Rienner.

Lynch, M. 2017: *The New Arab Wars: Uprisings and Anarchy in the Middle East*. New York: Public Affairs.

Lyth, P. 2013: Carry on up the Nile: the tourist gaze and the British experience of Egypt, 1818–1932. In M. Farr and X. Guegan (eds.), *The British Abroad Since the Eighteenth Century*, vol. I . Houndmills: Palgrave Macmillan (pp. 176–93).

Maalouf, A. 2001: *In the Name of Identity: Violence and the Need to Belong*. London: Arcade.

Mahmoud, M. 1996: Women and Islamism: the case of Rashid al-Ghannushi of Tunisia. In Sidahmed and Ehteshami (1996).

Maisel, S. 2016: *Yezidis in Syria: Identity Building Among a Double Minority*. London: Lexington Books.

Mansfield, P. 1969: *Nasser*. London: Methuen.

—— 1992: *A History of the Middle East*. Harmondsworth: Penguin.

al-Marashi, I., 2017: The impact of the Islamic State of Iraq and Syria's campaign on Yezidi religious structures and pilgrimage practices. In M. Leppakari and K. A. Griffin (eds.), *Pilgrimage and Tourism to Holy Cities: Ideological and Management Perspectives*. Wallingford: CABI, pp. 144–55.

Marlowe, J. 1954: *Anglo-Egyptian Relations, 1800–1953*. London: Cresset Press.

—— 1970: *Cromer in Egypt*. London: Elek.

—— 1971: *Perfidious Albion: The Origin of Anglo-French Rivalry in the Levant*. London: Elek.

Masoud, T. 2015: Has the door closed on Arab democracy? *Journal of Democracy*, 26:1, pp. 74–87.

Matar, D. 2012: Rethinking the Arab state and culture: preliminary thoughts. In T. Sabry (ed.), *Arab Cultural Studies: Mapping the Field*, London: I. B. Tauris, pp. 123–36.

Matthieson, T. 2013: *Sectarian Gulf: Bahrain, Saudi Arabia and the Arab Spring that Wasn't*. Stanford: Stanford University Press.

Mazzetti, M. and Kirkpatrick, D. 2015: Saudi Arabia leads air assault in Yemen. *The New York Times*, 26 March, www.nytimes.com/2015/03/26/world/middleeast/al-anad-air-base-houthis-yemen.html?_r=0.

McCants, W. 2015: *The ISIS Apocalypse: The History, Strategy, and Doomsday Vision of the Islamic State*. New York: Picador.

McDowall, D. 2007: *A Modern History of the Kurds*. London: I. B. Tauris.

McGarry, J. and O'Leary, B. (eds.) 1993: *The Politics of Ethnic Conflict Regulation*. London: Routledge.

McKiernan, K. 2006: *The Kurds: A People in Search of a Homeland*. London: St. Martins Press.

McMahon, A. H. 1939: The Mcmahon Correspondence of 1915–16. *Bulletin of International News*, 16:5, 11 March, pp. 6–13.

McMurray, D. and Ufheil-Somers, A. (eds.) 2013: *The Arab Revolts: Dispatches on Militant Democracy in the Middle East*. Bloomington: Indiana Uuniversity Press.

McNamara, R. 2003: *Britain, Nasser and the Balance of Power in the Middle East, 1952–1967*. London: Frank Cass.

McRobie, H. 2014: The common factor: sexual violence and the Egyptian state 2011–14. *Open Democracy*, https://www.opendemocracy.net/5050/heather-mcrobie/common-factor-sexual-violence-and-egyptian-state-20112014.

Mead, W. R. 2001: *Special Providence: American Foreign Policy and How it Changed the World*. New York: Alfred A. Knopf.

—— 2008. *The Israel Lobby and U.S. Foreign Policy*. Harmondsworth: Penguin.

Méouchy, N. and Sluglett, P. (eds.) 2004: *British and French Mandates in Comparative Perspective*. Leiden: Brill.

Middle East Report. 1992: The democracy agenda in the Arab world. *Middle East Report – MERIP*, 174, January–February, pp. 3–5.

Mernissi, F. 1985: *Beyond the Veil: Male–Female Dynamics in Muslim Society*. London: Saqi Books.

—— 1991: *Women and Islam: An Historical and Theological Enquiry*. Oxford: Blackwell.

Milani, F. 2011: *Words, Not Swords: Iranian Women Writers and the Freedom of Movement*. Syracuse: Syracuse University Press.

Miller, J. 1993: The challenge of radical Islam. *Foreign Affairs*, 72:2, Spring, pp. 43–56.

Milton-Edwards, B. 1991: A temporary alliance with the crown: the Islamic response in Jordan. In J. P. Piscatori (ed.), *Islamic Fundamentalism and the Gulf Crisis*. Chicago: The Fundamentalism Project, AAAS.

—— 1993: Jordan and façade democracy. *British Journal of Middle Eastern Studies*, 20:3, pp. 191–203.

—— 1996a: *Islamic Politics in Palestine*. London: I. B. Tauris.

—— 1996b: Climate of change in Jordan's Islamist movement. In Sidahmed and Ehteshami (1996).

—— 2004: *Islam and Politics in the Contemporary World*. Cambridge: Polity.

—— 2008: *The Israeli–Palestinian Conflict, A People's War*. Abingdon: Routledge.

—— 2010: The democratic freedom deficit in the Middle East. In Paya and Esposito (2010).

—— 2016a: *The Muslim Brotherhood: The Arab Spring and its Future Face*. Abingdon: Routledge.

—— 2016b: Is protecting Mosul minorities an excuse for partition? *Al-Jazeera*, www.aljazeera.com/indepth/opinion/2016/10/protecting-mosul-minorities-excuse-partition-161017074315301.html.

—— 2016c: Protests in Jordan over gas deal with Israel expose wider rifts. *Markaz*, 26 Oct. https://www.brookings.edu/blog/markaz/2016/10/26/protests-in-jordan-over-gas-deal-with-israel-expose-wider-rifts?

—— 2017: Jordan's troubles in its own backyard. *Markaz*, 22 Feb., https://www.brookings.edu/blog/markaz/2017/02/22/jordans-troubles-in-its-own-backyard.

Milton-Edwards, B. and Farrell, S. 2010: *Hamas: The Islamic Resistance Movement*. Cambridge: Polity.

Milton-Edwards, B. and Hinchcliffe, P. 2008: *Conflicts in the Middle East since 1945*, 3rd edn. Abingdon: Routledge.

—— 2009: *Jordan, a Hashemite Legacy*. London: Routledge.

Minces, J. 1978: Women in Algeria. In L. Beck and N. Keddie (eds.), *Women in the Muslim World*. Cambridge, MA: Harvard University Press.

Mirsepassi, A. and Fernee, T. G. 2016: *Islam, Democracy and Cosmopolitanism: At Home and in the World*. Cambridge: Cambridge University Press.

Mitchell, R. P. 1969: *The Society of Muslim Brothers*. Oxford: Oxford University Press.

Mitchell, T. 1988: *Colonising Egypt*. Cambridge: Cambridge University Press.

—— 2011: *Carbon Democracy: Political Power in the Age of Oil*. London: Verso.

Moaddel, M. 2005: *Islamic Modernism, Nationalism, and Fundamentalism: Episode and Discourse*. Chicago: University of Chicago Press.

Moghadam, V. 2003: *Modernizing Women: Gender and Society Change in the Middle East*. Boulder, CO: Lynne Rienner.

Moghissi, H. 1994: *Populism and Feminism in Iran: Women's Struggle in a Male-Defined Revolutionary Movement*. Basingstoke: Macmillan.

Molyneux, M. 1991: The law, the state and socialist policies with regard to women: the case of the People's Democratic Republic of Yemen 1967–1990. In D. Kandiyoti (ed.), *Women, Islam and the State*. Basingstoke: Macmillan.

Momani, B. 2016: *Equality and the Economy: Why the Arab World Should Employ More Women*. Doha: BDC.

Monem, A. 2013: *Arabs and Israelis: Conflict and Peacemaking in the Middle East*. Houndmills: Palgrave Macmillan.

Monroe, E. 1963: *Britain's Moment in the Middle East 1914–1956*. London: Chatto and Windus.

Moore, C. H. 1970: *The Politics of North Africa: Algeria, Morocco and Tunisia*. Boston: Little, Brown.

Moore, E. D. 2017: *Russia–Iran Relations Since the End of the Cold War*. London: Routledge.

Morris, B. 1988: *The Birth of the Palestinian Refugee Problem, 1947–1949*. Cambridge: Cambridge University Press.

—— 1998: Refabricating 1948. *Journal of Palestine Studies*, 27:2, Winter, pp. 81–95.

Moussawi, N. 2005: Interview with author.

Moynihan, D. P. 1993: *Pandemonium: Ethnicity in International Politics*. Oxford: Oxford University Press.

M'rad, H. 2015: *National Dialogue in Tunisia: Nobel Peace Prize 2015*. Lyon: Éditions Nirvana.

al-Muhajirah, U. S. 2015: Slave-girls or prostitutes? *Dabiq*, 9, p. 46.

Muhanna, A. 2016: *Agency and Gender in Gaza: Masculinity, Femininity and Family during the Second Intifada*. London: Routledge.

Mukhimer, T. 2016: *Hamas Rule in Gaza: Human Rights under Constraint*. Houndmills: Palgrave Macmillan.

Musa, C. 2010: *EU policy Towards the Arab–Israeli Peace Process: The Quicksands of Politics*. Houndmills: Palgrave.

Muslih, M. 1993: Palestinian civil society. *Middle East Journal*, 47, Spring, pp. 258–74.

Nakhle, C. 2017: Tunisia's fragile transition. *Carnegie* Endowment, 10 Feb, http://carnegie-mec.org/2017/02/10/tunisia-s-fragile-transition-pub-68070.

Nassar, J. and Heacock, R. (eds.) 1991: *Intifada: Palestine at the Crossroads*. New York: Praeger.

Nassar, M. 2017: *Brothers Apart: Palestinian Citizens of Israel and the Arab World*. Stanford: Stanford University Press.

Natali, D. 2005: *The Kurds and the State: Evolving National Identity in Iraq, Turkey, and Iran*. New York: Syracuse University Press.

Neep, D. 2015: Focus: the Middle East, hallucination and the cartographic imagination. *Discover Society*, 3 Jan., http://discoversociety.org/2015/01/03/focus-the-middle-east-hallucination-and-the-cartographic-imagination.

Nereim, V. and Carey, G. 2015: Saudi 2015 budget deficit is $98 billion as revenue drops. *Bloomberg Business*, 28 Dec.

Nevakivi, J. 1969: *Britain, France and the Arab Middle East*. London: Athlone Press.

Nisan, M. 2002: *Minorities in the Middle East: a History of Struggle and Self-expression*. Jefferson, NC: McFarland and Company Inc.

Noorani, Y. 2010: *Culture and Hegemony in the Colonial Middle East*. Houndmills: Palgrave.

Norton, Augustus R. 1993: The future of civil society in the Middle East. *Middle East Journal*, 47, Spring, pp. 205–16.

Noueihad, L. and Warren, A. 2012: *The Battle for the Arab Spring: Revolution, Counter-revolution and the Making of a New Era*. New Haven, CT: Yale University Press.

Odell, P. 1981: *Oil and World Power*. Harmondsworth: Penguin.

OPEC. 2015a: *Annual Statistical Bulletin*. Organization of the Petroleum Exporting Countries.

—— 2015b: OPEC share of world crude reserves, 2015, www.opec.org/opec_web/en/data_graphs/330.htm.

Orhan, D. D. 2010: *Dynamics and Evolution of the European Union's Middle East policy: Challenges, and Opportunities*. London: LAP Lambert Publishing.

Orr Commission. 2001: Orr Commission Report. *Israel Studies*, 11:2, pp. 25–53.

Osman, T. 2016: *Islamism: What it Means for the Middle East and the World*. New Haven, CT: Yale University Press

Ottaway, M. and Riley, M. 2006: *Morocco: From Top-down Reform to Democratic Transition*. Washington, DC: Carnegie Endowment for Peace

Owen, R. 1969: *Cotton and the Egyptian Economy 1820–1914: A Study in Trade and Development*. Oxford: Clarendon Press.

—— 1981: *The Middle East in the World Economy 1800–1914*. London: Methuen.

—— 1991: Epilogue: making sense of an earthquake. In Brittain (1991).

—— 2004: *State, Power and Politics in the Making of the Modern Middle East*, 3rd edn. London: Routledge.

—— 2012: *Rise and Fall of Arab Presidents*. New Haven, CT: Harvard University Press.

Ozcan, A. K. 2010: *Turkey's Kurds*. London: Routledge.

Paidar, P. 1996: Feminism and Islam in Iran. In Kandiyoti (1996).

Pappe, I. 1994: *The Making of the Arab–Israeli Conflict, 1947–51*. London: I. B. Tauris.

—— 2005: *Modern Middle East*. London: Routledge.

Parekh, B. 2010: Promoting democracy. In Paya and Esposito (2010).

Pargeter, A. 2012: *The Rise and Fall of Qaddafi*. New Haven, CT: Yale University Press.

—— 2016: *Return to the Shadows: The Muslim Brotherhood and An-Nahda since the Arab Spring*. London: Saqi Books.

Pawlak, P. 2016: Conflict in Syria Trigger factors and the EU response. *European Parliamentary Research Service Brief*, www.europarl.europa.eu/RegData/etudes/BRIE/2016/573924/EPRS_BRI(2016)573924_EN.pdf.

Paya, A. 2010: Islamic democracy: a valid concept or an oxymoron? In Paya and Esposito (2010).

Paya, A. and Esposito, J. (eds.) 2010: *Iraq, Democracy and the Future of the Muslim World*. Abingdon: Routledge.

Peretz, D. 1990: *Intifada: The Palestinian Uprising*. Boulder, CO: Westview.

Perthes, V. 1991: A look at Syria's upper class: the bourgeoisie and the Ba'th. *Middle East Report*, 170, May–June, pp. 31–7.

—— 1992: Syria's parliamentary elections: remodelling Asad's political base. *Middle East Report*, 174, January–February, pp. 15–18.

—— 1995: *Political Economy of Syria under Asad*. London: I. B. Tauris.

—— 2004: *Syria under Basher al-Asad: Modernization and the Limits of Changes*. Oxford: Oxford University Press.

Pesaran, E. 2013: *Iran's Struggle for Economic Independence: Reform and Counter-Reform in the Post-Revolutionary Era*. London: Routledge.

Pew Global Attitudes Project. 2004: A year after the war in Iraq, mistrust of America in Europe ever higher, Muslim anger persists. *Pew Global Attitude Survey*, Washington, DC: PRCP&P.

Pew Research Center. 2016: *Middle East Sympathies, 1978–2016*, www.people-press.org/2016/05/05/5-views-of-israel-and-palestinians/5_1.

Pfeifer, K. 1997: Is there an Islamic economics? In Beinin and Stork (1997).

Phillips, C. 2016: *The Battle for Syria: International Rivalry in the New Middle East*. New Haven, CT: Yale University Press.

Piazza, J. A. 2007: Draining the swamp: democracy promotion, state failure and terrorism in 19 Middle Eastern countries. *Studies in Conflict and Terrorism*, 30:6, June, pp. 521–39.

Picard, E. 1990: Arab military in politics: from revolutionary plot to authoritarian regimes. In Luciani (1990).

Piscatori, J. P. 1986: *Islam in a World of Nation States*. Cambridge: Cambridge University Press.

Podeh, E., 2014: Israel and the Arab peace initiative, 2002–2014: a plausible missed opportunity. *The Middle East Journal*, 68:4, pp. 584–603.

Polk, W. R. 1991: *The Arab World Today*. Cambridge, MA: Harvard University Press.

Pollack, K. M. 2016: Fight or flight: America's choice in the Middle East. *Foreign Affairs*, 95, pp. 62–75.

Pollack, K. M. and Byman, D. 2011: *The Arab Awakening: America and the Transformation of the Middle East*. Virginia: R. R. Donnelley.

Potter, D., Goldblatt, D., Kiloh, M. and Lewis, P. (eds.), 1997: *Democratization*. Cambridge: Polity.

Potter, L. G. (ed.) 2014: *Sectarian Politics in the Persian Gulf*. Oxford: Oxford University Press, USA.

Provence, M. 2005: *The Great Syrian Revolt and the Rise of Arab Nationalism*. Austin: University of Texas Press.

al-Qaradawi, Y. 2009: *Princeton Readings in Islamist Thought: Texts and Contexts from al-Banna to Bin Laden*. Princeton: Princeton University Press, 2009, pp. 230–45.

Qutb, S. 1978: *Milestones*. Beirut: Holy Koran Publishing.

—— 1988: *The Religion of Islam*. Kuwait: Holy Koran Publishing.

Rahnema, S. and Behdad, S. (eds.) 1995: *Iran after the Revolution: Crisis of an Islamic State*. London: I. B. Tauris.

Ramadan, T, 2012: *Islam and the Arab Awakening*. New York: Oxford University Press.

al-Rasheed, M. 2013: *A Most Masculine State: Gender, Politics and Religion in Saudi Arabia*. Cambridge: Cambridge University Press.

Reinl, J. 2015: Arab 'brain drain' accelerates after Arab Spring: U.N., 8 May, www.middleeasteye.net/news/un-arab-brain-drain-accelerates-after-arab-spring-1752815577.

Reuter, C. 2015: The terror strategist. *Spiegel Online*, 18 April, www.spiegel.de/international/world/islamic-state-files-show-structure-of-islamist-terror-group-a-1029274.html.

Richards, A. 1982: *Egypt's Agricultural Development, 1800–1980*. Boulder, CO: Westview.

—— 1993: Economic imperatives and political systems. *Middle East Journal*, 47, Spring, pp. 217–26.

Richards, A. and Waterbury, J. 1990: *A Political Economy of the Middle East*. Boulder, CO: Westview.

Riedel, B. 2017: *Kings and Presidents: Inside the Special Relationship between Saudi Arabia and America since FDR*. Washington: Brookings Institute.

Roald, A. S. and Longva, A. N. 2016: *Religious Minorities in the Middle East*. Boston: BRILL.

Robson, L. 2016: *Minorities and the Modern Arab World: New Perspectives*. Syracuse: Syracuse University Press.

Roded, R. 2008: *Women in Islam and the Middle East: A Reader*. London: I. B. Tauris.

Romano, D. and Gurses, M. (eds.) 2014: *Conflict, Democratization, and the Kurds in the Middle East, Turkey, Iran, Iraq and Syria*. New York: Palgrave Macmillan.

Roy, O. 1994: *The Failure of Political Islam*. London: I. B. Tauris.

—— 2012: The transformation of the Arab world. *Journal of Democracy*, 23:3, pp. 5–18.

—— 2017: *Jihad and Death: The Global Appeal of Islamic State*. London: C. Hurst and Co.

Roy, S. 2013: *Hamas and Civil Society in Gaza: Engaging the Islamist Social Sector*. Princeton: Princeton University Press

Russell, G. 2015: *Heirs to Forgotten Kingdoms, Journeys into the Disappearing Religions of the Middle East*. London: Simon and Schuster.

Sadiki, L. 2015: *Routledge Handbook of the Arab Spring: Rethinking Democratization*. London: Routledge.

Sadiqi, F. and Ennaji, M. 2010: *Women in MENA: Agents of Change*. Abingdon: Routledge.

Sadowski, Y. 1997: The new orientalism and the democracy debate. In Beinin and Stork (1997).

Sahliyeh, E. 1988: *In Search of Leadership: West Bank Politics since 1967*. Washington, DC: Brookings Institute.

—— 1992: Beyond the Cold War: the superpowers and the Arab–Israeli conflict. In Spiegel (1992).

Said, E. 1978: *Orientalism*, 1st edn. Harmondsworth: Penguin.

—— 1981: *Covering Islam: How the Media and Experts Determine How We See the Rest of the World*. London: Routledge.

—— 1982: Reply to B. Lewis. *New York Review of Books*, 12 August.

—— 1989: Intifada and independence. In Lockman and Beinin (1989).

—— 1993a: *Culture and Imperialism*. London: Chatto and Windus.

—— 1993b: Culture and Imperialism. *Times Literary Supplement*, 4 June.

Saikal, A. 2015: *Iran at the Crossroads*. Cambridge: Polity.

Saikal, A. and Acharya, A. 2014: *Democracy and Reform in the Middle East and Asia: Social Protest and Authoritarian Rule After the Arab Spring*. London: I. B. Tauris.

Saktanber, A. 2002: *Living Islam, Women, Religion and the Politicization of Culture in Turkey*. London: I. B. Tauris.

Salame, G. (ed.) 1994: *Democracy Without Democrats? The Renewal of Democracy in the Muslim World*. London: I. B. Tauris.

Salem, E. A. 1995: *Violence and Diplomacy in Lebanon: The Troubled Years 1982–1988*. London: I. B. Tauris.

Salem, N. 1984: Islam and the status of women in Tunisia. In Hussain (1984).

Salisbury, P., 2015. *Yemen and the Saudi–Iranian 'Cold War'*. Research Paper, Middle East and North Africa Programme. London: Chatham House, the Royal Institute of International Affairs.

Salloukh, B. F., et al. 2015: *The Politics of Sectarianism: Postwar Lebanon*. London: Pluto.

Salvatore, A. 1997: *Islam and the Political Discourse of Modernity*. Reading, NY: Ithaca Press.

Saouli, A., 2012: *The Arab State: Dilemmas of Late Formation*. Abingdon: Routledge.

Sardar, Z. and Wyn Davies, M. 2003: *Why Do People Hate America?* Cambridge: Icon Books.

Sater, J. N. 2007: *Civil Society and Political Change in Morocco*. London: Routledge.

Sayigh, Y. 1997: *Armed Struggle and the Search for a State: The Palestinian National Movement 1949–1993*. Oxford: Clarendon Press.

Sayre, E. A. and Yousef, T. M. (eds.) 2016: *Young Generation Awakening: Economics, Society and Policy on the Eve of the Arab Spring*. New York: Oxford University Press.

Sayyid, B. 1997: *A Fundamental Fear – Eurocentrism and the Emergence of Islamism*. London: Zed Books.

al-Sayyid, M. A. 1994: The third wave of democracy. In Tschirgi (1994).

—— 1995: The concept of civil society and the Arab world. In Brynen, Korany and Noble (1995).

Schafer, I. (ed.) 2015: *Youth, Revolt, Recognition: The Young Generation During and After the 'Arab Spring'*. Berlin: Mediterranean Institute Berlin (MIB) /Humboldt University Berlin.

Schanzer, J. 2008: *Hamas vs. Fatah: the Struggle for Palestine*. New York: St. Martin's Press.

Schiff, Z. and Ya'ari, E. 1984: *Israel's Lebanon War*. New York: Simon and Schuster.

Schneer, J. 2011: *The Balfour Declaration: the Origins of the Arab–Israeli conflict*. London: Bloomsbury.

Schwarz, R. 2008: The political economy of state formation in the Arab Middle East: rentier states, economic reform and democratization. *Review of International Political Economy*, 15:4, pp. 599–621.

Schwedler, J. 2006: *Faith in Moderation: Islamist Parties in Jordan and Yemen*. Cambridge: Cambridge University Press.

Seale, P. 1988: *The Struggle for Syria: A Study of Post-War Arab Politics 1945–58*. London: I. B. Tauris.

—— 1989: *Asad of Syria: The Struggle for the Middle East*. Berkeley: University of California Press.

Segev, T. 2000: *One Palestine, Complete*. New York: Henry Holt and Company.

—— 2010: Are Israeli Arabs the new African Americans? *Haaretz* [newspaper], 5 April.

Sensini, P. 2016: *Sowing Chaos: Libya in the Wake of Humanitarian Intervention*. Atlanta, GA: Clarity Press.

Shabi, R. 2009: *Not the Enemy, Israel's Jews from Arab Lands*. New Haven, CT: Yale University Press.

Shahin, E. and Esposito, J. L. (eds.) 2016: *The Oxford Handbook of Islam and Politics*. New York: Oxford University Press.

Shalaby, M. 2016: Women's political representation and authoritarianism in the Arab World. *Women and Gender in Middle East Politics*, POMEPS, https://pomeps.org/wp-content/uploads/2016/05/POMEPS_Studies_19_Gender_Web.pdf.

Shalaby, M. and Moghadam, V. (eds.) 2016: *Empowering Women after the Arab Spring*. New York: Palgrave Macmillan.

Shane, S., Rosenberg, M. and Lipton, E. 2017: Trump pushes dark view of Islam to center of U.S. policy-making. *New York Times*, 1 Feb., https://www.nytimes.com/2017/02/01/us/politics/donald-trump-islam.html.

Sharabi, H. (ed.) 1990: *Theory, Politics and the Arab World*. London: Routledge.

Sharp, J. M. 2016: *US Foreign Aid to Israel*. Washington, DC: Congressional Research Service.

—— 2017: *Jordan: Background and U.S. Relations*. Washington, DC: Congressional Research Service

Shehadi, N. (ed.) 1988: *Lebanon: A History of Conflict and Consensus*. London: I. B. Tauris.

Sheppard, S. 2016: What the Syrian Kurds have wrought: the radical, unlikely, democratic experiment in northern Syria. *The Atlantic*, 25 Oct., https://www.theatlantic.com/international/archive/2016/10/kurds-rojava-syria-isis-iraq-assad/505037.

Sidahmed, A. S. and Ehteshami, A. (eds.) 1996: *Islamic Fundamentalism*. Boulder, CO: Westview.

Sifry, M. L. and Cerf, C. (eds.) 1991: *The Gulf War Reader*. New York: Times Books.

Silverstein, P. A. 1998: The rebel is dead. Long live the martyr! Kabyle mobilisation and the assassination of Lounes Matoub. *Middle East Report*, 208, Fall, pp. 3–4.

SIPRI. 2002: *Yearbook 2002, Armaments, Disarmament and International Security*. Stockholm: SIPRI.

—— 2016: Fact Sheet. Trends in world military expenditure 2015, http://books.sipri.org/files/FS/SIPRIFS1604.pdf.

Sivan, E. 1985: *Radical Islam: Medieval Theology and Modern Politics*. New Haven, CT: Yale University Press.

Sluglett, P. and Farouk-Sluglett, M. 1993: *The Middle East, the Arab World and its Neighbours*. London: Times Books.

Small Arms Survey. 2015: *Policy Brief: Armed Violence in the MENA Region: Trends and Dynamics*, Nov., www.smallarmssurvey.org/fileadmin/docs/M-files/SAS-2015-Policy-BriefAV–MENA-Region.pdf.

Smith, A. D. 1979: *Nationalism in the Twentieth Century*. Oxford: Martin Robertson.

—— 1986: *The Ethnic Origins of Nationalism*. Oxford: Blackwell.

—— 1991: *National Identity*. Harmondsworth: Penguin.

Smith, C. D. 2004: *Palestine and the Arab–Israeli Conflict: a History with Documents*. Boston: Bedford / St. Martin's.

Smooha, S. 1990: Minority status in an ethnic democracy: the status of the Arab minority in Israel. *Ethnic and Racial Studies*, 13:3, pp. 389–413.

Spangler, E. 2015: *Understanding Israel/Palestine: Race, Nation, and Human Rights in the Conflict*. Rotterdam: Sense Publishers.

Spiegel, S. L. (ed.) 1992: *Conflict Management in the Middle East*. Boulder, CO: Westview.

Springborg, R. 2016: Globalization and its discontents in the MENA region. *Middle East Policy*, 23:2, pp. 146–60.

Stansfield, G. R. V. 2007: *Iraq*. Cambridge: Polity.

Steed, D. 2016: *British Strategy and Intelligence in the Suez Crisis*. Houndmills: Palgrave Macmillan.

Stent, A. 2016: Putin's power play in Syria: how to respond to Russia's intervention. *Foreign Affairs*, 95, p. 106.

Stepan, A. C. and Robertson, G. B. 2003: An 'Arab' more than a 'Muslim' democracy gap. *Journal of Democracy*, 14:3, pp. 30–44.

Stephens, R. H. 1971: *Nasser: A Political Biography*. London: Allen Lane.

Stetter, S. 2012: *The Middle East and Globalization: Encounters and Horizons*. Hound-mills: Palgrave Macmillan.

Stewart, F. 1995: *Adjustment and Poverty, Options and Choices*. London: Routledge.

Stokes, D. 2007: Blood for oil? Global capital, counter-insurgency and the dual logic of American energy security. *Review of International Studies*, 33:3, pp. 245–64.

Storm, L. 2005: Ethnonational minorities in the Middle East: Amazighs, Kurds and Palestinians. In Choueri (2005).

—— 2007: *Democratization in Morocco: The Political Elite and Struggles for Power in the Post-independent State*. London: Routledge.

Stowasser, B. 1993: Women's issues in modern Islamic thought. In Tucker (1993).

Suleiman, Y. 2004: *A War of Words: Language and Conflict in the Middle East*. Cambridge: Cambridge University Press.

Svolik, M. W. 2012: *The Politics of Authoritarian Rule*. Cambridge: Cambridge University Press.

Tabaar, M. A. 2017: *Religious Statecraft: The Politics of Islam in Iran*. New York: Columbia University Press.

Tadros, M. 2012: *The Muslim Brotherhood in Contemporary Egypt: Democracy Redefined or Confined?* London: Routledge.

Tahmasebi-Birgani, V. 2010: Green women of Iran: The role of the women's movement during and after Iran's presidential Election of 2009. *Constellations*, 17:1, pp. 78–86.

Tammimi, A. 2007: *Hamas: Unwritten Chapters*. London: Hurst and Company.

Tarock, A. 2016: The Iran nuclear deal: winning a little, losing a lot. *Third World Quarterly*, 37:8, pp. 1408–24.

Taylor, A. R. 1991: *The Superpowers and the Middle East*. Syracuse: Syracuse University Press.

Tell, T. M. 2013: *The Social and Economic Origins of Monarchy in Jordan*. Houndmills: Palgrave Macmillan, pp. 55–71.

Teo, H. M. 2014: *Desert Passions: Orientalism and Romance Novels*. Austin: University of Texas Press.

Tessler, M. 1994: *A History of the Israeli–Palestinian Conflict*. Bloomington: Indiana University Press.

Tessler, M. and Gao, E. 2009: Democracy and the political culture orientations of ordinary citizens: a typology for the Arab world and beyond. *International Social Science Journal*, 59:192, pp. 197–207.

Tetreault, M. A. and al-Mughni, H. 1995: Modernization and its discontents: state and gender in Kuwait. *Middle East Journal*, 49:3, pp. 403–17.

Thiele, B. 1986: Vanishing acts in social and political thought: tricks of the trade. In C. Pateman and E. Goss (eds.), *Feminist Challenges: Social and Political Theory*. Sydney: Allen and Unwin.

Thomas, H. 1986: *The Suez Affair*. London: Weidenfeld and Nicolson.

Tibi, B. 1987: Islam and Arab nationalism. In B. Stowasser (ed.), *The Islamic Impulse*. London: I. B. Tauris.

—— 1992: Major themes in the Arabic political writings of Islamic revivalism. *Islam and Christian–Muslim Relations*, 3:2, pp. 183–210.

—— 1994: Redefining the Arab and Arabism in the aftermath of the Gulf Crisis. In Tschirgi (1994).

— 1996: Old tribes and imposed nation states in the Middle East. In J. Hutchinson and A. D. Smith (eds.), *Ethnicity*. Oxford: Oxford University Press.

— (ed.) 1997: *Arab Nationalism: Between Islam and the Nation State*, 3rd edn. London: Macmillan.

Tignor, R. L. 1984: *State, Private Enterprise and Economic Change in Egypt, 1918–1952*. Princeton: Princeton University Press.

Touaf, L., Boutkhil, S. and Chourouq, N. (eds.). 2017: *North African Women after the Arab Spring: In the Eye of the Storm*. Houndmills: Palgrave Macmillan.

Transparency International. 2011: *Corruption Perceptions Index*, https://www.transparency.org/cpi2011/results.

Tripp, C. 2002: *A History of Iraq*, 2nd edn. Cambridge: Cambridge University Press.

Trump, D. 2017: Christians in the Middle-East have been executed in large numbers we cannot allow this horror to continue! @realDonaldTrump [Twitter], 29 Jan., https://twitter.com/realDonaldTrump/status/825721153142521858.

Tschirgi, D. (ed.) 1994: *The Arab World Today*. Boulder, CO: Lynne Rienner.

Tucker, J. (ed.) 1993: *Arab Women: Old Boundaries, New Frontiers*. Bloomington: Indiana University Press.

Tuncer, S. 2017: *Women and Public Space in Turkey: Gender, Modesty and the Urban Experience*. London: I. B. Tauris.

Turner, Barry. 2012: *Suez 1956: The Inside Story of the First Oil War*. London: Hodder & Stoughton.

Turner, Bryan. 1994: *Orientalism, Postmodernism and Globalism*. London: Routledge.

Tyler, P. 2009: *A World of Trouble: America in the Middle East*. London: Portobello Books.

UNDP. 2009: *Arab Human Development Report 2009*. New York: UNDP.

UN ESCWA. 2015: Against winds and tides: a review of the status of women and gender equality in the Arab region (Beijing +20), https://sustainabledevelopment.un.org/content/documents/2283ESCWA_Women%20and%20Gender%20Equality%20in%20the%20Arab%20Region_Beijing20.pdf.

United Nations Economic and Social Council. 2012: *Situation of and Assistance to Palestinian Women*. UN Commission on the Status of Women.

United Nation Human Rights Council. 2016: 'They came to destroy': ISIS crimes against the Yazidis. Thirty-second session: Agenda item 4.

United Nations Office for the Coordination of Humanitarian Affairs in Occupied Palestinian Territory. 2012: *Land Allocated to Israeli Settlements*, Jan., https://www.ochaopt.org/sites/default/files/ocha_opt_land_allocated_for_settlements_January_2012_english.pdf.

US Energy Information Administration. 2016: US imports from Saudi Arabia of crude oil and petroleum products, https://www.eia.gov/dnav/pet/hist/LeafHandler.ashx?n=PET&s=MTTIMU.S.SA2&f=M.

US State Department. 2012: National Security Strategy seeks to defend peace and prosperity. http://usinfo.state.gov.

Van Bruinessen, M. 1986: The Kurds between Iran and Iraq. *Middle East Report*, July–August, pp. 14–27.

Van Dam, N. 1996: *The Struggle for Power in Syria: Politics and Society under Asad and the Ba'th Party*. London: I. B. Tauris.

Varisco, D. M., 2017: *Reading Orientalism: Said and the Unsaid*. Washington, DC: University of Washington Press.

Vatikiotis, P. J. 1987: *Islam and the State*. London: Routledge.

—— 1988: Non-Muslims in Muslim society: a preliminary consideration of the problem on the basis of recently published works by Muslim authors. In Esman and Rabinovich (1988).

Vitalis, R. 1994: The democratization industry and the limits of new interventionism. *Middle East Report*, March–June, pp. 46–50.

Voller, Y. 2014: *The Kurdish Liberation Movement in Iraq: From Insurgency to Statehood*. London: Routledge.

Waldman, P. 2016: The $2 trillion project to get Saudi Arabia's economy off oil. *Bloomberg*, 21 April.

Walford, G. F. 1963: *Arabian Locust Hunter*. London: The Adventurers Club.

Walters, F. P. 1952: *A History of the League of Nations*. London: Oxford University Press.

Warburg, G. R. and Kupferschmidt, U. M. (eds.) 1983: *Nationalism and Radicalism in Egypt and the Sudan*. New York: Praeger.

Waterbury, J. 1994: Democracy without democrats: the potential for political liberalization in the Middle East. In Salame (1994).

Waylen, G. 1996: *Gender in Third World Politics*. Buckingham: Open University Press.

The White House: Office of the Press Secretary. 2017: *Readout of the President's Call with Prime Minister Netanyahu of Israel*, 22 Jan., https://www.whitehouse.gov/the-press-office/2017/01/22/readout-presidents-call-prime-minister-netanyahu-israel.

Wiktorowicz, Q. 2001: The new global threat: transnational salafis and jihad. *Middle East Policy*, 8:4, December, pp. 18–38.

Willis, M. 2012: *Politics and Power in the Maghreb: Algeria, Tunisia and Morocco from Independence to the Arab Spring*. London: C. Hurst and Co.

Wilson, K. M. (ed.) 1983: *Imperialism and Nationalism in the Middle East: The Anglo-Egyptian Experience 1882–1982*. London: Mansell.

Wilson, R. 1979: *The Economies of the Middle East*. Basingstoke: Macmillan.

Winiarek, C. W. 2015: *Examining Pseudo-Republicanism: Democracy and Civil Society in Tunisia*. London: Lambert Academic Publishing.

Woodhouse, C. M. 1959: *Britain and the Middle East*. Geneva: PIUHII.

World Bank. 2009: Unemployment, youth total (% of total labor forces ages 15–24), http://data.worldbank.org/indicator/SL.UEM.1524.ZS?end=2009&start=1991.

World Bank. 2016a: *Middle East North Africa (MENA) Overview*, www.worldbank.org/en/region/mena/overview.

World Bank. 2016b: World Bank, youth unemployment rates 1991–2016, http://data.worldbank.org/indicator/SL.UEM.1524.ZS.

World Bank. 2016c: *Migration and Remittances, Recent Developments and Outlook*. Washington, DC: World Bank.

World Bank, Vishwanath, T., Nguyen, N., et al. 2011: *Capabilities, Opportunities and Participation: Gender Equality and Development in the Middle East and North Africa Region*, No. 10870. Washington, DC: World Bank.

World Food Programme. 2015: *Yemen Overview*, https://www.wfp.org/countries/yemen/overview.

Wright, R. (ed.). 2012: *The Islamists Are Coming: Who They Really Are*. Washington, DC: United States Institute of Peace.

Yacobi, H. and Newman, D. 2008: The EU and the Israel–Palestine conflict. In A. Diez, M. Albert and S. Stetter (eds.), *The European Union and Border Conflicts: The Power of Integration and Association.* Cambridge: Cambridge University Press.

Yariv, A. 1992: The crisis experience in the Middle East: conflict management triumphant. In Spiegel (1992).

Yassin-Kassab, R. and Al-Shami, L. 2016: *Burning Country: Syrians in Revolution and War.* London: Pluto Press.

Yiftachel, O. 1993: Debate: the concept of ethnic democracy and its application to the case of Israel. *Ethnic and Racial Studies,* 15:1, pp. 125–36.

—— 2006: *Ethnocracy: Land and Identity Politics in Israel/Palestine.* Philadelphia: University of Pennsylvania Press.

Yom, S. L. 2009: Jordan: ten more years of autocracy. *Journal of Democracy,* 20:4, pp. 151–66.

Young, M. 2010: *The Ghosts of Martyrs Square: an Eyewitness Account of Lebanon's Life Struggle.* New York: Simon and Schuster.

Young, E. G. 2014: *Gender and nation-building in the Middle East: The political economy of health from mandate Palestine to refugee camps in Jordan.* London: I. B. Tauris.

Zabad, I. 2017: *Middle Eastern Minorities: The Impact of the Arab Spring.* London: Routledge.

Zacharia, J. 2010: New restrictions provoke unusually strong wave of criticism among Jordanians. *Washington Post,* 20 August.

Zaltsman, J. 2012: *Egypt: Women under Siege,* 6 Feb., www.womenundersiegeproject.org/conflicts/profile/egypt.

Zambelis, C. 2008: Attacks in Yemen reflect al-Qaeda's global oil strategy. *Terrorism Monitor,* 6:7.

Zartman, I. W. 2015: Mediation: ripeness and its challenges in the Middle East. *International Negotiation,* 20:3, pp. 470–93.

Žižek, S. 2016: *Against the Double Blackmail: Refugees, Terror and Other Troubles with the Neighbours.* London: Penguin.

Zubaida, S. 1993: *Islam, the People and the State.* London: I. B. Tauris.

—— 1997: Is Iran an Islamic state? In Beinin and Stork (1997).

Zunes, S. 2009: Peace or pax Americana? US Middle East policy and the threat to global security. *International Politics,* 46:5, pp. 573–95.

Index

Names with the initial articles 'al-' and 'el-' are alphabetized under the second element of the name.